SATAN'S RHETORIC

SATAN'S RHETORIC

A Study of Renaissance Demonology

ARMANDO MAGGI

THE UNIVERSITY OF CHICAGO PRESS

Chicago & London

Armando Maggi is associate professor of Romance Languages and Literatures at the University of Chicago. He is the author of several works, including *Uttering the Word: The Mystical Performances of Maria Maddalena de'Pazzi.*

THE UNIVERSITY OF CHICAGO PRESS, CHICAGO 60637
THE UNIVERSITY OF CHICAGO PRESS, LTD., LONDON
© 2001 by The University of Chicago
All rights reserved. Published 2001
Printed in the United States of America

10 09 08 07 06 05 04 03 02 01   5 4 3 2 1
ISBN (cloth): 0-226-50132-9

Library of Congress Cataloging-in-Publication Data

Maggi, Armando.
    Satan's rhetoric : a study of Renaissance demonology / Armando Maggi.
       p.   cm.
    Includes bibliographical references and index.
    ISBN 0-226-50132-9 (cloth : alk. paper)
    1. Demonology—History of doctrines.   I. Title.
BF1511 .M34   2001
133.4′2′09—dc21

                                                        2001000824

This book is for my dead:
for my beloved friend Marisa
my dear aunt Liliana
my friend Françoise
my grandfather Guido
and my father
Sergio

CONTENTS

vii

CONTENTS

MY FIRST AND MOST SINCERE THANKS go to Edward Peters, Charles Lea Professor at the University of Pennsylvania. Professor Peters has followed this project very closely. His support and corrections have been crucial to my work. I am also deeply grateful to the other scholars and friends whose comments have dramatically improved my text. In particular, Paolo Cherchi, professor of Italian and Spanish literature at the University of Chicago, and Victoria Kirkham, professor of Italian literature at the University of Pennsylvania, have helped me clarify the relationship between Maria Maddalena de' Pazzi and Dante's vision of purgatory. Ann Matter, professor of religious studies at the University of Pennsylvania, has kindly commented on the chapters on Manuel do Valle de Moura and Girolamo Menghi, and on the conclusion. With Bernard McGinn, professor of historical theology and history of Christianity at the University of Chicago, I briefly discussed Thomas Aquinas' demonology and the ritual of exorcism. Professors Gabriella Zarri and Pedro Loureiro have provided me with essential bibliographical information on Sylvester Prierio and the Portuguese Inquisition. Edward Gallagher of the Rhetoric Program at Purdue University has carefully read my entire manuscript. Finally, Dr. Monique Laberge helped me correct and strengthen the conclusion

Apart from the introduction and the conclusion, written in Florence and Chicago, I wrote this book at the University of Pennsylvania, where I taught from 1996 to 1999. This book could not exist without the phenomenal Charles Lea Collection located on the sixth floor of the Van Pelt Library at Penn. I thank Dr. Michael Ryan, director of Special Collections at the University of Pennsylvania, for his support, kindness, and friendship. I am also very thankful to Mr. John Pollack, responsible for the public services at the Department of Special Collections at Penn.

A special thanks to Dr. Grazia Visintainer of the Kunsthistorisches Institut in Florence. During a torrid morning of mid-July, Dr. Visintainer patiently showed me innumerable reproductions of Maria Maddalena de' Pazzi's demonic possession.

I am also indebted to the staff of the National Library of Lisbon for the bibliographical information on the Inquisitor de Moura.

I remember with sincere affection the sisters of the Convent of Santa Maria Maddalena de' Pazzi in Careggi (Florence), who several years ago let me read the original manuscripts of the Florentine mystic.

My most sincere thanks to Douglas Mitchell, executive editor at the University of Chicago Press, for his invaluable support, help, and friendship. I am very grateful to Dr. Lys Ann Shore for a wide range of suggestions and editorial corrections.

A final, filial thanks to my mother, Lina. When I was still a child in Rome, she took me to a memorable exorcism at a Roman basilica.

Words Beclouding the Eyes: An Introduction

"THE CONNECTION between the human kind expelled from the earthly paradise and the devil banished from heaven is founded on their common accident," Leon d'Alexis remarks in the opening section of *Traicté des energumènes*, a brief Renaissance essay on demonology that may serve as a basic introduction to this study.[1] "[T]his angelic spirit," d'Alexis continues, "is characterized by a relentlessly active nature, but he can neither turn to God who has abandoned him, nor can he converse with the good angels from whom he has separated himself, nor can he find any rest and solace in contemplating his deformed and disfigured image. As a consequence, he cannot help but turn his attention to our behaviors. Wandering on earth in search of rest, his sole activity is his interaction and dialogue with human beings."[2]

The book you are about to read is a linguistic and rhetorical analysis of this dialogue, as it was hypothesized and investigated during the Renaissance. In D'Alexis's words, no one is more similar to us than the devil, for no one but the devil shares our outcast condition. The devil, D'Alexis

---

1. Leon d'Alexis (pseud. of Pierre de Bérulle), *Traicté des energumènes, suivi d'un discours sur la possession de Marthe Brossier: Contre les calomnies d'un medecin de Paris* (Troyes, 1599), 19r.

2. D'Alexis, *Traicté des energumènes*, 19r–v. In *Dämonie und Transzendenz* (Stuttgart: Neske, 1964), Arnold Metzger dedicates an extremely insightful chapter to this subject ("Zur Philosophie der Symbolik," 181–86).

reiterates, "is forever removed from his center [that is, God]."[3] Could not we say that the innumerable treatises on demonology written in premodern and modern Europe—starting from the late fifteenth-century *Formicarius* and *Malleus maleficarum*, and continuing to the repetitious manuals still composed during the Enlightenment—are in fact grammar books, obsessive attempts to define the idiom exchanged between these two radical solitudes?

As the five treatises selected for this study will make clear, the linguistic field where these two exiles converge, where Satan and Adam's progeny gather in order to silence each other, is the human mind. The Foe announces his presence first and foremost in the mind. It is in the mind that devils try to articulate their idiom—and sometimes succeed in doing so. In a central passage from *Thesaurus exorcismorum*, the most authoritative Renaissance collection of exorcisms and the topic of the third chapter of this book, the Italian inquisitor Zacharia Visconti states that there are three forms of linguistic expression. Whereas God speaks the "language of things"—that is, He expresses himself through the created world—humankind can only pronounce the "language of the voice." In other words, if divine language at once makes and names reality, human language has no direct connection with the reality it describes through phonemes, syllables, and sentences. The third existing idiom, Visconti holds, is a nonlanguage, a nonexpression that takes place first in the human mind and subsequently in the creation. The fallen angels are the speakers of this paradoxical "language of the mind." Rather than engaging in some form of visible speech, the "speakers of the mind" communicate through the results brought about by their nonstatements. In other words, more than speaking, the "speakers of the mind" *are spoken*. And what their discourse "says" is the annihilation of the medium that has articulated it. The mind, the Italian demonologist is convinced, is that area of our being where we "recall" our unalterable status as pariah, for at any moment the mind may become the dwelling of the "speakers of the mind," who can erase our "language of voice" and make us articulate their silent idiom of solitude and devastation.

A brief pause is necessary before we proceed further. I am aware that defendants of the traditional, or "canonical," analysis of medieval and Renaissance witchcraft and demonology are likely to find my work preposterous, naïve, or simply laughable. Innumerable studies have taught us that the "correct" approach to this cultural phenomenon should be strictly

---

3. D'Alexis, *Traicté des energumènes*, 26v.

social historical or, at the most, psychoanalytical: minimizing the theological premises behind the criminal conduct of the Catholic Church first and then of numerous other Christian denominations, we should exclusively focus on the factual consequences of what many consider merely a form of mass hysteria that influenced the birth of, and coexisted with, modern European culture. In 1980, however, Jeffrey Burton Russell denounced the reductive character of this dogmatic investigation: "Most historians have emphasized the social history of witchcraft, an emphasis that has both virtues and limitations. . . . The chief dangers of this approach are that it has tended to be dogmatic, blocking or dismissing other approaches, and that in its search for the social mechanisms of witchcraft it misses the broader ethical, intellectual, and spiritual meaning of witchcraft."[4] If, as the Italian philosopher Gianni Vattimo writes, paraphrasing Nietzsche, "there are no facts, only interpretations"—that is, if it is true that "the present epoch . . . [has] renounce[d] the reassuring authority of presence" and identifies being and truth with hermeneutic—we may be ready to look back on the phenomenon of Renaissance demonology in order to review and rethink its spiritual, philosophical, and literary implications.[5] To say that hysteria obfuscated the minds of innumerable inquisitors and theologians should not prevent us from pursuing the possible sense of that hysteria. Additionally, *hysteria* is one of those big words, like *melancholy, folly,* or *depression,* that point more to our inability to fathom their rationale than to their actual meaning.[6] Why could we not at least try to walk through the "senseless" maze of this folly called demonology, which postulates the presence of a paradoxical "other," at once radically different from us and so close and similar to us, an enemy that finds in our mind its primary and most abhorred interlocutor?

It should be evident by now that my study is founded on a "credulous" suspension of disbelief, on the basic assumption that, in order to make sense of such an obsolete and "insane" intellectual system, we must endeavor to let it lay out its essential premises and obsessive goals without superimposing our "enlightened" beliefs on what those demonology books *really* meant to say. It may be useful to read this study as a form of intellectual and linguistic translation more than as an act of interpretation. The old-fashioned Husserlian process of "bracketing" and suspension

4. Jeffrey Burton Russell, *A History of Witchcraft* (London: Thames and Hudson, 1980), 109.

5. Gianni Vattimo, "The Trace of the Trace," in *Religion,* edited by Jacques Derrida and Gianni Vattimo (Stanford: Stanford University Press, 1998), 93.

6. See Elaine Showalter, *Hystories* (New York: Columbia University Press, 1997), 14–29.

has accompanied me throughout the composition of this book. The surprising result of this more discreet approach may be the recognition of some central similarities between, on the one hand, the sixteenth- and seventeenth-century theories on the linguistic confrontation between devils and humans, and, on the other, our contemporary obsession with concepts like "identity" and "self," "performance" and "being," "presence" and "narrativity."

All too often, though, the theoretical foundations that brought about the bloody persecutions of women, "sodomites," Jews, and other minorities are perceived as an ideological justification, a mere excuse for murder. Indeed, treatises on demonology are usually seen as divided into two major parts: First is an assortment of superstitious and even ludicrous anecdotes that acts to support the belief in the actual existence of a pact between humans and devils (for instance, how witches can actually fly to the sabbat or how the devils make them imagine the whole trip; if and how witches can cause diseases and storms; how succubi and incubi steal sperm from a man and insert it into the witch's vagina, thus bringing about the birth of some kind of half-human and half-demonic creatures). This is followed by a list of legal procedures concerning the detection, questioning, and punishment of the devil's followers. It is unquestionably true that even the most famous and most quoted Renaissance works on demonology linger on picturesque and gruesome narrations to convince the reader of the need for extreme measures. It is also true, however, that every treatise at least endeavors to explain why and how the devils and their disciples are able to subvert the natural, and moral, order of creation. Nonetheless, these more conceptual explanations are in most cases unsystematic, trivial, or simply inconclusive. As you will see, this study goes beyond the conventional texts of Renaissance demonology, such as Nider's *Formicarius* (1475), the *Malleus malleficarum*, Remy's *Demonolatriae* (1595), Guazzo's *Compendium maleficarum* (1608), and Del Rio's imposing *Disquisitionum magicarum* (1599–1600). To respond to my introductory hypothesis of an essential connection between human and demonic expression, I make these canonical books interact with other essential, though now almost or totally forgotten, texts that focus on the topic of demonic linguistics.[7]

At the origin of what we call modernity lies, as d'Alexis puts it, our "in-

---

7. In *Il Diavolo* (Rome: Newton and Compton, 1999), Alfonso di Nola gives a basic list of the "canon" of medieval and Renaissance literature on demonology (222–24). For an exhaustive outline of Catholic demonology, see Renzo Lavatori, *Satana. Un caso serio* (Bologna: Edizioni Dehoniane Bologna, 1995). In the fourth section of chapter 1 (46–53), Lavatori analyzes the most recent papal statements on this issue.

teraction and dialogue" with the Foe. In no other period of its history has Christianity been more obsessed with the idea that "he" is persistently watching, reading, and addressing us with his discourse of fall, solitude, and damnation. To make his language perceived and understood, however, the Enemy must decode "our behaviors," our physical and linguistic gestures. As I will explain in detail in chapter 1, dedicated to Sylvester Prierio's *De strigimagis* (1521), devils are skilled and astute semioticians. Angels, the Italian inquisitor reminds us, do not have an idiom of their own because they have no memory. Borrowing from Augustine's theories on language, Prierio underscores that to speak essentially means to perform an act of remembrance—that is, language first and foremost gives voice to the speaker's desire. But we must keep in mind that, according to the Church Fathers, angels (both the good and the fallen ones) possess no desire, and thus no language. What do angels actually say when they speak to us? In Prierio's view, angels simply deliver someone else's discourse. We all know that angels are messengers, vehicles, instruments of language. They are the voice and breath that carry words. We also know that the good angels limit themselves to pronouncing God's statements. The good angels do not need to double-check the validity of what they tell us; they do not need to know whether their discourse makes sense or not, because God would not allow them to mispronounce his words. The good angels speak, but they neither know nor remember what they say or are about to say.

But whose words do the fallen angels announce? As the opening pages of *De strigimagis* make vividly clear, the devil's discourse is a fire that devours both its speakers and its addressees. Like a flame burning everything it encounters, or a plague spreading through a city, demonic language utters chaos and annihilation. At the origin of a demonic statement lies its speaker's original confusion and exile. If a good angel is the linguistic statement connecting a speaker with his interlocutor, a devil is the memorial of a perennial exclusion from meaning. We will follow Prierio's close reasoning on how the devils succeed in articulating their non-idiom of devastation. Expanding Thomas Aquinas's angelology and medieval theories on human intellectual faculties, Prierio holds that devils, since they have lost their linguistic connection with the divinity, are unable to listen to their own voice—that is, they can never be certain whether they have actually "spoken" or not. Their utterances are syllogistic constructions whose validity is exclusively inferred from the results they exert on humankind first and then on the creation. By reading our external manners (how we look and walk, the words we use, the gestures we make, the people we associate with and how we relate to them), a devil posits a syllogism in which the *praemissa maior* is a universal statement and the *praemissa minor* is what he speculates about the identity of a specific human being. The *conclusio* is the cogent, though totally hypothetical, outcome of this reasoning. If the devil's syllogistic statement turns out correct, that particular human being will be infected with the devil's unspoken language. According to the specific *praemissae* stated in the syllogism, he or she may either become the devil's disciple and lover (witches, magicians, Jews, sodomites) or be the victim of a demonic possession, whose symptoms resemble those of a virulent melancholy. In either case, the human element is of central importance for the devil's linguistic expression. If a melancholic may be the tangible evidence of the devil's cancerous eloquence, a faithful disciple is the essential *medium* through which the "speaker of the mind" carries on and expands his syllogistic discourse. The *medium* or *local motion (motus localis)* is the transitional area between the two-part conjectural statement *(praemissae maior* and *minor)* and its result *(conclusio)*. Witches, Jews, magicians are not only the successful result of a demonic syllogism, they also identify with that local motion, enabling the "speaker of the mind" to express his idiom. Moreover, Prierio explains how the devil transforms the conclusion of the first syllogism (a magician, a witch, but also a possessed body) into the *praemissa minor* of a new syllogism, which will bring about a chain (a fire) of far-reaching adversities. In other words, the devils' disciples at once give voice to and are the voice of the "speakers of the mind." Witches, Jews, and sodomites are the "air" (which, according to the Augustinian tradition, is the quintessential local motion) carrying the devils' utterances.

According to Pierre de Lancre's popular *Tableau de l'inconstance des mauvais anges et demons*, the night before she gave birth to a demon, a witch could not help but scream words summoning the concept of chaos, such as "unstable!" "inconsistent!" or "senseless!"[8] This woman's outcry simply echoed the chaos (the devil's son) she was about to bring to life. Let us also remember, de Lancre continues, that "the devils made [sibyls] write down their oracles on leaves, marks of inconstancy and inanity. Moreover, when they possessed sibyls and prophetesses, the devils marked their bodies with puzzling and convulsive movements."[9] If devils utter chaos and incertitude, not even the notorious mark on the disciples' flesh can be read

8. Pierre de Lancre, *Tableau de l'inconstance des mauvais anges et demons* (1st ed., 1611; Paris: Nicolas Buon, 1613), 14. De Lancre finds this story in Del Rio, book 1, chap. 3, q. 2, on p. 18.

9. De Lancre, *Tableau de l'inconstance*, 14.

as the legal "signature" of a linguistic contract. If in theory the devil marks his followers so that they participate in "the destruction of God's laws and nature's rules," in fact these marks come and go at random, often disappearing suddenly and reappearing somewhere else at a later moment.[10] In some cases, Satan may even decide not to leave his mark at all.[11] Like the leaves on which the sibyls transcribed Satan's cryptic messages, a human body is an "inconstant" text whose "true" communication roams from one member or organ to another (for instance, from the shoulder to the ear, from the ear to the eyelid, from the eyelid to the pupil) and whose presence is paradoxically detected (when it is detectable) by its insensitivity to the inquisitor's needle.[12] De Lancre acknowledges that, after an inquisitor has poked a defendant's body for a long time in search of a nonresponse (the spot where pain is absent), the flesh bleeds so profusely that it is impossible to circumscribe the area of a possible demonic signature.[13] Furthermore, even when one finds the potential spot, it is hard to tell how deep the needle is supposed to go. Many inquisitors, de Lancre says, have the questionable habit of sticking the needle so deeply that it goes beyond the actual devil's mark and meets some sensitive organ or bone, thus causing a painful reaction in the defendant. In other words, to make the devil speak, one must be sure that he keeps silent.

More than actual symbols, these alleged marks are "indices," similar to what Peirce calls *indexes*—that is, "signs" summoning the remembrance of something else (as a hole in the wall may signify a bullet).[14] Asked to examine the eyes of a seventeen-year-old girl accused of being a witch, de Lancre saw in her left pupil "something like a small cloud" that somehow resembled a toad's leg, one of the possible indexes of a demonic pact.[15] That "cloud" lingering over the girl's left pupil was what remained of the devil's contract. Staring into the girl's eyes, de Lancre detected the shadow (a cloud) of a written text, the remembrance of a past event. As usual, the witch was then asked to unveil the whole story beclouding her eye. Satan marked her cornea the first time she went to the sabbat with her mother,

---

10. De Lancre, *Tableau de l'inconstance*, 187.

11. In his discussion on the devil's mark, de Lancre follows Henry Boguet's *Discours des sorciers*; I refer to the third edition (Lyon: Rigaud, 1610), 317.

12. See Jacques Lacan, "Seminar on 'The Purloined Letter,'" in *The Purloined Letter*, edited by John P. Muller and William J. Richardson (Baltimore: Johns Hopkins University Press, 1988), 28–54.

13. De Lancre, *Tableau de l'inconstance*, 190.

14. Compare De Lancre, *Tableau de l'inconstance*, 191.

15. De Lancre, *Tableau de l'inconstance*, 192.

herself a witch.[16] By "confessing" her crime, the girl assigned a linguistic coherence to the formless demonic statement.

Since the devil's mark is a cloud gliding through the flesh in an "inconstant" manner, a text erasing itself and rewriting itself at random, we may find it more pertinent to investigate the linguistic practices through which Satan's disciples communicate with their master. If the devil's followers coincide with his local motion—the connector enabling the Foe to complete his syllogistic reasoning—it is imperative to detect and to cancel every form of linguistic and performative expression that may fulfill this rhetorical role.

This is what the Portuguese inquisitor Manuel do Valle de Moura attempts to accomplish in *De encantationibus seu ensalmis* (1620), one of the most convoluted treatises of Renaissance demonology and the topic of chapter 2. No extensive study has ever been written on this crucial text. The Catholic inquisitor de Moura is convinced that Satan's followers, whom he identifies with the Jewish community, invoke their master by means of what he calls *ensalmi*—sly linguistic hybrids made of biblical quotations (primarily from the Book of Psalms), Catholic formulaic expressions and prayers, and segments of popular magic. De Moura likens an *ensalmus* to any form of invocative text, whose message may be directed either to God or to Satan. However, the essential ambiguity of an *ensalmus* lies in the fact that its linguistic performativity may hide a double interlocutor. As a petition, even the most lawful *ensalmus* may either miss its intended interlocutor or may reach two antagonistic listeners (God and Satan) at the same time. Therefore, an *ensalmus* presents two different fundamental problems: on the one hand, its unverifiable efficacy, and, on the other, its performer's hidden intentions.

Although these literary patchworks derive almost entirely from Catholic doctrine and thus always sound like legitimate expressions of a correct religiosity, Satan has instructed the Jews to deliver their *ensalmi* in ways that pervert the literal meaning of the text. In other words, whereas the literal level of a (Jewish) *ensalmus* expresses an apparently legitimate content, the performative one unfolds a totally opposite sense. The performance of an *ensalmus*, de Moura explains, is always accompanied by specific gestures and objects (for instance, candles, water, wine), whose intent is to bring to the fore the actual meaning of the written page. Like any other theatrical text, an *ensalmus* manifests itself as a speech act through the particular intonation of the speaker's voice, through his facial

16. De Lancre, *Tableau de l'inconstance*, 193.

8

expressions, his movements, and the actual "stage" on which he delivers his lines.[17]

If, like the devil's mark on the witch's flesh, the demonic undertone of an *ensalmus* affects (beclouds) the whole field of expression without necessarily residing in a specific area, how can the inquisitor catch a visible (readable) allusion to Satan's presence in the text? Although an *ensalmus* may manifest its ruinous message only when and if an *ensalmista* gives voice to it, at the beginning of *De ensalmis* de Moura still believes that some fundamental reference to its actual addressee must be detectable in the way the *ensalmista* has stitched its pieces together, since he can only investigate this invocative performance in its literary structure and theological references and not in its actual rendition. But the Portuguese inquisitor soon dismisses this structural analysis because he realizes that the main, and most insidious, problem of a demonic *ensalmus* lies in its phonetics and morphology and not in its narrative. De Moura comes to the conclusion that two similar accounts may hide two opposite ideological messages. Like the body of a young girl hiding a demonic mark on the cornea of her left eye, the perverted nature of an *ensalmus* can be unveiled only by dissecting it in its single "organs," its smallest units of signification (nouns, verbs, prepositions, adverbs).

What is essential to determine, de Moura emphasizes, is whether or not words, syllables, phonemes, possess some natural, if covert, power. Although at the outset he follows Martin del Rio in his strenuous attack against Marsilio Ficino's Neoplatonic theories of the "natural" powers of language, later de Moura acknowledges that words—at least some specific words such as *Jesus* or *Word*—do exert an undeniable influence over the created world. But not only God's holy names and the prayer He taught us possess this uncanny quality. Origen and Thomas themselves, de Moura continues, mention that magicians know how to manipulate the hidden faculties of language to tame snakes and other animals. It is thus evident,

17. Augustine broaches this essential problem in the second book of *On Christian Teaching (De doctrina christiana)*, where he speaks of those signs that "are not generally understood unless accompanied by agreement" (*On Christian Teaching*, book 2, chap. 25/39, translated by R. P. H. Green [Oxford: Oxford University Press, 1997], 53). According to Augustine, theater is based on this form of expression. These signs are particularly dangerous because they can be interpreted in different manners according to the subject's personal reaction: "[T]hey have different effects on different people, according to their particular thoughts and fancies" (52). Evil spirits play with this semiotic ambiguity: "So (by way of example) the single letter which is written like a cross means one thing to the Greeks and another to Latin speakers, and has meaning not by nature but by agreement and convention. . . . Likewise the signs by which th[e] deadly agreement with demons is achieved have an effect that is in proportion to each individual's attention to them" (52–53).

he infers, that Satan may instruct his disciples concerning how to perceive the language lying within language, an idiom that relies on human audible phonemes to cause effects that transcend the syntactical meaning conveyed through the primary oral level.

Given that, like his master, a demonic *ensalmista* speaks a silent, "intangible" idiom, the Mother Church can only succeed in erasing Satan's utterances by erasing its human speakers, the Jews. Like the sodomites infesting the Iberian peninsula, de Moura holds, the Jews speak a language "against nature," in that in their invocative intercourse with Satan they use their natural organs (the voice and language that God has granted them) in a deviant and harmful manner. What makes a given *ensalmus* a licit speech act, de Moura concludes, is neither its content nor its specific speaker, but only the fact that Mother Church has defined it as such. The legitimacy of language is thus an essentially legal procedure.[18] As the legitimate expression of God's will on earth, the Catholic Church is the sole institution enabled to utter a language in which orality and (natural and hidden) meaning coincide.

Exorcism is the ritual embodying the "natural" linguistic procedure through which Mother Church responds to the noxious effects of a demonic discourse. Exorcism is the topic of chapter 3 of this book. If a devil speaks (through) silence and his idiom is exclusively perceived as a signified (storms, diseases, possession, melancholy) and never as a signifier, since the devil has no memory, an exorcist tries to turn the diabolical statements written on a possessed body into audible utterances in the attempt to make the speaker pronounce his name and thus reveal his linguistic identity (**N**). Most treatises on exorcism recommend that the exorcist force the devil to move up to the victim's tongue, so that the "body in pain" may spit the devil (**N**) out through the mouth.

After tracing the origins and medieval developments of the practice of exorcism, chapter 3 turns to the *Thesaurus exorcismorum* (first published in 1608), the most influential collection of treatises on exorcism of the Renaissance. The *Thesaurus* is an imposing work of more than twelve hundred pages in which Valerio Polidori and Girolamo Menghi, two important Italian demonologists, assemble six fundamental texts written in the last quarter of the sixteenth century: Menghi's *Flagellum daemonum* and *Fustis daemonum*, Polidori's *Practica exorcistarum* and *Dispersio daemonum*, Zacharia Visconti's *Complementum artis exorcisticae*, and Antonio

18. Edward Peters offers a seminal analysis of this issue in *The Magician, the Witch and the Law* (Philadelphia: University of Pennsylvania Press, 1975).

Stampa's *Fuga Satanae*. Even though the *Thesaurus* is a landmark of Christian demonology, it has never been the object of a detailed investigation.

The numerous adjurations collected in the *Thesaurus* are linguistic constructions based on an unrelenting process of metaphorization. We will read and examine a powerful exorcism ("On the Life of Jesus") from Visconti's *Complementum*, the longest (more than seventy pages) and most compelling adjuration of the whole *Thesaurus*. This analysis will bring to the surface essential similarities between Florentine Neoplatonism and the practice of Catholic exorcism, two seemingly distinct areas of sixteenth-century culture. As we will see, metaphor is the rhetorical device founding both Neoplatonic philosophy and Catholic theory of demonic adjuration. In Florentine Neoplatonism, the created world is the visible manifestation of a universal "sympathy" *(sympathia)*, according to which everything is related to everything by means of metaphorical or analogical connectors *(like, as)*. Similarly, Renaissance demonologists believed that, to silence Satan's unheard discourse of annihilation, they had to bring to the fore the creation's narrative potentials, which unfold as a chain of extended metaphors. If the Church is the sole repository of God's unfathomable project, the Catholic Bible is the text that translates the creation into a narrative of salvation. In other words, the countless narrative units reported in the two Testaments are the most accurate reflections of the visible world. As we will see in chapter 3, for the two Italian exorcists the Book of Life develops as the dialogical relationship between biblical events and the created world. *Like* and *as* are the exorcist's essential healing instruments. In an exorcism words mirror things that mirror words.

The accuracy of this metaphorical proliferation can be monitored only through the possessed body, which is indeed the text that ratifies the exorcist's narrative correspondences. Since the secret (metaphorical) language of the created world utters God's ultimate message of redemption, through his narrations the exorcist aims to make the world's "sense" into a visible syntax.[19] The devil hidden in the body in pain must hear and thus "see" that his destructive eloquence is doomed to fail, because the Book of Life has already envisioned and recounted it.

According to the authors of the *Thesaurus*, the visible supremacy of the exorcist's speech, and the devil's subsequent withdrawal from the scene of language, is manifested by a sudden, cold exhalation of air coming out

19. On the syntactical structure of the world's "sense," see Jean-Luc Nancy, *The Sense of the World*, translated by Jeffrey S. Librett (Minneapolis: University of Minnesota Press, 1997), 12–15.

of the possessed body (through one of its orifices). This cold draft, which often extinguishes a candle placed next to the possessed, is the (visible) sigh of an extinct voice. If, as the Jesuit Petrus Thyraeus writes in *Daemoniaci cum locis infestis* (1627), a possessed body is nothing but a set of clamorous disturbances *(clamores)* lacking any coherent meaning, the final breath that marks the closure of a failed discourse.

The paradoxical condition of a human being tormented by the devil is that he is at once a vociferous text (the chaotic signs the devil marks in and on his body) and a silenced subjectivity. Although a body in pain is the essential means through which the exorcist articulates his language of metaphors, he or she is never more than an abstract physicality, an indistinct but necessary given. As every text in the *Thesaurus* emphasizes, what matters in an exorcism is the identity (the name) of the devil in the body, and not the body itself. However, every demonologist knows that the mind of the possessed is not a linguistic vacuum, for it is flooded with an unrelenting verbal production. Menghi and Polidori are aware that the victims are often unable to hear the priest's words because the devil is whispering, mumbling, or screaming in their minds. While the exorcist is haranguing against the chaos surging in the body in pain, the possessed mind passively listens to its own thoughts that have come to coincide with those of its aggressor. Indeed, more than thinking, the possessed mind echoes a discourse of self-annihilation.

A basic tenet of Renaissance demonology is the conviction that, although a melancholic is not necessarily a *maleficiatus* (possessed), every *maleficiatus* shows evident symptoms of melancholy. In other words, melancholy is not a univocal sign of demonic possession. That an individual is a melancholic does not mean that he or she is possessed by the devil, although demonic possession is always accompanied by melancholy. Melancholy, most treatises hold, can have natural causes. The exorcist must assess whether or not melancholy is a sign of the devil's presence—that is, he must understand if the symptoms of a given case of melancholy work as the satanic mark gliding through the body of the possessed. To detect a demonic melancholy, the priest must be able to determine if someone else is speaking through the melancholic symptoms.

It is difficult to find a Renaissance text detailing the devastating rhetoric articulated by the speakers of the mind. How the devil actually unfolds his discourse of despair and dissolution in the melancholic mind is something unknown to most treatises on demonology. Demonologists stress that melancholy can be either natural or demonic; they never address the problem of what actually happens when Satan takes hold of the mind. In this regard, *Probation* by the Carmelite mystic Maria Maddalena de' Pazzi is a precious and unique specimen. *Probation* reports the monologues this Florentine visionary delivered during her demonic oppression, which lasted more than five years, from 1585 to 1590.

A fundamental aspect of de' Pazzi's mysticism is her obsession with orality. She is convinced that the Word wants her to utter his Being through oral discourse. For Maria Maddalena de' Pazzi, the most important mystic of the Renaissance after Theresa of Avila, "to utter the Word" has indeed a literal, unmetaphorical sense. This is why she refused to write down her long and often obscure speeches revolving around the Word's essence and the occurrence of his human death. Once they realized that the core of her revelations lay in her spoken language, her convent sisters decided to take turns transcribing her discourses along with her pauses, exclamations, and repetitions.

Given the absolute centrality of verbal expression in her mystical "project" (the possible expression of the Word), for de' Pazzi a demonic possession presents itself as a defacement of her linguistic competence, a harrowing inability to construct an effective eloquence. More than active attempts to give voice to the divinity, the mystic's monologues turn into invocations structured as narrative reenactments of the Word's death and withdrawal from the visible world. We may say that de' Pazzi's demonic melancholy takes the form of a "memorial" of a lost interlocutor. As her convent sisters remark, Maria Maddalena has entered a state of "linguistic exile" in which she is the passive recipient of others' discourse. The silence of a demonic melancholy is an act of listening.

We have seen that, according to Sylvester Prierio, the devil himself "speaks" only insofar as he is able to listen to the signs we emit. Being exiled from the domain of language, both the devils and the mystic suffering from melancholy are receptive listeners, alert receivers of others' statements. The most striking phase of de' Pazzi's demonic possession is the moment when, silenced by her internal demons suggesting that she take her own life, the mystic suddenly perceives the voice of her brother, who had recently passed away. Finding himself in purgatory, he begs his sister to do something to alleviate the excruciating torments to which he has been subjected. Maria Maddalena understands that to respond to her brother's request essentially means to free him of the remembrance of his (sinful) existence. Purgatory is the place where the soul slowly "burns" the remembrance of itself and attains an everlasting oblivion.

We may thus say that to listen to a soul in purgatory entails an act of substitution. In *Probation*, the mystic oppressed by the demons of melancholy realizes that to answer her brother's entreaty, she must accept the burden of his memory—that is, she must recognize that his agonizing expressions of sorrow are hers, that he is voicing her own purgatorial torments. Similar to the pilgrim Dante, in a central rapture from *Probation* de' Pazzi decides to visit her deceased brother. Turning the kitchen garden of her convent into a purgatorial space, the mystic walks around meeting and conversing with souls. As we shall see in detail, in her journey through purgatory the mystic comprehends that her silenced word is uttered by the other (her brother, the souls immersed in the flames of purgatory), and that she can regain her voice only by letting the other articulate his demand to her.

The paradoxical identification between linguistic expression and the act of listening, between speaking and hearing, is a central aspect of Renaissance demonology. The devil at once deprives the subject of his or her own voice (the mind as echo of someone else's musing) and indirectly grants a different kind of idiom that posits the essential identification between speaking and being spoken. The "melancholic speaker" understands that his or her identity resides in the other's utterance. Being strictly linked to the overall problem of linguistic expression, the relationship between demonic possession and melancholy will be analyzed from a different angle in each chapter of this work.

So far we have identified the expression "Renaissance demonology" with the interpretation formulated by the Catholic Inquisition. Prierio, de Moura, Menghi, de' Pazzi all agree on the meaning of basic terms such as *demon* or *devil, possession* and *enlightenment.* Although their texts dwell on different facets of the linguistic interaction between fallen angels and human beings, they share an identical rhetorical system and theological background. In particular, as far as de' Pazzi's "melancholic substitution" is concerned, it is evident that the mystic's linguistic "exchange" with her brother (exchange both as interaction and as conversion) is an unexpected side effect of her demonic possession. Silencing her mind—that is, infecting it with melancholy—the devil paradoxically enables her to perceive the statements pronounced by someone sharing a similar "purgatorial" state. In other words, the mystic's melancholic insight results not from her demons' active participation, but rather from the weakened condition of her mind.

Florentine Neoplatonism, the fifteenth- and sixteenth-century philosophical movement stemming from Marsilio Ficino's translations and interpretations of Plato's and Plotinus' texts, both confirms and distances itself from the Catholic view on the essence of demonic beings and their rhetorical interaction with the human mind. In Renaissance Neoplatonism *devil* and *demon* have two distinct, though not opposite, connotations. While *devil* is usually used as a synonym for the Catholic "fallen angel," *demon* is a cluster of different meanings, which include but are not limited to the Platonic and Plotinian "daimon," the Christian "devil," and "spirit" according to medieval and Renaissance popular magic.

I must emphasize, however, that in Renaissance culture the Catholic *demon* or *devil* and the Neoplatonic *daimon* or *demon* do not embody two radically different beings and thus also two different forms of eloquence. It is thanks to a demonic possession that the Florentine mystic becomes able to perceive the request of the other (her brother, the souls in purgatory). It is the devil that makes her "inner senses" more alert and open to the language of the created world.[20] A closer look at the Neoplatonic interpretation of demonology may disclose further essential points of contact.

In the fifth and final chapter, we shall conduct this investigation by analyzing the "demonic philosophy" of the Italian physician Girolamo Cardano who, as Henry Charles Lea confirms in *Toward a History of Witchcraft*, exemplifies the highest intellect and culture of the sixteenth century.[21] In the introductory notes on Prierio's *De strigimagis*, I have alluded to the essential concept of "local motion," through which the devil succeeds in completing his syllogistic reasoning. In several passages from his diverse treatises, which range from astrology to medicine to moral and theological philosophy to mathematics and physiognomy, Cardano insists on the fundamental concept of *ratio*, which he explains as the capacity of connecting one mental image to another by means of intellectual "leaps" or "knots." This subtle principle *(tenuis principium)*, Cardano holds, ties images together with great swiftness. Through a close reading of several of his texts, we shall see that for Cardano the highest form of *ratio*, or "reasoning," visits the mind when it is almost (quasi) asleep in a form of ecstatic revelation. In the twilight zone between wakefulness and sleep, the mind discerns this seemingly spontaneous process of syntactical associations, according to which single images stored in memory come to formulate new, unexpected visual and/or verbal communications. In his

---

20. The notion of "inner senses" is present in Origen's *Commentary on the Song of Songs*, where he rephrases Paul's idea of the "outer" and the "inner" man (2 Cor. 4:16). See Origen, *An Exhortation to Martyrdom*, translated by Rowan A. Grean (New York: Paulist Press, 1979), 220. Compare my essay, "Blood as Language in the Visions of Maria Maddalena de' Pazzi," *Rivista di letterature moderne e comparate* 48 (1995): 219–35.

21. Henry Charles Lea, *Materials toward a History of Witchcraft*, vol. 2 (Philadelphia: University of Pennsylvania Press, 1939), 435.

Dialogus de morte, Cardano stresses that to be awake means to persist in a state of ecstasy, in which oneiric representations, remembrances, fantasies, and the actual messages conveyed by the real merge as linguistic segments of an identical visual and/or verbal idiom. In other words, for Cardano, the visible (dreams, memory, imagination, inner and outer sight) speaks only one language.

Cardano's "mind" is thus a form of intellectual insight occurring when and only when what we identify as "mind" is about to withdraw from the subject (almost asleep). Indeed, for Cardano, human consciousness (the mind) is divided into two different functions: "soul" *(anima)*, the faculty that simply enacts and influences the body, and "mind" *(mens)*, a sudden insight whose text is made of the (verbal and visual) phonemes already present in the subject's memory. To get an idea of how "soul" can affect the body, says Cardano, we do not need to go very far; let us simply look at the demoniac people, who usually present deranged eyes, swollen body parts, and a frantic demeanor. "Mind" is a much more complex idea. In a fundamental passage from *De subtilitate*, one of his major and most controversial texts, Cardano states that "mind" is made of four different faculties *(iunctio, iudicium, intellectus,* and *voluntas)* that describe the formation, apprehension, and conscious response to an inner enlightenment. In my detailed analysis of these four aspects, I will show that "intellect" *(intellectus)* is the key function of Cardano's "mind." "Intellect" coincides with an act of mental mirroring, when the subject recognizes and reflects (upon) the visual/verbal text the "mind" has constructed before his inner sight. For Cardano, there are three levels of "intellectual" representation. If the first kind occurs when the subject senses what "mind" has communicated, is communicating, or is about to communicate to another subjectivity, the second corresponds to a moment of self-reflection in which the mind receives and decodes, so to speak, the "mind's" text. In the third and final stage, Cardano envisions a total identification/reflection between mind and "mind," between alertness and sleep, between seeing and being seen. This is the most perfect form of ecstasy. In this third phase, "intellect" manifests a perfect coincidence among sight, being, and expression. To see, Cardano synthesizes, means to let our *visa* (our intellectual visions) speak themselves.

For Cardano, it is necessary to distinguish between four forms of *visum* (vision). If the first is when our inner sight sees something different from what our outer sight is perceiving, the second occurs when our mind sees what is actually out there. Cardano calls this insight *spectrum* (specter). The third vision occurs when our mind is not visualizing anything, but we suddenly see something. For Cardano, this visual manifestation is a *genius*. The fourth and highest form of sight takes place when we are deeply immersed in an act of meditation. In a state of total wakefulness, we are visited by a clear and imposing communication, which Cardano defines as *daemonium* (demon). A demon is the "mind's" most eloquent (in)sight, which uses its receiver as a vehicle of self-expression.

Cardano is convinced that the so-called demonic sight is a constitutional part of our subjectivity. In a central passage from *Contradicentium medicorum*, the Italian physician holds that "two things know in us," the mind and a demonic presence. Cardano also stresses that our demons inhabit our mind but are not controlled by it. Let us remember that for the Italian philosopher "demon" coincides with a kind of visual/verbal text in which the mind reflects and merges with the "mind's" enlightenment. Demons are therefore a form of potential expression that comes to us from within. In *Paralipomenon*, Cardano explains that *demon* means "wise man," thus positing a basic coincidence between the demonic (at once independent being and internal insight) presence in the subject and the subject himself. In the same passage, we also learn that a more specific definition of this demonic being is "lemur," who "is like our face reflected in a mirror."

To receive a demonic revelation, to perceive its message, is like looking oneself in the eye. In this act of self-reflection, the self is at once doubled and paradoxically divided into two almost identical images (by "almost" I mean the intellectual distance existing between the mind and its reflected [demonic] face). We shall see that *face* is a pivotal term in his philosophical system. For Cardano, to apprehend a given insight (granted by our inner demon) indeed means "to face" or to reflect (upon) it by an act of exegesis (Cardano's "intellect"). Cardano holds that a face is the most eloquent example of his famous concept of "subtlety" *(subtilitas)*, that "something" at once hiding and exposing the "truth" and inner destiny of any visible thing. In other words, a face speaks a "subtle" language in that it manifests its meaning (the subject's character, his past, his future intentions) without revealing it. By means of his "intellect" (the central faculty of the "mind"), the contemplative subject reads and verifies the truthfulness of the face's manifested message. Since the "mind's" ecstatic revelations are messages delivered by the demonic presences within us but independent from us, a face (the highest form of "subtle" manifestation) requires a form of authentication ("intellect"). Expressing a view reminiscent of Trithemius's *Steganographia*, Cardano is convinced that the demons residing in our mind may deliberately convey false and misleading communications.

If he wants to emphasize the possibly sinister nature of a demonic being, in some passages Cardano uses *devil* instead of *demon,* thus shifting to a more "lawful" rhetoric.

It is evident that even the supreme form of demonic revelation (the "lemur"), in which the contemplative subject mirrors his own face, necessitates an act of exegesis. According to Cardano's philosophical system based on the "sympathetic" relationship among all forms of visual manifestation, the visible (dreams, memory, external reality) articulates one and only one idiom. In his seminal *Synesiorum somniorum*, a crucial Renaissance treatise on dreams, Cardano states that the most eloquent form of oneiric message is what he calls the "specular dream," in which the dreamer sees his own face as if he were looking at himself in a mirror. This image always expresses a warning concerning the subject's future. Cardano adds, however, that in a "specular dream" what the subject perceives as his own face is actually someone else's. A "specular dream" delivers its message by showing the face of someone extremely close to the dreamer, usually his first son. In this kind of dream, then, the subject reads his face through his son's. This reflection is a warning that the contemplative mind will write out through its "intellect."

In *The Book of My Life,* his fascinating autobiography, Cardano writes that no painter has ever been able to draw his face, because it lacks any "recognizable" feature. A decent depiction of Cardano's face can be achieved only by comparing it with more defined faces holding some similarities to Cardano's. This is why the specularity with his son is an essential aid in the father's attempt to decode the destiny (the subtle language) written in his own face. In the same treatise, Cardano says that in oneiric terms "son" means "sight" or "to see." The practice of exegesis (the act of interpreting the idiom of our face) is thus a "filial" procedure, in that the "son" reflects and clarifies the foreboding hidden in the father's facial traits. In *De sapientia,* Cardano clearly states that the wise man always keeps the image of his son before his (inner) eyes. The father-son connection is a carnal one, says Cardano, for father and son are indeed one in the "soul," the part of the mind that vivifies the body.

It is difficult to convey the intensity of Cardano's obsession with the image of his first son. In almost every treatise Cardano reminds the reader of the devastating suffering he underwent when his son Giovanni Battista died at the age of twenty-six. The young man was executed in prison for having attempted his wife's murder. Premonitory signs had marked Cardano's body, one more time revealing the link between father and son in the "soul." In a passage from *Paralipomenon,* Cardano hypothesizes that

18

this union is based on a shared melancholic humor. Father and son speak to each other via their common melancholy.

If melancholy is the linguistic medium through which two subjects converse with each other (the Florentine mystic and her deceased brother, Cardano and his dead son), a demonic presence in the mind is an essential element of this dialogical event. If in the case of Maria Maddalena de' Pazzi the devil invades the mind with an excess of melancholy, for Girolamo Cardano a demon "occurs" when the son's reflected image arises in the wise man's (the father's) inner sight. A demon is the premonitory vision lying dormant in the subject's face. In the last part of the final chapter, we shall read Cardano's seminal treatise on metoposcopy, the art of reading the warning signs written on the forehead. Starting from the image of a wise man who, according to Cardano's description, is doomed to endure harrowing pains because of his sons, we shall trace a possible grammar of this art of divination. Like the souls in purgatory, the innumerable faces in Cardano's *Metoposcopia* expose themselves to the viewer in order to be recognized, remembered, and thus saved. Each face encapsulates a destiny, and many of them also unveil their impending violent end (by murder, drowning, execution, virulent disease). Cardano's doxology is both warning inventory and act of remembrance.

WE CAN SEE NOW the paradoxical nature of the devil's rhetoric according to Renaissance culture: If, on the one hand, Satan's nonlanguage attempts to silence the created world (Prierio, de Moura, Menghi), on the other it results in a different and much more expressive idiom (de' Pazzi, Cardano) in which to speak means to respond to the words uttered by the other in pain. In writing this book, I had a distinct narrative structure in mind. I wanted the reader to see that the devil's language has a salvific potential. I also wanted to clarify that this positive outcome arises only if we are "flooded" with a demonic discourse—that is, only if we oppose no resistance to Satan's linguistic invasion. In other words, only a "weakened" mind is able to translate a linguistic chaos into a message of redemption.

The first two chapters recount how, according to two major Catholic inquisitors, Satan "beclouds" human expression by means of a syllogistic "local motion," which is at once the rhetorical connector of an explorative reasoning and the actual speakers of a language "against nature." Demonic expression manifests itself as a trace signifying the disappearance of every form of expression (the mark overshadowing the young witch's pupil, according to de Lancre's story). We may say that the chapters on Prierio and de Moura speak of a forceful, repressive reaction with regard to the demonic discourse. Describing Satan's language as a disease, these Catholic inquisitors aim to detect and repress Satan's words. To do so, they cannot help but detect and repress those (Jews, sodomites, women) who support Satan's linguistic endeavors.

In chapter 3 we will see how, through the ritual of exorcism, a Catholic priest tries to impose a plausible narrative sense onto the "beclouded" world. According to the Catholic creed, the creation both speaks and is spoken by the sacred, mythic tales reported in the Catholic Bible, which foresee (Old Testament) and describe (New Testament) God's incarnation and sacrifice for all of humanity. To heal a possessed body thus means to turn it into a narrative unit of a past story of redemption. We must understand that the practice of exorcism is based on the assumption that the world has one and only one story to tell (Christ's death and victory over the forces of evil). An exorcist "reassembles" the pieces of a chaotic account (a body possessed by a demonic non-sense) according to a fixed narrative scheme.

But while a Catholic priest tries to force a credible (metaphorical) narration onto the body in pain in order to give it a curative meaning, the invaded body itself is asked to grant salvation—that is, to respond to a request for meaning coming from others. Only a mind emptied of any narrative meaning can listen to the suffering endured by the other. A "weak" mind rescues the other from his torment not by reading him through the lenses of some familiar story, but rather by making himself a receptacle of the other's disquiet. This is an essential trait present both in Christian demonology and in Florentine Neoplatonism. The highest form of knowledge, both Maria Maddalena de' Pazzi and Girolamo Cardano would say, is what comes to you once you have become a victim of the devil's discourse. According to Cardano's philosophy, the silent "cloud" of a demonic visitation is the brightest and most eloquent enlightenment.

ONE

The Devil's Perverted Syllogism:
Prierio's *De Strigimagis*

ONE OF THE CENTRAL ISSUES discussed in Christian theology is the nature of angelic language. In *On the Devils' Divination, On the Trinity, On the Literal Meaning of Genesis*, and primarily in *The City of God*, Augustine laid the foundations for the medieval and Renaissance debates on the ontological differences between good and bad angels, and thus also on their intrinsically different idioms.[1] Expanding Augustine's fundamental, yet rather general, theories on blessed and fallen angels, Thomas Aquinas first dedicated a considerable section of his *Summa* to the analysis of angelic beings (part 1, questions 50–64). Thanks to his seminal analysis, "angelology" became one of the most important branches of Christian theology. Still, in recent years, lay scholars, such as Michel de Certeau and Massimo Cacciari, have written fascinating studies on angelic creatures.[2]

By "angelology" students of Christian theology generally mean the investigation of the good angels' nature, mission, and language. Strictly speaking, angelology does not include the analysis of the fallen angels' ontology. The Church Fathers founded a second discipline of study, the so-called demonology, dedicated to the study of the rejected angels. But

1. For an introduction to Augustinian demonology, see Jeffrey Burton Russell, *Satan: The Early Christian Tradition* (Ithaca: Cornell University Press, 1981), 186–218.

2. Michel de Certeau, *Il parlare angelico*, translated by Daniela de Agostini (Florence: Olschki, 1989); Massimo Cacciari, *L'angelo necessario* (Milan: Adelphi, 1994).

angelology and demonology are not parallel areas of research. While angelology has a strongly theoretical character, and primarily examines the similarities and dissimilarities between God's unfathomable nature and the heavenly spirits' created being, demonology is the study of the devils' manifestations in the world. Church Fathers and demonologists attempt to understand how the devil influences and communicates with the creation.

Augustine explains how the Enemy rules over the world, in a crucial passage from *The City of God* (book 9, chap. 22). According to Augustine, whereas the good angels "look upwards"—that is, they constantly contemplate God's goodness—the fallen angels are entangled in the world's deceitful snares:

> [T]he good angels hold cheap all the knowledge of things material and temporal that gives the demons such a swollen notion of themselves; not that they are ignorant in such matters, but that the love of God whereby they are sanctified is dear to them. In comparision with its beauty, which is not only immaterial but also immutable and ineffable as well, and which makes them glow with a holy passion, they despise all things which are beneath it. . . . The devils on the contrary do not fix their gaze on the eternal causes, the hinges as it were, of temporal events, which are found in God's wisdom, though they do foresee many more future events than we do by their greater acquaintance with certain signs that are hidden from men. Sometimes too they announce in advance events that they themselves intend to bring about. Consequently the demons are often mistaken, the angels absolutely never.[3]

Augustine holds that, unlike the good angels, the fallen angels do not behold God's wisdom, and thus are intrinsically "worldly" creatures. Moreover, Augustine states that, given their "acquaintance with the signs that are hidden from men," the devils are able to foresee the future. In other words, while the good angels could be interpreted as linguistic devices through which the Divinity speaks to his creation, the fallen angels are keen interpreters of the world's signs.[4] As I shall show below, according to Christian theology, neither the good nor the bad angels possess a personal

---

3. Augustine, *The City of God against the Pagans*, translated by David S. Wiesen, vol. 3 (Cambridge, Mass.: Harvard University Press, 1982), book 9, chap. 22, 233–35. Augustine analyzes the devil's particular "skills" in the third chapter of *De divinatione daemonum* (PL 40), 584–85.

4. Prierio alludes to this point in several passages of *De strigimagis*. For instance, at the end of book 1 he says: "[D]emons are equal to the good angels as far as their nature is concerned, and in some cases even superior, since they fell from every [angelic] order and in particular from the highest one" (115).

idiom. But while the good angels *are spoken* by the Divinity to the world, the devils mime the "phonemes" of the world itself.

In book 10, chapter 12 of *The City of God* Augustine makes it clear that the blessed angels are nothing but that "matter" through which the Divinity hears us: "[W]hen His angels answer prayers, it is He Himself who answers within them" (trans. Wiesen, 311). If we interpret the angels' essence from a linguistic standpoint, we might say that the angels are both God's phonemes and the "air" that carries his phonemes to us.

Although he openly states that the bad angels are astute semioticians of the world's language, Augustine does not consider it necessary to investigate the nature of their semiotics. The two fathers of Catholic theology, Augustine and Thomas, primarily focus on God's "utterances" through his angelic messengers, whose essence lies in their being "mute matter."

THIS CHAPTER ANALYZES Sylvester Prierio's *De strigimagarum daemonumque mirandis* (Rome, 1521), a central, yet underestimated, book of Renaissance demonology.[5] As Henry Charles Lea reminds us, "Sylvester Mazzolino, known as Prierias from his birthplace, was one of the leading theologians of his time and papal champion against Luther. He was inquisitor in Lombardy, 1508–12."[6] The importance of Prierio's text lies in

---

5. The Italian scholar Giovanni Romeo believes that *De strigimagis* is one of "the most fanatic books written in Italy about witchcraft" (*Inquisitori, esorcisti e streghe nell'Italia della Controriforma* [Florence: Sansoni, 1990], 86). I quote from a later edition of Prierio's book (Rome, 1575). Compare Michael Tavuzzi, *Prierias* (Durham, N.C.: Duke University Press, 1997), 122–27.

6. Henry Charles Lea, *Materials toward a History of Witchcraft*, ed. Arthur C. Howland, vol. 1 (Philadelphia: University of Pennsylvania Press, 1939), 354. Prierio was born between 1456 and 1460 in the small town of Prierio in Piedmont. He became a Dominican at the age of fifteen. He taught theology in Bologna and Padua. Between 1508 and 1511, he was inquisitor in Brescia, Milan, Lodi, and Piacenza. In 1511 Pope Julius II invited him to teach theology in Rome. He died in 1522, during an outbreak of plague. See Attilio Agnoletto, Sergio Abbiate, and Maria Rosario Lazzati, eds., *La stregoneria. Diavoli, streghe, inquisitori dal Trecento al Settecento* (Milan: Mondadori, 1991), 362–64. Compare Federico Pastore, *La fabbrica delle streghe* (Paisian di Prato, Italy: Campanotto Editore, 1997), 199–200. Pastore notes that Prierio coined the expression *strigimagae*. Before *De strigimagis*, Prierio wrote *Sylvestrina summa, quae Summa summarum merito nuncupatur*, 2 vols. (Bologna, 1514). In his *Summa* Prierio broaches a variety of ecclesiastical problems, such as *indulgentia* (1:27–36), *matrimonium* (1:174–224), *missa* (1:233–41), *papa* (1:274–79), *religio* (1:332–57), *sepultura* (1:403–8), *simonia* (1:410–24), *absolutio* (2:4–10), *baptismus* (2:71–84), *clericus* (2:132–44), *divortium* (2:256–61). The longest entry is *excommunicatio* (2:350–422). Prierio was a very prolific writer. Along with *De strigimagis* and his *Summa*, he published several texts against Luther, such as *Epitoma responsionis ad Martinum Luther* (Perugia, 1519) and *Errata et argumenta Martini Luteris recitata, detecta, repulsa et copiosissime trita* (Rome, 1520). On Prierio's

its attempt to investigate how the devil constructs his own idiom through an ongoing process of semiotic interpretation. The treatise's very first sentence (book 1, chap. 1) is a dramatic biblical quotation (Ps. 13:4): "Devorant plebem meam sicut escam panis" ("they devour my people as if they were eating bread"). Prierio is convinced that this verse is more than a historical reference to "those who blaspheme God and are unjust against God's people." According to Prierio, if we interpret this verse allegorically ("in sensu, quem allegoricum dicunt," 1), it becomes a direct accusation against the devil and his followers, primarily the witches. What the devil "devours" is "the fruits of my people, their cattle, and both their bodies and their souls."

The devil devours humankind by means of his followers who "with words deny the true God [*Deum verum . . . verbis negant*]." From the outset, Prierio relates the image of the devils devouring God's creatures to an act of linguistic expression. In other words, the voice and the mouth, the site where the voice is articulated, are closely connected with each other. The voice, the devil's voice, is also the devil's mouth, which devours our body and soul.[7] As Louis Marin puts it, "[T]he voice is a 'thing of the mouth,' that is, a part of the body which consists of lips, teeth, a tongue, a palate, a glottis, and a throat. . . . The mouth and its various parts may thus be said to designate metonymically the specificity of a speaking voice, ranging between the scream on the one hand, a discharge of almost raw sound . . . and, on the other hand, an almost inarticulate whisper verging on silence. . . . The mouth is the locus of need, as well as the means by which this need is satisfied."[8] The devil's devouring idiom is predicated upon a fundamental premise: to speak the devil's language *is* as well as *means* to devour the creation (men's bodies and souls, their cattle). The good angels' language is a nonlanguage in that its speakers simply voice the Divinity's will by means of human signifying sounds. The devil's idiom is spoken by three categories of speakers: the devils themselves, the

---

position against Luther, see the entry "Mazolini, Silvestre" in *Dictionnaire de théologie catholique*, vol. 10, part 1 (Paris, 1928), 475–77; Tavuzzi, *Prierias*, 104–19.

7. As we shall see later, in order to construct sounds similar to a human voice, the devil may enter a human body and force it to produce some particular noises/sounds. The devil's saying is so base that, according to Jean Bodin, he may even "speak" through a witch's anus or vagina: "Et quelquesfois le malin esprit parle, comme dedans l'estomach estant la bouche de la femme close, . . . par les parties honteuses" (*De la démonomanie des sorciers* [Hildesheim: Olms Verlag, 1988], 76r–v). In other words, the devil's speaking is a form of defecation. The devil at once devours, speaks, and defecates.

8. Louis Marin, *Food for Thought*, translated by Mette Hjort (Baltimore: Johns Hopkins University Press, 1989), 35–37.

witches (along with sodomites and Jews), and those human beings who have been corrupted/devoured by this very language. This distinction is of crucial relevance.[9] As we shall see, the devil's idiom is similar to a historical language spoken in more than one geographic area (for instance, British English and American English, or Brazilian Portuguese, Continental Portuguese, and African Portuguese). Moreover, the devil's language distinguishes between a "native speaker" and a "foreign speaker."

These distinctions are based on the assumption that each of the three categories of speakers embodies a different ontological status. Whereas God's creature can be "devoured" by the devil's idiom and thus begins to articulate a language/mouth that devours its own body, both the devil himself and the witches are "native speakers" of this language/devouring mouth. Moreover, within this second category of speakers we must distinguish between speakers without a mouth (the devil has no body) and speakers with a mouth (the witches). As I will explain, these distinctions bear important theological and historical consequences.

Prierio notes that the name *strix* indicates an "avis nocturna a stridendo dicta, quod scilicet clamando stridat" (3). A "witch" is similar to a night bird whose screams produce harsh sounds. Her second common name *lamia* refers to a *bestia monstruosa* with horselike feet, who "tears to pieces her own children."[10] *Lamia*, Prierio infers, is equivalent to *lania* (female butcher). The two Latin definitions (witch as *strix* and as *lamia/lania*) thus compound the two major facets of the witch's essence: her being a "bird" (a nonhuman speaker) emitting harsh sounds that tear apart, "devour" her listeners.[11]

9. Compare Stuart Clark, *Thinking with Demons: The Idea of Witchcraft in Early Modern Europe* (Oxford: Clarendon, 1997), 285: "Knowledge consisted . . . in relating one form of language to another."

10. Compare Petrus Binsfeldius, *Tractatus de confessionibus maleficorum et sagarum* (Trier: Henricus Bock, 1605), 85: "*lamia* is a monster, whose superior part resembles a woman and his legs have feet similar to those of a horse."

11. In the short *De strigis* (c. 1505), the Dominican inquisitor Bernardo Rategno da Como shows a similar philological interest. He thinks that the word *strix* derives from *Styx (Stige)*, which either means "hell or infernal swamp, because these people are diabolical and infernal" or "it can come from the Greek *stigetos*, which corresponds to the Latin [for] 'unhappiness.'" I quote from the complete Italian translation of this work in Agnoletto, Abbiate, and Lazzati, eds., *La stregoneria*, 200–201. In Joseph Hansen's *Quellen und Untersuchungen zur Geschichte des Hexenwahns und der Hexenverfolgung im Mittelalter* (Bonn: Carl Georgi, 1901), we find another text specifically interested in the witches' possible names (195–200). In *Quaestio de strigis* (c. 1460), the Dominican Jordan of Bergamo mentions *maliarde* (something like "enchantresses") and *herbarie* (herbal practitioners) (Hansen, *Quellen*, 196). For an exhaustive analysis of the origin and development of *witch*, see Johannes Franck, "Geschichte des Wortes

Although a human being cannot learn the language of the good angels, who limit themselves to borrowing human phonemes in order to communicate someone else's communication to one specific interlocutor, a human being can certainly learn how to speak the idiom of the fallen angels, through an act of free will.[12] Indeed, unlike the language of divine angels, the devouring idiom of Satan is first and foremost a social occurrence. Before entering into a detailed analysis of the soul's essence according to Thomas's *Summa*, Prierio offers a graphic description of those gatherings, the notorious Sabbat, where the Enemy is called up *(vocatus)*. For this and subsequent narrative inserts Prierio refers to two basic texts: Kramer and Sprenger's infamous *Malleus maleficarum* (1486) and Nider's *Formicarius* (1475).[13] Following Sprenger, Prierio states that to become a member of the *diabolica religio* an individual must undergo two rituals, one private and one public (4).[14] In both cases, the person must call *(vocare)* the Enemy, who will appear to him or her "through a given image [*assumpta effigie*]." The effectiveness of the linguistic articulation is sanctioned by its ability to conjure an image. This is what Aristotle, a basic reference both for Thomas and Prierio, theorizes in the third book of *De anima*.

Quoting from Nider, Prierio writes that the devil's "novice" *(novitius)* must respond to the Enemy's *assumptam effigiem* by verbally abjuring the Catholic faith (5). The "disciple" is indeed engaged in a constant dialogue with his master, even when the devil is not visible to him or her. The ab-

---

Hexe," in Hansen, *Quellen*, 614–70. Although Franck primarily focuses on the relationship between Latin and German, his article is still extremely useful because it brings to the fore the innumerable connotations of this crucial term.

12. Bartholomeo Spina, Prierio's pupil, clarifies this central point. In *Quaestio de strigibus* (Venice, 1523), Spina explains that, by offering themselves to the devil, witches have abandoned their condition of human beings, for they have lost their free will forever: "[Witches] state that . . . those who have signed a pact [with him] . . . are not allowed to withdraw from their obligations. To give up one's own free will and thus to become a heretic is a manifest act against nature" (6).

13. As far as Nider's book is concerned, Prierio directly quotes it in the second part of *De strigimagis*, where he discusses the relationship between the devils and the witches. In this second section Prierio's style becomes less philosophical and much more narrative. Nider's *Formicarius* is a source of gruesome anecdotes and stories. For instance, on p. 154 Prierio relates the trial of two witches who had eaten babies who had not been baptized. He finds this story in book 5, chap. 3, 74v, of *Formicarius* (Strasbourg, 1517). Later (167) Prierio recounts the trial of a certain "maleficus Stadhin" who confessed that he had killed seven unborn babies (*Formicarius*, book 5, chap. 3). Other direct references to Nider's work are on pp. 2, 5, 172, 189, 198, 204, 205. I use the edition of *Formicarius* published in Helmstedt in 1692.

14. See, for instance, *Malleus maleficarum*, part 2, q. 1, chap. 2, "Of the Way whereby a Formal Pact with Evil is made." I quote from the English translation by Montague Summers (New York: Dover, 1971), 99–101.

sence of the devil's "image," Prierio says, is more alarming than its presence. This is why, when the novice does not see the image, he or she refers to him as *magisterolus*, a diminutive and thus more familiar form of *magister* (5). The absence of the Master's image is perceived as a linguistic void, the withdrawal of one's mother tongue.[15]

Once the apprenticeship is concluded—that is, the novice has completed a series of acts insulting Catholicism, such as spitting in church or crushing a crucifix under one's feet—the disciple encounters the Master in a "sexual" image. In other words, the disciple has succeeded in conveying his or her drives through the newly apprehended language. Prierio notes that the traditional distinction between *incubus* and *succubus* refers to two forms of sexual intercourse, *activus* or *passivus* (6). In other words, the Enemy's image "responds" to his disciple's phonemes of desire. Unlike other late medieval and Renaissance demonologists, Prierio believes that sexual encounters between the devil and a human being can give birth to "unnatural" creatures, similar to the biblical giants (described in Gen. 6).[16]

Referring to Origen's and Augustine's distinction between inner and outer senses, Prierio clarifies that the devil's "appearance" *(apparitio)* engages the physical senses and/or the spiritual ones.[17] The disciple is never granted a complete and direct view of the Master, but rather perceives him as if he were behind the disciple, who was looking into a mirror (8). If the Master primarily manifests himself as the phantasmatic embodiment of his disciple's desire, the language exchanged between the lover (disciple) and the beloved Master (Satan) enacts the grammar of missing signifieds typical of every erotic language. Prierio emphasizes that one of the most

15. Julia Kristeva, "En deuil d'une langue?" in *Deuils: Vivre, c'est perdre*, edited by Nicole Czechowski and Claude Danzinger (Paris: Éditions Autrement, 1992), 27–36.

16. Compare *Malleus*, part 1, q. 3, 21–28, "Whether children can be generated by Incubi and Succubi"; Augustine, *The City of God*, translated by Philip Levine (Cambridge, Mass.: Harvard University Press, 1988), vol. 4, book 15, chap. 23, 549: "[T]here is a very widespread report, corroborated by many people either through their own experience or through accounts of others of indubitably good faith who have had the experience, that Silvans and Pans, who are commonly called *incubi*, often misbehaved towards women and succeeded in accomplishing their lustful desire to have intercourse with them." In the same chapter, Augustine also tackles the thorny issue of the offspring (the biblical "giants") generated through an "angelic" intercourse.

17. The theory of "inner" and "outer" senses is present in Origen's *Commentary on the Song of Songs*. See Origen, *An Exhortation to Martyrdom*, translated by Rowan A. Greer (New York: Paulist Press, 1979), 220: "In his letters he [Paul] wrote more openly and clearly that every person is two different men. This is what he said, 'Though our outer man is wasting away, our inner man is being renewed every day' (2 Cor. 4:16)." Augustine refers to Origen's interpretation in several texts, for instance, in *De trinitate* (PL 42), 983.

common effects of the devil's missed presence is the sudden and inexplicable hiding of things. This phenomenon, Prierio explains, is called *acrisia* or *aorasia*, and may be interpreted as a form of temporary and "selective" blindness, as if "we were forbidden to see certain things but not others" (8).[18] The first biblical occurrence of *aorasia* is in Genesis (19:11) and refers to the destruction of Sodom: "And they struck the men who were at the door of the house with *blindness* [*aorasìa*], from the youngest to oldest, and they never found the doorway."[19] Prierio does not clarify how this temporary blindness affects the relationship between the two speakers, the devil and his human interlocutor. What this blindness certainly brings about is the subject's questioning of his or her own sight—especially if we remember that the devil's summoned image is able to intrude upon both our outer and inner senses.[20]

Prierio discusses the relationship between outer and inner senses, words and their related images, in the rest of the first book of *De strigimagis* (chaps. 3–5), which focuses on the nature of the human soul. Prierio's rather long, though necessary, analysis is heavily influenced by the first book (questions 75–89) of Thomas's *Summa*. The crucial issue discussed in this section is not just what the soul is, but also, and more important, whether both imaginary and real images affect the soul. Borrowing the definitions of Augustine (*On the Trinity*, book 10, 7) and Thomas (*Summa*,

18. The first commentary on the term *aorasia* is in *Commentii in Genesim in tres libros distributi* (PL 50), a work falsely attributed to St. Eucherius. On p. 962 the author explains that God sent *aorasia* to the sodomites who threatened Loth: "Those who desired Elisaeus were punished with 'aorasia.'" In *Disquisitionum magicarum* (Mainz: Petrus Henningius, 1617), 121, Martin del Rio discusses *aorasia* at length: "Forms of deception connected with visual perception . . . are indeed of various kinds. . . . As a result, it happens that a thing that is in one place is however seen in another, or a single thing is perceived as double. Similarly, if you press down a finger in the cavity where the eye is located and then, still keeping the finger there, you move your eye up and down you will see that things that are simple will look double. Second, if humors are stirred up or perturbed, things will be perceived not the way they actually are, as it happens to drunk or insane people. . . . [He] usually prevents the subject from perceiving a given affection by blocking its passage through a thicker humor so that that specific spirit be unable to reach its organ, or by dulling the subject's perception in other ways. How right were the angels when they hit the sodomites with 'aorasia.' When a demon convinces men that he has turned them into beasts, in fact he does not modify their organ, but only its functions, and always their imagination. . . . The devil can indeed arrange and order mental images [*phantasmata*], as in the case of those who, albeit awake, dream (as they say) as if they were asleep, and are convinced that they feel things that in fact they do not feel, as it happens to insane people."

19. Other occurrences: Deut. 28:28: "Yahweh will strike you down with madness, *blindness*, distraction of mind"; Wisd. of Sol. 19:16; 2 Macc. 10:30.

20. We have already mentioned *Quaestio de strigis* by Jordan of Bergamo (see note 11, above). Jordan reminds us that sometimes we have the impression that insects are passing over our eyes, though these are only what we now call "floaters" (Hansen, *Quellen*, 197).

q. 75, art. 2), Prierio states that the soul is primarily *principium nostrae intellectionis* and its operations are intrinsically independent from the body (12). Quoting Thomas, Prierio writes that the soul is a substance, without being a body. Referring to Aristotle's *De anima* (3.2.15–20), Thomas synthesizes this point as follows: "The soul understands just as the eye sees. . . . The body is necessary for the action of the intellect, not as its organ of action but on the part of the object; for the phantasm is to the intellect what color is to the sight."[21] The human act of perceiving and understanding is a two-sided process. The mind/soul, like its thoughts, is both passive and active. The mind (agent intellect) is a power of under-standing that abstracts the intelligible forms from the sensible world. In this process of abstraction the mind (possible intellect) is actualized by its own act of thinking/perceiving (agent intellect).[22] According to Prierio, the agent intellect, the active side of the soul, expresses the "incorruptible and nobler" nature of our soul, because it is totally independent from the body (16). Yet the possible intellect is "in potentiality to the determinate species of things" (Thomas, *Summa* V.1 [ed. Pegis], q. 79, art. 4, 752; com-pare Prierio, 31). The agent intellect's process of abstraction is predicated upon two fundamental procedures, reduction and dissection of the per-ceived phantasm through the possible intellect. "The phantasm itself," Thomas confirms, "is not the form of the possible intellect; the intellegible species abstracted from phantasms is such a form" (*Summa* V.1 [ed. Pegis], q. 76, art. 2, 702; compare Prierio, 21–22).

This process of dissection/reduction is essentially a form of grammati-cal analysis. However, a fundamental distinction subsists between the per-ception of the sensible by the good angels and by the human beings, and, as we shall see later, by the devils as well. As Thomas emphasizes (*Summa* V.1 [ed. Pegis], q. 85, art. 1, 813), the good angels "know material things, yet they do not know them save in something immaterial, namely, either in themselves or in God." Thus, God's angels do not share the human process of grammatical abstraction/dissection from the phantasms. The language of the angels is not a set of phonemes abstracted from the sen-sible; the angels need neither a possible intellect nor an agent intellect (Prierio, 43).

This central distinction is a cornerstone in Prierio's theory of demonic language. Indeed, we shall see that in the second part of his text Prierio

21. I quote from the partial translation of the *Summa* in Thomas Aquinas, *Basic Writings*, edited by Anton C. Pegis (New York: Random House, 1945), 686.
22. Speaking of the different forms of false images conveyed primarily through dreams, Nider mentions a sort of *caecitas mentis*, or "mental blindness" (*Formicarius*, 24v).

grants the devil a psychological structure very similar to that of the human beings. Moreover, since the devil perceives the world in a more than human manner, he is able to fabricate "phantasms"—that is, imaginary linguistic artifacts aimed to corrupt the grammar of our understanding (possible intellect) and our "uttering" (agent intellect) of the world. However, by stating that the soul is absolutely autonomous from the body's activities, and thus is not divided into "intellectual," "sensitive," and "nutritive" soul, Thomas and Prierio wish to emphasize man's potential freedom to process and judge any devilish utterance/phantasm (Prierio, 19–21; Thomas, *Summa* V.1 [ed. Pegis], q. 76, art. 3, 706). Indeed, Prierio claims that those who believe that the soul is divided into these three functions express a creed fostered by the devil (21). Through an intellectual act the soul gives form to the body without having any physical attribute.

The soul's central activity *(operatio)*, Prierio explains, is to understand *(intelligere)*, performing an act of abstraction from the sensible phantasms (55). In other words, although the soul has nothing to do with the body and limits itself to being the body's form, it takes from the body's interaction with the world its linguistic signifiers, the phantasms, through which it can perform its act of understanding (compare Aristotle, *De anima*, 3.15–20). The soul speaks/understands thanks to the body; it is the body's constant production of phantasms that grants the soul the signifiers of its language.

The *substantiae intellectuales*—that is, both the good and the bad angels—do not have a language of their own because they do not have phantasms. To admit that angels "remember" the language of the world would entail that the angels possess passions and memories, which are the primary signs of the soul's phantasmatic relation to the world. When the angels, first of all the fallen angels, seem to have entered a body, they have actually joined the body as forms and possess that body in an accidental manner (Prierio, 50–51).[23] While the soul can communicate with the body through its phantasms, the *substantiae separatae* can only communicate with the soul (54). Indeed, as Thomas emphasizes, angels have no memory, since memory is a product of the senses. God can instill a given remembrance in an angel only for a specific purpose and for a given time (Thomas, *Summa* 1, q. 54, art. 5, 515).

Memory is the phantasmatic field through which the soul "moves" in

---

23. In *Tractatus de sortilegiis* (Lyons, 1536), one of the most influential texts of Renaissance demonology, the Italian judge Paolo Grillando reminds us that the devils' bodies are "almost" natural *(quasi naturalia)*, in that they are able to move, make gestures, articulate sounds, eat. However, they are unable to perform other important activities. For instance, they cannot grow, sleep, or give birth (Paolo Grillando, *Tractatus de sortilegiis* [Frankfurt, 1592], 96).

its act of understanding. Following Thomas, Prierio distinguishes between *motus* (movement) and *movens* (moving), the former being the "drive" *(appetitus)* generated by the phantasmatic/linguistic signs, the latter being the actual act of moving one's *intellectus* in order to attain comprehension (73). In the angels the duality *motus/movens* does not entail a temporal distinction. The angels are in the act of performing their pure "intellectuality." [24] While the soul's process of moving from one phantasm to another in order to compose a thought is processed in time and engages both the agent intellect and the possible one, the angels at once think and "cross" a given area of intellectual existence. [25] In Thomas's words: "[A]n angel is of simpler substance than the soul. But our soul, by taking thought, can pass from one extreme to another without going through the middle: for I can think of France and afterwards of Syria, without ever thinking of Italy, which stands between them. Therefore much more can an angel pass from one extreme to another without going through the middle" (*Summa* V.1 [ed. Pegis], q. 53, art. 2, 504). As we shall see later, this passing "from one extreme to another without going through the middle" corresponds to the middle point of a perfect syllogism. [26] The inexistent "middle" embodies the "moment" when a deduction is going to be drawn. The angels live as subsistent syllogisms and are able to move through an act of what Prierio calls "self-reflection": "Nulla autem potentia iudicans seipsam ad iudicandum movet, nisi supra suum actum flectatur" (73–74). In the angels this "bending over his own act" is equivalent to phrasing the second *ratio* or *praemissa minor* of a syllogism, which follows the founding "act" of the syllogism *(praemissa maior)* and precedes its final "crossing" of the open field leading to its closure *(conclusio)*. [27] We shall see later how, while the good angels never construct a wrong syllogism, the fallen angels always formulate "perverted" syllogisms. [28]

24. On the notion of "intellectuality," see Thomas, *Summa* 1, q. 50, art. 4, 487.

25. In another passage Prierio states that (good) angelic minds are at once "above" time *(supra tempus)* and "in" time *(infra tempus)*, because of their dual way of thinking. On the one hand, (good) angels reflect divine wisdom; on the other, they produce an "almost" (quasi) syllogism, as if it took place in time (107–8).

26. On Aristotle's concept of syllogism, see Renato Barilli, *Rhetoric,* translated by Giuliana Menozzi (Minneapolis: University of Minnesota Press, 1989), 10–11.

27. Compare Heinrich Lausberg, *Elementi di retorica* (Bologna: Il Mulino, 1969), 198–201.

28. The Church Fathers often state that syllogism was the typical form of pagan reasoning. In other words, for Christianity syllogism was associated with any form of dishonest (unreligious) reasoning. For instance, in *The Life of Saint Anthony* (translated by Robert T. Meyer [Westminster, Md.: Newman Press, 1950], 84) Athanasius attacks the Greek philosophers in these terms: "We Christians . . . possess religious truth not on the basis of Greek philosophical reasoning, but founded on the power of a faith vouchsafed us by God through Jesus Christ. . . .

A fundamental rule of any syllogism is its derivation from an act of free will (Prierio, 74). Both the angels and the human soul act out of a private decision. This is why the angels may sin (76). Since the angels have no physicality, their hypothetical sin is a mere act of their intellect. However, an angelic intellect essentially differs from a human being's because it is deprived of memory and imagination. The angel's sin is much more radical and unforgivable because it is predicated upon a "pure" syllogism—that is, a syllogism that cannot be misconstrued because of a "strong imagination," of a rush of phantasms, which can even cause fever and leprosy (Prierio, 77). The phantasms, the basic components of a human syllogism, come from the body and affect the body. Again, the only possible "error" in a syllogism can occur "in the middle," as Thomas explains:

> To go from one extreme to the other it is necessary to pass through the middle. Now the being of a form in the imagination, which is without matter but not without material conditions, stands midway between the being of a form which is in the matter, and the being of a form which is in the intellect by abstraction from matter. . . . Consequently, however powerful the angelic mind might be, it could not reduce material forms to an intelligible being, except it were first to reduce them to the being of forms in the imagination; which is impossible, since the angel has no imagination. (*Summa* V.1 [ed. Pegis], q. 55, art. 2, 519)

Since the angels have no passions, memories, or imagination (Prierio, 91)—that is, they cannot produce phantasms, the signs and phonemes of any human interaction—they influence matter not directly, but rather by means of a "local movement" *(motus localis)*, which affects the form of a given matter.[29] For instance, Prierio explains, natural heat does not alter meat of itself, but rather through *virtute animae vegetabilis* (78). In other words, the devils can exert an influence on the creation only through an intellectual abstraction, a syllogism that gathers concrete conclusions from conceptual premises.

In rhetorical terms, the "local movement" is the actual *conclusio* deriving from two *rationes* linked through a *sed* or *et* (but, and), as in "all men are mortal, [and] Socrates is a man." It is the adversative connector

---

[Y]ou with your syllogisms and sophisms are not converting anybody from Christianity to Paganism." Compare Augustine, *Soliloquiorum libri duo* (PL 32), book 2, chap. 14, "Excutitur superior syllogismus."

29. Compare the entry "maleficium" in *Sylvestrina summa* (1:166–70): "The bad angel is able to produce all possible things by means of a local motion, or by making use of powers that are naturally active, such as rain or winds. . . . [Thus he can also] condense or rarefy the air. In the air he can appear in the form of a man or a woman" (1:167).

that brings about the "physical" conclusion "Socrates is mortal." Prierio stresses that language itself affects reality not because of its being a set of phantasms, but rather because it is directed *somewhere*—that is, it has an addressee.[30] Language itself is movement, an act of crossing intellectual boundaries, from a "wherefrom" to a "whereto," as Thomas says in question 53, 3. Attacking the Neoplatonics—in particular Marsilio Ficino, who claimed that matter, human voice included, has an actively signifying quality—Prierio believes that voice does not mean anything in itself; it has no "dynamic" connotation, unless it is intended as a form of "invocation" or "entreaty," as for instance in the magicians' utterances: "The sensible utterances that magicians use are in fact invocations, supplications, entreaties" (82).

Seemingly anticipating Searle's theories on illocutionary acts, Prierio highlights the intrinsic directionality of language. To mean something, language must be directed to someone.[31] According to Prierio, Ficino is mistaken when he states that pictures (*figurae*) are able to produce effects in the creation ("figura autem nullius actionis principium est," 82).[32] Language, phantasms, pictures are nothing but "signs" [*signa*] used to signify something for someone ("Signis autem non utuntur nisi ad alios intelligentes"). Therefore, when magicians recite some obscure verse or draw cryptic images, they are actually invoking, directing a request to a higher interlocutor, a fallen angel (85).

A common trait of every medieval and Renaissance treatise on demonology is the intrinsic dichotomy between the speaker, who is always either a human being or God himself, and the listener, who identifies with the angelic being.[33] Indeed, if the good angels are "interpreters of divine silence"[34]—that is, they constantly attempt to understand God's unspoken

---

30. "Speech has indeed an intrinsically rational nature." Prierio also stresses that man reveals himself through his words (79).

31. "Insofar as it conveys a meaning, voice can only derive its nature by the intellect, either the intellect of the speaker or that of his interlocutor" (Prierio, 81).

32. I analyze this aspect of Ficino's philosophy in "Impresa e misticismo nel *Settenario* di Alessandro Farra (1571)," *Rivista di storia e letteratura religiosa* (1997): 3–28.

33. For an interesting discussion on the language of the fallen angels, see Bartolomeo Sybilla, *Speculum peregrinarum quaestionum* (1499), especially q. 4: "Quarta questiuncula est: quotmodis potest aliquis spiritus alloqui hominem" (203r–v).

34. See Henry Corbin, *Avicenna and the Visionary Recital,* translated by Willard R. Trask (Princeton: Princeton University Press, 1988), 55. Corbin discusses Avicenna's Neoplatonic interpretation of the angelic beings: "The idea (common to Islam and Christianity) of the Angel as servant of the supreme God and messenger of His communications to the Prophets is replaced by the Neoplatonic idea of the Angel as "hermeneut of the divine silence"—that is, as

directions—the fallen angels listen to the signs sent out by the creation it-self. Pretending to articulate human language, the devils are actually re-sponding to a human speaker's request, even if it has not yet been uttered. In other words, the devils are able to read the signs that signify a "possible" human speaker. The devil's temptation is primarily a response, in that the fallen angel is capable of understanding if a given subject might be willing to direct his or her phantasmatic signs to him.

Prierio stresses the relevance of this point when he writes that, since the angelic beings do not draw their knowledge from the sensible but rather through a process of abstraction/purification from the sensible it-self, they cannot err in their cognition.[35] If they understand something, they apprehend it without any possible error.[36] When they enter the sen-sible world, the fallen angels act by means of "local movement," which embodies the *conclusio* of the devils' syllogistic procedure.[37] Before ana-lyzing how the devil constructs his syllogism, Prierio examines the means through which the devil formulates his analytic process. Whereas both the *praemissa maior* and the *praemissa minor* take place in the *substantia intellectualis* itself, the syllogism's conclusion occurs in the creation and identifies with the angelic being's "local movement" (161).

The medium of the devil's *conclusio* is the air. Starting from Augustine, all the Church Fathers are convinced that the good angels reside in a non-place located between the beyond-being divinity and the creation, and that the fallen angels are doomed to wander in the air.[38] The air signifies the devils' "ungroundedness," their identity as angelic substances "compelled"

---

annunciation and epiphany of the impenetrable and incommunicable divine transcendence." I examine the nature of angelic language in *Uttering the Word: The Mystical Performances of Maria Maddalena de' Pazzi, a Renaissance Visionary* (Albany: State University of New York Press, 1998), 37–72.

35. "The separate substances . . ., both the good and the bad ones, do not glean any form of knowledge from created things" (96).

36. "[T]hey understand everything they know. Indeed, you cannot err in something you know. Every mistake comes from a defect of knowledge. No error is present in the cognition of separate substances" (90).

37. In *De memoria et reminiscentia*, Thomas states that, unlike "memory" *(memoria)*, "rec-ollection" *(reminiscentia)* is similar to a syllogism because, like a syllogism, it derives from cer-tain principles. Thomas, *In Aristotelis libros de sensu et sensato, De memoria et reminiscentia commentarium*, edited by Raimondo Spiazzi (Turin: Marietti, 1949), *lectio* 8, chap. 399, 113.

38. See, for instance, Cassian, *De principatibus seu potestatibus*, in *Opera omnia* (PL 49), col. 12, 740: "The air is densely crowded with so many spirits scattered between heaven and earth. Anxious and industrious, they wander through the air"; Gregory the Great, *Moralia*, in *Opera omnia* (PL 75), col. 47, 590: "We know that the impure spirits, who fell from heaven, roam in the area between sky and earth." I analyze this point in *Uttering the Word*, 119–38.

to interpret the world's signs without possessing them.[39] We must bear in mind that the angels do not articulate any form of idiom, but rather are interpreters of all the world's idioms.

Air is the devils' most suitable dwelling because it is "shapeless" *(infigurabilis)* and the least material kind of matter (Prierio, 98 and 158). Indeed, air enables a series of different functions. First, devils, who are shapeless and immaterial like air, acquire a transient physicality by compressing and shaping air itself (158). Air is at once the place where the devils live and the body that they assume temporarily.[40] Furthermore, air is the medium that carries them through the world (98–99). Finally, air conveys the devils' responses to the creatures' phantasms. In particular, the language of the Enemy's response can be either verbal or corporeal: a devil can either "move the air" to reproduce a specific human idiom, or he can "move the air" to shape a bodily figure through which he can have sexual intercourse with a creature (158). In both forms of linguistic interaction, the devil relies on the essentially physical nature of voice, which is articulated through a complex interaction of several organs and parts of the human body (lungs, throat, tongue, teeth, lips).

When a devil assumes a given physicality to reproduce a series of sounds resembling a human language or to have a sexual encounter with a creature, he does not "speak" (he is not engaged in the production of any form of phantasms); rather, he speaks *per similitudinem*, mimicking a set of signifiers that have a certain impact on the human listener (Prierio, 159).[41] In other words, through a process of semantic abstractions the devil

39. On the relationship between air and demonic being, see Dyan Elliott, *Fallen Bodies: Pollution, Sexuality, and Demonology in the Middle Ages* (Philadelphia: University of Pennsylvania Press, 1999). As Elliott explains, "there is little doubt that both angels and demons had bodies in the first three centuries of the Christian era. . . . Augustine, though often speaking tentatively, tended to credit angels with ethereal bodies and demons with aerial bodies" (128). The essential ambiguity of air as demonic matter and as the dwelling of the demonic beings lasted until Thomas Aquinas, who "cut the Gordian knot, severing angelic nature from any vestige of corporeality" (ibid., 133–34).

40. In *Enarratio in Psalmum CIII* (PL 37), *Sermo* 4, 1382, Augustine reminds us that the air is the prison where the devil resides. Once they turned into devils, Augustine says, the fallen angels accepted to roam forever in this great and open sea [*in hoc mari magno et spatioso*]." Even Renaissance epic poetry appropriates the topos of the devil's airy body. See, for instance, Torquato Tasso's *Gerusalemme liberata*, canto 7, octave 99. In this canto Tasso writes that the magician Argante summons the devil, so that he constructs a false body out of nowhere.

41. In *Demonolatriae libri tres* (Lyons, 1595) Nicolas Remy describes the devils' voice as follows: "[J]ust as they [devils] can never so completely adopt a human appearance but that there remains something to expose the fraud and deception . . . , so they cannot so perfectly imitate the human voice that the falsity and pretence of it is not easily perceived by their

apprehends the possible human reaction to a given "linguistic" act. The angelic substances are unable to connect a signifier with its specific signified, because they lack both memory and imagination. This is why Prierio states that, more than speaking, the devils sing (159).[42]

This definition of angelic language is traditionally and exclusively referred to the good angels. Indeed, in many treatises the good angels' expression is compared with the birds' singing.[43] According to the most conventional interpretation, the good angels' singing reflects the harmonious movements of the celestial spheres, while the fallen angels utter screeching and cacophonous sounds, as Prierio himself states at the beginning of his text. When he comes to analyze the essence of angelic expression, however, Prierio does not see an essential difference between the two angelic categories. Both the bad and good angels "sing" in that what they "say" has no meaning per se. Prierio maintains that the angels' saying is similar to a baby's weeping or a man's laughing (159).

---

hearers. . . . [M]any women said that their Demons spoke as if their mouths were in a jar or cracked pitcher. . . . Or else their voice is feeble and weak." I quote from the English translation by E. A. Ashwin (London: John Rodker, 1930), book 1, chap. 8, 30.

42. In *De rerum subtilitate* (Basle, 1557) Girolamo Cardano, one of the major scientists of the Renaissance, likens the devil's language and understanding to a dog's. Cardano stresses that devils know reality in a way that is totally different from ours (chap. 93, 651). A dog does not understand the words two human beings exchange in a conversation, although it may grasp the feeling underneath the exchanged utterances. Yet a dog can perceive things a human being does not notice, such as some subtle smells or another dog's voice. In any case, in their understanding devils do not use our human reasoning: "Dogs are unable to understand the things concerning a human conversation. . . . However dogs do know things that men totally ignore, such as the smells of the house, the smell of a pregnant puppy . . . , the voice of another barking dog. In a similar way, men understand certain things that are completely unknown to demons" (652). For a detailed analysis of Cardano's demonology, see chapter 5, below.

In *Tractatus de sortilegiis* Grillando mentions the story of the prophet Balaam (Num. 22:21–35), whose donkey becomes possessed by an "angel" and starts to speak. Like many other demonologists, Grillando uses this biblical passage to prove that an angel can enter a body to reproduce sounds similar to a human voice: "The angel moved the ass's tongue . . . and through an intense stirring of the air he brought forth a set of distinct phonemes, which in that context sounded like natural words" (107).

43. The comparison between birds and good angels is a topos of Christian theology. See, for instance, Gregory the Great, *Homiliarum in Ezechielem* (PL 76), Homily 10, 901: "We have already stated that the spheres are marked with the holy language of the Testaments [Hom. 6, chap. 2 and following]. The voice of the spheres is indeed the discourse of the Testaments. Behind the voice of the birds one also perceives the voice of the spheres. . . . [T]he saints' virtues fly up to accomplish higher tasks, and constantly strive to attain their goal, which is the foundation of the Holy Church, so that the pages of the holy Testaments will be read throughout the creation. Everywhere resound the words of the holy Testaments, everywhere [resound] the maxims of the apostles, [God's] law and his prophets. Behind the voice of the birds follows the voice of the spheres, for behind the miracles of the apostles the words of the holy discourse openly and profusely resonate within the Holy Church."

To define the devil's specific idiom, Prierio must question the traditional and theologically ungrounded metaphors concerning the two categories of angelic beings. For instance, he does not see an essential difference between the devils' and the angels' phonetics, because neither group knows how to translate their phonemes into signifying expressions. Therefore, Prierio infers, both kinds of angels "sing."

The angelic beings' singing differs from a human being's laughing, weeping, or singing, in that the angels exclusively sing for someone in particular—that is, they can only articulate their phonemes to direct a message to a given creature. The fallen angels' process of syllogistic abstraction derives from their analysis of a given human speaker, and thus can never achieve a theory of the laws constructing a historical idiom. To clarify this central point, Prierio recounts two interesting events involving two friends of his. The first story revolves around a certain Hieronimus, a priest in the city of Bononia, who was a gifted flutist. In 1500 a sorcerer asked Hieronimus if he was interested in seeing and accompanying his musicians *(pulsatores)* with his instrument (159–60). The magician took the priest to a solitary clearing that overlooked the entire city. When the priest asked him, "When am I going to see your musicians?" the sorcerer answered, "Look up." Prierio's friend saw fifteen handsome young men descending from the sky, playing trumpets and drums, and fifteen beautiful girls intoning loud songs.[44] Since their music was extremely clamorous, the priest asked the sorcerer why the city seemed to be unaware of this noisy gathering (160). The magician explained that the devils addressed those obstreperous sounds only to a specific hearer; no one else could possibly perceive them ("omnia [sunt] in sensibus eorum, quos diabolus participes huius esse vult").

The second story concerns a man of humble origins, who suddenly became possessed by a devil. When, according to a basic procedure of every exorcism, the inquisitor directly addressed the devil inside the man's body, he noticed that the devil was speaking in a rather simplistic and unrefined manner. When the inquisitor asked him why he was articulating such an unpolished rhetoric, the devil answered that it was not his fault; he could not help but use the possessed man's "raw" language ("Non est [inquit daemon in illo] mea culpa, sed lingua huius rustici tam grossa, quod per ora eius vertere nequeo" [160]).

Prierio makes use of the stories to highlight the two fundamental aspects

---

44. In *De natura daemonum* (Venice, 1581) Laurentius Anania mentions a similar event that occurred in the Milanese area (84–85).

of angelic expression: they can only respond to one speaker at à time, and they imitate the speaker's particular language. A central question arises at this point. If they limit themselves to mimicking human signifiers without "possessing" them—that is, without being able to produce them independently—how can the angels understand what they are saying? This question, I believe, is the core of *De strigimagis*. I have already alluded to Prierio's belief that the angels understand through an act of abstraction. In chapter 13, analyzing this process in detail, he defines it as a form of "discourse" *(discursus)*. A discourse, Prierio explains, occurs when the subject comes to know something unknown from something known ("cognoscere unum ignotum ex alio prius noto, discursus est" [101]).[45] In other words, both the devils and the angels know through syllogisms *(syllogizare possunt)*, and thus are able to "know conclusions in principles and effects in causes" (compare Thomas, *Summa* 1, q. 58, art. 3, 541).

This explanation refers to the central difference subsisting between the syllogisms of the angels and those of human beings. A syllogism leads a human speaker to acquire knowledge of an unknown truth, but it never increases the angels' knowledge. This is a paradoxical aspect of the angels' perception/thinking. In reality, angels think *as if* they were constructing a syllogism, but they never move away from the abstracted ideas that form the *praemissa maior* and *praemissa minor*. The angels' *conclusio* is still in the realm of *entia*, never of matter (Prierio, 105). As Prierio states, angels "know conclusions in principles and effects in causes." As a consequence, an angelic syllogism does not derive from composing and dividing a discursive matter ("neque componendo aut dividendo intelligunt").[46] However, referring to Thomas, Prierio holds that the angelic minds read the creation as if it were a sentence, or an incomplete syllogism, in which one of the three parts is missing. Prierio explains that angels and devils process the world's signs as segments of a proposition (109). In most cases human speakers are able to complete a proposition lacking either the subject, verb, or (in)direct object by means of an *apprehensionem phantasticam*, based on our *appetitus sensitivus*, that is, on our phantasms.[47] Good and bad an-

45. Compare *De anima*, book 2, chap. 2 (413a 15). I refer to the translation in *Introduction to Aristotle*, edited by Richard Mckeon (Chicago: University of Chicago Press, 1973), 184.

46. Compare Thomas Aquinas, *Summa* 1, q. 58, art. 4. Thomas and Prierio refer to Aristotle's *De anima*, book 3, chap. 6 (430a 15): "But that which mind thinks and the time in which it thinks are . . . divisible only incidentally and not as such. For in them . . . there is something indivisible . . . which gives unity to the time and the whole of length; and this is found equally in every continuum whether temporal or spatial" (ed. Mckeon, 232).

47. On the various connotations of the term *phantasm* in Aristotle's *De anima*, see the insightful essay by Dorothea Frede, "The Cognitive Role of *Phantasia* in Aristotle," in *Essays on*

gels process reality's "propositions" not through their perception of the sensible, which they lack, but through their syllogistic reasoning.[48] We must remember here that the angels' propositions never reach the sensible. Indeed, the angels' knowledge is never affected by their reasoning. Although they act *as if* they were composing and dissecting a syllogism or a proposition, the angels limit themselves to completing a given proposition, but they do not achieve any form of knowledge (110).

Prierio reiterates that, when the angels articulate a voice by means of a given matter (air, a possessed body, a corpse), they affirm and deny, although the angelic substances do not learn anything through their act of affirming and denying ("[C]um voces in subiecta creatura corporea formant angeli, affirmando et negando loquuntur, quamvis non affirmando, aut negando intelligant" [101]).

If they do not apprehend anything through their linguistic acts, how do the angels perceive their own saying? The angelic utterances deny the essential nature of any form of discourse, if by "discourse" we intend an oral text through which its speaker at once develops and communicates his own thinking. Paradoxically, an angelic discourse "makes sense" for its hearer but not for its speaker. Through his discourse an angel utters his listener's, but never his own, desire, because an angel does not and cannot have memories or imagination.[49]

Aristotle's "De Anima," edited by Martha C. Nussbaum and Amélie Oksenberg Rorty (Oxford: Clarendon, 1995), 279–95.

48. Compare Thomas Aquinas, *Summa* 1, q. 58, art. 2.

49. In the seminal third volume of his *Seminar* (*The Psychosis 1955–1956: The Seminar of Jacques Lacan: Book III,* edited by Jacques-Alain Miller [New York: W. W. Norton, 1993]), Lacan analyzes the psychosis of Daniel Paul Schreber, who had detailed his mental disturbances in *Memoirs of My Nervous Illness.* It is interesting to note that the angels and Schreber's "God" share some interesting similarities. The most intriguing essay of the whole *Seminar III* is undoubtedly "On Nonsense and the Structure of God" (117–29), in which Lacan investigates how "God" relates to the psychotic Schreber. "God" speaks to Schreber in two distinct, though coexistent, ways. First of all, "God" talks to him through his "rays" or "divine nerves," which could be seen as some sort of angelic intellects; second, while his nerves are talking to Schreber, "God" utters his own sentences. As Lacan stresses, Schreber sees God as language; God is insofar as He speaks to Schreber. However, what "God" and his "nerves" have in common is their total ignorance of the world, including his human interlocutor (79). Schreber's God needs to talk, without knowing to whom he is talking (125). While according to the theological tradition, the angels speak without acquiring any knowledge from their own saying, which is exclusively significant for their interlocutors, Schreber's God constantly speaks without saying anything: "So, here is this God . . . [He] is who is always talking, who is forever talking without saying anything. That is so much so that Schreber dedicates many pages to considering what it might mean, that there is this God who talks without saying anything and who nevertheless never stops talking" (126).

Similarly, in a subsequent essay ("The Quilting Point"), Lacan studies what Schreber says

The linguistic interaction between a superior intellect and a human interlocutor is intrinsically jeopardized by a missing connection between
saying and understanding/perceiving. This miscorrelation can have two
different origins: first, that the superior mind does not know or does not
need to know what he is saying; second, that the superior mind's language
is obscure (devils or Holy Spirit speaking in tongues through a human
body). One must also bear in mind an important distinction between angelic and demonic expression. Paradoxically, a good angel speaks, even
though he does not need to speak. God's angels do not need us to confirm
the validity of their discourse and syllogisms. If, as Giorgio Agamben puts
it, a human being speaks to fill a void, to erase the absence brought about
by remembrance, the good angels announce a discourse that does not concern them directly. This is the fundamental difference between angels'
and devils' reasoning. The good angels do not need us, their human interlocutors, because the cogency of their thinking is validated by the Word
himself. The Word is the ultimate signified of the angels' "propositions"
(Prierio, 105). The Word is at once the source and the goal of the angels'
knowledge. In this atemporal process, the angels move away from the
Word and return to it, after having pronounced their language, which is its
language. In Augustinian terminology, this two-moment occurrence is
defined as the angels' "morning knowledge" and "evening knowledge."[50]

---

about divine rays' saying: "God's" nerves or rays constantly whisper in Schreber's ears. Their
sentences are truncated and repeated, as if these divine "nerves" had "learned them by rote,"
without really knowing what they mean (ibid., 258–59). These voices, Lacan stresses, "express themselves in striking formulas." Pier Aldo Rovatti, one of Italy's most prominent philosophers, offers a fascinating interpretation of Lacan's *Psychosis* in *Abitare la distanza. Per
un'etica del linguaggio* (Milan: Feltrinelli, 1994), 93–107.

It is impossible not to note that both biblical angels and Schreber's divine rays are somehow disconnected from their own language. Lacan underscores the central role played by the addressee of these divine voices. Human interlocutors (the Virgin, Schreber) validate or fail to
validate, so to speak, the angel's saying. Since to articulate language primarily means to direct
a linguistic message to someone, the angels do not reside in their own saying. According to the
Church Fathers, the angels do not know what they say in that they do not learn anything from
their interlocutors' reactions. As far as Schreber's divine nerves are concerned, they clearly utter "sounds in the air," as the Church Fathers define the devils' language.

50. For instance, see Augustine, *De Genesi ad litteram* (PL 34), book 5, chap. 18, 334; Augustine, *The City of God*, translated by David Wiesen (Cambridge, Mass.: Harvard University
Press), vol. 3, book 11, chap. 7, 451–53: "[A]lthough the Scripture enumerated those first days
in order, it nowhere inserted the word night. It never says: 'Night was made,' but instead:
'There was made evening and there was made morning, one day.' . . . We must note that the
knowledge of created entities when seen by themselves is dim and faded, so to speak, in comparison with their brilliance when seen in the realm of God's wisdom, and, as it were, in the de-
sign according to which they were made. Therefore the term evening is more appropriate than
night."

Thomas explains these definitions as follows: "[J]ust as in the ordinary day, morning is the beginning, and evening the close of the day, so, their [the angels'] knowledge of the primordial being of things is called *morning knowledge;* and this is according as things exist in the Word. But their knowledge of the very being of the thing created, as it stands in its own nature, is termed *evening knowledge*" (*Summa*, q. 58, art. 6). We might say that the angels' evening knowledge is the result of their process of abstraction (morning kowledge), through which they perceive the forms of the sensible.[51] However, since the angels have no direct knowledge of the sensible itself, the soundness of their syllogistic reasoning can only reside in (be granted by) the Word.

The fallen angels do not have a referential Word. Their syllogisms take place in the air where they are doomed to exist.[52] This is why the fallen angels must read the signs emitted by the world in order to verify their "propositions." Unlike the good angels, the devils need a human interlocutor to prove the validity of their saying. Prierio reminds us that, since they have abandoned the Word, the devils are unable to read supernatural signs. For instance, if they saw the Savior's corpse, the devils would never expect him to resurrect (102).

What the devils can easily read are the world's signs. The fundamental contradiction of the devil's being lies in that he aims to destroy what he understands. For the devil, an act of knowledge is always equivalent to an act of annihilation. The devil "reads" to erase what he is reading, primarily a human being's mind, but also all of nature's manifestations. By reading natural signs (winds, clouds, animals' expressions), devils are able to bring about storms, plagues, and floods. Moreover, by reading a human being's gestures, facial expressions, linguistic intonation, a devil can produce a "discourse" able to erase that human being's soul and body. Let us remember that Prierio's book opens with the biblical quotation "they devour my people as if they were eating bread" (Ps. 13:4).

51. Of course, the concept of "morning knowledge" and "evening knowledge" metaphorically relates to Venus, as Meister Eckhart says in his famous sermon "Quasi stella matutina": "The planet Venus . . . has many names. When it proceeds and rises before the sun, it is called the morning star; when it so follows that the sun set first, it is called an evening star. . . . [We] should be like the morning star; always present to God. . . . [We] should be an ad-verb to the Word" (Eckhart, *Teacher and Preacher,* edited by Bernard McGinn [New York: Paulist Press, 1986], 259). Meister Eckhart gives a grammatical interpretation of the relationship between the Word and his creatures, what Eckhart calls his "ad-verbs." Since the angels are dedicated interpreters of the Word's silence, their "grammatical" function is that of an adverb, which qualifies, and thus determines, the word (Word) it relates to.

52. Compare Augustine, *Enarratio in Psalmum CIII* (PL 37), *Sermo* 4, 1382.

The idea that a devil is capable of interpreting nature's signs is a topos of medieval and Renaissance demonology, founded on Augustinian theology.[53] As I have pointed out, the unique aspect of Prierio's analysis is his attempt to sketch the dynamics of the devils' intellectual practices. Prierio's *De strigimagis* focuses less on how we can defeat the devils' attacks than on how the devils think and manifest their thoughts. As the third and final book of his text (the witches' trial) shows, to develop a successful counterattack against Satan it is imperative to understand how the Enemy constructs his thinking.

In several passages Prierio emphasizes that the *substantiae separatae* (both angels and devils) have an intellect whose power is infinite (for instance, 47, 96), and that their primary activity is to comprehend the creation (53). But while human beings draw their knowledge from the phantasms of the sensible, both the good and the bad angels understand by means of reality's "species," which are the "signs of the things' essence" or *quidditas* (55). For instance, the concept/species "humanity" *(humanitas)* is something "superior" to the humanity embodied in a given being (68).[54] Like an Aristotelian syllogism, the angels' thinking is based on a process of composing different "sentences," rather than dissecting them: "[I]ntelligibiles rerum species . . . ad angelicum intellectum veniunt quasi per viam compositionis" (107).

A major contradiction arises at this point. As I have pointed out, both good and bad angels are granted neither memory nor imagination, because to posit the existence of a phantasmatic activity within the angelic minds would entail the presence of desire, which is absolutely denied by Christian theology. According to Augustine and Thomas Aquinas, in some rare cases the Word allows the good angels to formulate a specific memory in

---

53. An interesting description of the devil's process of exegesis is in *Specchio della vera penitenzia* by Jacopo Passavanti (1302–57), first published in Florence in 1495. In Passavanti's words, "the Doctors of the Church [believe] that thoughts can be understood in two ways. The first method is based on some kind of external effect. For that matter, not only the devil but men themselves are often capable of understanding someone else's inner thoughts, or at least those among us who have a subtle intellect resulting from their natural disposition, science, or from their knowledge of secret disciplines. But one can read someone else's thought also through some gesture, look, some facial expression. In a similar manner, by feeling our pulse expert physicians are able to understand the nature of our thoughts and our passions, and the affections of our soul, such as love, fear, sadness, among others." I translate from a later edition ([Florence: Tartini and Franchi, 1725], 237–38). On Passavanti, see Agnoletto, Abbiate, and Lazzati, eds., *La stregoneria*, 32–34.

54. In another passage Prierio says that the angels possess a *cognitio intellectiva*, which focuses on the species of the things observed (103). Compare Thomas Aquinas, *Summa* 1, q. 56, art. 3.

order to attain a particular goal.[55] Of course, since the fallen angels have rejected the Word, they are denied the gift of remembrance. Nevertheless, Christian demonologists are convinced that the bad angels can deceive us because, as the first creatures to be created, they have a much more developed memory of nature's "signs." Even those theoreticians who questioned the actual existence of witches and demonic possessions confirm this theory. For instance, in *De praestigiis daemonum* Johann Weyer states: "[A]s Augustine attests, their [the devils'] lifetime extends down from the very beginning of the world, and by virtue of the long passage of time they have acquired a remarkable familiarity with far greater things than men can know."[56] According to this interpretation, devils do have memories; they do store experiences in their intellect. We must also bear in mind another cornerstone of Christian theology: the devils want to harm us because they are envious of us. The devils "remember" that they have sinned and cannot be saved. As a revenge against the Divinity, they constantly try to annihilate what the Word has created.[57]

To resolve this apparent contradiction, it is necessary to understand the nature of the devils' (non)memory, and thus the way they turn their remembrances into linguistic acts devoid of passions and memories. Christian theology must interpret the devils' evil nature as a result of an act of free will (Prierio, 73–74). But since the devils are not granted memory, their primal rejection of God's Word must be interpreted as an "original sin" that compels them to formulate syllogistic reasonings meant to annihilate their own *conclusiones*. The devils' original sin has molded their thinking without producing an actual memory. As Augustine reiterates in many of his texts, evil is an absence, a void resulting from the lack of good. While the good angels think/reflect the Word's thought, the devils act out an immemorial, though constantly present, betrayal (Prierio, 75). If the good angels' reasoning springs from the Word and returns to the Word as a reflected thinking, the devils syllogize to reenact a past event, a treachery, which has been erased from their mind. Since the devils have no memory, their speaking does not express an inherent mourning. They "articulate evil" without knowing why.

The devils read their nonmemory in the act of combining the signs/

---

55. Augustine, *De trinitate* (PL 42), book 10, chap. 11, 983; Thomas Aquinas, *Summa 1*, q. 54, art. 5.

56. Johann Weyer, *De praestigiis daemonum*, edited by George Mora (Binghamton: State University of New York Press, 1991), 26. Weyer refers to Augustine's *De spiritu et littera*, chap. 28 (PL 44, 230).

57. Compare Augustine, *The City of God*, vol. 3, book 9, chap. 18.

sentences pronounced by the world into syllogisms. Borrowing the traditional terminology of the classical art of memory, we may say that the
world is an infinite set of *loci* where the devils find their memory images
(imagines). The creation is indeed similar to Plato's wax tablet, where impressions and perceptions are imprinted.[58] The devils' memory lies in the
world itself; the world manifests the devils' original abandonment from
the Word. Thus, the devils' strenuous attempt to erase the creation is nothing but an assault on their own memory.

The devil's nonmemory can only result in a nonlanguage, in a nonvoice.
In accordance with the tradition, Prierio states that the devils possess neither a language nor a voice; they limit themselves to articulating "sounds
in the air." The devils construct their illusive idiom by invading a body—
that is, by entering the materiality of the world and forcing it to utter a set
of phonemes that the world mistakes as expressions of its own being.

Let us clarify how the devil can act within the creation and articulate his
"worldly" idiom. In the first part of book 1 of his text, Prierio emphasized
that the devil essentially proceeds through an ongoing syllogism. Since he
cannot acquire any knowledge of the sensible, he works through conjectures *(coniecturaliter,* 108 and 125). Both his illusory, though "material,"
language and his noxious deeds result from a three-step reasoning, in
which both the *praemissa maior* and the *praemissa minor* are "formal"
propositions, generating a "physical" *conclusio*. Through his reasoning
the devil aims to bring to the fore his own memory, "inscribed" in the
world's physicality. But from this first "rhetorical" construction the devil
is able to deduce a second reasoning, in which the *praemissa minor* becomes a "physical" agent producing an effect on a third form, which thus
becomes the *conclusio* of the devil's thinking.[59] This second syllogism is
superior to the previous one, because it affects the forms of the world and
not its mere materiality. In other words, if the first syllogism brings about
storms, plagues, and phonemes, the second attacks the forms existing in
the world, including the human souls. After having produced a first syllogism whose result is a physical entity, the devil uses this physical entity
and makes it the second proposition of a new syllogism, which in turn af-

58. For a brilliant analysis of *memoria* in the Renaissance, see Renate Lachmann, *Memory
and Literature* (Minneapolis: University of Minnesota Press, 1997), 1–24.

59. "[T]he bad . . . angel . . . is unable to modify a corporeal matter in a formal way, that is,
from one form to another, without the medium of a corporeal agent" (112). Prierio also explains
that a form is not the thing in itself, but rather what the thing inhabits: "[S]trictly speaking, a
form is not, nor is it a 'thing' [*ens*], as if it actually were or existed. It is more that in which
something is" (ibid.).

fects the forms governing the physicality of the world. We might say that the devil operates by shifting the nature of the second proposition from a formal conjecture to a formal/physical one. The concept of *medius agens* (the *praemissa minor*, which connects the first *propositio* with the syllogism's *conclusio*) is indeed crucial in Prierio's investigation of the devil's thinking.

To clarify his interpretation of the devil's double syllogism, Prierio states that the devil's reasoning is like fire, which "devours" everything it encounters. As fire generates fire, Satan's thinking annihilates the results of its own thought (113). This fire/syllogism, Prierio reiterates, comes from a constant *addendo, subtrahendo, mutando,* or better yet, from a repeated *condensatione et rarefatione* (116 and 122).[60] Through a *medium agentem* or *localem motum* the devil endeavors to influence a human being's *sensum communem* (170).[61] As I have already mentioned, the devil can cause a partial and temporary blindness (aorasia), as in the case of Jesus' disciples when on their way to Emmaus they were unable to recognize him (Prierio, 123).

After having laid out his theoretical underpinnings in the first book, in the second Prierio analyzes the relationship between the devil and one of his mediums/local agents, the witches themselves (127–213). If, through the first form of syllogism, the devil succeeds in achieving a physical result (the conversion of a woman to Satan), through the second syllogism he uses the previous *conclusio* as a second proposition of a new syllogism, in which he aims to exert a larger and more deleterious influence on the creation. It is clear now that witches are key elements of the devil's ongoing reasonings. As Prierio explains, devils and witches "per mundum discurrunt et colligunt semina diversa, ex quorum adaptatione prorumpere possunt species diversae" (141). By means of the witches' support *(medio corpore)*, the devils are capable of moving from one physical form to another (145).[62] Moreover, witches help the devils collect "seeds" and alter them to create new and abnormal species (158, 164–66).

The major interaction between a devil and a witch concerns sexual

---

60. Prierio holds that this form of syllogistic reasoning is innate in the devil's being. According to Prierio, the devil acquires knowledge in three ways: through his own nature, God's revelation, and experience. This third kind corresponds to the devil's private reasoning, which is "ambiguous" because never confirmed by the Word (120).

61. On the concept of *motus localis,* see Grillando, *Tractatus de sortilegiis,* 99–100.

62. Synthesizing the devil's two syllogistic procedures, Prierio writes: "[B]y means of another corporeal matter, he can change things both in their accidents and in their substance. Also, he can give form to different species and affect our sight as he likes" (145).

activities, in particular the removal and transportation of a man's semen into a woman's vagina. Again, devils may proceed in one of several different ways. First, they can affect a man's phantasmata to arouse him sexually and induce him to an act of onanism (147). They can also acquire an "airy body" *(corpus aereum)* and have sexual intercourse with a man. As I explained at the very beginning of this chapter, the distinction between incubus and succubus primarily describes the sexual (active or passive) desire of a human subject. Indeed, in Prierio the traditional discussion of how and if a devil can generate abnormal creatures through a human medium acquires a clearly linguistic/rhetorical connotation. To introduce his semen into the female organ, a devil operates a syllogistic process. First, he takes up a female body; then, he has sexual intercourse with a man; finally, he removes that man's spilled semen and instills it into a female body.[63] If at the beginning of this process femininity was a "airy" entity, at the end she is the actual recipient of the devil's *conclusio*, obtained through the male "medium agent" (Prierio 165).

Prierio emphasizes that the devil could not accomplish this sexual process unless he knew how to modulate his (non)voice (150). In his double (active or passive) intercourse with a human being, the devil articulates either an "assertive" or a "recitative" voice, according to his human interlocutor's (active or passive) desire. We have seen that, according to Prierio, devils do not so much speak as modulate a sort of musical melody, close to an actual singing (159). Rather than articulating his own discourse, the devil interprets the other's desire. The devil's "language" is a reflection of the other's drive.

Prierio explains in detail why the devil's voice is neither a *dictio* nor a *locutio* (158–59). He stresses that to speak, an animal must breathe in a certain amount of air and channel it into its lungs. Then, after having cooled down its heart with the inhaled air, the animal breathes it out through its throat. On its way out, the air strikes the animal's vocal cords, passes through its tongue, teeth, and lips, and thus produces some kind of voice. For Prierio, *dictio* is the minimum linguistic unit of desire. If an animal is able to express a string of *dictiones*, it composes an actual *locutio*— that is, a discourse. Since the devil has neither desire nor memory, his

63. To confirm his theory on the transaction of semen from a male body to a female one, on p. 161 Prierio quotes a story from the *Bonum universale de proprietatibus apuum* (Koelhoff, 1477) of Thomas of Cantimpré (c. 1200–1270), book 2, chap. 56. Prierio refers to Thomas of Cantimpré's text (book 2, chap. 56) a second time on p. 199. The first quotation concerns a male witch, whose sperm had been used by a succubus; the second story relates the case of a virgin tormented by an incubus who wanted to sleep with her.

breathing in and out is a "melodic" response to the other's request, but not an actual utterance.[64] As we have seen, Prierio likens the devil's voice to singing. The devil's singing is interpreted by his human interlocutor as a seductive saying, although its alluring connotation lies in the interlocutor's interpretation rather than in the speaker's voice itself (164).

The success of this seductive (non)saying results in the extraction and transportation of male semen. Sperm becomes a sort of Lacanian signifier moving from one body to another *(per motum localem)*, and belonging neither to the male body from which it was removed, nor to the devil himself, nor even to the woman who will "give birth to" some form of monstrous being (Prierio, 166–67). I use quotation marks for the expression "give birth to" because, even though he believes that a woman infected by the devil may generate a monster, Prierio does not clarify this point fully, but rather limits himself to mentioning the giants from Genesis.[65] Other demonologists insist that the devil's removal of semen cannot produce a monstrous, devillike child, because in any case the semen belongs to a human being and not to the devil himself. However, these theologians do not explain why the devil should bother to extract semen from a man's member and insert into a woman's vagina, if in this process he could not "contaminate" that semen at all.[66]

The extracted semen becomes infected not so much through an actual contamination as by being exposed to the "local movement" *(motus localis)* itself. What taints a man's semen is not that the devil "pollutes" it in some way, because the devil cannot come in contact with matter; he can touch only matter's forms. What is unnatural, and thus perverse, is the act of inseminating a woman in an "artificial" manner. The devil's perversion lies

---

64. As a response to the Lacanian "mirror stage," in *Le stade du respir* (Paris: Minuit, 1978) Jean-Louis Tristani posits a "breath stage." In this underestimated text Tristani offers an insightful analysis of the erotic component present in the act of breathing. In particular, Tristani examines Freud's seminal interpretation of Dora's asthma. Freud thought that Dora had difficulty in breathing because she had overheard her father panting during sexual intercourse with her mother. Tristani holds that to breathe in corresponds to a form of oral ingestion and to breathe out signifies a metaphorical defecation (59). If the act of breathing entails a given erotic practice, "oral discourse [*la parole*]" may be seen as a response to a "respiratory" pulsion (54–55). In other words, breath does have a sexual expressiveness. Relating this theory to Prierio's discourse on the devil's breath/illusory idiom, we may say that the devil's (non)significant breath "echoes" his interlocutor's phantasmatic breath/desire.

65. For instance, Nider refers to the same biblical passage as clear evidence of abnormal creatures generated by devils (*Formicarius*, 85r).

66. It is almost superfluous to point out that, according to every demonologist, succubi and incubi do not feel any sexual pleasure, since they do not have a real body. The extraction, transportation, and insertion of semen is a mere "transaction" that the devil performs without "knowing" it.

in his attempt to modify natural laws of procreation. Again, in the devil's "hands" sperm becomes a perverse signifier, which can only generate aberrant signifieds.[67] In this way, the devil procreates not only in a female womb, but also, and more important, in the creation itself, bringing about contaminated crops, making cows and plants sick, and polluting water. The devil's "sperm" is even capable of affecting man's sperm itself (*virtus generativa*), in that the Enemy can make a man impotent, can prevent his penis from becoming erect or from ejaculating (Prierio, 168–72).[68] Influencing his phantasms through aorasia, a devil can go so far as to prevent a man from seeing his own member (171).

Human beings are unable to counteract the devil's syllogistic procreations with a different, "healthy" reasoning because, unlike the devils, they do not know how to affect the forms of matter. In the last part of the second section, Prierio draws up a list of possible remedies (*remedia*) against specific ailments, plagues, and natural catastrophes caused by the devil's intervention. As far as man's sexuality (*vis generativa*), Prierio suggests two concurrent responses. First, it is imperative to burn and destroy every sorcery created with the devil's support (200). Second, the man suffering from a sexual spell must fast, confess, and spend many hours in prayer. The two procedures are related to each other. On the one hand, one must annihilate the results of the devil's thought. On the other, one must rely on the Word's intervention. Unlike the good angels, human beings are not granted a constant contemplation of the Word. Therefore, men cannot deduce "good" reasoning by gazing at the (silent) Word. For Prierio every form of incantation is an illocutionary act, in which a magician or a witch directs a request to Satan, who is an "intellectual substance."

Paradoxically, Christian demonology implies that Satan is much prompter than the Word in responding to a human being's request. For a

67. Remy states that witches "are completely in agreement in saying that, if the Demons emit any semen, it is so cold that they recoil with horror on receiving it" (*Demonolatriae*, trans. Ashwin, book 1, chap. 6, 12–13). As a result of their sexual intercourse with devils, Remy is convinced, witches cannot help but give birth to witches. As Remy himself says, entire families can be "infected" by a single devil: "The taint of witchcraft is often passed on as it were by contagion by infected parents to their children. . . . There is almost no hope of ever purifying one who has once been infected" (ibid., book 2, chap. 2, 92). Francesco Guazzo shares the same opinion: "The infection of witchcraft is often spread through a sort of contagion to children by their fallen parents. . . . There are daily examples of this inherited taint in children" (*Compendium maleficarum*, translated by E. A. Ashwin [London: John Rodker, 1929], book 2, chap. 6, 96). We have already seen, in the introduction, how Martin del Rio reasons that imagination can bring about real effects. According to del Rio, devils can infect the fetus by affecting the mother's imagination (*Disquisitionum magicarum*, book 1, chap. 3, q. 3, 18).

68. Compare *Malleus* (trans. Summers), part 1, q. 8, 54–58.

human being it is much easier to achieve one's own perdition and annihilation than one's salvation. To invalidate the devil's *conclusiones*, we must become astute readers of evil syllogisms. In other words, we must isolate and undo those signs that testify to the devil's activity. For instance, if the devil has cast a "love spell" *(maleficium amoris)* on a male subject, we must investigate who would be interested in the man's ailment, whether or not his suffering subsides at night, if certain words or gestures can avert his distress, if this pain is somehow influenced by his age, if a particular woman upsets him more than others (200–201). Prierio examines other forms of enchantment, such as the sudden and illusory disappearance of a male organ (201), a man's metamorphosis into an animal, or an unexpected storm or hail (203).

In the case of a ruinous hail, Prierio offers a detailed formula of exorcism. Since I analyze the performative structure of a Catholic exorcism in chapter 3, I will simply highlight a few points of Prierio's description. First of all, an exorcist is asked to throw three grains of salt in a fire, saying out loud that he does this in the name of the Holy Trinity. This act embodies a double sign. On the one hand, it symbolizes the bad angels' fall into Hell, where they have been "thrown" forever. On the other, it signifies both the remembrance of the destructive hail—that is, its actual "falling" on earth—and the annihilation of that "falling." In the priest's hands, "to fall" becomes to "be thrown," so that from an active occurrence hail turns into a passive, self-erasing event.

We must bear in mind that our acts do not affect matter's forms; our gestures never attain a factual result, because they are simply reenactments of traumas. Our symbolic gestures are inevitably indexes, signs of memory. When, after having thrown salt in a fire, the exorcist prays to the Word and recites, "In principio erat Verbum; Verbum caro factum est," he asks the Word to participate in the memory of a given community, whose crops have been damaged by hail (Prierio, 203–4). In other words, an exorcism is the attempt to construct a remembrance for the Divinity. After having invoked the Word, the exorcist directs his speech to hail and winds themselves: "Adiuro vos grandines et ventos per quinque vulnera Christi" ("I summon you, hail and winds, through the five wounds of Christ).[69] The exorcist reminds hail and winds of their having been "misled" by Satan.[70]

---

69. We shall see that in *Thesaurus exorcismorum* the exorcist is requested to call "creatures" all kinds of natural occurrences, such as fire, hail, rain, and everything a devil can possess (houses, food, clothes).

70. Compare Stuart Clark, *Thinking with Demons*, 69–79.

Narrating how the Word has suffered and died for his entire creation, the exorcist wishes to make hail and winds aware of their "sin" due to the devil's perverse reasoning. By addressing hail and winds, Prierio holds, the exorcist aims to bring to the fore the devil's practices and thus to restore a "natural" discourse within the creation (Prierio, 203).

Concluding this second section of his text, Prierio makes some final remarks on the language suitable to any form of exorcism. If the Enemy's perverted thinking is primarily based on secrecy and ambiguity, the exorcist's rhetoric must be absolutely lucid and intelligible (209).[71] Prierio gives seven fundamental rules: First, it is imperative to use every word that could lend itself to an evil interpretation. Therefore, and second, no *ignota verba* (unknown words) can be mentioned during a "purifying" discourse.[72] Third, sentences cannot communicate any false statement *(falsitas)*, which may be appropriated by witches during their intercourse with Satan. Fourth, besides the cross no delusive pictorial sign *(vana characteres)* can be sketched on the page. Fifth, the exorcist must harbor no secret narcissism in his discourse to the Word, because his concealed self-conceit would mar the crystal-clear rhetoric of his saying. Sixth, as a consequence, a priest must exclusively strive to concentrate on the "correct" understanding of the sacred words he is pronouncing. In the attempt to "purge" a natural occurrence of the devil's corruption, the exorcist must focus on his own hidden drives, which may "stain" his utterances and thus make them useless. Finally, the exorcist must bear in mind that his words exert a successful influence on the world insofar as the Word allows them to do so. Again, Prierio understands that human language is nothing but a constant invocation to the Word; to speak means to engage the Word in a dialogue.[73]

If human language can be easily "mispronounced" and thus misled from its "natural path" (Prierio, 208), trials against witches, the Church's last resort in its fight against Satan, must follow strict and safe guidelines. This is the topic of the third and final book of *De strigimagis* (214–62). Prierio is adamant about the treatment witches deserve. Since they have supported the devil in his act of devouring the creation, witches deserve to

71. Other demonologists are also convinced that an exorcism can be successful only if its language avoids any kind of ambiguity. For a full discussion of this topic, see chapter 2, below, on Manuel de Moura's *De ensalmis*.

72. Grillando speaks of "verba extranea, vel ignota nomina, aut characteres, sive verba quaedam extranea" (187).

73. The Italian mystic Maria Maddalena de' Pazzi theorizes on the relationship between orality and divine being. For an analysis of this crucial theological point, see chapter 4, below.

be devoured themselves, eliminated through fire *(ignibus eliminentur)*.[74] Indeed, any attempt to erase the Enemy's attack on the world would be fruitless, if we did not "burn" the effects of the devil's double syllogism (214). As we have seen, witches are both the *conclusio* of Satan's first syllogism and the *praemissa minor* of his second reasoning. Thus, to burn a witch means to turn the devil's syllogism into an *entimema*, which is an imperfect and thus vulnerable syllogism, for it is deprived of one of its two propositions.

Although Prierio demonstrates an excellent knowledge of the legal procedures regarding a witch trial, he openly borrows his views from *Malleus maleficarum*.[75] Compared to the first two sections, the third part of *De strigimagis* is much less original. What is unique in Prierio's final chapter is not its content, but rather its status as the necessary conclusion of a theological examination. Most of the treatises on demonology are divided into two clear-cut sections: first, a series of narratives on witches' diverse ways of harming human beings; second, a perceptive examination of how to organize a trial against a witch. This second part is always heavily indebted to the *Malleus*. In Prierio's text, the legal procedures against heretics / witches become the natural conclusion of a "rhetorical" analysis of the relationship between devils and human beings. We might say that *De strigimagis* gives a theological / linguistic connotation to a rather conventional set of legal rules.

Before delving into juridical details, Prierio states that witches must be considered heretics, because through their practices they reject the Catholic faith (216). Witches and heretics are those individuals who have "perverted" their minds, consciously or unconsciously. They may have embraced the devil's religion through a double ceremony—that is, through a private pact with him and a public ritual with other heretics / witches— or they may actualize the devil's will without being aware of the meaning of their deeds. Paradoxically, a person may be a witch without knowing it.

---

74. Compare the entry *superstitio* in *Sylvestrina summa* (2:447–50): "I state that diviners and magicians must be subject to the capital punishment. If they bring about negative effects upon someone's household, they must be burned. All their goods must be confiscated" (2:450). Compare Andrea del Col and Marisa Milani, "'Senza effusione di sangue e senza pericolo di morte'. Intorno ad alcune condanne capitali delle inquisizioni di Venezia e di Verona nel Settecento e a quella veneziana del Cinquecento," in *Eretici, esuli e indemoniati nell'età moderna*, edited by Mario Rosa (Florence: Olschki, 1998), 141–96.

75. Lea confirms Prierio's significant debt to Kramer and Sprenger's work: "He [Prierio] is fully imbued with the doctrines of the *Malleus Maleficarum*, which he quotes" (Lea, *Material toward a History of Witchcraft*, 1:358). However, Lea examines only the third part of *De strigimagis*, giving no reference to the first two chapters.

What matters are the results of her perverted mind, not whether her intellect is aware of its deviating status (Prierio, 218). It is important to remember that witches and heretics are mere means through which the devil completes his devastating reasonings. Prierio vigorously attacks those who believe that we should distinguish between those individuals who have formulated a pact with Satan and those who think that they are faithful Catholics but in fact are not.[76] In a sense, Prierio's views are even more radical than those of Sprenger and Bodin, who postulate the necessity of a conscious, although secret, agreement between a human being and Satan.[77]

Following Sprenger, Prierio states that a judge can proceed against a witch in three different manners, through accusation, denunciation, and inquisition (223).[78] In his precise analysis of each procedure, Prierio reproduces the *Malleus* almost verbatim. If the first two sections of *De strigimagis* are a theological discussion of the devil's thinking and his interaction with human beings, the third is a manual describing how to annihilate that interaction. And no book could serve this purpose better than the *Malleus*, given its detailed analysis of specific trials and technical aspects, and its status as the semi-official guidebook of the Catholic Church.[79]

---

76. Prierio, *De strigimagis*, 218–19. Prierio had already expressed a similar view in the entry *haeresis* in *Sylvestrina summa* (2:477–90). He writes that the Church has the right to define what is illegal from a theological standpoint (2:479).

77. Kramer and Sprenger clearly state: "[I]n the practice of this abominable evil, four points in particular are required. First, most profanely to renounce the Catholic Faith, or at any rate to deny certain dogmas of the faith; secondly, to devote themselves body and soul to all evil; thirdly, to offer up unbaptized children to Satan; fourthly, to indulge in every kind of carnal lust with Incubi and Succubi and all manners of filthy delights" (*Malleus* [trans. Summers], part 1, q. 2, 20–21). In *De la démonomanie des sorciers* Bodin basically reproduces Sprenger's definition: "Sorcier est celuy qui par moyens diaboliques sciemment s'efforce de peruenir à quelque chose" (1). Bodin stresses that witches operate *sciemment* (consciously).

Prierio's definition of heresy/witchcraft is more subtle than Sprenger's and Bodin's. While they hypothesize the actual occurrence of base rituals granting a human being the status of witch, Prierio understands that Satan essentially uses humans to "complete" his projects. Satan does not need an "eloquent" deed, such as the murder of children, to pervert a person's intellect.

78. Kramer and Sprenger explain the three methods as follows: "The first is when someone accuses a person before a judge of the crime of heresy . . . offering to prove it, and to submit himself to the penalty of talion if he fails to prove it. The second method is when someone denounces a person, but does not offer to prove it and is not willing to to embroil himself in the matter; but says that he lays information out of zeal for the faith. . . . The third method involves an inquisition, that is, when there is no accuser or informer, but a general report that there are witches in some town or place" (*Malleus*, trans. Summers, part 3, q. 1, 205). They add that the third method is "the most usual one" (207). Prierio confirms: "As far as the third method is concerned, it is ordinary and common" (*De strigimagis*, 225).

79. Prierio had already referred to the *Malleus* in *Sylvestrina summa* (entry *inquisitio*, 2:40–46).

Let us remember that Innocent VIII's bull (*Summis desiderantes affecti-bus*, 1484) was printed as a preface encouraging and praising Kramer and Sprenger's action against "heretical depravity." [80]

Prierio's discussion of the examination of witnesses and the prosecution of witches, including the legal remedies meant to overcome discrepancies among different witnesses' depositions and witches' denial of any wrong-doing, derives from part 3 of the *Malleus*.[81] As we shall see in chapter 2, the most accomplished books on demonology ingeniously merge a theo-retical analysis of Satan's pernicious influence on the world with a vehement attack against those individuals who, according to the Church, embody the devil's malevolence. The legal means through which the Inquisition feels entitled to persecute women, Jews, Muslims, and sodomites are always posited at the end of the treatise, and are borrowed from the *Malleus*. Even though Prierio must have witnessed quite a number of trials, given his striking knowledge of their technical aspects, *De strigimagis* fundamen-tally reiterates Kramer and Sprenger's sinister precepts on how to set up a successful trial.[82]

Although its final section concerning the legal precepts for trials against witches does not modify what the *Malleus* had already established, *De strigimagis* is a cornerstone of Renaissance demonology because it suc-ceeds in offering an original interpretation of Satan's linguistics. Before Prierio, no demonologist had broached the challenging topic of the devil's reasoning and of his linguistic interaction with the creation. Unlike most of the medieval and Renaissance books on this topic, *De strigimagis* is not a descriptive account of the devil's innumerable crimes, but rather an ana-lytical discussion of how Satan's infectious language is articulated in the world.

---

80. *Malleus* (trans. Summers), xix.

81. For example, for the legal number of witnesses, usually two, see *Malleus* (trans. Sum-mers), part 3, q. 2, 208 (Prierio, *De strigimagis*, 226); for the questioning of witnesses, part 3, q. 6, 210–11 (Prierio, 228); for the so-called *maleficium taciturnitatis*, part 3, q. 8, 214–16 (Prierio, 235–36); for the discordant interpretations of the witch's tears, part 3, q. 15, 227–28 (Prierio, 237); for an analysis of the three kinds of sentences (interlocutory, definitive, and pre-ceptive), part 3, q. 18, 235–36; q. 20, 240–41; q. 21, 241–42; q. 22, 242–44 (Prierio, 240–43).

82. Compare Lea, *Toward a History of Witchcraft*, 1:359.

The Word's "Ceremonies":
Natural and Unnatural Language
according to de Moura's *De Ensalmis*

THE DEVIL constructs his nonlanguage by interpreting nature's and human beings' signs and turning them against creation itself. In Prierio's words, the devil's perverse idiom is a fire that burns both its own speakers and its addressees. Demonologists recognize that even the most revered linguistic expressions, such as sentences taken from the Bible or from the Church Fathers' texts, can be contaminated by the devil's syllogism. Like every other aspect of creation, words are totally exposed to the Enemy's possible appropriation and infection. Prierio has shown that to complete his noxious syllogism, Satan needs a human speaker. Someone must utter the transition (the so-called local motion) between the syllogism's two premises and its possible conclusion. To eradicate Satan's language necessarily means to attack and eradicate his human speakers.

If verbal language is not immune from Satan's possible pollution, how can human beings protect their private dialogue with the Divinity? How can they be sure that their words do not articulate the Enemy's idiom? *De incantantionibus seu ensalmis* (1620) by Manuel do Valle de Moura, general inquisitor and bishop of the city of Evora in Portugal, is certainly the most detailed treatise on this subject.[1] In *De ensalmis* de Moura shows a

1. Manuel do Valle de Moura was born in Villa de Arrayolos in 1564 and died in Evora in 1650. After studying theology at the University of Evora and pontifical jurisprudence at the University of Coimbra, he was elected deputy of the Inquisition of Evora in 1603. When he was still a student at Evora, de Moura wrote with three other students a rather mediocre parody of

remarkable knowledge of medieval and Renaissance demonology. This fundamental text of the Portuguese Inquisition is characterized by a circular and obsessive reasoning.[2] In the first section de Moura's analysis seems to have reached a definite conclusion on the nature of the devil's influence on human language. In the following chapters, however, discussing the implications of his first statements, the author ends by questioning his initial results. Comparing any form of invocative act, what he calls *ensalmus*, with a theatrical performance *(comoedia)*, de Moura concludes that it is impossible to posit an invocative act devoid of its performer's private musings, reasonings, and first of all conscious and subconscious desires. At the end of the first part, de Moura feels compelled to modify the structure of his inquiry. Realizing that it is difficult to determine when and how Satan undermines human beings' invocative acts, the Portuguese inquisitor shifts his study from the *ensalmus* to the *ensalmista* himself—that is, from a given speech act to its speaker. For de Moura, a wicked *ensalmus* is an act of sodomy, primarily performed by the Jewish people.

DE MOURA'S TEXT IS a convoluted and thus often digressive analysis of those linguistic materials (primarily biblical passages and prayers, but also formulaic expressions both from Catholic rites and popular magic) that, when combined with ritualized gestures and objects (among others candles, water, and wine), aim to affect reality in a positive or a negative manner.[3] To synthesize this rather complex field of performative acts, de Moura makes use of the term *ensalmus*, which he defines as follows:

> Ensalmi are benedictions or evil invocations (imprecationes) composed of a certain formula of words, primarily holy ones, and sometimes also of some material things, like wine or a cloth. . . . Many individuals, first of all, Spaniards, make use of these [ensalmi] to heal wounds and different

---

the first canto of *The Lusiads* by Camões (*Paródia ao primeiro canto dos Lusiadas de Camões por quatro estudantes de Evora* [Lisbon: Martins, 1589]). Among his other publications are *De stigmatibus Sancto Francisco impressis ab Angelo, non ab ipso Jesu Domino nostro crucifixo; Tractatus de filiatione dubia;* and *Dous tratados sobre a expulsão dos Judeos*. See Diego Barboso Machado, *Biblioteca lusitana,* 2d ed. (Lisbon, 1933), 3:392–93.

2. The Portuguese Inquisition had four major locations: Evora, Lisbon, Coimbra, and Goa. For a detailed analysis of the structure of the Portuguese Inquisition, see António Borges Coelho, *Inquisição de Evora* (Lisbon: Caminho, 1987), 1:47–75.

3. Thomas Aquinas' *Summa theologiae* is the fundamental reference for de Moura. In particular, see *Summa,* 2.2, q. 96, art. 4, in which Thomas stresses that in some cases diabolic invocations merge oscure words and holy expressions and gestures, such as the sign of the cross.

diseases, and to remove various forms of injuries, that may result from tempests, poisons, and wild beasts. They also use ensalmi to obtain good things, primarily worldly ones. (1r)

These practices are called *ensalmi* because their primary source is the Psalms, texts characterized by a strongly invocative character.[4] The performers of *ensalmi* are called *ensalmistae* or *ensalmadores*. Although de Moura recognizes that an *ensalmus* is the combination of verbal language and bodily expression, he focuses almost exclusively on the linguistic component. Indeed, de Moura believes that an *ensalmus* is a performance primarily determined by its linguistic constituent.

De Moura's interpretation is predicated upon an ideological premise. Indeed, if he saw the *ensalmus* as a perfomance somehow influenced by the *ensalmista's* personal skills, de Moura would be compelled to admit that this practice escapes the Inquisition's rationalization and subsequent control and repression. In a central passage de Moura clearly states that neither the performer's *imaginatio*—that is, his private way of visualizing the images summoned by his words—nor the tone of his voice exerts any influence whatsoever on his *ensalmus* (183–84).[5]

De Moura holds that an *ensalmus* can be performed according to two different procedures, which he calls *benedictio invocativa* (invocative benediction) and *benedictio constitutiva* (constitutive benediction). The first performative act is a private invocation directed either to God or to the devil. It can be either a request *(per modum orationis impetrativae)* or a narrative deploring God's or Satan's insensitivity toward the *ensalmista* himself *(per modum deprecationis)*. The second kind of *ensalmus* is an actual ceremony aiming to "bring about effects" *(effectos operari)* by mimicking or reproducing parts of Catholic rituals and sacraments *(instar sacramentorum vel sacramentalium)*.

Much later in the text (341–42) de Moura transcribes a lawful *ensalmus*

4. De Moura writes that, according to Martin del Rio, the term *ensalmus* derives from a sort of magical practice that soldiers frequently use to heal even the most serious wounds: "[P]raxis quotidiana militum, qui solo afflatu, osculo, aut nudi linthei appositione sanant etiam atrocissima vulnera." Del Rio states that these rituals are called *ensalmi* from the so-called *ars S. Anselmi* (Martin del Rio, *Disquisitionum magicarum libri sex* [Mainz: Petrus Henningius, 1617], book 1, chap. 3, q. 4, 24). In *Reprobacion de las supersticiones y hechicerias* (1530), Pedro Ciruelo also condemns this practice.

5. For a fundamental discussion of the role of *imaginatio* in Platonism and Neoplatonism, see Eugenio Garin, "*Phantasia* e *Imaginatio* fra Marsilio Ficino e Pietro Pomponazzi," in *Phantasia-Imagination*, ed. Garin (Rome: Ateneo, 1988), 3–22.

performed in his country during a pernicious plague. Let us read how a Catholic *ensalmista* (a priest) formulates an acceptable request to the Divinity:

† O Cross of Christ, set me free.

O Jesus, home of God, rescue me.

O God, my God, expel the plague from this place, and rescue me.

Into thy hands, o Lord, I commit my spirit and my body.

Before the sky and the earth were, my God had the power to free me from this plague.

† The Cross of Christ has the power to expel the plague from this place and from my body.

It is good to implore God for help in silence, so that He expel the plague.

I devote myself to obeying your laws, so that I shall not be ashamed because I invoked thee.

Envying the arrogant as I did, and seeing the prosperity of the wicked, I hoped in you.

† The Cross of Christ casts out the devils and the impure air, and expels the plague.

I am your salvation, the Lord said. Invoke me, call me Father, and I shall respond to you, and shall free you from this plague.

Deep is calling to deep, and in your name you expelled the devils and rescued me.

Blessed are those who place their hope in God, and do not regard vanities and false insanities.

† O Cross, first you were a scandal, and now [you are] glorified and exalted. Be my salvation, and expel the devil from this place and from the impure air, and [expel] the plague from my body.

Let the zeal for your glory consume me. Before my death I shall offer my vow to God and my expression of penance to him, who has the power to rescue this place and myself from this plague, because those who do not confide in him shall be ashamed.

May my tongue remain stuck to my palate if I do not keep you in mind and do not exalt your name, because you are holy, and rescue those who believe in you. I confide in you, my God; eradicate the plague from me and from this place, where your name is invoked.

A dark night descended upon the world at the day of your death, my Lord. God, my God, observe the deceitful and dark power of the devil, and since you, son of the living God, came for that, to dissolve the work of the devil; that your power expel from this place and from me the plague and the corrupt air into the external darkness. Amen.

✝ O Cross of Christ, defend us; expel the plague from this place, and rescue your servant from the plague, because you, God, are good and compassionate, and very merciful, and truthful.

How blessed are those who put their trust in God and those who have not followed vanities and have not gone astray in falsehood; and the Lord rescued them from their evil night. O God, I have put my trust in thee. Rescue me from this plague. O God, you listen to me, because I have put my trust in thee. Rescue me from this plague.

Look at me, and take pity on me, and rescue me from this plague.

You are my salvation, save me, o Lord, and I shall be cured. Save me and I shall be saved.[6]

A central aspect of any invocative text is its rhythmical structure. A first clause (Cross of Christ; O Cross), a constant reference to the absolute power of the incarnate Word, introduces each section of the invocation, which always concludes repeating a request for help (set me free; free me from this plague; expel the devil; expel the plague). The terms used to indicate the specific affliction distressing the speaker are also repeated throughout the *ensalmus*. The bulk of the text is a series of quotations and variations from the Psalms, for instance, "Into thy hands, o Lord, I commit my spirit and my body" (compare Ps. 30:6); "I devote myself to obeying your laws" (compare Ps. 118:112); "I shall not be ashamed" (Ps. 118:80); "Deep is calling to deep" (Ps. 41:8); "Envying the arrogant as I did, and seeing the prosperity of the wicked" (Ps. 72:3); "How blessed are those who put their trust in God . . . and those who have [not] gone astray in falsehood" (Ps. 39:5); "May my tongue remain stuck to my palate if I do not keep you in mind" (Ps. 136:6); "Look at me, and take pity on me" (Ps. 24:16). According to de Moura's distinction, the above

6. Scholars believe that some psalms themselves were originally used for magical purposes. For instance, in *Spuren Magischer Formeln in den Psalmen* (Giessen: Alfred Töppelmann, 1927) Nicolaj Nicolsky studies several psalms (7, 35, 58, 59, 69, 91, 109, 141) and interprets their invocative expressions as "traces" of previous magical compositions (16). Particularly interesting is Nicolsky's analysis of "the Name of God," a clearly magical expression of the Jewish tradition (27–29). See also Eli Davis, "The Psalms in Hebrew Medical Amulets," *Vetus Testamentum* 42 (1992): 173–78; Alexander Fodor, "The Use of Psalms in Jewish and Christian Arabic Magic," in *Jubilee Volume of the Oriental Collection, 1951–1976* (Budapest: Library of the Hungarian Academy of Sciences, 1978), 67–71.

Treatises on demonology usually limit themselves to stating that the words used in such forms of invocations are not becoming. Read, for instance, Girolamo Menghi's *Compendio dell'arte essorcistica*. Examining the rituals performed by Satan's disciples, Menghi writes that these people "baptize certain images in the name of the great devil . . . using some dishonest words that we refrain from mentioning out of modesty" (230–31). I quote from the 1650 edition (Venice: Bertano).

ensalmus corresponds to an "invocative benediction," since it does not include any form of theatricality, and it could be performed in silence as a prayer.[7]

As de Moura emphasizes in the first section of his work, both forms of *ensalmi* are invocations, similar to traditional Catholic prayers (3v). De Moura understands that, like every other illocutionary act, an *ensalmus* requires both a speaker and a hearer, in this case either God or the devil.[8] However, *De ensalmis* is almost exclusively interested in fathoming the nature of the speaker's language, without considering how the performer's utterances affect their addressee.

Unlike any other illocutionary act, an *ensalmus* doubts the presence of its addressee. This explains de Moura's choice of focus. As de Moura stresses throughout the more than five hundred pages of his book, it is difficult to define the nature of the language of an *ensalmus* because all too often it is impossible to characterize its addressee. As we shall see, in some cases an *ensalmista* may be unaware that his invocations are directed both to the Divinity and to his Enemy. A given invocation may be received by both interlocutors, thus producing undesired results. In other words, the *ensalmista* articulates a language whose nature is determined by its absent hearer and not by its present speaker.

The first section of *De ensalmis* attempts to formulate a general theory of linguistic expression. The first chapter is particularly significant, because it constitutes the theoretical foundation of the entire text. The following parts either repeat or expand the premises stated in this introductory section. Following previous demonologists, de Moura initially attacks those who believe that a prayer inevitably brings forth good effects. De Moura states that some people are convinced that every prayer always produces positive results, not because God necessarily grants his believers' requests, but rather because "through the words and desire expressed in our prayer to God some sort of rays come down to us and . . . realize what we desire" (3v). Moreover, referring to Martin del Rio's *Disquisitionum magicarum*, de Moura writes that, according to other thinkers, Mass and all the sacraments "allow us to obtain a supernatural knowledge of all arts

---

7. The symbol of the cross at the beginning of every paragraph of an invocation or exorcism is not a performative indication, but rather a visual and rhythmical reminder of the gravity of that expression. See chapter 3, below.

8. De Moura repeats the same concept on p. 254: "Since it is a 'constitutive benediction' [*benedictio constitutiva*], an ensalmus does not have any specific or unique quality. It is not the manifestation of an inexpressible act of grace given to a particular individual. An ensalmus is not independent from certain words . . . unlike the sentences uttered by the apostles."

and sciences."[9] Therefore, de Moura infers, one might come to the conclusion that an *ensalmus* has the "natural" power to remove every form of evil and to obtain all kinds of good results (4r).

The unacceptable assumption inherent in this optimistic belief in the "natural" power of invocation is that it makes the role of Catholic authorities superfluous. Indeed, as we shall see later, for de Moura the Catholic Church embodies the power that authenticates any linguistic expression. If, as Augustine says, any form of language is an invocation to the Divinity, the Catholic Church grants any invocative act its foundation and validity, or better yet, its directionality. In other words, the Catholic Church allows an *ensalmus* to reach its necessary interlocutor. Clearly referring to the Protestant movements identified with the Waldenses later in the book, de Moura criticizes those who think that by means of a simple prayer one can attain eternal life even without any sacrament, including baptism (4r).

According to de Moura, language does not reflect the world; it neither influences creation nor is influenced by it. In a later passage he directly rejects Ficino's Neoplatonic view of the world's hidden correspondences. For de Moura, no word necessarily results from or responds to the world. De Moura finds in del Rio an adamant defense of his view on language's ineffectiveness. Attacking those who use *ensalmi* to heal a physical ailment, del Rio states: "*No word has the natural power to heal wounds or diseases, or to expel any other offense. I say, No word . . .* either spoken or written; either by itself and, as they say, incomplete, or complete and in a sentence (verse or prose); either with or without meaning; either in Hebrew or in any other idiom."[10] In this passage from *Disquisitionum magicarum* de Moura finds a succinct but quite eloquent rejection of every form of linguistic composition aimed at a possible impact on the world. No language (Hebrew included), no specific syntax or literary form participates in the "meaning" of God's creation.

De Moura recognizes, however, that according to the Church Fathers, language may exert "meanings" that transcend its merely communicative level. In some cases, de Moura writes, an *ensalmus* does affect reality; it does receive a response from its theoretical interlocutor. For instance, he mentions miraculous events occurring thanks to the articulation of an *ensalmus*, composed by a prominent religious figure. As del Rio himself recounts, St. German brought back to life an ass by pronouncing an

9. Del Rio, *Disquisitionum magicarum*, 20.
10. Del Rio, *Disquisitionum magicarum*, 48 (emphasis in original).

ensalmus "instituted against animals' diseases" (4v).[11] De Moura also stresses that in the validation or institution of a "legal" *ensalmus*, some jurists are not against the direct invocation of a devil, if the *ensalmista* is able to force the devil to perform a good deed (4v–5r).[12] For instance, de Moura writes, the blessed Dominick forced a devil to hold a candle while he was reading his night prayers.

In the introductory pages the Portuguese inquisitor faces two crucial problems. Not only must he define what and when an *ensalmus* "means," he must also characterize its legal signification. Referring to the example of the ass resuscitated through an *ensalmus* pronounced by a virtuous person, de Moura questions animals' ability to understand the language of the *ensalmus*. Moreover, what one perceives as miraculous could be simply a "natural virtue" of a given linguistic expression (5r). De Moura seems to contradict his previous statements concerning language's lack of intrinsic meaning. If language means insofar as it expresses a human speaker's intention, how can it possibly possess a sense transcending what the speaker has meant to express? And if every linguistic expression necessarily entails a listener, how could one consider an animal as a possible addressee of a human utterance? More important, if an *ensalmus* is exclusively directed to God or the devil, why should we care whether or not an ass understands the *ensalmista's* words?

De Moura's apparent contradictions are already present in del Rio's *Disquisitionum magicarum*, one of de Moura's primary references. In reality, in their examination of verbal intentionality, demonologists face a double impasse. First, they cannot help but see language as a clean slate on which human beings impress their good or bad designs. Human language must either speak to God or to the Enemy. Second, demonologists aim to interpret any linguistic expression from a legal standpoint—that is, they see the Catholic Church as the sole speaker of a legally "good" word. Only the Church is able to articulate a "good" utterance.

11. Del Rio, *Disquisitionum magicarum*, book 3, part 2, q. 2, sec. 8, 460–68. Del Rio analyzes if and how an exorcism can be applied to animals. He mentions expressions commonly used in a Catholic *ensalmus*, such as "si sancta Maria virgo puerum Iesum vere peperit: liberetur animal hac passione. In nomine Patris, etc." and "Christus fuit natus, Christus fuit amissus, Christus fuit inventus: ipse benedicat et consignet haec vulnera, in nomine Patris, etc." Del Rio also cites one *ensalmus* directed to worms afflicting an animal: "Ego adiuro vos vermes, per omnipotentem Deum, etc." (460).

12. De Moura refers to Thomas Aquinas, *Summa* 2.2, q. 90, art. 2, 645. Compare Augustine, *The City of God*, book 10, chap. 10 (theurgy, which promises a fraudulent purification of souls by the invocation of demons), 293–97.

However, both del Rio and de Moura recognize that language has also a "natural" character, previous to any form of intentionality. Words mean notwithstanding a human speaker. Therefore, words do pertain to the world, and thus "signify" without needing a human being's intervention. We might say that, according to Catholic demonology, language possesses two levels of expressivity. First, it manifests a "potential" meaning—that is, a meaning that exists apart from a specific speaker. Second, it has an "intentional" meaning that it receives from human speakers. Inquisitors must peel off, so to speak, the first layer of language to understand whether a speaker and/or the devil has infected language with a wicked intentionality.

The reference to language's "natural virtue" serves a second, ideological goal. By introducing and removing the concept of "naturality" from his text, de Moura endeavors to undermine any linguistic expression that has attained positive results without having originated from a representative of the Church. When an *ensalmista*, whose conduct cannot possibly be interpreted as a result of Satan's influence, achieves a good action, he has simply referred to the natural, though unknown, properties of language.

Language and animals pertain to the "natural," unintentional realm of creation. Going back to the episode of the saint who resuscitated an ass, de Moura concludes that animals must have some sort of knowledge of human language. Although they do not possess a language, beasts must be able to receive a human message, otherwise it would be difficult to explain why Psalm 58 (57) states:

> their poison is the poison of the snake;
> they are deaf as the adder that blocks its ears
> so as not to hear the magician's music
> and the clever snake-charmer's spells. (4–5)

This psalm, de Moura is convinced, clearly posits that animals "can be naturally enchanted"—that is, they can be restrained by how certain words sound and not by what they actually mean (5r). De Moura briefly refers to a second passage, this time from Jeremiah: "Yes, now I send you / serpents, adders, / against which no charm exists" (8:17). De Moura has purposefully chosen two passages that lend themselves to more than one interpretation. He first supports a literal interpretation of these verses. Accordingly, the adder is first and foremost the actual animal, as Thomas confirms.[13] As

---

13. Thomas Aquinas, *Summa* 2.2, q. 96, art. 4. Compare Del Rio, *Disquisitionum magicarum*, book 2, q. 13 ("An magi valeant incantare animalia bruta), 152–54.

Origen himself states, certain words, even unintelligible ones, have the power to put serpents to sleep and to remove their poisons from the human body.[14]

De Moura is evidently aware that this passage from Psalm 57 presents some rather thorny problems to a modern interpreter. He adds that the terms *adder* and *serpent* may also be meant as a metaphor *(metaphora)*, indicating all those that operate in favor of evil (5v). However, the main obstacle de Moura must overcome is less the identification between serpent and evil (sinners and the devil) than that between "natural" and "magical" language. One of the fundamental tenets of demonology is the condemnation of any practitioner of magic that does not express the language of the Church. The psalm, the passage from Origen, and that from Grillando clearly state that the speakers of those allegedly natural utterances were magicians. And only magicians—that is, witches—supposedly understand and articulate the devil's (the adder's) language. The magicians are able to express "natural" words only because they know that those words would be effective in a certain way. In other words, the speakers of healing words are magicians who entertain a special relationship with the "adder" itself.

At this point of his text de Moura does not yet need to condemn the magicians as heretics, as he will do later. For the moment, he need only state that, in order to tame adders and all other beasts, these magicians simply make use of the "natural magic and virtue . . . of words, whose meaning is not always detectable" (6r).[15] Supporting his argument with the authority of the Philosopher, de Moura explains that certain verbal expressions, such as laughter and sighing, have a primary meaning that "does not report the thing external to that expression itself."[16] Only at a second level of signification may an expression such as laughter or moaning manifest the speaker's intentionality. Beasts, de Moura concludes, express themselves not only through their specific sounds, but also through their performance of those sounds.

---

14. Origen, *Homiliae in librum Iesu Nave* (PG 42), Homily 20, chap. 15, 921–23. De Moura also cites a passage from Grillando's *De sortilegiis* (Frankfurt, 1592), book 2, q. 8, n. 2, 143, on a magician who mastered the most rebellious bulls with the sole use of language.

15. De Moura mentions an important passage from the *Summa* in which Thomas states that it is lawful to influence the natural qualities of things. However, things have some hidden qualities that man is not aware of ("Licitum enim est uti naturalibus virtutibus corporum ad proprios effectus inducendos. Res autem naturales habent quasdam virtutes occultas"; *Summa* 2.2, q. 96, art. 2).

16. Aristotle, *Politics*, translated by Ernest Barker (Oxford: Clarendon, 1961), book 1, chap. 2, 6.

Let us remember that Prierio's *De strigimagis*, written almost a century before *De ensalmis*, had compared the devil's language (that almost idiom the Enemy formulates to communicate to human beings) with preverbal expressions such as laughter or moaning. The devil's temporary language, Prierio had said, is similar to a singing that says nothing. In other words, for de Moura "natural magic" is what language is not—that is, "natural words" are those that speak without being aware of their speaking. It is evident that animal intelligence is "in slumber and imperfect." More than a logical conclusion, de Moura's discourse tries to attain an ideological effect. He first says that language does not possess any specific meaning, and thus *ensalmi* are nothing more than mere invocations to an uncertain addressee; then he states that words have a natural expressivity that exceeds the speaker's understanding. A burst of laughter means something, but its meaning is "in slumber" in that it does not need an act of rational intentionality.

The magician, the adder, the devil communicate with each other by means of a prelinguistic exchange. The magician does not know the animal's idiom, posited that such a thing exists; he merely knows how to use certain "natural" linguistic gestures that have an impact on the animal behavior (6r). De Moura hints that a magician or an *ensalmista* may receive this irrational knowledge from the devil through an "unspoken pact" *(tacito pacto)*. Indeed, it is fundamental to assess where the *ensalmista* has acquired the language he uses in his ceremonies. It is evident, de Moura reminds us, that sometimes the Divinity does grant certain "human beings' minds the power to do miracles" (7r).[17] Let us imagine, de Moura says, that an *ensalmista* has received a vision or an inspiration; will he be able to discern by himself whether this communication comes from God or from Satan?[18] It is clear that the Portuguese inquisitor doubts that an *ensalmista* may assess the truthfulness of a superior communication without the support of the "Holy Court" *(sacrum Tribunal)*. In most cases, de Moura is

17. Throughout *De ensalmis*, de Moura supports his ideas by mentioning well-known Counter-Reformation texts against Protestantism. The first is *Consultatio de vera fide et religione* by Leonardus Lessius (1554–1623). According to Lessius, miracles are "seals and certain divine evidences, whereby [Catholic] Religion is authorized and approved." I quote from the English translation by Edmund Lechmere: *A Consultation about Religion* (London, 1693), 29.

18. "[If] an individual receives a visitation, a vision, or a revelation, will he be able to discern whether it comes from God or from another source? It is thus reasonable to ask ourselves whether an ensalmista has the ability to have and to recognize any form of divine inspiration, through which he is moved by God either to use the ceremony of the ensalmus in order to achieve the effect wished by God himself, or to ask God for that ability" (7r).

convinced, not only does the *ensalmista* ignore or mistake the nature of his revelation and thus of his speech, he intentionally fails to manifest the unlawful sources of his language. Throughout *De ensalmis* de Moura refers to Jews as the quintessential unreliable speaker. Following a quite common view of those Jews who had converted to Catholicism, de Moura states that many "Judaizers" officially embrace the true religion, only to continue to profess their "detestable" creed secretly (7r–v).[19]

The Jewish *ensalmi*, which allegedly are able to help a woman become pregnant, are inevitably expressions of a secret and doubtful idiom, since their interlocutor is missing. The *ensalmus* is a linguistic artifact that has two different listeners. Although he needs his actual or imagined presence, an *ensalmista* does not speak to the beneficiary of his discourse. Even in the case of a favorable or noxious intervention of nature (such as a storm or the healing of an animal), the *ensalmista* primarily directs his words either to God or to the devil. A second addressee of his speech is a social construction: the Catholic Church or a heretical community, the latter embodied in the "synagogue" where, according to almost every book on demonology, witches and other heretics gather to perform their devilish rituals.

Moving away from his initial statements about the nonsignificant nature of language, de Moura says that some words, inspired by God and "inserted in certain prayers in a certain way," do possess potentially healing powers (8r–v). The first two words that have this capacity are *Jesus* and *Verbum* or the expression *Verbum divinum incarnatum*. De Moura backs up his statement on the intrinsic holiness of the word *Jesus* by quoting from Bozio's *De signis ecclesiae Dei* (book 15, chap. 71).[20] In Bozio, de Moura finds a list of assertions taken from the Church Fathers on the supposed sacredness of this term.

Bozio's work is based on the assumption that God constantly reveals his

---

19. The core of de Moura's attack against the Jews is his belief that through their heretical procedures Jews aim to attain "wordly goods" (*bona temporalia* [7v]).

20. Tommaso Bozio, *De signis ecclesiae Dei* (Cologne: Ioannes Gymnicus, 1593), book 15, chap. 71, 314: "Indeed, who will ever repel the very name 'Jesus,' which we so ardently revere, and its utterance, remembrance, and reading, acts that we all perform on our knees?" Bozio (1548–1610), a native of Gubbio and an Oratorian, was a famous historian of the Church. He studied with St. Filippo Neri and besides *De signis* composed *Annales antiquitatum* and a series of texts against Machiavelli. On Bozio, see Gabriella Zarri, "Living Saints: A Typology of Female Sanctity in the Early Sixteenth Century," in *Women and Religion in Medieval and Renaissance Italy*, edited by Daniel Bornstein and Roberto Rusconi (Chicago: University of Chicago Press, 1996), 222.

direct presence in the Catholic Church. The Catholic Church is the sole site inhabited by divine presence. Intended as a vehement attack againt Protestantism, Bozio's *De signis* intends to present the Catholic Church as the natural manifestation of Augustine's concept of the city of God. Apart from describing in detail the Church's hierarchy and its specific powers, Bozio's text draws upon an innumerable series of miraculous stories concerning God's intervention in his Church. Along with del Rio's *Disquisitionum magicarum*, *De signis ecclesiae Dei* grants de Moura narrative support for his definition of "natural" versus "unnatural" language.

Using Bozio's rhetoric, de Moura mentions the healing properties of saints' relics, kept in almost every Catholic sanctuary. The saints' corpses are God's natural and everlasting idioms. It is not rare, de Moura says, to find that the body of a saint, still intact centuries after his or her death, "pronounces" good and curative words—that is, a saint's corpse is God's direct response to human requests for help.[21] De Moura transcribes the following passage from Bozio's *De signis:* "I saw the pure and incorrupt body of a virgin . . . , who had ascended to heaven more than 300 years before. This body is in the monastery of the Holy Spirit. It is wrapped in a cloth, which often times shows drops of blood. The virgins take care of washing the cloth, and keep the water, because it has the amazing power to heal any form of disease."[22] This holy corpse constantly exudes drops of blood that are absorbed by the linen gown. The corpse is, so to speak, ever able to articulate syllables that are a direct expression of God's presence. The virgins transfer this idiom from a motionless medium (the cloth) to another (water) that allows the drops/syllables to flow into any ailing body.[23]

Other "utterances" whose validity is unquestionable are the Catholic Church's official prayers. Considering unnecessary an analysis of "Pater Noster," given its indisputable prominence among invocations, de Moura focuses on "Salve Regina" because it has both a juridical and a medical competence. The devotion to Mary—both in a personal and spontaneous manner, and in all "institutionalized" invocations, such as the crucial part of the rosary (*per orationes aliquas . . . institutas vel comprobatas* [12])—

---

21. On this subject, see Caroline Walker Bynum, *The Resurrection of the Body* (New York: Columbia University Press, 1995), 59–114.

22. Bozio, *De signis*, book 15, chap. 66, 283–84; de Moura, *De ensalmis*, 9r.

23. Reproducing a topos present in many books on demonology, de Moura also speaks of the healing powers of some church bells, which are able to protect entire villages from the devils' incursions (*De ensalmis*, 9r–v).

brings about innumerable positive reactions in the world. Here we must remember that the cult of the Virgin is one of the major sources of discordance between Catholicism and Protestantism. Since the Virgin Mary is inevitably connected with the Catholic creed, de Moura does not dare to question the consequences of any invocation directed to her. Accordingly, he emphasizes that, according to the Church, souls in Purgatory receive plenary indulgence thanks to the prayers directed to the Mother of God.[24] Mary embodies the "legal," and thus "natural," power of the Church's language. The Trinity cannot help but respond to Mary's requests received from human beings. Mary's intercessions are indeed "infallible" (13).[25] As a consequence, since it is the sole religion that sustains the cult of the Virgin, Catholicism is also the sole path through which a believer can see his or her invocations answered.

However, de Moura does not fail to stress that all these healing utterances (the word *Jesus*, relics, and prayers to the Virgin) may contain a very distressing element.[26] In some unexplainable cases, in the act of pronouncing even the most sacred utterances, a human speaker may be unaware that his or her first addressee, and thus primary benefactor, is not God, but the devil. The devil, de Moura says, often grants "benefits," even "ecclesiastical ones" *(ecclesiastica beneficia)*. De Moura recounts the poignant case of a monk called Gerebertus who, supported by the devil who convinced him to perform magical activities, succeeded in becoming an archbishop *(Archiepiscopus* [8v–9r]). But Gerebertus' contract with the Enemy had a fundamental and deceitful clause: he could not say Mass in Jerusalem. Years later Gerebertus found himself in a "certain place in Rome called Jerusalem that had a church called Saint Cross," where he was asked to say Mass. Again, the devil's deceit is essentially based on misinterpretation or double interpretation. Gerebertus thought that the word *Jerusalem* referred exclusively to the Holy City, while the devil had intended this term both literally and metaphorically. At the end of the Mass, Satan rushes down on Gerebertus in front of the crowd gathered for that celebration and demands his life. The story ends with Gerebertus' official repentance. Although the sinful monk wished his body to be dismembered, God showed his clemency by directing the animals that carried Gerebertus' corpse toward the Church of St. John Lateran *(ecclesiam Lateranensem* [9r]).

24. De Moura (15–16) speaks of "Salve Regina" and its beneficial influences on our sins.

25. After fol. 11v, *De ensalmis* follows the modern pagination.

26. De Moura reiterates the indisputable power of the term *Jesus* and that of relics in several other passages of his work (e.g., 41, 76–77, 252–53).

What de Moura intends to convey through this story and the preceding long citations from Bozio is that, although the *ensalmista's* invocations have an uncertain addressee, they are always listened to, even when they are not answered. At least in this passage, by the term *ensalmista* de Moura clearly intends all those who are engaged in an act of invocation, including priests, magicians, witches, and so forth. The monk Gerebertus is somehow symbolic of a liminal identity, whose act of invocation (Mass) at once involves the divinity and his Enemy. Was Gerebertus' devotion directed to both addressees? Were his religious rituals always marred by his pact with the Enemy, or did Gerebertus manage to split his identity into two areas of performativity? De Moura does emphasize that the "effect of a prayer" *(effectus orationis)* depends on the subject's "devotion" *(devotione)*, but he does not and cannot analyze devotion's possibly contradictory and subconscious intentions, which may mislead a speaker from the Catholic Church, the only "natural" institution (10r).[27] It is evident that the Portuguese inquisitor's interest in language transcends a merely legal intention. De Moura identifies a "clean" or "cleansed" utterance with the natural expression of a Catholic idiom. Since he understands that he cannot offer an objective analysis of man's conscious and subconscious intentions, de Moura focuses his examination on words themselves and their diverse "ceremonies" (65).

As we have seen, in the second part of the introductory section de Moura states that words do have some sort of "natural force" (23). This inherent quality is first and foremost detectable in "names"—that is, those words that point to a specific being. Referring to Origen, de Moura writes that "certain names, both of angels, cities, places, and human beings, are certainly distributed by God."[28] Not only "certain" names, but all names result from God's wisdom. For de Moura, it is irrelevant that every human language gives each thing a different name or pronounces it in a different manner, because both names and words derive their being from an act of divine wisdom. Thus, we might infer that a "name" possesses two kinds of existence, its divine essence and its phonetic representation. Words, de Moura means to say, exist before being articulated by man's intentionality. Words come before the mouth and the tongue that express them. De

27. In a later passage de Moura clearly says that the authorities are unable to speculate on an *ensalmista's* deepest intentions: "[Q]uis poterit iudicare de animo operantis" ("Who will be able to judge of the performer?" [65]).

28. Origen, *Selecta in Genesis* (PG 12), chap. 1, 87–90; compare Origen, *Commentaria in evangelium Ioannis* (PG 14), 147–48.

Moura, like Origen, states that those who believe that "names and nouns signify according to man's imposition and thus produce different effects in different idioms" are totally mistaken.[29]

De Moura's discussion of the origin of verbal expression is crucial to an understanding of how the devil manipulates language against human speakers and the world itself. Unlike Aristotle, de Moura sees human idioms not as fundamentally ungrounded and thus intrinsically devoid of any essence, but rather as echoes of divine goodness and presence. Even those who hold that Adam was the first speaker to impose names on things cannot help but believe that in his activity Adam followed "reason" *(ratio)* and thus his "names interpreted life" (24).[30] To support his view on the "natural" being of words, de Moura cites a long passage from Ioannes Goropius' *Hieroglyphica*, a long and involved discussion of the mystical origins and goals of language (28–29).[31] At the end of the first book, Goropius mentions the dialogue between Socrates and Protarchus in Plato's *Philebus*. In a famous passage (16c–d), Socrates explains to Protarchus that "the men of old, who were better than ourselves and dwelt nearer the gods, passed on this gift in the form of a saying. All things, so it ran, that are ever said to be consist of a one and a many, and have in their nature a conjunction of limit and unlimitedness."[32] De Moura interprets Goropius' quotation from *Philebus* as a clear reference to the divine origin of language and to the "unlimited" power of its syntactical constructions. The natural influence of words on reality is somehow enhanced or modified by their becoming parts of a sentence, what de Moura calls *artem sermocinandi* (29).

Both words and sentences have an existent, though imperceptible, quality *(proprietatem)*, which the devil and his followers endeavor to pervert

---

29. Origen, *Contra Celsum* (PG 11), chaps. 5 and 6, 663–67. Compare Origen, *Selecta in Genesis* (PG 12), 90: "How ridiculous are those who investigate the qualities of certain words in different idioms, examining them and carefully dissecting their meanings." De Moura also mentions Marsilio Ficino's *Iamblicus. De mysterii* (in *Opera omnia*, vol. 2, part 2 [Turin: Bottega d'Erasmo, 1959]). See the chapter "De nominibus divinis" (1902) where Ficino writes that each word possesses a certain superior quality, which is not transferable from one language to another ("[S]i significationum proprietas per aliam linguam interpretari possumus, non tamen eadem conservant permutata potentiam").

30. For an introduction to this topic, see Umberto Eco, *The Search for the Perfect Language*, translated by James Fentress (Cambridge, Mass.: Blackwell, 1997), 7–9.

31. I use the 1574 edition: Ioannes Goropius, *Hieroglyphica*, in *Opera omnia* (Brussels, 1574), 15–16.

32. I quote from Plato, *Philebus*, in *The Collected Dialogues of Plato*, edited by Edith Hamilton and Huntington Cairns (Princeton: Princeton University Press, 1996), 16c–d, 1092.

against creation. Since words, like magnets, attract and influence things, the devil's maleficent activities are nothing but the result of a sensible interpretation of their natural—that is, divine—essence (25). However, the spiritual properties of words are not "naturally" available for everyone. Although nouns and names naturally echo God's mysterious wisdom, they act out their divine essence only if and when their speakers are able to summon that essence. De Moura reminds us that an *ensalmus*—meaning here both a legal and an illegal invocation—often does not achieve its goal. The reason is that an *ensalmus* is a nonsignificant statement, unless at least one of its two addressees (God and/or Satan) is willing to listen to it. Furthermore, if a given sentence sometimes "works" and sometimes does not, for de Moura this is a sign that it has probably been inspired by the devil, because the devil constantly attempts to blur the unequivocal nature of words (26). De Moura mentions the typical case of exorcisms that the Church often must perform more than once.[33] It is a given, de Moura says, quoting from Raphael de la Torre's *De potestate Ecclesiae*, that an exorcism can be seriously jeopardized if its human addressee is deaf or deafened by the devil. However, de la Torre says, an exorcism "is directed to" *(dirigetur)* the obsessed and "meant for" *(destinatur)* the devil inhabiting the possessed person's body. Thus, although the exorcism is rendered much more difficult because of the possessed person's lack of collaboration, the inquisitor can still force the devil to let the possessed one perceive the Church's "natural," and thus healing, words.[34]

The Church authorities "possess" verbal expression in that words are God's direct creation. De Moura believes that in its rituals, including exorcisms and institutionalized prayers, the Catholic Church simply articulates the world's idiom and prevents the devil from perverting that language. Although he focuses on verbal expression, de Moura is aware that creation expresses itself through an infinite number of other languages, including

33. De Moura, *De ensalmis*, 26: "The Church repeats the application of an exorcism not once, but rather several times." Compare Petrus Binsfeldius, *De confessionibus maleficorum et sagarum* (Trier: Bock, 1605), 121–22: "The words of an exorcism do not have . . . the infallible attribute . . . to constrain and oppose demons."

34. Raphael de la Torre, *De potestate Ecclesiae*, in *Diversi tractatus* (Cologne, 1629), 58. For instance, a method frequently used to compel the devil to set the possessed person free is to perform some melodious music during the exorcism itself. This is a rather common view among demonologists. De Moura finds it in Christobal Suarez de Figueroa's Spanish translation of *Piazza universale* by the Italian Tommaso Garzoni. I use the 1630 edition: Suarez de Figueroa, *Plaza universal de todas ciencias y artes* (Perpignan: Luys Roure, 1630), 141. The most accurate edition of Garzoni's essential treatise is Tommaso Garzoni, *La piazza universale di tutte le professioni del mondo*, edited by Paolo Cherchi and Beatrice Collina, 2 vols. (Turin: Einaudi, 1996).

human beings' gestures, movements, and nonverbal rituals. He is convinced that "vulgar treatments" *(vulgares curationes)*—that is, *ensalmi* that, although successful, have been performed outside the jurisdiction of the Church—are usually "constitutive benedictions" and not "invocative benedictions"; that is, they are rituals that avoid any verbal expression and simply rely on "unclear" and thus suspicious gestures and *mises-en-scène* (42). Nonverbal expressions defy any form of grammar and thus cannot be defined in an unquestionable manner. De Moura condemns all those "verbal ceremonies" that also "depend on some material things" that have a role in the happening of the *ensalmus* itself (65). In de Moura's opinion, these forms of performances are dubious because "in all the signs instituted by the devil the [*ensalmus'*] power [*vis operandi*] solely depends on that very sign." De Moura means that, while the Church's *ensalmi* transcend any specific ritual because they are inspired by God's free act of grace *(gratia gratis data)*, a perverse *ensalmista* must confirm his or her dedication to the devil's prescriptions by acting out Satan's orders. In other words, a diabolic *ensalmista* exclusively relies on the theatricality of his gestures, prayers if any, and use of certain objects, such as candles, animals, and so forth. The devil's signs are in fact ungrounded expressions in that, unlike the Church's rites, they are not "signs," as Augustine says, of the only existing "thing," God himself. However, de Moura adds, a legal *ensalmista* is allowed to make use of illegal, diabolic signs, in order to summon the devil's presence and to erase him and his ungrounded "signs" (60).

To clarify the ungrounded nature of the devil's sign, de Moura uses the metaphor of the circular movement that moves away from itself and returns to itself (72). This image of a circular sign has more than one implication. First, it indicates the devil's inability to move outside of his pride. The circle, de Moura reminds us, is the form that is closed in on itself in apparent perfection (73). However, to move in a circle also means to circumvent—that is, to encircle/ensnare others, namely human beings, into one's abysmal circle.[35] "The devil makes use of circumvolution in himself and circumvention in us. He uses that [circumvolution], because it is inherent to the personal will; he uses this [circumvention], because sometimes it ascends and sometimes it descends." Since the devil's signs mean

---

35. De Moura mentions Ps. 11:10: "The impious men walk in circles according to your profound wisdom." The word *circuitus (in circuitu)*, which I translate as "in circles," can mean "a going round," a "revolving," but also the English "circumlocution." De Moura knows Bernard of Clairvaux's commentary on this psalm. See Bernard's *On the Song of Songs* (Kalamazoo, Mich.: Cistercian Publications, 1981), 69–76.

only insofar as they annihilate those who perform them, since they have no natural referent, it is obvious that devils tend to gather around those places or objects that signify creation's loss of sense, such as corpses, cemeteries, tombs, and funerals (75). The devil's signs find in these places the sudden lack of sense that constitutes the devil's essence. Like a vulture that flies around "decomposed cadavers and putrifying human flesh" before devouring it, a devil "circles around" his prey and then "swallows" it by convincing it to perform his gratuitous signs. The most eloquent example of a devilish absorption in a radical nonmeaning is certainly the biblical account of Sodom's metamorphosis into a "fetid and nauseating lake" that in its circular form seems to have ingested every form of life (78–79).

De Moura dedicates only a small portion of his work to the topos of the unforgivable practices of sodomites. As I will show in detail later, according to de Moura no actual distinction exists between the Jewish people and the sodomites. The term *sodomite* designates all those individuals who have given themselves to Satan. Having abandoned the "natural" practices of the Church, these abominable individuals—including, of course, the Jews—indulge in what we now call homosexuality. De Moura's *De ensalmis* mirrors a deep-rooted hostility of the Portuguese religious and political authorities against the Jews. We should recall that de Moura was active in the city of Evora, where the Inquisition established its Portuguese headquarters. In Evora Catholic preachers produced a body of anti-Semitic sermons delivered at the periodical autos-da-fé, during which the Church staged "its obsessive hatred against the Jews and their baptized descendants," the so-called "Judaizers" or "new Christians" *(cristãos novos)*.[36]

36. According to Borges Coelho (*Inquisição de Evora*, 1:20), the violent attack against the so-called new Christians was triggered by the papal bull *Cum ad nihil magis* (1531). The popes Clement VII and Paul III supported the persecution that followed the publication of the bull. For a good introduction to the problem of the "new Christians" in Portugal, see António José Saraiva, *A inquisição portuguesa* (Lisbon: Publicações Europa-America, 1956), 14–43; Saraiva, *Inquisição e cristãos-novos* (Porto: Editorial Inova, 1969), especially chap. 1 (27–46); José Lourenço D. De Mendonça and António Joaquim Moreira, *História dos principais actos e procedimentos da Inquisição em Portugal* (Lisbon: Imprensa Nacional–Casa da Moeda, 1980), 115–44. See also Edward Glaser, "Portuguese Sermons at Autos-da-Fé," *Studies in Bibliography and Booklore* 2 (1955–56): 53. For an exhaustive analysis of the auto-da-fé in Portugal and Spain, see Francisco Bethencourt, *L'inquisition à l'époque moderne* (Paris: Éditions Fayard, 1995), 241–306. Bethencourt stresses that at the beginning the ritual of the auto-da-fé focused exclusively on the execution; slowly, however, the Spanish and Portuguese Inquisition developed a rather complex performance that aimed to occupy the whole public space. Every social class participated in the "theater" of the Inquisition. Given that it did not take place in a specific space, the annual auto-da-fé could be staged either in a church or in a square. Compare Henry Kamen, *The Spanish Inquisition* (New Haven: Yale University Press, 1998), 206: "The scene would invariably be set in the biggest square of public space available. The elaborate and im-

As Henry Kamen notes, "Lisbon witnessed the first great massacre of New Christians in 1506."[37] However, the Portuguese Inquisition celebrated its first auto-da-fé only thirty-some years later, in 1540. Moreover, as Kamen points out, "[o]nly on 16 July 1547 did the pope issue the bull which finally settled the structure of an independent Portuguese Inquisition."

Like exorcism, the auto-da-fé was a propaganda performance aimed to represent the Catholic Church's all-encompassing and thus inescapable power. The Inquisition's performances against the Jews were exclusively oral; more than seventy sermons were printed between the end of the sixteenth and the first half of the seventeenth century.[38] An auto-da-fé was officially meant both to represent the Jews' capital punishment and to compel them to abandon their creed. The preacher, however, almost always stated that the Jews, like the witches and the sodomites, were unable and unwilling to repent and embrace the "natural" faith.[39] The Jews' unyielding language, the inquisitors were convinced, could not possibly convert to Catholicism's "natural" idiom.

De Moura connects the Jews' "inflexible" language with their way of performing an *ensalmus*. It is impossible to believe, de Moura writes, that a prayer "naturally" *(naturaliter)*—that is, inevitably—produces the effects invoked (89). After all, "very often nothing is obtained through a given *ensalmus* or prayer" (92). De Moura portrays the Inquisition as the institution whose expression is ductile and open to Divinity's unfathomable decisions, while the Jews possess the rigid language of a false law. Paradoxically, for de Moura those who are persecuted by religious and civil institutions speak the (false) law, whereas Church law is seen as the language of freedom. The Jews still believe, de Moura says, that God is willing to answer all their requests. At the time of the Old Testament God granted the Jews, his people, all kinds of worldly goods, but after their murder of the Son, God rejected them forever (90). According to de Moura, in their prayers the Jews still limit themselves to asking the Father for mundane things, without understanding that God may respond to his believers' requests in many different ways, both visibly and invisibly. This

---

pressive staging of the proceedings . . . made for heavy expense and because of this public autos were not very frequent. Their frequency depended entirely on the discretion of individual tribunals and . . . the availability of prisoners."

37. Kamen, *Spanish Iniquisition*, 287.

38. See Maria Lucília Gonçalves Pires, *Xadrez de palavras. Estudos de literatura barroca* (Lisbon: Cosmos, 1996), 121–41.

39. Gonçalves Pires reminds us that, by denying them the possibility of a sincere conversion, the Inquisition prevented the Jews from becoming part of the Portuguese nation (*Xadrez de palavras*, 138).

is the "natural law" established by Christ with his death on the cross (109).
When they crucified the Savior, the Jews actually distanced themselves
from nature and fell into the devil's circular process of seduction.

To explain the point more clearly, de Moura quotes two powerful verses
from the Psalms. The first is Ps. 71:9: "[I]nimici . . . terram lingent," which
literally means "his enemies lick the ground" (101). Highlighting the connection between the verb *lingere* and the noun *lingua* ("tongue" and "language"), de Moura states that the Lord's "enemies"—that is, the Jews—
"lick" the earth without being allowed to swallow it *(deglutire);* that is, the
Jews' deceitful language/tongue merely grovels in the "world's" transient
wealth (102). According to de Moura, the Jews see no difference between
an *ensalmus* and their immoral practice of usury (103, 119). For the Portuguese inquisitor, usury symbolizes the Jews' corrupt use of language/
tongue, because language/tongue is the means through which they try
to enhance their worldly abundance, through their hypocritical discourse
about money and their materialistic conception of language (118–19). According to de Moura, the Jews believe that the words present in their invocations have a "physical" meaning—that is, their utterances are at once
requests and responses to those requests. The Jews do not understand that
they are not God's chosen people any longer.[40] Like the devils, the Jews express a circular language, which denies any actual interlocutor and thus
any possible denial or miscommunication (105).[41]

For the second citation De Moura chooses Ps. 16:14: "Saturati sunt
filii" ("their sons have plenty"). De Moura interprets this verse in the
context of the whole psalm, in which an innocent man asks God to rescue
his soul from wicked people (verse 13). "They" store up wealth, while for
himself, he only wishes to see God's face (verse 15). In a sense, de Moura
infers, we could interpret the term *saturati* as "sated," as if the Jews fed on
their own sons (110).[42] De Moura clearly states that, the Jews being the
Church's main enemy, the Inquisition has the duty "to exterminate this
injurious sacrilege" (123). The "injurious sacrilege" is primarily the Jews'

40. Compare Lessius, *A Consultation about Religion,* 91: "When the religion of the *Old
Testament* amongst the *Jews* was to be changed, and to pass from the *Shadow* to the Truth . . .
he [God] was pleased to confirm the fame with many and great miracles."

41. As is well known, Derrida discusses a similar problem. See *"The Purloined Letter": Lacan, Derrida, and Psychoanalitic Reading,* edited by John P. Muller and William J. Richardson
(Baltimore: Johns Hopkins University Press, 1988), 173–212.

42. De Moura supports his argument by quoting Ezek. 5:11: "[P]atres comedent filios . . .
and filii patres suos" ("fathers will eat their children, and children eat their fathers"). Verse 12
of the same psalm compares "them" to a "lion hungry for prey."

allegedly "perverse" use of language. Like devils, the Jews devour their own language, in that their expressions do not exceed the circularity of a solipsistic practice. Paradoxically, according to the Catholic de Moura, the Inquisition is the institution that protects the freedom of linguistic expression, including its errors and miscommunications. Thus, the Inquisition's fundamental role is to repress any practice that disclaims the absolute freedom of language.

As noted above, de Moura's discourse is also directed to the Protestant movement, which he identifies with the Waldenses. De Moura's paradoxical reasoning aims to refute Protestantism's central premise: that the relationship between God and his creatures is a private exchange, transcending any form of social construction. For the Roman Inquisition, any linguistic practice needs to be validated to guard against the unpredictability of its nature. The Jews, the witches, the sodomites, and the Waldenses are supporters of Satan's perversion, in that they do not perceive the risks inherent in verbal language.

After having clarified the gravity of his linguistic investigation, de Moura moves to analyze a crucial aspect of linguistic exchange—the relationship between words and images. An *ensalmus*, he writes, involves two forms of representation, *internae illustrationes* and *externae apparitiones* (138). The former are the images evoked in the minds of both the speaker and his listeners; the latter are the potential images conjured up by the *ensalmus* itself. To fully understand de Moura's examination, we must keep in mind that he interprets an "internal representation" both as the Aristotelian phantasm (the images summoned by verbal language) and pictorial communications sent either by God or by a devil (142–43).[43] It is well known, de Moura states, that the devil can exert an enormous power on a human being's internal representations (144). As he will state in a later passage of *De ensalmis*, "the devil can influence our intellect only through *phantasms*" (189). In other words, every time a human being rationally or spontaneously formulates a linguistic expression in his or her mind, his or

---

43. *De ensalmis*, 142–43: "It is a given that inner manifestations and revelations are sometimes granted by God or by a good angel. . . . It is also a given, however, that inner visions and external apparitions may have a demonic origin." Compare Augustine, *De cura pro mortuis gerenda (PL* 40), chap. 12, 602–3; del Rio, *Disquisitionum magicarum*, book 2, chap. 24 ("Quid magia, vel daemon, possit circa animam corpori iunctam, idque informantem?"), 207–17. Del Rio summarizes the different means through which the devil can influence a soul. First, the devil can deceive our external senses (207). Second, he can pervert our internal senses (207–8). Third, he can perturb our spirits (209). Fourth, he can enhance or blur our memory. He can also corrupt our will and our intellect (210–15).

her sentences may be engaged in a dialogic exchange with an interlocutor (God, angels, devils) who is at once internal and external to the thinker's mind. However, de Moura believes that human beings' internal representations may also result from the inability of human beings to think without producing images (as Aristotle states in the third book of *De anima*). Following a topos of medieval and Renaissance demonology, de Moura reminds us that an excessive production *(excessum)* of internal images is usually present in melancholics, who are often overwhelmed by their private reasonings.[44]

For de Moura, melancholics suffer from a natural corruption of their phantasms (143). Thus, their often irrational and disturbed utterances do not necessarily result from the devil's intervention. However, melancholics personify a liminal, borderline identity, which, because of the nature of its mental disease, lends itself to the Enemy's attack, since the devil primarily attempts to undermine the natural course of our thoughts. According to Renaissance demonologists, melancholics have a fluctuating identity, ranging from individuals prone to solitary musings to people who, suffering from hallucinations, believe that they have been turned into animals. Thus, it is extremely difficult to determine whether a melancholic is naturally sick or is affected by a devilish perversion.[45] As I will ex-

44. For an interesting analysis of melancholia in early modern Europe, see Stanley W. Jackson, *Melancholia and Depression: From Hippocratic Times to Modern Times* (New Haven: Yale University Press, 1986), 78–103. A further discussion of melancholia is found in chapters 3, 4, and 5, below.

45. Almost every text on demonology mentions the melancholics' tendency to become prey to the devil's mental intrusion. However, the actual process of visual perversion is interpreted in more than one manner. For instance, in *Compendium maleficarum* Francesco Guazzo states: "Many such persons [possessed people] . . . have debased imaginations, especially in their sleep, and so betray the presence of a demon: but this indication by itself is not enough, since it is common also to sufferers from melancholia" (167). For Guazzo, "[the devil] induces the melancholy sickness by first disturbing the black bile in the body and so dispersing a black humour throughout the brain and the inner cells of the body" (106). I quote from the English translation by E. A. Ashwin (John Rodker: London, 1929). In *De natura daemonum* (Venice, 1581) Laurentius Anania offers a different interpretation. Physicians are convinced, Anania states, that the devil does not cause melancholia, but rather uses this disease to enter a person's mind. According to Anania, a melancholic has a particularly thick phlegm that sticks to the patient's midriff and affects his heart, his lungs, and thus also his respiration and voice. More important, the brain is not aired as it should be. Hence the melancholic's obfuscated mind, dejected appearance, negative thoughts, and difficulty in speaking and moving. Because of the weakened condition of a melancholic's mind, an incubus can easily defeat it, triggering false but disturbing images (119). In *De rerum varietate* (Basle, 1575) Girolamo Cardano, the most influential physician of the Italian Renaissance, does not state that the devil has a direct responsibility for melancholia. He believes that melancholia may be caused by an excessive solitude, which facilitates the devil's attack against the subject's mind (650). For an analysis of the relationship be-

plain later (see chapter 4), demonologists believe that the devil can easily creep into a "natural" melancholy and thus turn a natural ailment into a demonic possession. Clearly, the melancholic identity directly reflects demonologists' difficulty in distinguishing between "lawful" and "unlawful" phantasms.

We have seen that in *De strigimagis* Sylvester Prierio discusses one form of perverted visuality, the so-called aorasia, or partial blindness, brought about by the devil. While Prierio analyzes how the devil perverts creation, including human beings, by interpreting the signs emitted by the world, de Moura focuses more on the "internal" nature of representations.[46] For de Moura, both "internal" and "external" representations are phantasms that essentially affect the subject's process of absorption and interpretation of phantasms themselves. Examining the so-called external apparitions, de Moura distinguishes among five kinds of visual visitations that take place in the subject's mind. An apparition can be either "visual," "physical," "auditory," "imaginary," or "intellectual" (144). The definitions relate to the possible ways through which the mind's internal processes may be modified. In other words, both internal visions and external apparitions may be nothing but demonic attempts to taint the human process of understanding. Following the Aristotelian reasoning of Franciscus Suarez's *Metaphysicarum disputationum*, de Moura distinguishes between *intellectus agens* or *potentia activa*, which provides the mind with internal images, and *intellectus possibilis* or *potentia receptiva*, the "passive" part of the mind, which accepts and processes the images deriving from the *intellectus agens* (Suarez, 2:322–23). The devil, Suarez says, may lead the *intellectus agens* to mistake the nature of a given external message, either visual, auditory, or totally intellectual.[47] The latter form of external message directly affects how a human being, after having accepted a given image as a truthful reflection of a real physicality, turns this image into a verbal statement and thus formulates a particular conclusion. This is why, referring to *Summula caietani*, de Moura believes that the interpretation

---

tween melancholia and possession, see the beginning of chapter 4, below. On Cardano's concept of melancholy, see chapter 5.

46. In *Summula caietani*, another important source of de Moura's text, the cardinal Tommaso de Vio (1469–1534) dedicates an entire chapter to the dangers of "the mind's disquiet" *(inquietudo mentis humanae)*. According to de Vio, a mental uneasiness is often connected with a sinful nature, which is unable to attain a perfect composure, always resulting from a contact with God. I refer to the 1584 edition (Venice: Nicolinus), 323.

47. Compare Franciscus Suarez's *Metaphysicarum disputationum* (Paris: Somnium, 1605). Apart from a brilliant analysis of angelic nature, Suarez offers invaluable insights on the mind's way of processing the Aristotelian phantasms. In *Disputatio* 9 ("De falsitate"; 2:216–26)

of images seen in a dream is always sinful, because in a dream images attain their most tenuous and dubious manifestation.[48]

Given the ambiguous nature of external/internal images, de Moura recognizes that it is difficult to distinguish between prophecy, which has always a divine origin, and prediction *(vaticinium)*, which can only spring from a demonic source (146).[49] Both forms of supernatural perception are the human response to an external message, in that both a prophet and a witch react to an imaginary input. It is thus imperative, de Moura states, to define a set of signs *(signa)* through which the Inquisition can characterize the actual nature of a prophetic speech.[50] In his examination, de Moura makes constant use of mystical literature, because it always relies on an external and superior message. As Henry Charles Lea notes, this is one of the most original aspects of de Moura's *De ensalmis*.[51]

To support his view on the relationship between mysticism and demonology, the Portuguese inquisitor first mentions the opinion of Gregory the Great (*Moralia*, book 28, chap. 2). Gregory's personal experience is that the Word does not communicate with his creatures' hearts through language ("de verbo eius sine verbis ac syllabis cor docetur").[52] The human subject discerns the Word's message without perceiving any form of im-

---

Suarez discusses how the subject can distinguish between truth and falsehood. He admits that many thinkers believe that the subject may be affected by an "external cause" *(extrinseca causa)*, either God, an angel, or a devil (2:223). Suarez states that God can only direct a human mind toward truth, and never toward falsehood. A devil *(malus angelus)* cannot blind the subject's mind. He can try to mislead an *intellectus* by means of deceitful images *(suggestiones)*.

48. *Summula caietani*, 469. De Moura also quotes from Cardano's *De rerum varietate*. Cardano is convinced that demons can easily interfere with a subject's mind in all those conditions in which the mind is momentarily weak (asleep or under the influence of alcohol [595]). However, it is essential to bear in mind the difference between the strictly Catholic "demon" and Cardano's Neoplatonic/Catholic interpretation of the term. Finally, de Moura mentions the opinion of the theologian Thomas Sanchez, who writes that the analysis of dreams *(somnia observare)* is a form of superstition. I refer to the 1661 edition: Thomas Sanchez, *In praecepta decalogi* (Lyons: Laurentius Anisson, 1661), book 2, 1:289.

49. Again, the distinction between prophecy and prediction reflects a social and political difference. We might say that, according to de Moura, our "legal status" is defined by how we relate to images. De Moura finds a direct reference in Bernardus Comensius' *Lucerna inquisitorum haereticae pravitatis* (Milan: Valerius et Hieronius fratres, 1566). For Comensius, those who work with "illusionary" images are heretics. To summon the devil, heretics give the holiest Catholic rituals a demonic twist. They use Christ's blood and rebaptize their children in the name of Satan (24r).

50. Del Rio as well believes that the Inquisition must define "safe" signs to interpret prophetic statements (*Disquisitionum magicarum*, book 2, q. 26, sec. 3, 235).

51. Lea, *Materials toward a History of Witchcraft*: "Valle de Moura is one of the few demonologists who seem to recognize the relations between sorcery and mysticism" (1:432–33).

52. Gregory the Great, *Moralia* (PL 76), 452.

age/word (147), as if verbal expression were always subject to Satan's possible infection. De Moura reminds us that God often speaks to us through his angels, who do not possess any language at all. However, de Moura fails to specify whether God's nonverbal communication corresponds to one of the five possible forms of external messages (listed above) or whether it transcends those categories. Although we might infer that God's speaking is close to a sort of intellectual insight, by quoting Gregory's text de Moura seems to indicate that God enlightens the emotional substance (the soul) of human subjectivity more than its intellectual and thus linguistic production. In other words, by stating that a sign of God's intervention is its affecting the subject's "internal senses" without communicating anything to him or her, Gregory implies that language, any form of language, is dubious and exposed to Satan's aberrant reasoning.

De Moura questions Gregory's definition of a divine sign. In his interesting approach to mystical experiences, de Moura mentions a series of female visionaries, whose internal dialogue with the Divinity was often disturbed by the devil's presence.[53] Referring to Teresa of Avila, de Moura reminds us that the Spanish mystic's "internal consolations and internal visions" were sometimes distraught because of a devil's intrusion (147–48). Even the holiest person's thoughts, de Moura infers, may be affected by the Enemy's illusions.[54] "Quod visio [est] divina?" ("What vision is divine?"), de Moura finally asks himself (148), and admits that all phantasms/signs are equivocal. As we will see later, at the end of his discussion on divine versus demonic signs the Portuguese inquisitor will rely on those physical signs, primarily relics, that must have a divine nature because of their healing qualities, but also because they have been legalized by the Church authorities.[55]

---

53. De Moura believes that in the special case of a prophet inspired by divine will, God does not allow Satan to intrude upon the human being's thoughts.

54. In *De spectris*, a popular text on spirits and demonic apparitions, Ludovicus Lavater believes that one must avoid any linguistic interaction with spirits or devils: "Spiritus qui apparent, merito nobis suspecti esse debent: non sunt conferendi sermones cum ipsis: nihil ex ipsis est discendum." I quote from the 1669 edition (Lyons: Henricus Verbiest), 217.

55. In *Tractatus de superstitionibus* (Frankfurt, 1581) Martin de Arles offers a detailed discussion of the relics' lawful and unlawful uses. See, in particular, pp. 390–91. The role of relics in the Catholic cult was discussed during the Council of Trent, as a direct response to the attacks of the Protestant movements. As Stéphane Boiron notes, the Catholic Church broached this topic at the very last session of the council (session 25). The Church issued a decree stating that the Catholic community had to revere the saints' bodies, since through them God had manifested his grace and support. However, every believer had to refrain from any kind of superstition. The decree did not mention any explicit form of fallacious behavior. See Stéphane Boiron,

Indeed, de Moura knows that, like God, the devil can grant some form of consolation to those souls afflicted by a private torment. In some cases, God himself allows the devil to support a holy person who, in conversation with God, undergoes some emotional turmoil (149). With this statement de Moura indirectly undermines the foundations of his inquiry. If the devil is allowed to participate in the believer's dialogue with the Divinity, how can we possibly understand when and if a given sign has a positive source? We might even doubt the healing powers of human remains—that is, the saints' relics—which do confer positive gifts but whose nature may be far from divine.

Sometimes both divine and demonic signs are difficult to interpret; their message is sibylline and open to more than one interpretation. De Moura recounts the biblical story of Nabuchodonosor, who questioned the revelations received from God.[56] Another possible way of discerning a sign's properties, de Moura writes, is to examine how the recipient responds to that sign. As I pointed out earlier, to dissect a given sign de Moura cannot help but focus on the relationship between an internal/external sign and its human reception. A sign *is* insofar as it affects the world. A sign may be either good or bad, or even both good and bad, according to its mental and physical effects on a human listener. Borrowing from Thomas Aquinas, de Moura states that, according to some Church Fathers, prophets and magicians speak in a very different manner (150).[57] While a prophet, during his speech, maintains a clear and composed mind even though he is removed from his senses *(cum abstratione a sensibus)*, a sorcerer speaks without being aware of what he or she is saying and acts in "unusual" ways.[58] The devil invades the human mind; God enlightens it. However, for de Moura,

---

La controverse née de la querelle des reliques à l'époque du concile de Trent (Paris: Presses Universitaires de France, 1989), 59–68.

56. Dan. 7:2–4.

57. Thomas Aquinas, *Summa* 2.2, q. 174, art. 6. Compare Del Rio, *Disquisitionum magicarum*, book 4, q. 6: "De speciebus divinationis, in quibus aperta invocatio intervenit" ("On the different forms of divination, which contain a direct invocation" [534–43]).

58. De Moura refers to Caietanus' commentary on the Book of Numbers (chap. 11), where he writes that the "good" prophets can be detected by their gestures and behavior. Speaking of 2 Kings 18, Caietanus reminds us that, when Saul "was invaded by an evil spirit, he started to prophesy in the middle of his house." However, he spoke "unbecoming" words *(insolentia)* and his gestures were "unusual" *(insolitis)*. I quote from the 1639 edition: *In Scriptura commentarii* (Lyons, 1639), 367. In *Tractatus de indiciis et tortura*, a detailed analysis on when and how a judge is supposed to submit a defendant to torture, Franciscus Bruni de Sanseverino states that the "art of divination" is not always a negative sign. The judge must look at the facial expressions of the defendant (for instance, whether he or she becomes pale or blushes while speaking). I use the edition published in Venice in 1549 (17r). Compare Thomas Aquinas, *Summa* 2.2, q. 173, art. 3.

"this sign is not satisfactory" *(hoc signum non est adequatum)*. Indeed, although God tends to visit the human mind without intoxicating it, sometimes God's communication temporarily shatters human rationality and a prophet's external composure.[59]

According to de Moura, another "unsatisfactory" sign is the widespread belief that a divine communication always affects the mind in a positive way, while a message coming from the devil can only result in a negative event (150–51).[60] The ambiguity of this sign lies in the fact that every sign may have more than one temporal meaning, because a sign that triggers negative effects now may bring about extremely positive conclusions in the future (151). Clearly, de Moura's answer to the enigmatic nature of signs concerns their legal status rather than their being. Unlike other demonologists, the Portuguese inquisitor understands that phantasms cannot be defined a priori, but only according to what they become in their interaction with the human subject. A human being's mind collects the (divine or demonic) sign through its *intellectus agens* and then turns it into verbal language by means of the *intellectus possibilis*. In this passage a sign has not revealed itself yet; it has merely acquired a physicality that neither a devil nor an angel can grant to it. We might go so far as to say that the human recipient of an external sign becomes him or herself a sign, given that to read a sign the Catholic Inquisition can only read its effects.

To support his legal interpretation of a sign's being, de Moura quotes Ioannes Turrecremata's prologue to *Revelationes S. Brigittae*, a significant book recounting the Swedish saint's life, miracles, and revelations (de Moura, 151 and 156–57).[61] Turrecremata lists five essential points for distinguishing between a divine and a demonic revelation. First, a sign is what the "experts" believe it is. Second, a sign is defined by its effects. Third, the good or bad nature of a given sign is determined by the "truth" it communicates. A divine sign conveys a "pure and sound truth," while a bad sign contains errors. The fourth element derives from the third, for a good sign is always respectful of the Scriptures. The fifth and final point concerns the Church's approval of the sign itself (compare De Moura, *De*

---

59. This part of *De ensalmis* uses del Rio as a basic reference (*Disquisitionum magicarum*, book 4, chap. 1, q. 3, sec. 5, 514–24). Del Rio's interpretation of the "satisfactory" signs, however, is more simplistic than de Moura's. Del Rio believes that while a divine communication makes its human recipient more humble and devout, a devilish message enhances the subject's bad qualities, primarily pride.

60. Compare Caietanus, *In Scriptura commentarii*, 435.

61. On St. Bridget's prophetic language, see Tommaso Campanella, *Theologicorum liber XIV*, edited by Romano Amerio (Rome: Bocca, 1957), 54, 68, 248.

ensalmis, 162). When the Church canonizes a given visionary, it means that the signs emitted by that person were lawful.[62] Contradicting what other theologians and he himself had stated in a previous passage, de Moura says that, according to Turrecremata, St. Bridget often received God's phantasms in a state of trance, as if she were dreaming. Bridget dreamed, we may say, divine images. For instance, once she saw a temple whose columns bent downward, thus endangering the life of the people praying and walking through its arcades. A thick fog rendered the temple almost invisible (*Revelationes S. Brigittae*, 294). In her own interpretation, the temple was the Church, whose priests (the columns) failed to sustain it against Satan (the fog). Turrecremata did not doubt that St. Bridget's vision had a divine origin, because of her attack against both the Enemy and the questionable morality of some of the Church's ministers.[63]

However, de Moura understands that, being a product of the mind, exegesis does not possess a "conservative quality" *(qualitatem conservativam)*—that is, an unquestionable and firm status of significance (160). As a result, he inevitably goes back to those signs—namely, relics and popular anecdotes—that have somehow become incontestable thanks to their public reception. We have seen that this was exactly how de Moura began his analysis of divine and devilish phantasms. He examined those physical signs, primarily relics, which had come to embody a sort of derivative status of "sure" signs because of their reception. However, in his attempt to define what makes a given event a positive or negative sign, de Moura came to the conclusion that such definition was impossible to obtain. As a consequence, those signs (relics) that he had posited as (almost) indisputable became questionable and precarious.

As I have noted, according to de Moura, it is time that turns relics into signs. A corpse needs to be narrated in order to be turned into a "speaking" sign. What makes a body or a bodily part a sign is the phantasms carved in it. While in his first examination of physical signs de Moura recounted the beneficial effects of some blessed soul's corpse, in a sort of follow-up he exclusively recounts stories concerning the bodies of royal personalities— Spanish and Portuguese kings, queens, and their closest relatives—whose pure souls had been seen "migrating," flying up in the sky to heaven (162– 66). According to de Moura, these miraculous occurrences had been wit-

---

62. *Revelationes S. Brigittae olim a card. Turrecremata recognitae* (Antwerp: Keerbergius, 1611), n.p.

63. On St. Bridget's visions, compare Tommaso Campanella, *Theologicorum liber XXV*, edited by Romano Amerio (Rome: Bocca, 1973), 202–4.

nessed by male members of the Church. The first story concerns King Philip II, who migrated to heaven with his wife Seraphina after four years of Purgatory (162). The archbishop of Evora himself had seen the couple flying up in the sky. The external and subsequently internal phantasms, which were brought about both by the royal family's bodies/souls and the narrations assigned to these bodies, become divine phantasms because of the political and religious power possessed and expressed by those bodies.

Concluding section 3 with an exclusively political explanation of a phantasm's essence, de Moura starts his text over, resuming his initial discussion on the natural versus unnatural properties of words. However, in this new analysis he does not limit himself to reiterating his first interpretation on verbal expression; he simplifies some of his central views in a rather strict and uncompromising way, and tackles a crucial aspect of verbal expression. As noted earlier, for de Moura, to analyze the notion of linguistic expression primarily means to bring to the fore its ideological connotations; thus he modifies his definition of *ensalmus* according to the political message he aims to convey. In particular, in this second version de Moura erases any favorable reading of the performativity of *ensalmi*.

At the beginning of the new section, de Moura restates that names and words do not have the power to produce any natural effect (180). Contradicting his own previous view, he also emphasizes that even divine names have no "active quality, neither natural nor supernatural" (181).[64] *God, Jesus, Word* possess no intrinsic might. Certain *ensalmistae*, de Moura states, believe that the written and oral words express two different aspects of the natural power of language. For de Moura, to write *Jesus* and to say *Jesus* are two variations of the same ungrounded word.

In his first analysis of the nature of an *ensalmus*, de Moura distinguished between negative and positive *ensalmi*, the latter coinciding with authorized prayers and rituals, which could also spring from the subject's spontaneous faith. In his second interpretation *ensalmi* are exclusively illicit expressions of an alternative language, which is defined and articulated by Satan and his followers. It is revealing that only at this point does de Moura narrate the origin of this allegedly ignominious practice. Stating that this story can be found in Pliny (who along with Galen was a fundamental reference in the Renaissance scientific discourse), de Moura recounts that the first *ensalmus* was created by a "certain woman" (*foemina*

---

64. Compare Ioannes Goropius, *Hermathena*, in *Opera omnia*, 16: "[W]ords, that is, oral statements articulated through natural instruments, do not contain other characteristics beyond their sounds and the meaning they convey."

quaedam) in ancient Athens. The Athenian authorities accused this woman of practicing illegal and perverted acts, because in her *ensalmi* she mixed up naturally signifying things, such as herbs and stones, with unexpressive objects, such as words (182).

In de Moura's view, the woman's aberrant rituals defied the state's "natural" and thus constitutional rhetoric. As a consequence, the Athenian government could not help but interpret her practices as an attempt to found an alternative and thus alarming discourse. It is apparent that the mythical founder of this deviant language can only be an outcast, in this case a woman, someone who cannot articulate the (male) discourse of law. Interestingly, the *Malleus maleficarum* comes to a similar conclusion. According to the *Malleus*, the cult of impure images was a creation of King Ninus, who had "an insane love for his father."[65]

More than articulating the devil's idiom, women, Jews, and homosexuals—those whom the Inquisition also defines as heretics—are articulated by the Enemy's idiom itself. In other words, their devious identities directly result from their signifying Satan's rhetoric. The Portuguese inquisitor vehemently emphasizes that the "heretics," including the Protestants, are means through which the Enemy generates a social and political construction that opposes the Church's natural power (210). The primary trait of this alternative discourse of power is its doubleness—that is, its tendency to blur the "adamant" signs of Catholic eloquence. Like the Athenian woman, the speakers of this deviant idiom merge natural and unnatural signs, legal and illegal "linguistic ceremonies" in the attempt to neutralize any possible detection of their unlawful practices.

As noted earlier, in his first analysis on the nature of signs de Moura admitted that the Inquisition possessed no crystal-clear method to determine a sign's intrinsic performativity. He concluded that relics were the sole clear signs of God's intervention in the created world. In this new discussion of the devil's alternative social and political power (sec. 2, chap. 6), he attributes the sign's irreducible ambiguity to the devil's appropriation of God's idiom. First of all, de Moura is convinced that in their devilish ceremonies *ensalmistae* often recite the "Pater Noster" or "Ave Maria" to heal a sick person (213). Even though he uses words that seem to speak to the Divinity, the *ensalmista* does not direct his illocutionary act to God. The possible success of an *ensalmus* lies in its perverse performativity. Satan, de Moura explains, asks his disciple to prove his or her loyalty by pro-

---

65. *Malleus maleficarum*, translated by Montague Summers (New York: Dover, 1971), part 1, q. 2, 15.

nouncing prayers whose natural addressee (the Trinity) is denied. In other words, the *ensalmista* invokes the Divinity, but does not speak to it. The "abuse of sacred words" even includes invocations or ceremonial expressions created by the first Christian communities, such as *In nomine Iesu omne genuflectatur, coelestium, terrestrium, et infernorum* or *Veni creator Spiritus* (217).

The appropriation of "natural" words is the main characteristic of the first form of *ensalmi*, what at the beginning of his work de Moura had called "invocative." The second and more complex kind is the "constitutive," which is structured as an actual ceremony. A "constitutive" *ensalmus* "abuses" both words and ritualized gestures. *Ensalmistae* go so far as to copy the Church's sacramental performances without modifying any of their aspects, in order to *mis*-direct their invocative message (213). *Ensalmistae* baptize babies, marry couples (an incubus or succubus and a human being), perform the Mass using consecrated hosts, and even confess their followers (what de Moura defines as *confessio diabolica* [214–18 and 256]).[66]

The same words and gestures used in Catholic rituals are appropriated and "doubled," so to speak, according to a new rhetoric that deletes its own original. As de Moura explains, this procedure of duplication and annihilation operates at the "connotative" level of every linguistic and performative expression, without modifying the "objective" one (222). The "objective" (denotative) aspect of a given utterance is what it "says" without any specific interpretation. For instance, words such as *God, saints*, and *sacraments* naturally mean holy things. At their "connotative" level, however, utterances or gestures may refer to the Divinity, but their significance is indirect and necessitates an act of interpretation. At this level an *ensalmista* may corrupt a given expression by attributing unnatural meanings to it. As an example, de Moura mentions *per ipsum et cum ipso et in ipso*, one of the fundamental expressions uttered during the Mass (224). Instead of speaking these words to invoke God so that He "mystically" turns bread and wine into his flesh and blood, *ensalmistae* often articulate these words to heal physical ailments (225).[67] De Moura does not say that the *ensalmista* necessarily misdirects the words, shifting their addressee from God to Satan, but rather that the actual procedure of misplacing these words or rituals is itself an unnatural, and thus diabolic, per-

---

66. De Moura amplifies a topos of medieval and Renaissance demonology. Every treatise on demonology discusses the "diabolic confession."

67. Compare Menghi, *Compendio dell'arte essorcistica*, 226.

formance.[68] It is a given, de Moura reminds us, that sorcerers often steal the débris of consecrated hosts and reuse them for their private *ensalmi*. Not only do *ensalmistae* use this débris of divine significance to achieve their dubious tasks, they also need it to neutralize and pervert the Catholic ritual itself (219). In other words, fragments of hosts work as a sort of diabolic vaccine, through which holy words are transferred from one field of meaning to another. This is why, says de Moura, a host is not always successful against devils and witches, because they have already absorbed and neutralized the powerful meaning of that very divine débris (219–20).

We might say that *ensalmi* are first and foremost acts of ambiguous exegesis. It is unquestionable, de Moura stresses, that exegesis is an indispensable expression of Catholic faith. How could we possibly understand the *Book of Revelation* unless we read it through the numerous "ingenious" interpretations offered by the Church Fathers (223)? More than saying something, words signify according to the context in which they are uttered. It is evident that, if on the one hand de Moura cannot deny that exegesis is a cornerstone of Catholicism, on the other he must define and restrict its practices. What ritualized expressions lack is an unquestionable referent—an ultimate meaning that prohibits any further exegesis.

De Moura's answer to this apparent dilemma is a legal tautology. Only the Holy Spirit can grant an unflinching, and thus successful, meaning to a given performance. Since the Catholic Church is the unique recipient of God's Spirit, only the words uttered by the Church have, at least in theory, an unquestionable expressivity. God's *gratia gratis data* "naturalizes" human linguistic performance. Through his Spirit, God legalizes the Church's rituals and grants its ministers the right to discern between natural and unnatural exegesis. Moreover, God's Spirit sometimes *(aliquando)* visits those performances that take place outside the realm of Catholicism (260). However, we must bear in mind that even when He grants a favorable expression to an unnatural *ensalmus*, God exclusively applies "natural causes"—that is, He only makes use of those natural signifieds that solely belong to and strengthen the Church (267 and 300).[69] In some cases, God may wish to express his will through a depraved *ensalmista*, who temporarily comes to utter the natural language of God's Church (279).[70] Even when the *ensalmista* exclusively directs his or her words and gestures to

---

68. Gregory the Great, *Moralia* (PL 76), book 22, chap. 31, 246–47 ("Si fructus eius comedi absque pecunia").

69. Compare Thomas Aquinas, *Summa* 2.2, q. 177, art. 1, where Thomas discusses the relationship between *gratia gratis data*, prophecy, and rhetoric.

70. Compare Thomas Aquinas, *Summa* 2.2, q. 172, art. 5.

Satan, God may allow his Enemy to intervene in the sorcerer's performance. However, only God knows the final effect and meaning of every given gesture or word, since He is the sole signified of every human expression. Therefore, even when a devil seems to overthrow God's natural and lawful will, he is in fact responding to God's wish (270).

The meaning of de Moura's second interpretation of the performativity of *ensalmi* is determined by the necessity to restate the Church's omnipotent presence in every possible utterance. Since the Catholic Church is a synonym for God's Church, even the most unlawful and perverse practices are monitored and interpreted by God's Spirit, which inspires and rules the Catholic Church through its ministers and inquisitors. De Moura makes it clear that no private individual may be granted the right to construct an *ensalmus*, because only the Church's ministers are entitled to offer God the Church's accomplishments, sanctity, and faith (286 and 289).[71]

According to de Moura, neither single individuals nor the representatives of the secular power may institutionalize an *ensalmus*, because this practice transcends political and temporal competence. Only the pope has the absolute authority to legalize a given ceremony in order to defeat physical or spiritual calamities caused by Satan, or to attack Satan's followers (Muslims, Jews, and so on [311]). De Moura directly cites session 25 ("De invocatione et veneratione sanctorum") of the Council of Trent, according to which a bishop is allowed to create only one form of invocative ceremony—that is, exorcism—because exorcisms may be necessary to respond to a specific emergency, a sudden attack of the Enemy (290 and 304–5). Indeed, the Council of Trent specifically asserts that a bishop does not have the authority to legalize *ensalmi*. De Moura reminds us that before the Counter-Reformation some bishops allowed *ensalmistae* to practice their healing ceremonies, without knowing that most of these performers were Satan's disciples (294). He mentions the case of Petrus Eanes Mayo do Covaõ, a Portuguese *ensalmista*, whose ceremonies had been legalized by the bishop of Evora, Henricus, in 1534. As we have seen, according to de Moura the apparently positive effects of an *ensalmus* do not necessarily entail that the *ensalmus* has a divine foundation. Indeed, nineteen years later (1555) the same *ensalmista* was accused of performing demonic ceremonies. When he was arrested, do Covaõ confessed that he had a secret pact with the devil and that his rituals were successful because of Satan's support. After being tortured, the *ensalmista* also admitted to having

---

71. "Privatus non habet potestatem ad instituendum Ensalmos, sacramentalia, aut sacrificium" (286); "non potest Deo offerre Ecclesiae merita, sanctitatem, et Fidem" (289).

sodomitical intercourse with the devil. We shall see later that at the end of
De ensalmis sodomy comes to signify the irreducible perversion of the
ensalmistae. The bishop of Evora justified himself by explaining what cri-
teria he had followed in order to understand whether a given *ensalmista*
was a virtuous practitioner or not:

> I have a great respect for the name and reputation of the people who live
> where these *ensalmistae* practice their benedictions. . . . They [*ensalmis-
> tae*] present [to me] the words they utter during their benedictions.
> [I check] if there is something disrespectful, dubious, or scandalous. . . .
> Then [I examine] those words and gather information about the *en-
> salmista's* life or grace that God grants those who have served Him. For,
> if I find that the *ensalmista* has helped his people, I do not see why we
> should prevent them from practicing their *ensalmi.* (294–95)

De Moura emphasizes that the bishop of Evora had failed in his analysis
of the defendant's conduct, because he had not examined the words of his
ensalmi in detail. For de Moura, more than being a merely social occurrence (the *ensalmista's* reputation, his lifestyle), *ensalmi* are first and foremost linguistic constructions that claim to have a direct impact on creation.

A paradoxical difference between the signs expressed through an *ensalmus* and those articulated by a Catholic ritual is that the former are considered infallible, while the latter, which signify the Church's infallible
power over the created world, are fallible. At the beginning of chapter 13,
de Moura writes that "when an *ensalmus* promises infallible effects, it
must be condemned" as an expression of Satan's pride (327). Catholic
sacraments, he says, work but "not always" *(non semper)* because, following the Augustinian model, the Catholic Church believes that any utterance is an invocation to the Divinity *(per modum impetrationis* [330, 333,
337]), who may or may not respond to a priest's ritual—that is, He may or
may not translate human invocations into visible signs.[72] For instance, mentioning the beneficial effects that Communion sometimes brings about, de
Moura warns the reader not to consider them a necessary outcome of this
Catholic ceremony. Of course, he writes, "Christ's flesh can resuscitate
corpses" and "send away storms caused by Satan" (331).[73] However, these
results do not depend on a priest's specific performance *(ex opere operato),*
but exclusively on God's unfathomable decision to validate a priest's litur-
gical act. De Moura comes to the same conclusion when he analyzes bap-

72. Compare Thomas Aquinas, *Summa* 3, q. 60, art. 2.
73. Compare Bozio, *De signis ecclesiae Dei,* book 14, chap. 7, 170–76; book 15, chap. 2:
"Miri esse effectum Eucharistia sumptae" (228–35).

tism, holy water,[74] and the practice of exorcism (332–37).[75] Speaking of exorcism, de Moura makes it clear that "the Catholic Church prohibits that the exorcist add any new word to any given exorcism" (334).

We might say that the Portuguese inquisitor theorizes a linguistic performance that speaks itself through a superfluous speaker's voice. The invocations established by the religious power (sacraments, prayers, exorcisms) acquire a metaphysical status that at once shuns and necessitates human presence. A typical example of the human subject's contradictory performativity is the recital of the rosary (358). This ritual, as de Moura reminds us, is a rote repetition of a set of canonical prayers. However, a certain physical posture is also required. While the believer's mouth repeats the words of a prayer, his or her fingers hold the bead corresponding to that particular prayer. At the end of that prayer, the fingers move to the next bead. The rosary, we may say, enacts itself by means of a human subject's performance. *Rosary* is both the object and the performance embodied in the object itself, which must be "voiced" by a mouth and a hand.

It has been proved, de Moura claims, that the rosary may produce miraculous effects. The author himself witnessed a wondrous event during the composition of *De ensalmis*. In 1614, during a fierce tempest in Evora, lightning struck two rosaries. The first one broke, but the second protected the woman who was wearing it around her neck. According to de Moura, this double result clearly proves that God may grant the status of signified to one rosary and deny it to another. Therefore, it is incorrect and unlawful to use the rosary as a shield against physical ailments, plagues, and diabolic temptations. In other words, legitimate *ensalmi* are rites in which the subject is at once absent as such and present as the essential actant of the *ensalmus* itself.

In both forms of *ensalmi (benedictio invocativa* and *benedictio constitutiva)* a fundamental tension exists between the structure of the *ensalmus* and its performer, whose identity—that is, his or her desire—may pervert the *ensalmus* itself. While an invocative benediction is less risky when its performer limits him or herself to repeating a fixed text (349), a constitutive one is more complex and hazardous, since it has a theatrical character involving words, gestures, and objects. De Moura is convinced that a Catholic *ensalmista* should conceive of his performance as an "absolute act" (*actus absolutus* [428]), meaning that he should "bracket" his will (*voluntas suspensa* [426]) and enact two forms of "doubt" (*dubia*),

---

74. Compare Menghi, *Compendio dell'arte essorcistica*, 468.
75. Compare Del Rio, *Disquisitionum magicarum*, book 6, chap. 2, sec. 3, q. 3, 992–93.

both before *(dubium speculativum)* and during/after the performance of the *ensalmus (dubium practicum)*.

In a crucial passage from chapter 16, de Moura directly compares the theatricality of the *ensalmus* with forms of lay theater, in particular *comoedia*: "materia ensalmorum [est] simil[is] materiae comoediarum" (397).[76] Expressing a view shared by several Church Fathers, de Moura believes that "comoediae . . . damnandae s[u]nt," because, by representing human beings' intimate life, they stage man's scandalous and sinful behaviors without condemning them.[77] However, discussing the nature and goal of theater, de Moura concedes that, rather than damning theater per se, the Inquisition should analyze the content of each specific play (398). Of course, he says, it is often laborious to determine whether a given play has been written with Satan's direct or indirect support. Although *ensalmi* and plays share a similar theatricality—that is, both are based on words and gestures constructed by an author for an audience—their main goal is different, at least from a theoretical standpoint. While an *ensalmus* is an invocation directed to the divinity or to Satan, a play simply tries to entertain its audience. In other words, the problematic nature of *ensalmi* lies in their addressee, for the addressee molds the character of every *ensalmus*. Thus, it is crucial to assess whether or not a given play hides an additional listener.

De Moura studies the relationship between *ensalmi* and lay theater with subtlety and insight. Theater, he writes, is not necessarily a diabolic expression, even though it does lend itself to diabolic interference. Theater is a performance made of three major components, an author, his *ministri mediati* (the director and actors), and an audience (398). It is clear, de Moura infers, that the devil may pervert all three levels of theater. First, he may force perverse thoughts into the author's mind. This first influence often results in the use of vulgar words, lewd acts, and effeminate gestures (398 and 401). Even when the text contains no reference to indecorous situations, the actors themselves may portray a certain scene in a manner that perverts its original nature.

76. Compare Thomas Aquinas, *Summa* 2.2, q. 168, arts. 2 and 3. In particular, in art. 2 Thomas states that it is imperative to watch one's own gestures, which must be becoming and never offensive to the human nature.

77. In book 2, chap. 27 of *The City of God*, Augustine reminds us that ancient Romans used to stage plays for ten days in a row to placate their idols' wrath. In chapter 13 of the same book Augustine had already spoken of "the filth of the stage" on which the Romans paid tribute to their false gods with descriptions of their vulgar conduct. Compare Thomas Aquinas, *Summa* 2.2, q. 164, art. 2.

The Portuguese inquisitor is especially concerned with the effects a play may produce in the audience, since the audience is the indubitable addressee of every theatrical performance. Indeed, a play may affect a viewer's morality in several different ways. Although the essential purpose of theater is pure pleasure, it is almost impossible to assess what kind of delight *(delectatio)* arises in the viewer's mind and in what way. Of course, de Moura says, the audience may simply be impressed by the author's literary style, his cunning narration, or the actors' performance. Yet words and gestures are never devoid of images; bodily and verbal statements always refer to an image signifying the signifier expressed by a (verbal) gesture ("in delectatione . . . verborum et gestorum *in actu signato*").[78] I have already analyzed de Moura's concern with the ambiguous nature of imagination in both Catholic and diabolic *ensalmi*. However, he is aware that a play is much more complex than an *ensalmus*, given that a play is capable of producing multiple forms of images. First, if a play is devoid of any perversion, it simply shows, without referring to anything beyond the stage. In other words, in this rather hypothetical case of "chaste" theatrical production, the image brought about by a scene is the scene itself, and the viewer's pleasure exclusively derives from the scene's beauty. Nonetheless, when a scene does provoke a rush of phantasmatic thoughts in the viewer's mind, the Inquisition must take into account the author's intentions, the actors' interpretation, and possibly also the viewer's personal creation of imaginary signifiers. This is why, de Moura copiously repeats, to see a play always entails a serious risk of venial and mortal sins (399). By staging a daily situation—that is, by merely reflecting the viewers' life—a play may induce them to complete an apparently innocent scene with licentious and sinful images that, without being actually staged, are present in the viewers' memory. In this sense, it is not inappropriate to state that Satan may be the indirect addressee of a theatrical production, for beyond the audience itself the Enemy may "listen to" the phantasmatic effects arising in the viewers' minds. In this case, the play, the stage, the actors, and the audience participate in a performative act that aims to summon the Enemy's presence in the world.

Fantasy, de Moura reiterates, is the major means through which the devil creeps into the mind of an *ensalmista* (priest, sorcerer, playwright, actor) and of his or her audience. De Moura is aware that any language, any verbal or physical gesture, articulates an imaginary discourse, whose

---

78. De Moura, *De ensalmis*, 400 (emphasis mine).

grammar cannot be fully investigated. He understands that it is impossible to posit an *ensalmus* devoid of any phantasmatic expression, a set of gestures that never become (private) images. Every ritualized performance, including theater, acquires its complete expression when, in the here and now of its actual performance, it opens itself to Satan's hazards.

Throughout *De ensalmis* de Moura attempts to unveil Satan's snares inherent in every invocative act, without being able to formulate a structure of surveillance, so to speak, to overcome those pitfalls. Indeed, the final sections of *De ensalmis* no longer focus on the performativity of *ensalmus*, but rather on the *ensalmista's* identity. Since it is arduous to determine what an *ensalmista* actually says, de Moura defines what an *ensalmista* is. Where at the beginning of *De ensalmis* a given *ensalmus* characterized an *ensalmista's* morality, at the end of the text an *ensalmus* is defined a priori by the *ensalmista's* being.

If to name means to grant a detectable identity, for de Moura an *ensalmista's* name is *sodomita* (sec. 3, chap. 4).[79] The connotative level of the term *sodomite* in medieval and early modern Europe has been analyzed at length by several scholars, first of all Michel Foucault. *Sodomy*, Foucault and others claim, has a large and contradictory connotation that transcends the mere sense of "anal sex between two people, especially two men." Still, in most treatises on demonology and in the final part of *De ensalmis*, sodomy clearly refers to male homosexuality. It connotes the ultimate form of depravity, which occurs when two men have anal intercourse.[80] Mentioning the expression *caro altera* present in Jude 1 ("Abeuntes in carnem alteram"), de Moura states that a man can never be united with another man, because his body is irremediably "other" to every man's (489). *Luxuria*, the worst and most unforgivable (irremissible) sin because it turns a human being into a beast, primarily occurs when two men practice *Venus ridiculosa* (504). A topos of medieval and Renaissance demonology is the belief that even devils refrain from any sodomitical intercourse with their disciples because of its indecency (486). Devils, says de Moura, go so far as to avoid a man for three days when he has practiced depraved acts with another man.

79. On the "name," see my "Performing/Annihilating the Word: Body as Erasure in the Visions of a Florentine Mystic," *TDR: The Drama Review* 41, no. 4 (1997): 110–27.

80. Del Rio inserts an important reference to sodomy in his analysis of aorasia, a phenomenon discussed in chapter 1. Like Prierio, del Rio believes that the devil can distort a human being's sight (aorasia). The two angels imposed aorasia on the inhabitants of Sodom (book 2, q. 8, 121). Compare Augustine, *The City of God*, book 1, chap. 30.

The identification between sodomy and Judaism is also present in the contemporary *Short Discourse against the Heretical Treachery of Judaism* by Vicente da Costa Mattos. Published in Lisbon in 1623, this treatise holds that the Bible, primarily the Old Testament, was written *against* the Jewish people—that with the Bible God meant to leave an everlasting evidence of the Jews' perverse nature.[81] Innumerable Portuguese travelers in Northern Africa, Mattos adds, have reported that the Jews indulge in this unspeakable sin even with their own children.[82] According to Mattos, it is evident that in the Bible the word *sodomite* equals *Jew*.

In de Moura's book, an *ensalmista* is a sodomite in the sense that he perverts language by merging "other" *(altera)*—that is, holy and demonic—linguistic gestures. The outcome of this corrupt misuse is a degeneration of language, which is a gift God has granted to human beings. De Moura also believes that one of the two angels that knocked on Loth's door in Sodom was the Word (498). As a consequence, by offending the Word, the sodomites rejected God's idiom. It is clear, de Moura infers, that *ensalmistae/sodomitae* must be "suspected of a light heresy at least," because in most cases their sexual acts reflect a degraded morality (485; compare 491 and 496). In other words, in *De ensalmis* anal sex between two men becomes a sort of "Ur-sign," an icon that signifies a variety of depraved acts. Therefore, it is incorrect to think that, in de Moura's book, the term *sodomy* means a number of possibly contradictory signifieds (anal sex between a man and a woman and between two men, sex between two women, all forms of nonreproductive sexuality, atheist beliefs, Protestant religiosity, Judaism). For de Moura, sodomy at once indicates a specific form of sexuality and an act that originates many other sinful acts. It is thus secondary to assess whether or not a heretic, a Protestant, or a Jew actually practices sodomy, because in any case his or her behavior is an unquestionable index of a perverted sexuality.

Citing Thomas Aquinas, de Moura reminds us that it is imperative to extirpate sodomites—that is, Protestants, heretics, *ensalmistae*, and Jews—because they prevent the city they live in from thriving and remaining "healthy" (503).[83] That sodomites are the actual cause of plagues and all kinds of natural disturbances is a common belief in medieval and early

---

81. Vicente da Costa Mattos, *Breve discurso contra a heretica perfidia do iudaismo* (Lisbon, 1623). In particular, see chapter 16 ("On how the Jews are both idolatrous and sodomites"), 118v–22r.

82. Mattos, *Breve discurso*, 121v.

83. Compare Thomas Aquinas, *Summa* 1.2, q. 92, art. 4.

modern Europe.[84] Consider, for instance, that in fifteenth- and sixteenth-century Florence and Venice the authorities attempted to eliminate sodomy by instituting the so-called Officials of the Night (Ufficiali della Notte), whose task was to investigate the nocturnal sexual activities going on in the streets, taverns, and parks.[85]

In *De ensalmis* the discussion of sodomy and sodomites is a function of a much more pressing task, the Inquisition's attack against the Portuguese Jews. Jewish people are the actual target of de Moura's disquisition on the biblical origins and hideous consequences of sodomy. Indeed, the two final chapters of the book (sec. 3, chaps. 5 and 6) are a fierce denunciation of the Jews' diabolic and bestial practices. It is a fact, de Moura claims, that Jewish people are *socii daemonum* (allies of the devils), and that the Kabala is nothing but a form of devilish divination (509). According to de Moura, "among the Jews nothing is more common than magic."[86] To support his argument, de Moura quotes a notorious passage from Grillando: "These people [the Jews] are those who celebrate . . . these sacrifices with their own hands, and follow the cult of the devil, as if he really were their god. After having completed their sacrifices, they posit questions about those they want to hurt."[87] This description of the Jews' alleged pact with the devil follows a long introduction that reiterates a series of received ideas concerning the secret bond between sorcerers and devils. Indeed, medieval and Renaissance books on demonology usually open with a similar account relating how these perverted people renounce the Catholic faith, are baptized in the name of Satan, are asked by the devils to perform nefarious acts (such as shedding the blood of their own children or stealing and crushing consecrated hosts under their feet) in order to prove their faithfulness to their master, and engage in sexual intercourse with incubi and succubi. What differs in *De ensalmis* is not the content of this description, but rather its rhetorical position in the economy of the book. Positing the trite

84. For an interesting analysis of homosexuality in Portugal and in the Portuguese colonies during the late Renaissance, see Luiz Mott, *O sexo proibido. Virgens, Gays e Escravos nas garras da Inquisição* (Campina, Brazil: Papirus, 1988), 75–130.

85. On the *ufficiali della notte* in Venice, see Guido Ruggiero, *Boundaries of Eros: Sex, Crime, and Sexuality in Renaissance Venice* (Oxford: Oxford University Press, 1985). On their role in Florence, see Michael Rocke, *Forbidden Friendships: Homosexuality and Male Culture in Renaissance Florence* (New York: Oxford University Press, 1996). Pat Robertson the leader of the Christian Coalition, recently stated something similar. See conclusion, below.

86. On p. 524 de Moura transcribes a passage from *Hermathena*, in which Goropius describes how Kabala analyzes divine names (6). Distorting Goropius' text, de Moura claims that Kabala is a devilish practice that dissects divine names to attack the Divinity himself.

87. Grillando, *Tractatus de sortilegiis*, q. 5, sec. 1, 46; de Moura, *De ensalmis*, 517.

account of *ensalmistae's* diabolic nature in the chapter on the Jews, which is also the last section of the whole text, de Moura makes his view of the Jewish people's identity much more graphic and forceful.

In *De ensalmis* both the traditional discourse on sorcerers' depraved behavior and de Moura's original analysis of invocative ceremonies acquire a distinctly historical connotation, an assault against the Jewish community in Portugal. Having realized that it is impossible to construct a systematic analysis of Satan's "linguistics," de Moura shifts his attention toward those who, in his belief, are the actual speakers of the devil's invocative speech acts—the Jews.

The Portuguese inquisitor turns the final section of *De ensalmis* into a sermon that he imagines himself delivering before the Portuguese Catholics on Ascension Day. For de Moura, through the ascension to heaven the incarnate Word clearly and distinctly confirms that the Inquisition's fight against the Jews is the right response to their betrayal and murder of God. To inflict the death penalty on the Jews, says de Moura at the very end of his book, is the suitable *(iustissime)* punishment for their unforgivable crimes (552).[88] Not only do the Jews believe that Jesus deserved to die on the cross, they also pervert the creation with their diabolic *ensalmi*.

As the final part of *De ensalmis* clearly shows, de Moura interprets his investigation of the ambiguous relationship between Catholic and diabolic verbal "ceremonies" as a direct attack against the Jewish community in Portugal. As the Word ascends to heaven, *De ensalmis* arises from a merely theoretical investigation of the dangerous ambiguities of language to a comprehensive denunciation of those people, the Jews, who corrupt God's language. The Jews are sodomites in that, like the inhabitants of Sodom, they have rejected God's message and have embraced Satan's alluring and misleading enticements.

De ensalmis is a key text in the history of the European Inquisition. Before de Moura, no one had connected a theoretical investigation of the nature of invocative acts, a cornerstone of Catholic doctrine, with an unflagging justification of capital punishment for those *ensalmistae* who did not belong to the Catholic hierarchy. Unlike other books written by the Roman Inquisition, *De ensalmis* offers a linguistic clarification for the Church's hatred of women, homosexuals, and Jews. More than for what they do, women, homosexuals, and Jews deserve to die for how they speak.

88. Compare Borges Coelho, *Inquisição de Evora*, 195. Borges Coelho emphasizes that, out of a total of 8,210 trials that took place in Evora, 7,269 (84 percent) were against the Jewish people.

THREE

To Vomit the Name of the Morning Star:
Creation as Metaphor in Menghi
and Polidori's *Thesaurus Exorcismorum*

IN OUR READING OF DE MOURA'S *De ensalmis* we have seen that the Portuguese inquisitor constructs his text as a literary performance taking place at a given time and in a given place, on Ascension Day in the Portuguese city of Evora. De Moura emphasizes that his book against the sodomites/Jews—the speakers of a duplicitous idiom at once invoking and denying the Divinity—is a response to a state of emergency. The Jewish people, he says, must be eradicated because they speak a language *contra naturam*, in that, like sodomy, it functions against creation. To "finish" *De ensalmis* means to celebrate the "ascension" of the book's "Truth"—that is, the need for the annihilation of the Portuguese Jews as a theological urgency.

Rather than achieving an actual dissection of the Jews' demonic language, *De ensalmis* theorizes its unheard but eloquent phonemes, sentences, reasonings. The Jews speak when and if "we" cannot hear them. Indeed, this paradox is the central premise of demonic linguistics. If to articulate language inevitably means to allude to an objective presence through the materiality of sounds, demonic utterances remove their signifieds from the realm of presence. As Prierio says in *De strigimagis*, devils use syllogism to "burn" their own statements—that is, they speak in order to subtract presence from the created world. As a consequence, we may say that books on demonology bring to the surface of conscience the unspoken and contagious presence of evil. As Francesco Guazzo writes in the preface to *Compendium maleficarum* (Milan, 1608), "[a]mong the countless blessings which the divine mercy daily confers upon the whole human race," the most important one is to become aware of and confront the Enemy's wicked presence in the world.[1] Paraphrasing an unfortunately familiar slogan of contemporary activism, for Renaissance demonologists silence does equal death.[2]

As a literary and theological genre, books on demonology emphasize their "necessary" existence in the here and now of a perennial state of crisis. Indeed, the rhetorical foundation of this literature is its possibly imminent erasure, its constant risk of having been written too late. If creation, the Book of Life, is at once dominated and attacked by the Fallen Angel, treatises on demonology are theoretical reportages of the ongoing tension between creation and de-creation, between language as order and language as chaos. As we have seen both in Prierio and in de Moura, demonologists perceive themselves as advocates of a pristine idiom at risk in an age of decadence and illiteracy. As "purists," demonologists write at the moment when that linguistic classical age, that symbiosis between divine unsaying and human response, has been and is being tainted. Paradoxically, like every purist, a demonologist believes that innocence (a "perfect" and thus "natural" syntax, morphology, faith, soul) is lost and is about to be lost forever.

The corrupted idiom of our times is not only the most frequent topos of this literary genre, it is its essential rhetorical foundation. A central, though not always expressed, tenet of demonologic creed is the concept of *postremus furor Satanae* derived from Rev. 12:12.[3] If time past is dominated by oblivion and sin, time present is perceived as an intrinsically brief and transient occurrence, during which Satan is allowed to articulate his silent idiom against divine creation before Michael's (Christ's) final triumph. Thus, a treatise on demonology is not only a theological investigation of the nature of fallen beings, it is first and foremost a vade mecum, a manual to be used here and now against those demonic beings whose

1. Francesco Maria Guazzo, *Compendium maleficarum,* translated by E. A. Ashwin (London: John Rodker, 1929), vii. For an excellent discussion of the eschatological aspects of books on demonology, see Stuart Clark, *Thinking with Demons: The Idea of Witchcraft in Early Modern Europe* (Oxford: Clarendon Press, 1997), 401–22.

2. In *Homographesis* (New York: Routledge, 1994), Lee Edelman offers an insightful analysis of the slogan "Silence = Death" in the contemporary debate on AIDS. Edelman reminds us that, similar to what I have said about de Moura's interpretation of Jews and sodomites, "the homosexual [discourse is viewed] as a parasite waiting to feed upon the straight body" (87). See in particular chapter 4, "The Plague of Discourse" (79–92).

3. Clark, *Thinking with Demons,* 409. Compare Jeffrey Burton Russell, *Mephistopheles: The Devil in the Modern World* (Ithaca: Cornell Uiversity Press, 1986), 56.

speech is bringing the world to its end. As we shall see, one of the most powerful and "eloquent" remedies examined in almost every treatise following the *Malleus* is the ritual of exorcism.

The "applied" nature of demonology is evident in the structure of the *Malleus maleficarum* (1486), the text that founded modern demonology and outsold every other book except the Bible.[4] I have already made frequent use of the *Malleus* in chapters 1 and 2, in discussing Prierio and de Moura. But the treatise becomes of primary relevance for a comprehensive analysis of demonic adjuration in the Renaissance. To understand the role of exorcism in the *Malleus,* it is necessary to read this book, the primary and unquestioned model of Renaissance demonology, as a sermon with three major subsections not coinciding with the treatise's three parts: "Treating of the Three Necessary Concomitants of Witchcraft" (1); "Treating of the Methods by Which the Works of Witchcraft Are Wrought and Directed, and How They May Be Successfully Annulled" (2); "Relating to the Judicial Proceedings" (3).[5] Pope Innocent VIII's infamous bull *Summis desiderantes affectibus* constitutes the first segment of the introductory section, in which readers are warned of Satan's growing power over the world because of the increasing number of witches and heretics: "[M]any persons of both sexes . . . have abandoned themselves to devils, incubi and succubi, and by their incantations, spells, conjurations, and other occursed charms and crafts, enormities and horrid offences, have slain infants yet in their mother's womb."[6] The first two questions of part 1 uphold the bull's discourse on the sweeping degradation brought about by witches' activities. The second section of the treatise (the rest of part 1 plus

---

4. Jeffrey Burton Russell, *The Prince of Darkness* (Ithaca: Cornell University Press, 1988), 165–66.

5. The major treatises published before the *Malleus* have quite incongruous structures and primarily focus on magic and superstitious practices. See, for instance, the influential *Formicarius* by Nider, printed about 1475. The text wanders through the themes of magic, superstitions, and remedies against demonic attacks without following a well-defined project. Witchcraft is the topic of book 5. Nider first speaks about exorcism in chapter 6, dedicated to diabolic charms and to the roles of good and bad angels (78r–8or). On fol. 78v Nider analyzes some of the legal questions concerning exorcism (who is allowed to perform it, and its validity). Nider later mentions exorcism in passing as one of the remedies against a diabolic possession, along with communion, confession, relics, and prayer (87v). *Formicarius* concludes with chapter 12, on roots, herbs, fruits, and melodies beneficial against the devil, and on the most important remedies against "mania" (90r). I refer to the 1517 edition: Johannes Nider, *Formicarius* (Strasbourg, 1517). Nicolao Iaquerio's *Flagellum hereticorum,* written in 1458, deals exclusively with the theological aspects of demonology. However, unlike *Formicarius, Flagellum hereticorum* dedicates one of its last chapters to the legal persecution of heretics and witches ([Frankfurt am Main, 1581], chap. 27, 175–81).

6. *Malleus maleficarum,* translated by Montague Summers (New York: Dover, 1971), 43.

the entire question 1 of part 2) expands this premise by detailing the numerous ways in which the devil's disciples are able to harm and even murder human beings.

After having "proved" the existence and extreme wickedness of witches, the third and final section (question 2 of part 2 and the entirety of part 3) examines the "methods of destroying witchcraft." It includes both the physical and psychological treatments against demonic ailments, and the legal persecution of witches and heretics. If we read the *Malleus* according to this three-part division, we infer that no essential difference exists between the practice of exorcism, the application of specific herbs, and the extermination of witches through juridical channels. Herbs, relics, exorcisms, torture, and trials all work as a response to Satan's contagious, albeit unuttered, idiom. In particular, exorcism is part of what the Dominican authors define as "the verbal remedies" against all kinds of infirmities, including epilepsy (179).[7] Unlike relics, stones, and herbs, however, exorcism and witch trial are active procedures aiming not only to repel evil, but also to annihilate it. Exorcism is similar to a witch trial in that both operations compel devils to manifest their language, and thus to become vulnerable to human counter-rhetoric. In other words, exorcists and inquisitors are able to eradicate evil only insofar as evil turns into visible (linguistic) signs and thus becomes prey of a discourse invoking the extinction of evil itself.[8] By burning evil's signifiers (witches' bodies marked by their succubi or incubi), inquisitors momentarily erase evil's being itself, since devils exist only as they affect the created world. Similarly, an exorcist "burns" evil by using its signs (the possessed person's body and mind) to make evil pronounce its own erasure. Exorcism and witch trial are the two natural outcomes of demonology as the act of recognition, mentioned in Guazzo's text.

The exorcism that the *Malleus* outlines ("And then *may* be said the following . . .") is of primary importance in Renaissance demonology less for its formal and literary structure than for its legal status within the ample range of possible treatments against diabolic assaults. Indeed, the authors of the *Malleus* emphasize that exorcism deserves a unique place within the Church's strategy against witches' attacks. They discuss the practice of exorcism in book 2, question 2, chapter 6, which is dedicated to the most

7. Compare Henry Charles Lea, *Materials toward a History of Witchcraft* (Philadelphia: University of Pennsylvania Press, 1939), 1:326–27.

8. Compare Carlo Maccagni, "Le razionalità, la razionalità" in *La strega, il teologo, lo scienziato*, edited by Maurizio Cuccu and Paolo Aldo Rossi (Genoa: Ed. Culturali Int., 1986), 329–38.

beneficial methods against withcraft. This chapter, entitled "Prescribed Remedies; to Wit, the Lawful Exorcisms of the Church, for All Sorts of Infirmities and Ills due to Witchcraft; and the Method of Exorcising Those Who Are Bewitched," is by far the longest of the whole section (179). From the outset, the authors stress that, although "lawful exorcisms are reckoned among the verbal remedies and have been most often considered by us, they may be taken as a general type of such remedies" (179).

The practice of exorcism thus exceeds and summarizes every other "lawful" practice the Catholic authorities may use against Satan. The *Malleus* offers the first and most detailed analysis of both the religious and the legal aspects involved in the ritual of exorcism: who may perform it, what words to utter, what to do when the exorcism is not successful, and who is to be blamed for its failure (179–88). Exorcism of bewitched people, the authors stress, is a common and "abused" practice. Their goal is to establish a "lawful exorcism," which will replace the innumerable "unlawful charms and unlawful conjurations and exorcisms" still performed throughout Europe. The two inquisitors make it clear that their instructions for how to conduct a legitimate exorcism have a binding connotation: "[L]et no one meddle with such sacred offices by any accidental or habitual omission of any necessary forms or words; for there are four matters to be observed in the right performance of exorcism, namely, the matter, the form, the intention and the order, as we have set them out above" (185–86).

As far as the formal aspect of exorcism is concerned, the *Malleus* considers this "verbal remedy" as an invocation divided into three segments, directed to three different interlocutors. The exorcist first addresses the possessed person, who "is to remain bound naked to a Holy Candle of the length of Christ's body or of the Cross": "I exorcise thee, Peter, or thee, Barbara, being weak but reborn in Holy Baptism, by the living God, by the true God, by God Who redeemed thee with His precious Blood" (183). The priest next invokes God, and then adjures the devil tormenting the victim: "O God of mercy and pity, Who according to Thy tender lovingkindness chastenest those whom Thou dost cherish. . . . Therefore, accursed devil, hear thy doom, and give honour to the true and living God." After repeating these prayers two more times, the exorcist finally recites a conclusive short prayer: "God . . . incline Thine ear to our prayers and look in mercy upon Thy servant labouring under the sickness of the body" (183).

Notwithstanding its rigorous script, this exorcism still retains a fundamental trait of medieval demonic adjuration: its explicit and daring theatricality, which in the *Malleus* focuses less on the exorcist than on the possessed person, who is asked to stand naked next to a cross or a candle "of the length of Christ's body." The Dominicans' exorcism merges the two essential versions of medieval exorcism: either a mise-en-scène with a variable number of actants, or a rather obscure text to recite with or without someone else. What medieval rituals lacked was a textual reference, a literary model. Indeed, as Richard Kieckhefer notes, "before the fifteenth century . . . the techniques [of exorcism were] in large measure improvised."[9]

Let us mention only two strikingly different examples.[10] First, about 1169 the mystic Hildegard of Bingen inserted a rather long and quite "personal" exorcism in a letter to Gedolphus, abbot of Brauweiler, who had asked her for advice on how to free a woman from evil spirits. The mystic emphasizes that she has not made up this ritual; rather, "the One who is" has granted it to her.[11] Hildegard conceives of exorcism as a highly symbolic and ritualized performance. Since she believes that the spirits tormenting the woman somehow correspond to the seven deadly sins, Hildegard suggests that the abbot "choose seven priests of good repute, recommended by the quality of their life, in the name and order of Abel, Noah, Abraham, Melchisedech, Jacob, and Aaron, for these offered sacrifice to the living God. The seventh priest will represent Christ" (149). After having fasted, prayed, and offered oblations—the typical practices of every exorcism of the Christian tradition—the seven priests, symbolizing the seven cardinal virtues, will celebrate Mass.

> [They then] approach the suffering woman with their eyes averted. They are to stand around her, each one holding a rod in his hand in figure of that rod with which Moses struck Egypt, the Red Sea, and the rock at God's command [Exod. 7:8–10:23, 14:16–29, 17:6–7; Num. 20:11] so that, just as there, God revealed his miracles through the rod, so also, here, He may glorify Himself when that foul enemy has been cast out through these rods. These seven priests will represent the seven gifts of the Holy Spirit, so that the Spirit of God which in the beginning "moved over the waters" [Gen. 1:2] and "breathed into his face the breath of life" [Gen. 2:7] may blow away the unclean spirit from the wearied person.[12]

9. Richard Kieckhefer, *Forbidden Rites: A Necromancer's Manual of the Fifteenth Century* (University Park: Pennsylvania State University Press, 1998), 149. Compare Nancy Caciola, "Wraiths, Revenants and Ritual in Medieval Culture," *Past and Present* 152 (1996): 3–45.

10. Compare Clark, *Thinking with Demons*, 414.

11. *The Letters of Hildegard of Bingen*, translated by Joseph L. Baird and Radd K. Ehrman (New York: Oxford University Press, 1994), 148.

12. In a subsequent letter, Gedolphus informs Hildegard that the devil had left and invaded the victim again, right after the performance of Hildegard's exorcism (*Letters*, 151–52).

Hildegard believes that exorcism must stage a metaphorical reading of a biblical narrative. For the author of *Ordo virtutum*, exorcism is synonymous with theater, seen as the embodiment of an act of exegesis. Moses' rod *means* God's power over sin (Egypt) and creation itself (Red Sea, rock).[13] Thus, when the priest "and the other six standing around strike her lightly with their rods upon the head and upon the back, upon the breast and upon the navel and upon the kidneys, upon the knees, and upon the feet," they give body to a metaphor, or better yet, they participate in a process of biblical metaphorization. The woman must be beaten lightly *as if* she were the Red Sea or the Rock hit by Moses' rod, and the priests act *as if* they were both Moses moving the waters apart and the Spirit of God "which in the beginning 'moved over the waters.'" While the seven priests are *like* Moses and the Holy Spirit, the obsessed woman lacks any symbolic transference. The woman is herself—that is, she is the irreducible irruption of reality (what has not yet become a metaphor) within the field of a pure and purifying narration. This is why, Hildegard stresses, when they order the devils to leave the woman's body ("Now, you, O satanic and evil spirit, you who oppress and torment this person, this form of a woman, depart!"), the priests must avoid making eye contact with her. The evil eye is more frequently mentioned in the descriptions of witch trial than in the performance of exorcism. The witch, the *Malleus* suggests, "should be led backward into the presence of the Judge and his assessors."[14]

As I will show below, Hildegard's ritual differs from the Renaissance forms of exorcism more in its structural aspects than in its intrinsic ideology. To find theologically dubious forms of exorcisms, we must look at the medieval and Renaissance books of magic. We may take as an example of this second type of medieval exorcism a fifteenth-century manuscript from Woltsthurm Castle in the Tyrol. This text suggests that the exorcist whisper the following words in the possessed person's ear: "Amara Tonta Tyra post hos firabis ficaliri Elypolis starras poly polyque lique linarras buccabor vel barton vel Titram celi massis Metumbor o priczoni Jordan Ciriacus Valentinus."[15] This sort of exorcism contradicts a central tenet of Renaissance theory of demonology, and thus can be found in no Renais-

---

13. For the connection between Christ's cross and Moses' rod in medieval exegesis and magic, see Valerie I. J. Flint, *The Rise of Magic in Early Medieval Europe* (Princeton: Princeton University Press, 1991), 177–78.

14. *Malleus* (trans. Summers), part 3, q. 15, 228.

15. Richard Kieckhefer reports this exorcism in *Magic in the Middle Ages* (New York: Cambridge University Press, 1989), 4.

sance collection of exorcisms. As I have pointed out in chapter 2, incomprehensible words must be avoided in any form of invocation.[16] However, the act of whispering a conjuration in the possessed person's ear is still present in *Thesaurus exorcismorum*, the most authoritative collection of exorcisms of the Renaissance (1608). In the *Thesaurus* exorcisms acquire a distinctly narrative structure, which is missing from medieval demonic adjurations. For example, during the "secret exorcism" the priest whispers the story of Eve's original pact with Satan and the consequently evil nature of women.[17] Although from the third century on it was part of the baptismal ceremony, the ritual of expelling devils never became a sacrament of the Catholic Church, and this helps explain the rather improvised and often unstructured nature of medieval and early Renaissance exorcism.[18]

Although the *Malleus* emphasized the importance of exorcism among all verbal remedies against witches, its analysis of demonic adjuration was too synthetic and focused much more on its legal connotations than on its linguistic and theological aspects. It is toward the end of the sixteenth century, during and after the Council of Trent, that exorcism acquired its status of primary "verbal treatment" and became the theme of a new theological and literary genre. If the *Malleus* founded modern demonology, Girolamo Menghi and Valerio Polidori's *Thesaurus exorcismorum* is the undisputed reference for the ritual of Catholic exorcism. A short but very

---

16. Compare *Malleus* (trans. Summers), 181. Every book on demonology transcribes one or more of these conjurations. Martin de Arles discusses this matter at length. As an example of suspicious exorcism, he mentions the following text: "Coniuro te, alligo te per aelim, per olin et per saboan, per aelion, per adonay, per alleluia, per tanti, per archabulon, per tetraggramaton, per mare, per mundum, per crura, per tibias" (*Tractatus de superstitionibus* [Frankfurt, 1581], 395).

17. Girolamo Menghi and Valerio Polidori, *Thesaurus exorcismorum* (Cologne: Lazari Zetneri, 1608), 1111–16.

18. Jeffrey Burton Russell, *Lucifer: The Devil in the Middle Ages* (Ithaca: Cornell University Press, 1984), 124–25. Martin del Rio offers a brief but clear summary of early Christian practice of exorcism (*Disquisitionum magicarum* [Mainz: Petrus Henningius, 1617], 992). Del Rio mentions the fourth Council of Carthage (398), whose seventh canon prescribed the rite of ordination for exorcists. Compare the entries "Exorcisme" and "Exorciste" in the *Dictionnaire de spiritualité* (Paris: Beauchesne, 1932), 1762–80 and 1780–86. For a brief description of exorcisms in the Gospel, see Jeffrey Burton Russell, *The Devil* (Ithaca: Cornell University Press, 1977), 237–39.

The *Rituale romanum* was published in 1614, a few years after the *Thesaurus*. For a brief analysis of exorcism in contemporary Catholicism, see Emil J. Lengeling, "Der Exorcismus der Katholischen Kirche" *Liturgisches Jahrbuch* 32 (1982): 248–57; Adelbert Scholz-Dürr, "Der traditionelle kirchliche Exorcismus im Rituale Romanum—biblisch-systematisch betrachtet," *Evangelische Theologie* 52 (1992): 56–65; Cécile Ernst, *Teufelaustreibungen. Die Praxis der katolischen Kirche im 16. und 17. Jahrhundert* (Bern: Huber, 1972), 17–23.

popular exorcism published in Venice in 1532, *Exorcismo mirabile da disfare ogni sorte de maleficii et da caciare li demonii*, had already appropriated the apocalyptic rhetoric expressed in the *Malleus:* "God showed us that the solution against such excess of evil, which had grown beyond any possible limit, was the practice of exorcism, as it had been established by the Church."[19] While in 1486 the *Malleus* still envisioned a complex strategy of "verbal," "practical," and legal procedures to counteract *postremus furor Satanae*, less than fifty years later the anonymous author the *Exorcismo mirabile* recommends exorcism as the sole "solution" to demonic persecution. This new emphasis on the therapeutic qualities of exorcism will find its undisputed point of reference in *Thesaurus exorcismorum*, compiled and published in Italy at the very beginning of the seventeenth century.

Students of European witchcraft have failed so far to study the crucial role played by exorcism in early modern demonology. As the historian Giovanni Romeo points out, scholars have primarily examined the inquisitors' and exorcists' abuses, in part because these alleged legal violations were the major theme of Protestants' attack against the Catholic Church.[20] Romeo mentions the vehement defense of exorcism written by the Franciscan inquisitor Girolamo Menghi in the preface to *Flagellum daemonum* (1578), "the most celebrated treatise of the day" and one of the texts collected in *Thesaurus exorcismorum*.[21] Dedicating his work to Cardinal Gabriele Paleotto, Menghi advocates a much more aggressive promotion and publication of books of exorcisms in the Church's attempt to eradicate the deadly and mysterious disease *(aegritudo)* that has been mowing down innumerable victims.[22] It is impossible to extirpate this plague unless the art of performing exorcisms *(ars exorcismorum)* is fully known and appreciated throughout the Catholic world. Menghi, one of the most impor-

19. *Exorcismo mirabile da disfare ogni sorte de maleficii: et da caciare li demonii* (Venice: Bernardinus Vercellensis de Lexona, 1532), n.p.

20. Giovanni Romeo, *Inquisitori, esorcisti e streghe nell'Italia della Controriforma* (Florence: Sansoni, 1990), 115. Romeo dedicates an entire chapter to Menghi's role in the Italian Counter-Reformation (109–44).

21. Romeo, *Inquisitori, esorcisti e streghe*, 114; John Tedeschi, *The Prosecution of Heresy: Collected Studies on the Inquisition in Early Modern Italy* (Binghamton, New York: Medieval and Renaissance Texts and Studies, 1991), 235.

22. Girolamo Menghi, *Flagellum daemonum* in *Thesaurus exorcismorum*, 286–87. Girolamo Menghi was born in Viadana, Italy, in 1529, and died there in 1609. He entered the Franciscan Order in 1550 and was elected provincial in Bologna (1598–1602). Menghi performed exorcisms in Bologna and in northern Italy for more than forty years. On Menghi's *Flagellum daemonum*, see Lea, *Materials toward a History of Witchcraft*, 3:1055–56; Clark, *Thinking with Demons*, 389; D. P. Walker, *Unclean Spirits* (Philadelphia: University of Pennsylvania Press, 1981), 2.

tant inquisitors and theoreticians of his time, had already dwelled on the apocalyptic urgency motivating his activity both as an exorcist and as a writer of exorcisms, in *Compendio dell'arte essorcistica* (first published in 1576). He wrote this work in Italian and not in Latin to make his dramatic message available to the largest audience possible.[23] Following and expanding the rhetoric of the *Malleus* and *Exorcismo mirabile*, at the beginning of this book Menghi states that the devil is invading human bodies more than ever before "[I]n our tempestuous times, in which our cruel Enemy has become more powerful than ever against our human bodies . . . by means of his wicked deeds, which he uses to insult the divine authority and to murder the souls who had been saved through the precious blood of the immaculate Lamb Jesus Christ."[24] Writing in the post-Tridentine era obsessed with the risks of physicality, in his opening remarks Menghi paradoxically emphasizes that demonic possession is first and foremost a carnal, and thus totally private and incommunicable, occurrence. Flesh, Menghi understands, is where language fails to utter the Enemy's intrusion.[25] If the *Malleus* was primarily concerned with the juridical aspects of demonic adjuration, the *Thesaurus* conceives of exorcism as the ritual staging the (exorcist's) self as the locus of inner and irreconcilable voices. As we shall see in the texts collected in the *Thesaurus*, the body possessed by invisible spirits is only the silent, though necessary, matter through which the exorcist gives a voice to evil.

Thesaurus exorcismorum contains two works by Menghi, *Flagellum daemonum* and *Fustis daemonum*. Each was previously published as an independent book, the *Flagellum* in 1578 and *Fustis* in 1584. The *Thesaurus* also includes four more treatises: *Practica exorcistarum* (1585) and *Dispersio daemonum* (1587) by Valerio Polidori, *Complementum artis exorcisticae* by Zacharia Visconti (1589), and *Fuga Satanae* by Pietro Antonio Stampa (1597). The *Thesaurus* is an imposing book, totaling 1,272 pages excluding the indexes, and represents one of the first collections of exorcisms to be published in book form.[26]

23. Compare Alfonso Di Nola, *Il diavolo* (Rome: Newton and Compton, 1999), 292–98.

24. Girolamo Menghi, *Compendio dell'arte essorcistica* (Venice: Bertano, 1605), 2–3.

25. Mary R. O'Neil studies the relationship between popular culture and ecclesiastical beliefs in "*Sacerdote ovvero strione*: Ecclesiastical and Superstitious Remedies in Sixteenth-Century Italy," in *Understanding Popular Culture: Europe from the Middle Ages to the Nineteenth Century*, edited by Steven L. Kaplan (New York: Mouton Publishers, 1984), 53–84. O'Neil stresses that "for Menghi, the *medicine ecclesiastiche* are sufficient to thwart or reverse the actions of demons and witches" (54).

26. Compare Romeo, *Inquisitori, esorcisti e streghe*, 116.

Instead of analyzing this linguistic artifact as a rather haphazard compilation of books on related topics, I read the *Thesaurus* as the coherent and unequaled monument erected by Catholicism to language as the field where sense and chaos, discourse as remembrance and discourse as erasure of any remembrance, confront each other in and through the exorcist's voice. The voice of the exorcist is the medium through which evil's being is summoned in the here and now of its real but invisible invasion of a body. One of the most eloquent philosophical explanations of the healing character of the exorcist's voice is found in *Compendium coniurationis contra daemones vexantes humana corpora* (1598) by Thomas Tropianus, a less well-known collection of exorcisms. According to Tropianus, Adam could be considered as the first exorcist, because he received from God the power to name each aspect of creation *(authoritatem imponendi nomina)* according to its inner properties, and thus he was enabled to dominate and direct nature by means of his voice.[27] Similarly, the exorcist's voice calls reality by its name—that is, he speaks the pristine order of things, which has been disrupted by the devil's invasion:

> Who instituted exorcisms and the things that were exorcised.
> Some theologians are convinced that exorcism already existed when nature was still untouched. God disclosed this to Adam and granted him the knowledge of every attribute of all natural things, which became subject to him. God gave him [Adam] the authority to impose names upon all the animals and things depending on him. According to these names, everything will naturally obey man. And remnants of this natural power still lie in the exorcist's words, when they naturally obey his reciting voice and his orders, unless sin obstructs them.

The devil's unnatural presence is spoken in the exorcist's voice and is manifested in the possessed person's body. While the priest reminds his listener (Satan) that his sudden and violent irruption is illicit and transitory, the body in pain shows evil's "unnatural" presence through its obscure but injuring signs, what demonologists often define as the devil's "local motion" *(motum localem)* within the victim's flesh (for instance, something crawling from the stomach to the throat and vice versa, a feeling of being stabbed and jerked around, voices speaking in the mind, sudden images of despair and desire in the internal sight).[28] However, the body's presence is

27. Thomas Tropianus, *Compendium coniurationis contra daemones vexantes humana corpora* (Palermo: Baptista Maringhinus, 1598), 1.

28. For a detailed description of the devil's local movements, read the "Quarta Advertentia" in *De potestate ecclesiae coercendi daemones circa obsessos* (Cologne: Constantinus, 1629) by the Spanish Dominican Raphael de la Torre (172). I use the expression "body in pain" as a

simply assumed, without active participation in the utterance itself. The body testifies that Satan is either there or has left the place where the voice has spoken his being. Although most secondary literature on possession and exorcism primarily focuses on the social and psychoanalytic aspects of the relationship between the priest and the (female) possessed, if we actually read the fifteenth- and sixteenth-century manuals and treatises founding the practice of deliverance from evil spirits, we find that the victims of the devil' attacks are given very little analysis. As we shall see later, references to the possessed person's physicality are generally limited to a distinction between *daemoniacus* and *maleficatus*.[29] In *Daemoniaci cum locis infestis* (1627), the Jesuit Petrus Thyraeus offers the best and most synthetic definition of a possessed person. A victim of a devilish possession, says Thyraeus, is nothing but *clamores* — that is, irrational and bothersome linguistic expressions, bits and pieces of a text that make no sense at all.[30]

After a publisher's note recommending a thorough reading of the entire volume as a therapeutic process of enlightenment, the *Thesaurus* opens with the central quotation from Matthew (17:14–21), recounting Jesus' exorcism of a young man possessed by a mute and deaf spirit (compare

direct reference to Elaine Scarry's seminal book *The Body in Pain* (New York: Oxford University Press, 1985). I have found particularly inspiring her analysis of the relationship between God's voice and the Jewish people in the Old Testament. Speaking of the frequent "sign of the weapon," Scarry reminds us that "God's invisible presence is asserted, made visible, in the perceivable alterations He brings about in the human body" (183).

In *The Possession at Loudun*, Michel de Certeau describes how exorcists and physicians tried to read the symptoms of the nuns possessed by the "devil" Grandier. The physicians called to the convent of Loudun tried to "make the body" speak, so that it should confess what they already knew according to what they saw. Michel de Certeau, *The Possession at Loudun*, translated by Michael B. Smith (Chicago: University of Chicago Press, 2000), 109–21, 127–28. On the names of the devils inhabiting the nuns of Loudun, see de Certeau, *The Writing of History*, translated by Tom Conley (New York: Columbia University Press, 1988), 244–68.

29. For a feminist interpretation of the relationship between (male) exorcist and (female) possessed, see Lyndal Roper, *Oedipus and the Devil* (New York: Routledge, 1994), 171–98. Compare Giovanni Romeo, *Esorcisti, confessori e sessualità femminile nell'Italia della controriforma* (Florence: Le Lettere, 1998). In particular, see chap. 3 on "exorcists and female sexuality in early seventeenth-century Italy" (86–127).

30. Petrus Thyraeus, *Daemoniaci cum locis infestis et terriculamentis nocturnis* (Cologne, 1627), 162. In *Inferno atlântico. Demonologia e colonização. Séculos XVI–XVIII* (São Paulo: Companhia das Letras, 1993) Laura de Mello e Souza reports the story of a woman from Lisbon who had been possessed by the devil since she was a child. What made her case particularly interesting was the violence of her language. Not only did she insult her numerous exorcists with uncommon eloquence, she also spoke in tongues and imitated animals, including dogs and lions. "In the *grammar of the possession*," de Mello writes, "the possessed woman speaks an idiom that she does not know, for it [the language of possession] is a closed system, which can be entered only through the unconscious, like in a dream" (153; emphasis in original).

Luke 9:37–43; Mark 9).[31] The very first quotation of the *Thesaurus* thus presents exorcism as the performance through which a victim of demonic possession may regain his lost voice. In *Complementum artis exorcisticae,* the fifth treatise of the *Thesaurus,* Zacharia Visconti considers the loss of voice as one of the most frequent effects of demonic possession (771–74). Influencing our humors, devils can blur our senses and thus make us feverish, mute, deaf, and obsessed by internal images; in a word, they make us sick with melancholy (773). Visconti is convinced that melancholy is very difficult to eradicate and can cause deadly diseases (774).[32] To alleviate the victim's melancholic symptoms and to prepare him or her for the rite of exorcism, Menghi recommends in *Flagellum daemonum* the use of certain kinds of herbs, among others rue, and first of all music (*armonia, melodia* [296–98]).[33] Devils, whose sole idiom is chaos and deceit, cannot tolerate music (298). Given that the victim has been deprived of his phonemes and of the internal harmony of his mind, the exorcist makes him listen to the world's natural melody as it is articulated in music. If the possessed person cannot express himself because he has been silenced by a mute spirit, the exorcist speaks the loss of the victim's voice, as Jesus himself did for the man visited by a deaf and mute spirit. Exorcism, as the *Thesaurus* emphasizes from the outset, is an act of substitution.

The six treatises collected in the *Thesaurus* must be read as interdependent texts on the healing art of substituting silence with voice, the deaf and mute occurrence of chaotic signs with a set of meanings structured as a sermonic discourse based on two essential devices, repetition and variation. Although the six texts were originally separate publications, they have an

---

31. *Thesaurus exorcismorum,* n.p. Most books of demonology refer to Petrus Chrysologus's interpretation of this biblical passage. Petrus Chrysologus emphasizes that the young man is not mute and deaf because he is possessed by a spirit, but the spirit itself is mute and deaf (Petrus Chrysologus, *Sermo* 52 ["De daemoniaco surdo et muto curato"] [*PL* 52], 345). I discuss this passage in *Uttering the Word: The Mystical Performances of Maria Maddalena de' Pazzi, a Renaissance Visionary* (Albany: State University of New York Press, 1998), 127–28.

32. In *De potestate ecclesiae,* De la Torre reminds the reader that melancholy is more than one illness. Indeed, he speaks of *morbi melancholici* (melancholic diseases). De la Torre believes that the devil is able to combine different symptoms in one single disease (*De potestate ecclesiae,* in *Diversi Tractatus* [Cologne, 1629], 173).

33. Compare Thyraeus, *Daemoniaci cum locis infestis,* 177–79. To justify the use of herbs, Menghi notes that in the Book of Tobit, Tobias exorcised the devil Asmodeus from Sarah by taking a fish's heart and liver and "put[ting] some on the burning incense. The reek of fish distressed the demon, who fled through the air to Egypt" (Tob. 8:3). Smell, Menghi infers, should play a role in every exorcism. On the differences between Menghi's and Ficino's theories on the healing effects of music, see Gary Tomlinson, *Music in Renaissance Magic* (Chicago: University of Chicago Press, 1993), 125–26.

almost identical structure, made of two fundamental sections: the theoretical analysis of demonic adjuration and the transcription of a variable number of exorcisms. This repetition and variation not only dominates the overall structure of the *Thesaurus* but also corresponds to the internal melody of the individual chapters. In each, the string of exorcisms vary and repeat similar themes, rhetorical shifts, prayers, gestures, as if each set of conjurations were meant to be read as a narrative continuum whose healing effects resulted from the internal rhythm of the book.

The *Thesaurus* has a unique character in being at once a text to be read and a script to be performed. In the preface to *Fuga Satanae*, the final treatise of the book, Stampa notes that his work is meant both for exorcists and for lay people, who can find in it a series of inspiring prayers (1194). In the *Thesaurus* words have a double temporality, as lines to be uttered both in the future of a sudden emergency and in the present of the reader's mind. As Zacharia Visconti explains at the beginning of *Complementum artis exorcisticae*, there are three kinds of words: "Threefold is language. The first kind is the language of deed; the second of the voice, and the third is of the mind. God speaks with the language of deed. Human beings speak with the language of the voice, and angels speak with the language of the mind" (761).[34] The three levels of language correspond to three different forms of physicality. While God speaks being itself, humans speak the memory of being, the mourning of and the longing for being's presence. Good and bad angels alike limit themselves to reminding humans of their desire for being. More than speaking, angels collect, modify, shift humans' remembrances in order to affect human minds in beneficial or noxious manners.[35] As a consequence, even though exorcisms are made of "words and things" (holy water, candles, relics, crucifixes, herbs), as Petrus Thyraeus writes, both words and things are invocations to God so that He will prevent the bad spirits from "speaking" to the possessed person's body— that is, prevent them from summoning virulent remembrances in the subject's physicality.[36] Indeed, in the *Complementum* Visconti states that the final goal of every exorcism is "to impose silence on the devil" (*taciturnitas daemoni imponenda est* [781]). The devil's most powerful weapon is

34. "*[T]riplex est verbum, operis, oris, et mentis:* verbo operis, loquitur Deus; Verbo oris, loquuntur homines, et verbo mentis, loquuntur Spiritus" (original emphasis).

35. In *The Origin of Satan* (New York: Vintage, 1995), Elaine Pagels analyzes the political aspects of Satan as "speaker of the mind" in early Christianity. In chap. 40 of *Prescription*, for instance, Tertullian labels as heretics all those who question the Church's prescriptions. Tertullian, Pagels notes, states that devils inspire the heretics' mind (165).

36. Thyraeus, *Daemoniaci cum locis infestis*, 164.

his utterances *(loquutiones)*, with which he tries to darken our intellect (*rationem obtenebrare* [782]).

We must understand that from a grammatical point of view, in an exorcism two past tenses confront each other. I have explained that the malady tormenting the possessed is nothing but a perverse form of remembrance. The devil has brought back and manipulated a set of memories sitting in the back of the victim's mind. Therefore, the *present* of the victim's ailment is the perverse reenactment of a series of *past* occurrences. The healing core of an exorcism is an act of remembrance as well. Since evil originally manifested itself as an absence (if God is presence, when Satan fell out of Heaven, he withdrew from being), what is the meaning of the devil's *present* assault? Does the devil not realize that his current *presence* contradicts his *past* absence?

In short, in the exorcist's voice the present of a torturous remembrance clashes and converses with the past of the devils' absence. An exorcist narrates the occurrence of a sudden perversion, the manifestation of evil not in its natural, albeit negative, outcomes (storms, deadly plagues, sexual impotence), but rather in its real and autonomous being. In chapter 1 I explained that devils first and foremost exist as semioticians of the world's signs. Devils solely live in their interpretations, in their destructive syllogisms. As Visconti puts it, devils speak the idiom of the mind.[37] An exorcism aims to restore Satan's natural, and absent, idiom. Forcing the devil to erase his presence from the possessed person's body, an exorcist articulates the world's natural order, its well-structured discourse made of symbolic gestures and unambiguous sentences. The exorcist's healing voice states that Satan has always been absent from the world, that his disturbing and unclear manifestations in the possessed person's physicality are really nonexistent occurrences, nothing but disturbances of the mind, since evil itself is a lack of being.

Every book of the *Thesaurus* highlights how, to restore the natural order of things that has been perverted by the revelation of devils' being, an exorcist must purify himself. His voice must become the stainless vessel through which creation speaks its natural and divine presence. As Hilarius Nicuesa states in *Exorcismarium in duos libros dispositum* (1639), the

---

37. It is necessary to distinguish the devils' "language of the mind" and Augustine's *verbum mentis* (word of the mind), as he theorizes it first of all in *On the Trinity* (book 15). The devils' language of the mind disturbs the subject's internal and preverbal discourse. For a good analysis of Augustine's *verbum mentis*, see Giorgio Santi, *Dio e l'uomo. Conoscenza, memoria, linguaggio, ermeneutica in Agostino* (Rome: Città Nuova, 1989), 92–99.

exorcist must bear in mind that he is a nothingness and that he does not have anything good in himself.[38] An exorcist succeeds in casting devils away less because of his personal qualities and virtues than because of his being the representative of Christ's church *(in persona ecclesiae)*.[39] What matters is less the exorcist's identity than his religious function. However, every demonologist recommends that the exorcist undergo some form of spiritual purification, because in any case, as Menghi writes in *Flagellum*, exorcisms go better if the exorcist has purged his soul (293). In *Practica exorcistarum*, Polidori suggests that the exorcist cleanse his conscience *(de puritate conscientiae)* through prayer, confession, fasting, and a costant self-analysis (3).[40] The exorcist must monitor his own behavior and make sure that neither his gestures nor his words are scandalous (4). Furthermore, the exorcist must refrain from any form of vainglory deriving from his pivotal role in the war between God and Satan (4–5).

Exorcism is a performance whose two human actants (the priest and the possessed) exist only as generic, unspecified presences. The ritual requires that an exorcist and a body in pain be present so that evil may be invoked, spoken, and silenced. What matters is not who these performers are and what has brought them together (whether or not the priest is pure, what thoughts cross his mind while he is performing the ritual, what kind of disease the victim suffers from), but rather the event of their meeting and performing together.[41] If the goal of every exorcism is to expose evil's real and unnatural presence, this objective is attained in the "void" of two generic individualities.[42] As an exorcism from Menghi's *Flagellum* clearly shows, the ritual of diabolic adjuration is first and foremost the unfolding

---

38. Hilarius Nicuesa, *Exorcismarium in duos libros dispositum: quorum annuale alterum, alterum sanctuarium dicimus coniurationum* (Venice: Iuntas, 1639), 2.

39. However, as André Goddu reminds us, most treatises on demonology believe that the failure of exorcism can also be attributed to the unclean status of the performer's soul ("The Failure of Exorcism in the Middle Ages," in *Possession and Exorcism*, edited by Brian P. Levack [New York: Garland, 1992], 2–19).

40. Compare Tropianus, *Compendium coniurationis*, 3.

41. In *Inheriting Power: The Story of an Exorcist* (translated by Lydia G. Cochrane [Chicago: University of Chicago Press, 1988]), Giovanni Levi recounts the story of a seventeenth-century Italian exorcist, Giovanni Battista Chiesa, who performed innumerable, and very questionable, exorcisms in various areas of northern Italy. Chiesa believed that the devil was responsible for every form of evil, including physical illnesses. According to this exorcist, almost everybody was possessed by one or more devils (20–25).

42. In *A Declaration of Egregious Popish Impostures* (London, 1603), Rev. Samuel Harsnett calls exorcism a "puppet-play." As John L. Murphy explains in *Darkness and Devils: Exorcism and King Lear* (Athens, Ohio: Ohio University Press, 1984), Harsnett criticizes the highly theatrical nature of the Catholic ritual of exorcism (186–87).

of the devil's biography.[43] In this exorcism, after pronouncing an introductory prayer, the priest is supposed to ask the devil a series of questions regarding his decision to enter that body. First of all, the devil must reveal his name: "At this point the exorcist will ask the devil to reveal his name; if he has accomplices; what is the name of his master; which role he plays in the demonic order; why he has chosen this obsessed . . . how long he has been residing in this obsessed . . . who are his worst enemies in heaven and in hell; how he will signify his departure" (336–37). The name of the devil plays a fundamental role in the *Thesaurus*.[44] The devil's name at once hides and epitomizes his biography and his destiny.[45] Even the body in pain, says Hilarius Nicuesa in *Exorcismarium*, is nothing but a name of the devils inhabiting the body in that, by reading the symptoms expressed by the possessed *(daemonum naturae observationem)*, the exorcist can glean some information on the devils themselves.[46] Nicuesa is convinced that the exorcist must understand if the devils are "shy, daring, silent, loquacious, stubborn, compliant, blithe, noisome, wild, mendacious . . . if [they live in] the air, waters, on earth, in fire; [if they come] from the North, from the South, from East or from West . . . if they are free or bound to some pact; [what are] their nature, kind, and tendencies."

We have seen that in Visconti's *Complementum* devils, humans, and God embody three different forms of language, according to their three different forms of being. As the Book of Genesis confirms, God does not distinguish between creating and speaking. Things indeed spring from an act of speech. Humans, on the contrary, use what Peirce calls "indexical" phonemes, an idiom made of acts of remembrances. According to Peirce, an *index* is a sign that marks the past presence of an object (as a hole in the wall might be a reminder of a bullet). A name, a first name, at once says

43. In *Das Reich Satans* (Graz: Akademische Druck- und Verlangsanstalt, 1982), Karl R. H. Frick notes that the Latin *ritus* (rite) "probably derives from the Indo-european concept rta = 'Truth' or 'Right'" (18). The ritual of exorcism, we may infer, conjures up the truth of evil, or better yet, evil as truth.

44. In his fascinating *Demons and the Devil* (Princeton: Princeton University Press, 1991), Charles Stewart offers an exhaustive analysis of Orthodox demonology with a special focus on contemporary Greek culture. In chap. 8 ("Exorcism: The Power of Names"), Stewart highlights the importance of names in the practice of demonic adjuration: "Exorcism texts constantly reproduce th[e] struggle of names. . . . Sometimes, in texts that seemingly exceed the bounds of Orthodox tolerance, the demons are given many names, all of which the priest must recite" (214–15).

45. Compare de Certeau, *Possession at Loudun*, 85–100.

46. Hilarius Nicuesa, *Exorcismarium*, 6.

everything and nothing about its object.[47] A first name exclusively points to a presence; it says that someone with that name exists. This is why, in an exorcism based on the repetition of the "holy and terrible mystery of the sacred names" of God (62), Polidori feels compelled to insert a grammatical analysis of the possible linguistic constructions expressing God's names. This exorcism, the very first adjuration of the *Practica* and thus of the entire *Thesaurus*, opens with the priest addressing the "cruel beast" and his acolytes. The primary and the secondary devils are one identity, which is marked on the page as **N** *(nomen):* "I exorcise you, **N**, cruel beast along with all your acolytes, and all the other evil spirits present in the body of this creature of God, so that you immediately leave this body modeled by God and regenerated through the baptismal bathing" (63). While "this creature" (the victim) is an indistinct gesture of divine intervention in history (the possessed is "molded" and re-created in baptism), the devil is a common name, an **N**, the sign indicating that someone is indeed receiving the exorcist's speech. "This" creature, the possessed, is the carnal means through which the performer delivers his discourse to a name (**N**). Thanks to the presence of a common name (that of the devil), the exorcist is able to enumerate God's "incomprehensible," "ineffable," "holy," "inexpressible" names, which either allude to a specific quality of his divine being, or refer to the biblical event in which they were uttered for the first time:

> I exorcise you through the unfathomable name *Schemhamphoras* †, which signifies the pure and perfectly simple essence of God. . . .
>
> I summon you through the name *Agla* †, [which signifies] the omnipotent eternity and the eternal power, as it was wonderfully revealed in the mystery of Daniel's nocturnal vision. . . .
>
> I exorcise you . . . through the virtue of the name *Adonai* †, which the Lord spoke to Moses as follows: I am the Lord who appeared to Abraham, Isaac, and Jacob as almighty God, but I did not reveal my name Adonai to them. . . .
>
> I command you through the ineffable name *Iehova* †, or *Tetragrammaton*, that is, Iod, Hè, Vau, Hè, whose mysterious meaning manifests the trinity of the divine persons and the unity of the divine essence. . . .
>
> I summon you through the virtue of the name *Alpha et Omega* †, *Alpha*, I say, without Alpha, *Omega* without Omega, Alpha without Omega, Omega without Alpha. (63–66)

47. Compare Louis Marin, *Sémiotique de la passion* (Aubier Montaigne: Éditions du Cerf, 1971), 25.

If the addressee *vos* is a cluster of **N**s, God's names are either invocations of isolated qualities of God's being (his existence beyond time or his perfect purity), or reminders of God's historical manifestations (Agla, Adonai). No name is able to point to God's being as a whole, that is, as an essence. This is why, at the end of a long list of divine names, Polidori adds that God's "essential names" *(nomina essentialia)* can acquire several different morphological constructions: "I exorcise you and summon you through all the other essential names of God, both as essential substantives, as essential adjectives, as essential concrete substantives and as essential abstract substantives, as essential concrete adjectives and as essential abstract adjectives, as personal names and as notional names, as personal notions, as notions of notions, and also as attributes" (66–67).[48] Instead of mentioning "all the other names," Polidori resorts to a grammatical categorization of all their possible forms, from the most abstract and general ("essential substantives") to the most specific and secondary ("attributes").[49] We may infer that Polidori turns a grammatical analysis into an invocative expression to God.

Both **N** and God's innumerable "substantive and adjective essential names" are common names. Like the exorcist and the body in pain, God must be present in the ritual of exorcism through his common names so that **N** may be forced to utter his first name and thus his being. Indeed, while God's first names (Iehova, Agla, Adonai) are nothing but invocations and thus do not guarantee that God is present when they are uttered, exorcism as a linguistic performance comes to an end only if **N** reveals itself. In the dramatic concluding part, the exorcist attacks **N** ("**N**, cursed Prince!") and orders him to disclose his name.

Polidori recommends that the exorcist have some holy paper handy and write down in capital letters the name or names coming out of the possessed person's mouth, and draw a picture showing some "horrible and base" devil *(effigie horribili et turpi* [25]). By sketching the figure of a hypothetical devil, the exorcist tries to enhance his power over the devil himself. If a name points to a presence without actually showing it, the exorcist attempts to give a signified (an image) to its signifier (a name).[50] By connecting a name with its image, the priest believes that he has finally "possessed" the being of the devil himself. At the end of the ritual, the

---

48. Compare *Thesaurus*, 154.

49. In *Flagellum*, Menghi reminds us that God has also "unknown" names (*Thesaurus*, 305).

50. I discuss the role of the name in mystical language in "Performing/Annihilating the Word: Body as Erasure in the Visions of a Florentine Mystic," *TDR: The Drama Review* 41, no. 4 (1997): 110–27.

priest will exorcise a burning candle, a "fire" *(coniuratio ignis)*, with which he will destroy the written name and the sketched picture.[51] In the act of purifying the flame, the exorcist reminds the devil (the sheet with the name and the image) that God revealed his name to Moses in a burning bush ("I conjure you † with fire in the name of God Omnipotent Father, who appeared to Moses in the form of fire,"), and that "fire is His abode, fire is His dwelling, He is fire."[52] Being fire, God's name has the power to burn the Enemy's name and image. According to Menghi's *Flagellum*, before throwing the devil's name and image on the pyre of God's name, one more time the exorcist asks **N** to acknowledge his defeat and withdraw from the body in pain (415). **N**, Menghi believes, cannot resist the "virtues" of God's name.

For Hilario Nicuesa, **N** must ratify the annihilation of his own name through a legal and solemn confession *(solemni iuramento)*, made through the obsessed person's voice. While the victim stands with his hands on the altar or on the Bible, **N** must recite the following text: "Having completely abandoned every secret deception, I demon **N** in the name of the malignant spirits . . . invoke God's furor against me and call forth His wrath, so that he send the archangel Michael, Prince of his army, to overcome me. His messenger will hand me over to my enemies and will thrust me in the lake of the eternal fire, in which my infernal suffering will incessantly increase until the day of our final judgment."[53] In Nicuesa's *Exorcismarium*, fire at once burns a name and embodies its temporal existence. Exposed to the flame of God's name, **N** becomes subjected to history, and thus to its final erasure.[54]

If ambiguous signs marked the opening of the exorcism (the possessed person's indistinct symptoms and his annoying and meaningless utterances), unquestionable signs indicate that the ritual has come to an end. After having burned the sheet with the devil's image and name, the exorcist expects the devil(s) to send a sign of his (or their) departure. Paradoxically, the devil is supposed to blow out the flame on which his name has been burned. For an exorcism to be successful, the devil's name must be expressed twice, first by the victim's mouth and finally by the devil himself, who must exhale both his name and his being in a clear and distinct manner. Rather than actually hearing the devil pronouncing his own name,

---

51. Compare Menghi, *Flagellum*, 316; Visconti, *Complementum*, 984–85.
52. *Thesaurus*, 414; compare 870 and 876.
53. Hilarius Nicuesa, *Exorcismarium*, 30.
54. In *The Possession at Loudun*, de Certeau recounts the case of a devil who had "lost his name" (43–44).

however, the minister "hears" a "very cold" breath coming from nowhere. The draft is "very cold" because it carries **N** as a corpse. The draft is the visible manifestation of a dead name. Sometimes, instead of blowing out the candle, the devil limits himself to exhaling his very cold name through the possessed person's anus, vagina, nostrils, or ears (*Thesaurus*, 797).

In the act of breathing out his name, the devil finally erases the unclear signs he had written in the possessed person's body.[55] The "very cold" wind coming out of the victim's anus or ears signifies that the devil has exhaled his language from the possessed person's flesh—that is, he has stopped speaking to the humors in the victim's mind. If God's idiom can be both creation and annihilation (the fire burning **N**), and humans' voice is only the memorial of the past, demonic language is the process in which syllables turn (clot) into clauses and clauses turn into sentences attacking the mind that hosts them. It is the mind itself that produces these noxious statements, since the devil lacks a language. The "virus" assaulting the mind is the mind itself. In a demonic possession, the mind listens to its own annihilation.

The ritual of exorcism is first and foremost a dialogic performance involving two idioms and two names, God's and the devil's. As I have pointed out, the body in pain is a necessary, though silent, presence. The only remarks concerning the victim revolve around the introductory distinction between *maleficiatus* and *daemoniacus*. While the former is the victim of some sort of sorcery or enchantment, the latter is actually possessed by one or more devils. Although all six texts of the *Thesaurus* draw up detailed lists of symptoms identifying an "obsessed person" *(obsessus)* as *maleficiatus* or as *daemoniacus*, the two categories present very similar traits.[56] In both cases, the individual shows signs of a foreign presence

55. Compare Augustine, *On Free Choice of the Will*, translated by Thomas Williams (Indianapolis: Hackett Publishing, 1993), book 3, chap. 25: "We must . . . distinguish between two classes of things seen. One originates in the will of someone who is attempting to persuade. An example of this class is the suggestion of the devil. . . . The other class originates in the things that are present to the attention of the mind or the senses of the body."

56. In *Manuale exorcismorum* (Antwerp: Balthasarius Moreti, 1648), Maximilianus ab Eynatten believes that to define the nature of a given possession, exorcists should work with physicians. Although his theories are heavily indebted to Menghi's and Polidori's works, in his distinction between *maleficiati* and *daemoniaci* Eynatten chooses a more "scientific" style, identifying three different kinds of signs. The first signs are no more than speculations *(pariunt solum suspicionem)*, the second symptoms are much stronger conjectures *(coniecturam vehementiorem)*, the third signs are certain inferences *(certitudinem nonnullam* [11]). For instance, if a patient shows some kind of knowledge transcending human capability (such as future events or new and successful medicines) and does not remember what happened when he had an attack of diabolic frenzy, he is definitely possessed by Satan (12).

within his or her flesh. The "patient," as Menghi calls the obsessed person in the fourth exorcism of *Fustis daemonum,* acts as if his or her identity were suddenly doubled, and both body and mind had become the field where two adverse identities attempted to prevail over each other (681). In the fifth chapter of the *Complementum* ("On the signs by which one can recognize a *daemoniacus* and a *maleficiatus*"), Visconti states that one of the most revealing signs of the devil's presence in the patient's body is that the patient cannot understand his own behavior anymore. In addition to abhorring relics, prayers, and holy water, a *daemoniacus* often cries without knowing why; speaks incessantly, making little or no sense at all; looks "deprived of his senses" for long periods of time; suddenly tears his hair for no specific reason; foams at the mouth; feels as if insects, snakes, or frogs were moving through his body; feels a cold or burning gust rush through his entrails (777–78).[57] A *maleficiatus,* Visconti continues, may sense something like wool in his stomach or throat, without being able to cough it out. He may also feel that his heart is being bitten by snakes or dogs (779–80). Both "patients" suffer from severe forms of melancholy, Visconti concludes, and no medical treatment seems to be successful.

Besides these "external signs," in the *Flagellum* Menghi makes clear that an exorcist must also take into serious consideration the devil's "internal signs"—that is, the single words, sentences, or monologues N utters in the obsessed person's mind. Once his or her malady has been diagnosed as demonic possession, the victim is asked to verbalize the signs N is manifesting inside his or her mind. The possessed must echo the thought of his or her "guest" *(hostis).* Menghi recommends that the exorcist constantly ask the obsessed person to vocalize the devil's words (314).[58] The victim must try to focus on what the priest is saying and to avert his or her attention from the thoughts the devil is pursuing in his or her mind.[59] The possessed must at once repeat the sentences N is formulating in his or her mind and follow the priest's instructions. Caught between two counter-discourses, the possessed person's identity is reduced to the awareness of having been dispossessed of him or herself. During the exorcism,

---

57. Compare *Thesaurus,* 9–10, 201–2, 295. In his *Practica,* Polidori does not hide the fact that these lists of symptoms derive from the Gospel narrations of Jesus's exorcisms (Mark 9, 10, 12; Matt. 12; Luke 9).

58. For those patients who have been struck by "the charm of silence" *(maleficio taciturnitatis),* in *Fustis daemonum* Menghi reports a specific exorcism *(Thesaurus,* 751–56).

59. In the third exorcism of the *Practica,* Polidori invokes the "discourse of all holy angels" *(omnium sanctum Angelorum locutionem),* whose mind language *(verbo mentis)* engages the devils in a silent debate taking place in the possessed person's intellect (87–88).

the obsessed silently listens to the two (external and internal) voices and also to the persistence of his or her own despair. A demonic possession presents itself as an overwhelming revelation. *Now* the victim knows that his being was nothing but a false appearance. *Now* he knows that to exist means to mourn over the loss of existence. This revelation is a name (**N**).

During the exorcism, the priest may address single organs of the patient's body in which devils may hide their names. Once he has detected their exact location, the exorcist's voice leads **N** from a given organ up to the patient's throat and then to his mouth, so that **N** can be finally uttered and then marked on the page. In *Exorcismarium,* Nicuesa believes that the most critical moment in the act of expelling the devil is to push **N** to the obsessed person's tongue.[60] This is the prayer he recommends to achieve this goal:

> God is truthful and no thought is hidden to Him. He fathoms the heart and the loins. From heaven His eyes examine the earth, and no one can hide from His knowledge. Through the virtue of the names *Yschiros* † *Agios* † *Otheos* † *Alpha* † *Omega* † *Iesus* and through the great virtue of that Who summons the things that are not and those that are, I thus order you not to hide the truth from me with any form of [secret] pact and to disclose the actual number of demons present in this body. I want all of you and each of you to ascend immediately to the superior part [of this body]. I do not want one to speak for all, but each will speak for himself.[61]

God's names compel the devils to move from the most hidden recesses of the possessed person's body up to his mouth, and to "breathe forth" their names one after the other so that, as Polidori theorizes in his own version of this exorcism, the devil's name can be exposed to a divine trial *(ante tribunal domini nostri)* and finally "thrown" *(praecipitatus)* into the flames of hell (51). In the *Complementum,* Visconti makes the exorcist tie a *stola*

---

60. *Trophaeum Mariano-Cellense,* or *The Trophy of Mariazell,* a manuscript work in the Austrian National Library in Vienna (n.14.084), offers a different interpretation of the devil's presence on the possessed person's tongue. This manuscript contains the fascinating self-analysis of a seventeenth-century German painter, Christoph Haizmann, who became possessed with the devil. As is well known, Freud studied this case of possession at length. One morning Haizmann went to the Franciscan fathers to confess and take communion. "When I wanted to confess," Haizmann writes, "the priest ordered me to say the confession-prayer. But I could not pray it although I started four times." Four devils had assailed him. "One of them sat on my tongue, so I took my hand and tore out the evil spirit." I quote from the edition by Ida Macalpine and Richard A. Hunter, *Schizophrenia 1677: A Psychiatric Study of an Illustrated Autobiographical Record of Demoniacal Possession* (London: Dawson, 1956), 81.

61. Hilarius Nicuesa, *Exorcismarium,* 13.

(long upper garment) around the patient's neck with three knots and say: "As the Lord Jesus Christ captured the ancient snake and tied it up with a chain, so will I tie you up with this *stola*" (929).[62] In the *Flagellum* Menghi offers a variant on this procedure. If the devils are not willing to express their names, the exorcist must order them to descend to the victim's toenails, so that they can be cut out and burned, as if the nail were a sheet on which the devil had inscribed his name. He must order them "to withdraw from the head, the heart, and the stomach, and to go down to the inferior parts of the body . . . the toenails of the foot" (448). In the sixth exorcism of the *Flagellum*, Menghi is much more specific about the removal of any diabolic presence from the patient's organs.[63] At the beginning of this adjuration, the priest reminds the devils hiding in the body that the words he is about to pronounce "are a powerful fire, which will burn you [N] in a horrid and effective way" (425). The exorcist's words, uttered in the name of God, "make the world shudder." Indeed, in Menghi's fascinating exorcism the priest first conjures the four basic elements of the world: air ("I conjure you, air, in the name of the Father . . . so that you become unable to tolerate this evil spirit in you" [404–5]), earth ("I conjure you, earth, in the name of the Trinity . . . so that you absorb this rebellious spirit" [405–6]), water ("I conjure you, water . . . in the name of Christ's sweat and the water that came out of his side"), and fire ("I conjure you, fire, wherever you are in the name of God the Father" [408]). After having asked the whole creation to reject the evil spirit inhabiting the body in pain, the exorcist then addresses hell itself: "Oh Hell, and infernal fire, and you, infernal suffering, and all of you, princes and demons of hell, listen, listen to me, and understand the words of my mouth. . . . In the name of the words, with which you, hell, infernal fire, and you all, demons of hell, and suffering of hell, can be conjured and bound. . . . [I order you] never to release this wicked spirit, but rather to call it back to you" (409–10). Since the whole creation has been turned against them, the devils (**Ns**) cannot help but abide by the minister's words and manifest their names: "I force you . . . to tell me your names without any further delay" (432). However, Menghi is aware that the exorcist's invocations "in the name of God's names" are effective only insofar as God is willing to inhabit his own names. In other words, the exorcist can ascertain the devil's presence by analyzing the

---

62. Compare *Thesaurus*, 793. For the theme of "binding" in exorcism, see Richard H. Hiers, "'Binding' and 'Loosing': The Matthean Authorizations," *Journal of Biblical Literature* 104, no. 2 (1985): 233–50.

63. Menghi reproduces the same detailed list in the first exorcism of the *Fustis* (609–10).

possessed person's symptoms, but he cannot determine whether God is responding to his own names or not. Paradoxically, God's "language of things," as Visconti says, is much less detectable than the devil's idiom of the mind. Since no clear sign reveals that God has actually spoken his healing language, the sixth exorcism of the *Flagellum* concludes with an obsessive description of all the possible locations where devils could be hiding their names: "Oh God, expel the devil . . . from his [this creature's] head, hair, skull, forehead, eyes, tongue, epiglottis, ears, nostrils, neck, jaws, teeth, throat, gums, mouth, palate, brain and its recesses, eyelids, eyebrows, hair, feet, knees, legs, genitals, kidneys, sides, upper and lower intestines, thighs, belly, stomach, heart, shoulders, chest, breasts, arms, hands, nails, bones, nerves, veins, intestines, lungs, . . . from every juncture of his body" (426). According to Polidori, if the exorcist fails to detect the devil's name, he can simply "rechristen" the devil with a new name: "If he [the devil] does not reveal it [his name], it is necessary to impose a base and contemptible name, such as Source of Vices, Father of Deception, Bestial Beast, and the like, and this name will be used and written down" (13).[64] In the act of renaming the devil, the exorcist/Adam speaks in the name of Christ (*ad instar Christi, ex parte Christi* [300–301]). Of course, to speak in the name of Christ primarily means to ask Christ to inhabit his own name—that is, to respond to the priest's invocation of the name of Christ (436). However, the expression *to speak in the name of Christ* has a second, central sense, resulting from the four Italian inquisitors' view of linguistic expression. In the *Thesaurus*, the exorcist at once speaks in the name of Christ and like Christ. Indeed, when he addresses the devil in a given body, the exorcist reenacts the memory of the Savior adjuring demons, as recounted in several Gospel narrations.[65] However, the exorcisms transcribed in the *Thesaurus* show that, according to Polidori, Menghi, Visconti, and Stampa, to reenact a narrative is not a mere act of remembrance, a memorial of the Word's biography. For these authors reality is an infinite process of metaphorical displacements, in which every thing, every word, and every event may influence and echo past, present,

---

64. Exorcisms abound with seemingly incomprehensible names. For an excellent explanation of this subject, see Karel van der Toorn, Bob Becking, and Pieter W. van der Horst, eds., *Dictionary of Deities and Demons in the Bible* (Leiden: E. J. Brill, 1995).

65. The "healing" properties of memory play a fundamental role in most forms of shamanistic performances. For a fascinating analysis of this theme, see Carol Laderman and Marina Roseman, eds., *The Performance of Healing* (New York: Routledge, 1996). I am particularly indebted to the following essays: Thomas J. Csordas, "Imaginal Performance and Memory in Ritual Healing" (91–114); Robert R. Desjarlais, "Presence" (143–64).

and future things, words, and events.[66] *Like* is the word that holds the creation together.

AS A VADE MECUM to understand and control the created world, the *Thesaurus* itself is a metaphor extending over twelve hundred pages. This fundamental text of the late Italian Renaissance aims to show that, *like* the evil spirits, things, words, and gestures express a hidden, unheard idiom, whose essence is metaphorical and whose temporality is at once within and without history. Reproducing a clearly Augustinian view, the *Thesaurus* is based on the assumption that things are what they are able to say. Things, words, gestures are essentially groundless, since their being is a linguistic gesture.[67] In the second exorcism of the *Flagellum*, one of the most poetic texts of the whole *Thesaurus*, we find this opening passage: "In the name of the Fa † ther, and the Son †, and the Holy † Spirit, Amen. God rise, and his enemies be overthrown, and those who hated him flee from his face. *As* smoke becomes extinct, so will they become extinct. *As* wax flows down from the substance of fire, so will all the devils die away from our face" (345, emphasis mine). This introductory invocation is based on a series of metaphorical parallelisms springing from the word *sicut* (as, like).[68] The smoke of the candle (on which N will be burned) goes up in the air, *as* God rises over his enemies. Moreover, the smoke disappears *as* God's enemies are defeated by his rising power. If the first metaphor speaks of an ascension (God, the smoke), the second focuses on a descent (wax, the devils going down back to hell). The text also plays with the figurative meaning

66. Compare David Tracy, "Metaphor and Religion: The Test Case of Christian Texts," in *On Metaphor*, edited by Sheldon Sacks (Chicago: University of Chicago Press, 1979), 89–104; Paul Friedrich, *The Language Parallax: Linguistic Relativism and Poetic Indeterminacy* (Austin: University of Texas Press, 1986); Thomas J. Csordas, *Language, Charisma, and Creativity* (Berkeley: University of California Press, 1997), 157–246. Particularly interesting is Csordas's analysis of the relationship between "motive" and "act" (192–94).

67. In *Vom exorcismo. Ein Christlicher nötiger und in Gottes Wort wohlgegründter Bericht* (Jena: Thobias Steinman, 1592), Polycarpus Leysern D. makes a fundamental distinction between what he considers a "Papist" exorcism and a Christian, that is, Protestant, one. Leysern first speaks of the alleged "Jewish" exorcism, a ceremony based on magic and sorcery. Then he writes that the main difference between a "Papist" and a "Christian" exorcism is that "Christians" believe that an exorcism is an invocation and has no "substantial" character (chap. 6, n.p.). An exorcism, Leysern stresses, is a "spiritual" practice in that "in our Church" words have no *sonderbare Kraft* ("special power" [chap. 5, n.p.]). What Leysern finds particularly questionable is the utterly theatrical nature of a "Papist" exorcism (herbs, candles, gestures, holy water).

68. Compare Brian Vickers, "On the Function of Analogy in the Occult," in *Hermeticism and the Renaissance*, edited by Ingrid Merkel and Allen G. Debus (Washington, D.C.: Folger Books, 1988), 265–92.

of *facies*, which is used both to indicate God's and men's "face" (face as presence or being), and fire's "face" (its matter or substance).

"The paradigm of signifying by improper names," as Giorgio Agamben defines Renaissance literature on emblems, shares interesting elements with the interpretation of metaphor formulated in the *Thesaurus*.[69] Sixteenth- and seventeenth-century emblematists were convinced that "a representation that proceed[ed] by discrepancies and shifts would be more adequate to its object than a representation that proceed[ed] by analogies and resemblances."[70] This view of visual expression had a clearly mystical connotation, following Dionysius the Areopagite's concept of negative theology. Although both Renaissance emblematists and the authors of the *Thesaurus* based their discourse on a metaphorical model, their reasonings bore radically different consequences. While an emblem reflects an act of meditation moving from verbal and visual language toward a state of wordless and imageless contemplation, exorcism proceeds from a condition of confused and silent signs (the body in pain, the hidden and real presence of devils) to a metaphorical narrative that both discloses and erases evil's unheard language. We may say that, in an exorcism, metaphor is anything but "metaphorical" in that, more than being a simple similitude, it tells that *this* and *that* at once recount similar stories and share similar essences. In the exorcisms of the *Thesaurus*, things are stories that may turn into things that may turn into stories. Let us remember that "the language of things" pertains only to God. If syllogism belongs to the devil, metaphor is a divine construction.[71]

The stories merging past, present, future things and events derive exclusively from the Bible. The Old Testament and the Gospels are the narrative models repeated and varied ad infinitum in the history of creation. The Bible was recounted by God himself, the sole speaker of the "language of things." God has unfolded, revealed his being in a narrative form. Divine being, we may say, is a narrative that is reflected in every form of the created world. An example from the *Thesaurus* will clarify this crucial point. We have seen that *maleficiati* often feel something like wool moving up and down their throat. In the *Dispersio*, Polidori mentions a short

69. Giorgio Agamben, *Stanzas: Word and Phantasm in Western Culture*, translated by Ronald L. Martinez (Minneapolis: University of Minnesota Press, 1993), 141–51. I analyze this problem of emblematic literature in *Identità e impresa rinascimentale* (Ravenna: Longo, 1998).

70. Agamben, *Stanzas*, 141.

71. In the opening pages of *Fustis daemonum*, Menghi underscores that "the Holy Scripture is full of metaphors [*plena est metaphoris*] and other figurative expressions, in which, given a certain agreement [*convenentiam*] between two things, the name of one thing stands for the other thing (*Thesaurus*, 536).

exorcism to be used when a patient has difficulty in coughing out this un-pleasant presence. The exorcist makes the obsessed drink a healing potion made primarily of vinegar and olive oil. Before giving it to the obsessed, the priest exorcises the beverage with the following words: "I exorcise you, natural blend, which is able to induce vomit, in the name of God the Almighty, creator of your healing virtue. God ordered the big fish to vomit the prophet Jonah, who had been in its belly for three days and three nights. God wanted him to preach to the Ninevite people. *In a like man-ner,* deriving your virtue from the same creator, you will induce vomit at every sip" (279–80, emphasis mine). The healing "virtues" of the potion result from its having been connected to a biblical event through the ex-pression *in a like manner.* According to Polidori's prayer, the drink is a re-minder of the fish holding the prophet in its stomach. The "big fish" and the drink do not play the same grammatical role; the drink is not "like" the fish (the fish vomited the prophet, whereas the drink is the means through which the obsessed will vomit the devil). The act of vomiting is similar to what Claude Lévi-Strauss calls a *mythème,* the smallest unit of a mythic story.[72] The difference between Lévi-Strauss's and Polidori's views of nar-rative is that for Lévi-Strauss the *mythème* "to vomit" designates a prera-tional and thus prelinguistic narration, while for Polidori "to vomit" is an event whose essence coincides with God's story of Jonah in the fish's belly.[73] Unlike a *mythème,* in the *Thesaurus* the narrative unit "to vomit" is not a sort of Platonic idea with infinite possible incarnations. Divine "language of things" spoke/manifested the act of vomiting once and for all in the Jonah story.[74] When he mentions the Jonah episode, the exorcist ac-tually reminds God of his own narration—that is, he asks God to turn a

72. Compare Manfred Frank, *What Is Neo-structuralism?* (Minneapolis: University of Minnesota Press, 1989), 43; Claude Lévi-Strauss, *Structural Anthropology,* translated by Claire Jacobson and Brook Grundfest (New York: Doubleday, 1967), 205–6.

73. A fascinating collection of essays on the relationship between anthropology and spirit possession is *Spirits in Culture, History, and Mind,* edited by Jeanette Marie Mageo and Alan Howard (New York: Routledge, 1996). In particular, see the essays by Liko Besnier, "Heteroglossic Discourses on Nukulaelae Spirits" (75–97), and Alan Howard, "Speak of the Devils: Discourse and Belief in Spirits on Rotuma" (121–45). In the "Afterword," Michael Lambek writes: "[Spirit possession] combines spirits as a semiotic system and an order of col-lective practice whereby hosts are initiated, particular voices are legitimated, and spirits are pro-vided with spaces in which to perform. Possession thus provides a context in which contem-porary experience is actively mediated by past myth models, and vice versa" (238). Compare Manfred Frank, "Die Dichtung als 'Neue Mythologie,'" in *Mythos und Moderne* (Frankfurt am Main, 1983), 17.

74. I find fascinating similarities between my interpretation of the *Thesaurus exorcismo-rum* and Joel C. Kuipers's *Power in Performance* (Philadelphia: University of Pennsylvania Press, 1990), an analysis of the ritual speech performed by the Weyewa people of western

story made of words (human language) into one made of things (divine language). We may thus say that evil's name can only be vomited or spoken through divine idiom. *As* the fish made the prophet visible, *so* does God's language (embodied in the patient's throat) spit out the devil's real presence. Evil's name, we infer, can be uttered only by God.

At this point it is evident that what Visconti defines as three distinct idioms (language of things, language of words, and language of the mind) can also be seen as three essential facets or potentials of language itself. While the human "language of words" corresponds to grammar and syntax, the demonic "language of the mind" is the intentional component hidden in a given utterance—that is, it is what the mind wishes to attain when it formulates a "sentence of the mind." Finally, the divine "language of things" is what language actually does, what language succeeds in accomplishing beyond being thoughts, desires, and phonemes.

This interpretation of Visconti's three forms of language helps us highlight the essential connection between demonic and human expression. While divine idiom exceeds the linguistic realm because it manifests itself as things, human and demonic expression are two moments of the same speech act. The tongue articulates what the mind has suggested. If we follow this reasoning, every human statement is inevitably exposed to the devils' "language of the mind." This is why the authors of the *Thesaurus* require that the exorcist speak with a detached and unperturbed voice, as if the exorcism recited itself—that is, as if the speaker were simply the physical means through which a divine message reaches and defeats its addressee (the devil tormenting the body in pain).[75] According to Polidori, the priest is not supposed to show any curiosity or resentment toward his demonic interlocutor (the speaker of the mind [10–11]) and must make sure that his discourse does not expand into lengthy and spontaneous di-

---

Sumba (an island in eastern Indonesia). As Kuipers explains, "in their rites of atonement [Weyewa spokesmen] struggle to identify, reaffirm, and enact the *li'i* 'words of the ancestors'— by which they mean a connected body of teachings, promises, and obligations set down— fixed—by the ancestors and expressed in narrative form" (167). And again, "one of the important senses of *li'i* 'word, voice' . . . is 'promise,' as in 'plant the word' *(katukku li'i)*" (139).

75. In *Modus interrogandi daemonem ab exorcista* (Venice: Turrinus, 1643), Carolus de Baucio, a priest in the city of Capua, summarizes the canonical views on how to question devils during an exorcism. In a few instances, however, de Baucio introduces some interesting and less frequent variants. For instance, he believes that the exorcist may ask the devil which priest will succeed in expelling him from the obsessed person's body ("per quem exorcistam, aut Sacerdotem erit expellendus" [4]). De Baucio also underscores that the exorcist's questions must be succinct and unequivocal (5). If curiosity leads the priest to futile inquiries, he will commit a venial, and not mortal, sin, for his unnecessary requests simply reflect an imperfect behavior.

gressions (12).[76] In *Compendio dell'arte essorcistica*, Menghi reports the eloquent case of an exorcist who yelled at the devil, "Va al cesso!" ("Go to the lavatory!"), a very disrespectful expression used in Italian to send someone away (something like "Get out of my face!"). When the exorcism was over, the priest went to the bathroom. Awaiting him there, the devil jumped to the priest's throat and killed him.[77] In other words, during the exorcism the priest had brought to the fore the "linguistic presences" lurking in his own mind, which then strangled him in the washroom.

The priest was throttled, we may infer, by his own language. As soon as a discourse becomes the discourse of someone, it may be invaded by the speakers of the mind, who turn it against its own speaker. In the exorcisms of the *Thesaurus*, human identity interferes with the metaphorical re-enactment of an original "narrative gesture," a divine *mythème* whose articulation has the power to annihilate Satan's name (**N**). Of course, *Jesus* is the name that synthesizes God's victorious narrative. To say *Jesus* is *like* recounting how God's language has turned and constantly turns words into things, "the speakers of the mind" into wax flowing down to hell or into smoke disappearing up in the air.

JESUS IS THE THEME of exorcism 13 in Visconti's *Complementum* ("On the Life of Jesus Christ"), the longest and most compelling adjuration of the whole *Thesaurus* (1042–1111). The exorcism opens with the priest placing the Eucharist on the altar and praying silently *(in spiritu)*. This "extremely powerful" *(efficacissimum)* exorcism narrates Jesus' life starting from its conclusion—that is, it begins with the exorcist showing what Jesus has become at the conclusion of his biography. The wafer is Jesus' body *(manifestum signum,* "visible sign" [1052]) in that it *embodies* his life history, what will be told and "shared" throughout the exorcism. Exorcism as communion, as reenactment of the Savior's life and death.

Indeed, Visconti's adjuration is a double ceremony. If to say Mass means to ask the Word to incarnate his story in the here and now of the ritual, Visconti's exorcism is a Mass that opens with the Word already present (in the wafer on the altar) and develops as a reiterated invocation to the Word so that it may finally become present (in the priest's words). In Visconti's ritual, the exorcist's voice turns into a "linguistic Eucharist" recounting the Word's biography, as if the wafer were a metaphor for the

---

76. In *Daemoniaci cum locis infestibus,* Thyraeus recommends that the exorcist also watch his body language (203).

77. Menghi, *Compendio dell'arte essorcistica,* 472.

actual Eucharist, the exorcist's discourse.[78] Indeed, we shall see that, by telling and retelling the Word's story, the exorcist's language becomes *like* the wafer on the altar.[79] Visconti writes this "Mass" for the devils obsessing the body in pain, so that they "share" the Word with the priest, and thus acknowledge the necessity of their own erasure. Like a Mass, this exorcism is an act of remembrance.

After a long litany based on the repetition of the words *restrain them* ("Jesus bread of life, restrain them; Jesus firm faith, restrain them; Jesus our hope, restrain them . . . Jesus extirpation of vipers, restrain them; Jesus executioner of demons, restrain them; Jesus hammer of spells, restrain them" [1044]), the exorcist raises the Eucharist and with a menacing tone recites a long text (twenty-one pages) divided into innumerable short paragraphs, each introduced by the expression *Hic est Jesus* (This is Jesus), a variant of *Hoc est corpus meus* (This is my body) pronounced during the offertorium (the offering of the wafer). This "hymn to the Savior" opens with a reference to John's definition of Jesus as the Word:

> This is Jesus, from whose holy chest John drank and, like an eagle, in his beginning said "In the beginning was the Word, and the Word was with God, and the Word was God." . . . Everything was made by him, and nothing exists without him. . . .
>
> This is Jesus, inseparable Word of the Father. . . .
>
> This is Jesus, eternal splendor of the Father. (1046)

78. In "The Devil's Contemplatives: The *Liber Iuratus*, the *Liber Visionum* and the Christian Appropriation of Jewish Occultism," in *Conjuring Spirits: Texts and Traditions of Medieval Ritual Magic*, edited by Claire Fanger (University Park: Pennsylvania State University Press, 1998), 250–65, Richard Kieckhefer examines a text found in a manuscript of the late thirteenth or early fourteenth century (Oxford, Bodleian Library, MS e Mus. 219, 186r–87v). This text describes a "proved exorcism taught by a demoniac, [which] involves writing sacred words from the beginning of John's gospel on a piece of parchment, then scraping the letters into a bowl and administering the scrapings to the energumen with holy water" (251). We may say that in this ritual the scrapings containing débris of John's gospel indeed turn into a sort of blessed wafer.

79. As far as the relationship between the real presence, invisible presence, and visible absence of the thing according to the "Logic of Port-Royal," see Louis Marin, *La critique du discours. Sur la "Logique de Port-Royal" et les "Pensées" de Pascal* (Paris: Minuit, 1975), 290–99. Marin offers a brilliant analysis of the expression *hoc est corpus meum*. Marin believes that this sentence synthesizes "the equivalence of being and of its representation in and through the subject of the enunciation. This equivalence is attained in the double transformation of being into representation and representation into being" (297). The grammarians of Port-Royal attempt to distinguish between "sign-word," "word-sign," and "sign-image" *(signe-mot, chose-signe, signe-image)*. Marin writes that, according to Arnaud and Nicole, "like writing, the Eucharist is the body of a word and, like drawing, it is the soul of a picture, although the wafer is invisibly present as the body of Jesus Christ" (76).

John, at once author of the gospel and Jesus' beloved apostle, "drank" the opening sentence of his text from the bleeding chest of the Word. The wafer *(this is Jesus)* is *like* the blood from which the apostle acquired the Word's biography. Indeed, the wafer held in the exorcist's hand harbors a narrative, whose divine and healing essence needs to become incarnate in the priest's voice. *Hic est Jesus* is the present of the wafer and the future of the exorcist's voice. In the first case, *Hic est Jesus* identifies with a real presence; in the second, it says what it is about to become.

Jesus is the name announced by the archangel Gabriel to Mary. *Jesus* was before the Word's birth; it was before the beginning of his story. "This is Jesus," the exorcist recites, "whose arrival was announced by Gabriel, one of the major angels. . . . He said to Mary: 'Hail Mary, full of grace. . . . You will conceive a child in your womb, and will give him the name "Jesus"'" (1047). In Visconti's words, the birth of Jesus was a paradox. It was a "hidden" revelation in that the devil "thought that a woman, and not a virgin, had given birth to the child." *Jesus*, Visconti believes, was and is a narrative whose goal and closure (the annihilation of the Enemy) were and are attained only insofar as its plot unfolded and unfolds secretly. Although Jesus spoke marvelous words from his birth (his cries expressed "incomprehensible and wondrous things" [1048]) and throughout his life (his teaching among the doctors came "from the mouth of the Almighty" [1049]), "the enemy of the human kind heard his [Jesus's] voice" when the Savior told the thief crucified next to him that he would follow him to heaven (1063).

The Enemy "hears" the Word when his story comes to an end. Satan himself, we may say, "makes sense" of the Scriptures, which "were fulfilled" (literally "consumed" [*consummaretur*]) when the Word "exhaled his soul" on the cross (*emisit spiritum* [1064]). *Hic est Jesus*, the obsessive incipit repeated throughout the first section of Visconti's exorcism, is what Satan is asked to perceive at the beginning of a ceremony focused on the recollection of the Word's death. The first addressee of the Word's word, as Thomas Aquinas says, is Satan, because for the Enemy to listen to the Word's story (how he had been *figuratus* [symbolized and announced] by Noah, Abraham, David, Daniel, and John the Baptist; how he was born in the womb of a virgin; how he died on the cross) means to realize that *Jesus* is the story of a deception.[80] Like Oedipus unveiling the meaning of incomprehensible signs (the plagues tormenting the city of Thebes), the

---

80. Thomas Aquinas, *Summa contra gentiles* 4.14.

speaker of the mind reads the created world as a text secretly written against him.

As we have said, the first section of Visconti's exorcism concludes with the words *emisit spiritum. Spiritum* is also the key word of the following "intermission," in which the priest is asked to pray *in spiritu* for a short while. The pause of silence following a long rhythmical discourse *(Hic est Jesus)* at once marks the end of a narrative (the birth, life, and death of the name *Jesus*) and alludes to the possible presence of the very spirit "exhaled" at the end of the first part of the adjuration. In the opening part, the wafer is more an index of the Word than the Word himself—that is, it is the sign of what the Word has been. We may go so far as to say that in the initial narrative (centered on what the name *Jesus* was before its death on the cross) the Eucharist *partially* embodies *Jesus*, because its story and destiny have not been fully recounted yet. Indeed, if the first section was exclusively based on the rhythmical expression *Hic est Jesus*, the second opens with the same expression but later shifts to *Ecce qui*, by *ecce* meaning that the name *Jesus* has finally become visible ("Behold him who . . .").

While in the first part *hic* (this) was a term expressing a future tense (the exorcist's voice is about to speak *Jesus*), in the second *hic* has a past connotation, in that the narratives introduced by the incipit *Hic est Jesus* now tell how the end of the story *Jesus* coincided with the manifestation of its miraculous "signs" *(signa* [1066]). The signs of the dead Word/Jesus revealed and reveal his irresistible power over the Enemy. "In the name of" the dead Word, Visconti writes, new languages are spoken, snakes are eradicated, devils are expelled. Indeed, the dead Word first manifested himself to devils, when He descended to hell and "terrified its legions" (1065).[81] Because of the Word's horrifying presence, devils started to speak:

> Who is he that shines with such a luminous splendor? . . . A bright presence never appeared in this blind and caliginous place. He is here to prevail over us, not to succumb to us. He is a judge, not a sinner. . . . If he is God, what does he do here? If he is a man, how can he be so presumptuous? If he is God, what does he do in the sepulcher? If he is a man, how could he absolve men? . . . Oh, our Prince, did you not gloat over his fu-

81. Clement of Alexandria was one of the first theologians "to integrate Christ's descent into Hades as part of the act of redemption" (Russell, *Satan,* 117). Although the New Testament alludes to this myth (Eph. 4:8–9; Heb. 13:20; 1 Pet. 3:17–22; Rev. 1:18), its meaning was left unexplained. As Russell points out, "by the second century the belief had already become the most widespread and popular explanation of what Christ was doing between the crucifixion on Friday afternoon and his resurrection on Sunday morning" (Russell, *Satan,* 118–19).

ture death? Did you not think that after his death you would possess the entire world? Did you not promise us a wonderful future after his departure? What did you mean to do? (1065–66)

This account of the Word's mythical descent to hell is of great relevance. Fear and disorientation, caused by the Word's sudden invasion of hell, compel the devils to speak. Indeed, the Word's descent to hell corresponds to the devils' "ascension" to the realm of language. In Visconti's text, the devils' language is nothing but questions following an unexpected and unsettling revelation. *As* the angel Gabriel had descended upon the Virgin to announce to her that she would become pregnant with the Word, *so* did the Word descend to hell to grant devils the gift of language.

If demonic language is a question directed to the Word who has enlightened hell with his "luminous" being, *Hic est Jesus* is an indexical sentence. More than announcing the forthcoming presence of the Word, it gives voice to a primordial, mythical trauma. Darkness (hell) and light (Word) correspond to two different temporal stages of demonic linguistics. By descending to hell ("blind" place, in Visconti's words), the Savior has made the fallen angels see their being as a fundamental lack (of sight), that is, as a request. The devils' real, and unnatural, presence in the possessed person's body and mind are manifestations of their question to the Word. The devils' language is indeed a request for meaning. In the ritual of exorcism the priest recites a text meant to remind the devils that their real presence in the world signifies a trauma, their originary and sudden awareness of being deprived of sense. It is a given that an exorcism does not and cannot annihilate a demonic presence, it simply attempts to erase his (meaningless) utterances.

Hic est Jesus becomes *Ecce qui . . .* after the exorcist has voiced the devils' request for meaning. When he visited hell, Visconti writes, Jesus marked it with "his sign of Victory." It is the Word's "victorious sign" *(signum victoriae)* that urged devils to language:

> Behold him, who placed his sign of Victory in hell. . . .
> Behold him, who defeated death and the devil. . . .
> Behold him, whose blood destroyed the Dragon. . . .
> Behold him, who took his human body to the cross, so that he could take you, old serpent, to your death. . . .
> Behold him, whose name is admired by the whole universe. . . .
> Behold the Word of God. . . .
> Behold him, who is offered every day in every part of the world. . . .

Behold him, whose holy and sweet name is praised and extolled by
every people, tribe, and idiom with an immense exultation and a
fervent devotion.

Behold him, who cannot be comprised by the skies and is revealed by
the angels and archangels; who is feared by the saints and the just.
Yet, so friendly he calls us, poor and miserable sinners, to the communion with his holy body. (1071–75)

The end of this hymn to the Word's dominion over heaven, earth, and hell
corresponds to the conclusion of the offertorium, when the priest raises
the consecrated wafer and shows it to the audience. In Visconti's exorcism/
Mass, the "consecration" of the wafer signifies that the narrative of the
Word's victory over hell and its inhabitants has come to its conclusion. The
wafer "becomes consecrated" in the moment when the Savior enlightens
the devils in hell with the gift of language.

Visconti defines the new section of his exorcism as *Exprobatio* (Reproach). Holding the wafer in his hands, the exorcist speaks to the devils
with a direct and accusatory tone. The unnatural presences in the obsessed
person's body have become interlocutors of the priest's discourse after he
has celebrated the Word's enlightening descent to hell. This new part of the
ritual presents more than one essential change. Not only does the exorcist
address the devil as "you," he also gives the evil spirit a name: Lucifer, the
brightest star, the morning star. Visconti's narrative discourse defies any
linear narrative. If in the previous section the devil inhabited the caligi-
nous and blind areas of hell, now he is what he was before he fell to hell,
that is, at the origin of creation. Speaking in mythical terms, Christ's descent to hell is the *Ur-Geschichte*, the mythical occurrence at the basis of
any possible narrative on the relationship between the created world and
its "Prince." Lucifer, the morning star, is what the devil became when God
sent the light of his "luminous" Word to visit the regions of hell. The
devil's startling "wisdom" *(sapientia)*, as Visconti says at the outset of this
new segment, is what the devil learned when God "announced" his Word
in hell.

As a consequence, we may say that Lucifer's "bright light" is in fact
God's gift of language. The new section begins as follows: "Oh Lucifer, oh
miserable you, oh you all, cursed devils, listen to your miseries. . . . Listen
to the Lord through the mouth of Ezekiel, who said: 'You were once an example of perfection, full of wisdom, perfect in beauty; you were in Eden,
in the garden of God. A thousand gems formed your mantle, sard, topaz,
diamond, chrysolite, onyx, jasper, sapphire, carbuncle, emerald. . . . You,
cherub . . . I placed you on the holy mountain of God'" (1075–76). Going

back to a tradition founded by Origen, Visconti merges the "Prince of Tyre," the actual addressee of Ezekiel's text, with Lucifer, the morning star.[82] He also modifies the passage from Ezekiel. Whereas the prophet states, "I had provided you with a guardian cherub" (28:14), Visconti identifies the cherub with Lucifer himself ("You, cherub . . ."). In Visconti's interpretation, the morning star was a bright gem, like the precious stones (topaz, diamond, chrysolite, onyx) that adorned his mantle. Lucifer, Visconti continues, lived in "the holy Jerusalem, whose doors are made out of sapphire and emerald." In Jerusalem, "life was joyful, vital, and eternal" *(vita jucunda, vita vitalis et sempiterna)*. Lucifer was a "star shining with an everlasting light" (1076).

When he was part of the holy Jerusalem, Lucifer was one with its "immense, incorporeal, incorruptible, unfathomable . . . light" (1077). The radiance proceeding from Jerusalem, its bright gems, its luminous doors, its angelic stars, and their precious mantles, are an expression of their longing for the Word of God. Jerusalem burns with its desire for the Word. When Lucifer and his cohort denied their own desire, they were thrown down to earth *(in terram proiecti sunt* [1078]). In his description of Lucifer's fall, Visconti does not distinguish between earth and hell. When he was rejected from heaven, Lucifer fell to earth, in a deep lake *(profundum lacum* [1079]), where the air is dark and gloomy.[83] Thus, in Visconti's exorcism, Lucifer's fall echoes and reflects man's banishment from the garden of Eden. As Adam and Eve first perceived their flesh when they were exiled, so did Lucifer and his angels pass from being pure light to possessing a physical body at the moment of their fall.[84]

Borrowing from Genesis, Visconti describes the fallen angels' metamorphosis: "Your faces were blackened as charcoal. Tears will be always on your cheeks. Every day you will cry without solace. . . . The Lord has made your skin aged. Your flesh is charred like an oven. He has fed you with ashes and has made you drunk with absinthe. . . . [God] has broken your teeth. He has injected fire in your bones" (1079). When they became bodies marked with age and lust (the fire burning in their bones), Lucifer and his followers also acquired a desire for expression. Their minds started to harbor "useless thoughts" *(cogitationes inutiles* [1080]) and to articulate a

---

82. Origen, *An Exhortation to Martyrdom,* translated by Rowan A. Grean (New York: Paulist Press, 1979), 18. Compare Henry Ansgar Kelly, "The Devil in the Desert," *Catholic Biblical Quarterly* 26 (1964): 190–220; Russell, *Satan,* 131–32.

83. Compare Rev. 12:19 and 20:3.

84. In *Fustis daemonum,* Menghi asks Lucifer: "how can you, wretched and foul spirit, tolerate the memory of your past joy?" (*Thesaurus,* 703).

"language of iniquities" *(lingua iniquitatum)*, whose first addressees were and are "ignorant women" *(mulierculas)*. It is evident that, in Visconti's exorcism, devils and human beings share a similar biography. Our body, our mind (our "useless thoughts"), and our language result from our having being rejected by the Word. We *are*, we may infer, the rejection of the Word. The "useless" language of the fallen angels is the topic of Visconti's second *Exprobatio*. If in the first "Reproach" the exorcist reminded the devils of their disgraceful metamorphosis from bright stars to foul inhabitants of the blind regions of earth, in the second the priest attacks the "false arguments of the devil's language" (1081). Devils "silence the words of the just" and express not what "the Law requires but what the mind covets." "You, heretic," the exorcist exclaims, "invite men to investigate . . . the profound and hidden mysteries of God, which the human mind cannot comprehend." At Doomsday, God will "confound the language of the devils" and will send them back to their blind and dim realm (1083). We may say that the language of the mind proceeds from the Word, who has enlightened it when He visited hell, and returns to the Word, who at the end of time will deprive the devils of their idiom. Surviving without a language, Visconti continues, devils will live an "immortal death" (1085). The fallen angels will literally regress to indistinct and disordered phonemes, cries and moans with no meaning (1086). "No one," Visconti concludes, "can elude what is written in the Scripture."

The second "Reproach" envisions the final erasure of demonic expressivity. At the end of the world, the language of the mind, which defies the written Law, will be unlearned. When Lucifer and his devils go back to a "blind"—that is, imageless—place, demonic signifiers (phonemes, words, sentences) will fail to summon any possible image. The devils' final metamorphosis will be into a moan. Indeed, in the following section of the adjuration the exorcist speaks to the evil spirits *as if* their final defeat had already taken place—that is, *as if* the language of the mind had already succumbed to divine Law. It is clear that the metaphorical component of the *Thesaurus* involves its temporal categories as well. To speak of Doomsday is *like* speaking of the chaos brought about in the possessed person's mind and physicality. What will happen at the end of time has already happened and is about to happen at the end of this very ritual.

If we look at the title of this new section, we understand another essential aspect of Visconti's text. The Italian inquisitor calls this segment *Peremptorium,* a juridical expression that can be translated as "conclusive argument denying any further debate." What we have read so far is in fact a trial. While the previous parts examined the devils' felony and the evi-

dence against them, in the *Peremptorium* the exorcist/attorney launches his
last attack against the defendants. The *Peremptorium* is divided into three
structurally similar sections. The exorcist is first appalled that the devils
have not perceived the gravity of their offenses and are still harassing the
victim, and later demands that they leave the scene of their crime and go
back to hell. The unique aspect of this form of trial is that, by simply re-
constructing their biography, the exorcist may succeed in leading the defendants to confess their error and depart from the victim.

The success of the attorney's speech lies in its summoning the memory
of a forthcoming defeat. The defendants must see, must remember that
the luminous Word has already blinded their language at the beginning of
time, and that He will blind it again at the end of time. Mirroring each other,
past and future are reenacted through a speech act. The exorcist *orders* the
devils to remember their defeat, which will take place in an indefinite future. If and when the devils come to recall their future loss of language,
they will revoke, delete the signs of their presence from the possessed:

> Flee, flee down to the Netherworld, because the Lord is about to send
> marvels down from heaven. Blood and fire will rain. The sun will darken;
> the moon will turn into blood. The earth will mourn; the skies will fall
> down; humans will cry out of terror, as if they were giving birth. . . . The
> day of revenge is imminent. . . . God's voice will roar like a sea. Any moan
> or lament will be useless. . . . Thus, wretched creatures, go, go down to
> hell, where moans and cries are forever. (1087–89)[85]

In the following *Peremptorium*, realizing that the evil spirits have failed to
abide by his orders ("Oh you, proud creature, you then persist in your ob-
stinate attitude?" [1090]), the exorcist brings suit againts them ("I take
you to the court of our Lord Jesus Christ, who has prevailed over your
iniquities"). *Withdraw* is the key word of this second *Peremptorium*:
"Withdraw then, you abominable whisper, you, full of every iniquity.
Withdraw, you, cause of men's perdition and father of every crime. You
were expelled from the Angels. Withdraw, ancient serpent."

A fascinating rhetorical shift takes place in the third and final *Peremptorium*. After the common incipit ("Then, you, perverted insect, you still
resist the Creator?" [1092]), the exorcist addresses the evil presences still
lingering in the body in pain *as if* the diseases they have brought to the
body were affecting the devils themselves and not the possessed: "Until
you delay your departure, fever will plague you; your spirit will burn; confusion and lethargy will burden you. . . . Apoplexy, paroxysm, migraine,

85. Compare Rev. 8:6–12, 16:2–4.

and every sort of pain will exhaust you. . . . Epilepsy will possess your substance; melancholy, your spirit; folly, your mind and intelligence. A constant hemorrhage will shed your blood, along with an agonizing atrophy and paralysis" (1093). This passage describes the most common symptoms associated with possession. In Visconti's *Peremptorium*, the body in pain manifests the devils' "substance," as if, by invading the victim's flesh, the evil spirits had become incarnate. If the Word spoke his being in and through Jesus ("And the Word became flesh"), Lucifer reveals his substance in and through human bodies. However, his revelation is marked by decay, illness, and imminent death. If the devil's language first and foremost aims to uncreate the creation, the most eloquent signs of his idiom are spoken in its speaker's physicality, what Visconti calls his "substance."

We have seen that Visconti's exorcism is first and foremost an act of remembrance based on a prolonged course of metaphorization. In the *Peremptorium*, the tormented body is *like* the spirit tormenting the body, *as if* cause and effect coincided, *as if* speaking and being spoken were the same act. Apoplexy, fever, lethargy, hemorrhage, are both the results of the devil's presence and the origin of those results. The speakers of the mind at once bring about symptoms and are symptoms. The phonemes of the devils' language are symptoms.

If evil words are symptoms, the exorcist reminds these "linguistic symptoms" that the Word may grant human voice the power to efface them.[86] As the priest persists in reminding the devils of their original and forthcoming subjugation to the Word, so did Joshua and his people succeed in conquering Jericho, stronghold of the power of evil, by walking around its walls seven times and by uttering a final and "mighty war cry" (1094).[87] This parallel between the priest's speech and Joshua's "besieging" the walls of Jericho with his war cry marks the effective victory of the human "language of words," as Visconti says, over the idiom of the mind. Like the exorcist's *Peremptorium*, Joshua's victory manifests the veritable—substantial, we may say—power of metaphor. Indeed, after having recounted the story of Joshua, the exorcist makes the devils "swear" their own defeat, and their subsequent and irrevocable withdrawal from the possessed person's body (1096). The exorcist's vehement *Peremptorium* (which is like Joshua's war cry, which is like an irresistible weapon) com-

---

86. In the seventh exorcism of *Flagellum daemonum*, Menghi distinguishes between the exorcist's voice, his words, and the speech he delivers. The exorcist asks God to compel the devils to pay respect to his voice and to his words, and to obey the orders expressed through his sentences (*Thesaurus*, 436).

87. Josh. 6:16.

pels the devils to disclose their names (**Ns**) and to suggest a suitable image of their invisible substance.

Like the walls of Jericho, at this point of Visconti's adjuration the evil spirits give in and lead the exorcist's hand to draw three pictures of their hidden being. A pious person present at the exorcism will hit the first portrait with an olive branch. Two other religious persons will spit and step on the second and third picture. Finally, the priest lights three candles on which he will burn the names and the portraits of the devils (1096–97).[88] As the flames consume the sheets with the drawings and the names, the exorcist "burns" the linguistic residues of the devils' infectious presence by "disinfecting" the whole creation with his words:

> Oh, wretched and damned creatures, who have refused to obey God's will as it was communicated to you through me, I curse you and send you away. Be banned from the West and from the East, from the North and from the South, and from the impious realms. [Be banned] from every state, every province, every island; from every city, town, and village; from every building and every house; from every valley and every hill; from every mountain and every land; from every kitchen garden and every field; from every desert and every cave; from every ruin and every abyss; from every sepulcher and every statue . . . from every tree and every plant; from every fruit and every flower and every seed; from dust, ashes, air, clouds; from every thunder and every lightning . . . from every river, stream, spring, cistern, wave, rain, foam, hail, snow, storm. (1102)

After having banned the devils from every aspect of the creation, the priest takes the holy communion and places it over the obsessed person's head (1109–10). This gesture marks the conclusion of the ritual. As the Enemy was unable to face Jesus, the exorcist recites, so will the devils' faces and names, burned in the flames of the candles, withdraw into the fires of hell (1110).[89]

WE HAVE SEEN THAT in *De strigimagis* Prierio compares demonic language to a fire consuming the creation. Fire also signifies the conclusion of a successful adjuration, the annihilation of the devil's name and face. If the

---

88. In *Fuga Satanae*, Stampa offers a different version of this ritual. Instead of burning three pictures of the devils, Stampa suggests that the exorcist draw two portraits, one of the devil and the other of the possessed himself. Both images must be burned at the end of the exorcism (*Thesaurus*, 1247).

89. Compare Lambek, "Afterword," in *Spirits in Culture, History, and Mind*: "If spirits are imagined, they may become like works of art that, in turn, seize our imaginations, then seduce and overwhelm us with their power. . . . They may indeed 'possess' us" (239).

morning star, the brightest star, speaks a language of flames, flames will consume flames, fire will burn fire. *Thesaurus exorcismorum*, the majestic monument built to the power of metaphor, sees the created world and its immemorial history as an ongoing process of procreation, in which language and things, thoughts and words, time present and time past, memory and desire converse with each other and affect each other. The healing power of an exorcism lies in its bringing to the fore reality's infinite and hidden connections. According to the *Thesaurus*, the Scripture is the narration founding God's eternal will for metaphorization. As Visconti's powerful exorcism shows, reality is first and foremost the innumerable stories recounted in the Bible. The Word of God has become flesh in the act of recounting his contentious relationship with his chosen people. The exorcisms of the *Thesaurus* make the creation tell its silent and constantly renewed autobiography.

FOUR

Walking in the Garden of Purgatory: The Discourse of the Mind in the *Probation* of St. Maria Maddalena de' Pazzi

MEDIEVAL AND RENAISSANCE DEMONOLOGY sees possession as the physical manifestation of a demonic "language of the mind," as Visconti defines it in *Thesaurus exorcismorum*. I have emphasized that both *maleficiati* and *daemoniaci*—the former indicating victims of a spell and the latter referring to subjects invaded by one or more demonic beings—are the linguistic matter through which the exorcist can impose the discourse of divine law upon the speakers of the mind. As the books collected in the *Thesaurus* prove, an exorcism is primarily affected by the priest's and devil's identity, not that of the victim. The thoughts rushing through the exorcist's mind and his sins may have a negative influence on the adjuration, which is totally successful only if the devil hidden in the body unveils his biography (his name). The victim is first of all a cluster of symptoms, the medium allowing the exorcist to monitor his linguistic attack on the demonic presence.

Renaissance treatises on demonology are much less interested in defining the physical and psychological effects of a diabolical possession than in stating that a possession has actually taken place. The history of the confrontation between humans and devils still needs to be written. Witches are individuals who have willingly agreed to articulate Satan's discourse and thus cannot be considered as possessed or obsessed. But the demonologists never draw up a specific list of those human beings "at risk," as we would say today, of those people whose mental constitution may be easily corrupted by the devil's rhetoric. A commonplace of early modern demonology is that women in general are easy targets, given the fragility of their intellect. Since they are mentally weak, women can easily turn into witches or possessed persons.

This distinction between witches and possessed or obsessed individuals is important when we look at the lives of most Catholic saints, whose stereotyped hagiographies based on Athanasius' *Life of Saint Anthony* inevitably include a victorious confrontation with the Enemy.[1] In every saint's life the devil is nothing but a failed obsessive reasoning; he never succeeds in jeopardizing the "blessed soul's" rationality through his diabolic "local motions," as Prierio clearly explains in *De strigimagis*.

In a crucial passage from the *Malleus maleficarum*, the authors use a seemingly Aristotelian system to explain how the devil can enter the human body without causing any physical injury:

> [T]he devil can draw out some image retained in a faculty corresponding to one of the senses; as he draws from the memory, which is in the back part of the head, an image of a horse, and locally moves that phantasm to the middle part of the head, where are the cells of imaginative powers; and finally to the sense of reason, which is in the front of the head. And he causes such a sudden change and confusion that such objects are necessarily thought to be actual things seen with the eyes. This can be clearly exemplified by the natural defect in frantic men and other maniacs.[2]

"This theory of localization," as Klibansky, Panofsky, and Saxl call it, presupposes Galen's anatomy of the brain and is an essential facet of

---

1. As Michel de Certeau points out, hagiographies are "tautological tombs" in that "th[ese] literary 'monument[s]' [are] saturated with meaning, but with *identical* meaning" (*The Writing of History*, translated by Tom Conley [New York: Columbia University Press, 1988], 269). Compare my *Uttering the Word: The Mystical Performances of Maria Maddalena de' Pazzi, a Renaissance Visionary* (Albany: State University of New York Press, 1998), 67–68.

2. Heinrich Kramer and James Sprenger, *Malleus maleficarum*, translated by Montague Summers (New York: Dover, 1971), part 2, q. 1, chap. 9, 125. In *On Memory*, Aristotle believes that "memory belongs incidentally to the faculty of thought, and essentially it belongs to the primary faculty of sense-perception" (in *The Complete Works of Aristotle*, edited by Jonathan Barnes, vol. 1 [Princeton: Princeton University Press, 1985], 450a, 10, 715). It is also evident, Aristotle holds, that memory is a function of imagination, which he had already analyzed in *On the Soul*. The process of pictorial transference (local movement) occurs as the transportation of an image, "a sort of impression of the percept, just as persons do who make an impression with a seal" (*On Memory*, 450a, 30). "Remembering," Aristotle stresses in a later passage, "is the existence of a movement capable of stimulating the mind to the desired movement" (452a, 10). On the Aristotelian interpretation of the relationship between memory and medicine in the Middle Ages, see Paolo Rossi, *Clavis Universalis. Arti mnemoniche e logica combinatoria da Lullo a Leibniz* (Milan: Ricciardi, 1960), 32–35.

scholastic psychology.[3] According to this structure, "the human intellect comprised three distinct functions, each located in a different part of the brain: 1) Imagination . . . in the warm and dry ventricle of the forebrain . . . ; 2) Reason . . . located in the warm and moist "cellula logistica" in the middle-brain; and 3) Memory, located in the cold and dry ventricle of the back part of the head."[4]

In reproducing this typical subdivision, the authors of the *Malleus* consider man's internal "phantasms" as material units kept in the "back part of the head," which is the place of memory.[5] Memory is a physical storage of visual segments or remembrances, which the devil moves to the central part of the brain/mind in order to reuse them as visual *praemissae* of his ruinous syllogisms. We have seen how Prierio describes this process of demonic rhetoric in *De strigimagis*. But what distinguishes a simple *maleficiatus* from a "blessed soul" attacked by an evil presence is that in the latter the newly manipulated remembrances do not reach the "front of the head," that is, reason. While a blessed soul is still aware of the difference between external images and internal phantasms, a *maleficiatus* is blinded by his own memories.[6] In other words, a *maleficiatus* has absorbed and recognized the devil's visual discourse as a truthful, and devastating, insight.

According to the *Malleus*, *maleficiati* are similar to "frantic men or maniacs." It is difficult to draw a distinct line between "natural" and "unnatural" obsession. Demonologists reiterate that devils try their best to hide in a human body under a veneer of plausible symptoms. Mania and frenzy are the most evident signs of a blurred system of expression. Chaos is

---

3. Raymond Klibansky, Erwin Panofsky, and Fritz Saxl, *Saturn and Melancholia: Studies in the History of Natural Philosophy, Religion, and Art* (New York: Basic Books, 1964), 69. This specific description of the three functions of the human brain is taken from *De naturis rerum libri duo* by the thirteenth-century philosopher Alexander Neckham. Klibansky, Panofsky, and Saxl quote from the edition of T. Wright, in *Rerum Britannicarum Medii Aevi Scriptores,* vol. 24 (London, 1863).

4. Klibansky, Panofsky, and Saxl, *Saturn and Melancholia,* 68–69.

5. Compare Nancy G. Siraisi, *Medieval and Early Renaissance Medicine* (Chicago: University of Chicago Press, 1990), 82: "The division of mental activity into distinct processes which were allocated among specific sites within the brain was a medieval concept that derived from Galenic ideas about brain function." On Galen's psychological materialism, see Owsei Temkin, *Galenism: Rise and Decline of a Medical Philosophy* (Ithaca: Cornell University Press, 1973), 17–19.

6. In *Theologia platonica* (18.4), the bible of Renaissance Neoplatonism, Marsilio Ficino writes that hell is an eternal nightmare, from which the subject will never awaken. The damned soul is tormented by a constant flux of disturbing and frightening images deriving from the evil presences of the netherworld.

indeed the language articulated by the maniac's body and mind. Let us remember in this context that memory, the primary source of human imagination, is made of material linguistic segments, each of them marked with the picture of a past experience.[7]

The chaos of memory is called melancholy.[8] Let me explain this essential point. Melancholy, we could say, is what the body in pain fails to communicate.[9] Like N refusing to speak from the obsessed person's flesh, melancholy is a language producing infinite signs without saying anything. Melancholy testifies only to the unrelenting production of chaotic phonemes. One of the most accurate syntheses of Renaissance interpretation of melancholy is found in Johann Weyer's *De praestigiis daemonum* (1568). For the Lutheran physician Weyer, melancholics suffer from a "perverted imagination," whose origin is dubious and thus inherently suspicious:

> [C]onsider the thoughts, words, sight, and actions of melancholics, and you will understand how in these persons all the senses are often distorted when the melancholic humor seizes control of the brain and alters the mind. Indeed, some of these melancholics think that they are dumb animals, and they imitate the cries and bodily movements of these animals. Some suppose that they are earthen vessels, and for that reason they yield to all who meet them, lest they be "broken." Others fear death, and yet sometimes they choose death by committing suicide. Many imagine that they are guilty of a crime, and they tremble and shudder when they see anyone approaching them, for fear that the person may lay hands upon them and lead them off as prisoners and haul them before the tribunals to be punished.[10]

7. In *Demonolatriae,* Remy repeats that "it is certain that Demons often insinuate themselves into men's minds and, with God's permission, impress upon them and mark them with whatever thoughts they please." Remy refers this process of demonic "imprinting" to Girolamo Cardano's concept of "subtlety," which the Italian physician examines in his famous *De subtilitate* (Nicolas Remy, *Demonolatriae libri tres,* translated by E. A. Ashwin [London: John Rodker, 1930], book 1, chap. 14, 52). For an analysis of "subtlety," see chapter 5, below, on Cardano's *Metoposcopia.*

8. I have hinted at the relationship between melancholia and demonology in chapter 2, above.

9. For an accurate and succinct list of the major Renaissance medical treatises broaching the problem of melancholia, see Gustavo Tanfani, "Il concetto di melancholia nel cinquecento," *Rivista di storia delle scienze mediche e naturali* 39 (1948): 145–68. Among the texts examining melancholia's demonic components, Tanfani mentions *Praxeos Medicae* by the Swiss scholar Felix Plater (159–61).

10. Johann Weyer, *De praestigiis daemonum et incantationibus ac veneficiis,* edited by George Mora (Binghamton: State University of New York Press, 1991), 183. Compare Sydney Anglo, "Melancholia and Witchcraft: The Debate between Weyer, Bodin, and Scott," in *Folie*

The most interesting aspect of this description is what Weyer says about the melancholics' perception of their own flesh. Apart from producing an array of symptoms nowadays related to the similarly all-encompassing term *depression*, the melancholic humor "melts" the body into a fluid and fragile receptacle of images.[11] If, as Husserl states in the *Fifth Cartesian Meditation*, the subject's physicality is divided into "flesh" *(Leib)* and "body" *(Körper)*, the former expressing the image that the subject believes others have of his physical self and the latter indicating the body as mere matter, a melancholic perceives his "flesh" as a blind, imageless matter or "body" (an "earthen vessel") at the mercy of others' unpredictable interpretation.[12] In a healthy subject, "flesh" and "body" support each other—that is, the subject thinks that he knows how others see him, he knows what others think about his physical appearance. This is not the case of a melancholic person, who perceives the others' gaze as an uncontrollable and thus menacing presence. If "flesh" is the visual text we are given from "them," the melancholic body is prey to infinite ominous discourses.

The melancholic is essentially "possessed" by his own physicality, in that his flesh has become a presence imposed upon the subject by someone else.[13] As Weyer explains, the melancholic avoids any physical contact that may deform his body "of clay" and cause his death, which he perceives as

---

et déraison à la Renaissance (Brussels: Éditions de l'Université de Bruxelles, 1976), 209–22. Extremely interesting also is Winfried Schleiner, *Melancholy, Genius, and Utopia in the Renaissance* (Wolfenbüttel: Herzog August Bibliothek, 1991), 181–90.

11. In his section on "religious melancholy," Robert Burton states that the devil uses the melancholy humor to tempt human beings, by identifying those who are naturally inclined toward melancholy. For Burton, the melancholy humor is "the Devil's bath" (*The Anatomy of Melancholy*, edited by Floyd Dell and Paul Jordan-Smith [New York: Tudor Publishing House, 1938], part 3, sec. 4, member 2, subsec. 3, 938). However, in other sections of his treatise, Burton is much more cautious toward the allegedly demonic component of melancholia. See, for instance, the chapter "A Digression of the Nature of Spirits, Bad Angels, or Devils, and How They Cause Melancholy" (157–76).

12. Edmund Husserl, *Cartesian Meditations*, translated by Dorion Cairns (The Hague: Martinus Nijhoff, 1960). I use Husserl's concepts of "flesh" and "body" in my analysis of Renaissance literature on emblems and devices (*Identità e impresa rinascimentale* [Ravenna: Longo, 1998], 14 and 66).

13. In *Malinconia* (Milan: Feltrinelli, 1992), the Italian psychiatrist Eugenio Borgna analyzes what he calls "the demonic experience in psychopathology" (125–26). Borgna recounts a series of cases of melancholia based on the alleged presence of a diabolic being in the patient's body. Borgna's patients sense that their body is subject to a "demonic metamorphosis and to an irreversible destruction." Angela, a patient in her thirties, states: "This morning I lost my I . . . a devil is laughing inside of me . . . I can't find myself anymore. I'm scattered and annihilated. My mind is empty. I'm a nothingness" (127).

imminent.[14] This is why, according to Raphael de la Torre's *De potestate Ecclesiae*, baths are extremely soothing for melancholics because water, gently caressing their "feverish" flesh, makes them sense their body as a familiar and unthreatening presence.[15] The unquestionable pain a melancholic feels derives from his paradoxical condition, in which he at once fears and longs for his own flesh. A melancholic senses that his flesh is an external and hostile presence against his identity, but he also feels that flesh is something he has lost forever.[16] For a melancholic, death is indeed the victory of flesh over the subject.

Given melancholy's inherent ambiguity, it is quite easy for the devil to possess a melancholic mind. What started as a case of "natural" melancholy may turn into a form of demonic possession. Weyer says that although not every melancholic is possessed by the devil, every possessed person is a melancholic. The devil can easily insinuate himself into the melancholic humor, whose matter is suited to his "abuses."[17] It is interesting to note that Weyer's term for "abuses" is *ludibria*, which usually describes an act of violence done to a woman, as if Weyer meant to underscore that the devil's infection involves the subject's mind and the perception of his own "flesh," as Husserl says. The devil "speaks" violence, we may say, into the obsessed person's body. In some hagiographies of medieval and Renaissance mystics, this merging of the physical and mental symptoms of an "unnatural" melancholy is often recounted as a two-act solo play, in which the woman mystic is first tormented with a sudden and inexplicable sadness, which later materializes itself into an actual devil assailing the woman (Weyer's *ludibria*) in a physical manner.

Scholastic theologians often characterize the first phase of this form of melancholy as "acedia," what Thomas Aquinas calls *tristitia de spirituali bono* ("sorrow about one's spiritual good").[18] The key elements of this

---

14. In Levinus Lemnius' *De miraculis occultis naturae* (Frankfurt: Hofmann, 1604), we find a rare expression of sorrow for those who suffer from melancholia (104). For the physician Lemnius, melancholics are not *daemoniaci* (140).

15. Raphael de la Torre, *De potestate Ecclesiae coercendi daemones circa obsessos*, in *Diversi Tractatus* (Cologne, 1629), 173.

16. According to Burton, "fear and sorrow are the true characters, and inseparable companions, of most melancholy" (*Anatomy of Melancholy*, part 1, sec. 1, member 3, subsec. 1, 149).

17. Weyer, *De praestigiis* (ed. Mora), chap. 7, 183–86. In this English translation *ludibria* is translated as "purposes." Compare Weyer, *De praestigiis* (Basle: Officina Operiniana, 1568), 425.

18. Compare Thomas Aquinas, *Summa* 2a2a–e. I find this reference to acedia in Martina Wagner-Egelhaaf, *Die Melancholie der Literatur* (Stuttgart: Verlag J. B. Metzler, 1997), 42. See

mental state are thus sadness and distance from the divinity.[19] In *De malo*, Thomas emphasizes that this lack of happiness and of faith in God is also related to how the subject suffering from acedia senses his flesh as an unbearable burden.[20] Acedia is a sorrowful thought, a grievous obsession both affecting and deriving from the body. The mystic Hildegard of Bingen links acedia to Adam's expulsion from the earthly paradise and thus to Satan's intervention in the human body.[21] When Adam ate the apple, Hildegard says, melancholy "curdled in his blood."[22] More specifically, Hildegard believes that at the time of man's fall the devil "blew" melancholy into Adam. By "blowing" melancholy she means that Satan succeeded in "explaining" to Adam his irredeemable failure.[23] In other words, although sadness can be the most visible sign of a natural and "healthy" process of self-awareness, at the same time it can be the first symptom of the invasion of a demonic reasoning.

This blending of normal and and abnormal acedia is documented in many hagiographies. As an example, after a period of gloomy thoughts, Benvenuta Bojanni (Civilidade of Friuli, 1255–92) was taken up in the air by a devil and then thrown on the floor. Respecting a fundamental rule of hagiography, Benvenuta finally responds to the devil's assaults: "[I]t happened that [the devil] took her and rose her up, and then with great violence he hurled her down . . . once . . . she stood up against him, grabbed him and pushed him down under her feet. Then, putting a foot on his neck, she scolded him with outraged words."[24] In *The Life of the Blessed Benvenutae Boianne* the devil ends up begging the mystic for mercy. The devil of melancholy has been unveiled and humiliated by the

---

also Noël Brann, "Alchemy and Melancholy in Medieval and Renaissance Thought: A Query into the Mystical Basis of Their Relationship," *Ambix* 32, no. 2 (1985): 127–48.

19. For a thorough analysis of acedia in Thomas Aquinas, see Siegfried Wenzel, *The Sin of Sloth: Acedia* (Chapel Hill: University of North Carolina Press, 1967), 47–67.

20. Thomas Aquinas, *De malo*, q. 11, a. 2.

21. Hildegard of Bingen dedicates an entire chapter to melancholia/acedia in her *Causae et curae* (French translation: *Les causes et les remèdes*, translated by Pierre Monat [Grenoble: Millon, 1997], 167).

22. Compare Klibansky, Panofsky, and Saxl, *Saturn and Melancholia*, 79. Compare Wagner-Egelhaaf, *Die Melancholie der Literatur*, 43.

23. Hildegard of Bingen, *Les causes et les remèdes*, 168. Siegfried Wenzel reminds us that, according to the fourth-century theologian Evagrius Ponticus, who holds a position of primary importance in the history of the deadly sins, acedia is an evil spirit. Evagrius speaks of the "demon of acedia" attacking monks during their spiritual retreats (*The Sin of Sloth: Acedia*, 12).

24. Giovanni Pozzi and Claudio Leonardi, eds, *Scrittrici mistiche italiane* (Genoa: Marietti, 1989), 189. I use my own translation from *Uttering the Word*, 122.

energetic woman. Instead of wrestling with the fallen angel, Teresa of Avila sprinkles holy water on her insidious melancholy.[25] In these narratives, the materialization of an unnatural melancholy identifies with "his," the devil's, defeat. The devil comes out of the woman's body when she succeeds in "coming out" of her devil of melancholy.

No hagiography recounts what thoughts had "done violence" to the mystic, either because the author wished to protect the reader from the same affliction or because the reader already knew what these internal images might say, or simply because what mattered was the description of the final victory over the Foe. In any case both demonology books and saint's lives fail to analyze the internal evolution of (a demonic) melancholy. Having a body "of clay," the melancholic subject withdraws from the scene of narrativity, because to be a "narrative flesh," so to speak, primarily means to be molded, deformed, and possibly destroyed by that very narrative. As a consequence, in order to protect itself, the melancholic flesh becomes a visible, but speechless, presence.

In the history of Western spirituality, we find only one detailed description of how a demonic discourse may unfold as a melancholy disturbance. This is *Probation*, a two-volume reportage on St. Maria Maddalena de' Pazzi's excruciating combat with the devils of melancholy, which spanned five long years, from 1585 to 1590. The relevance of *Probation* results also from de' Pazzi's unique mysticism, which revolves around the power and essence of language. In another context, I have defined this Florentine mystic of the late Renaissance as "the mystic of the Word," because she is convinced that the sole goal of her life is the articulation of the Word through her voice, that is, through oral language.[26] Her existence is a constant effort to give voice to the Word through complex and poignant monologues in which she reenacts the most significant moments of the Word's experience: his passion and death. For this mystic, the Word may become incarnate first and foremost in human oral discourse, in what we say and how we say it. If the most distressing aspect of a demonic melancholy is the ceaseless "melting" of the subject's flesh, the case of Maria Maddalena de' Pazzi clarifies the essential connection between physical decay and linguistic disarray, between disease and inability "to speak the Word's flesh" in the here and now of oral language. The most

25. Teresa of Avila, *The Life of Saint Teresa of Avila by Herself*, translated by J. M. Cohen (New York: Penguin Books, 1957), 223.

26. Maggi, *Uttering the Word*, 49.

disturbing element of the saint's melancholy (her probation) is indeed the obfuscation of her mystical discourse.

CATERINA DE' PAZZI, born on April 2, 1566, in Florence, took the name of Maria Maddalena when she became a nun. When she was still a child, the Jesuits introduced her to their meditation techniques and to some of their basic writings. At the age of eight she had already contemplated embracing the religious life, and she joined the convent of Santa Maria degli Angeli when she was sixteen (in August 1582), taking the veil the following year. She chose this convent because it was remote and rigorous, and because it gave her the opportunity to have communion more often than in other convents.[27] Very soon after entering the convent, Maria Maddalena had intense mystical experiences, which led her to a mysterious and almost fatal disease.[28] When she recovered from this illness, the young mystic started to have daily visions, during which she spoke to and with the Trinity, and in particular to Christ, whom she generally refers to as the Word.[29]

Her obsession with the Word is indeed the fundamental aspect of de' Pazzi's mysticism. God, Maria Maddalena holds, has asked her to utter his Word through her voice. Three short passages from *The Dialogues (I colloqui)* will elucidate this essential point:

> [Y]our idea, your might, your goodness, everything is a language in the Word's God . . . the Word proceeding from the Word communicates the Word to us and unites Him with us.

27. Maggi, *Uttering the Word*, 4–5. Other important studies on this Italian mystic are the following: Claudio Catena, *Santa Maria Maddalena de' Pazzi carmelitana: Orientamenti spirituali e ambiente in cui visse* (Rome: Institutum Carmelitanum, 1966); Catena, "Ambiente del monastero di S. Maria degli Angeli ai tempi di S. Maria Maddalena de' Pazzi," *Carmelus* 13 (1966): 21–96; Ermanno del S.S. Sacramento, "I manoscritti originali di Santa Maria Maddalena de' Pazzi," *Ephemerides carmeliticae* 7 (1956): 323–400; Bruno Secondin, *Santa Maria Maddalena de' Pazzi: Esperienza e dottrina* (Rome: Institutum Carmelitanum, 1974); Giovanni Pozzi, *Le parole dell'estasi* (Milan: Adelphi, 1988); Antonio Riccardi, "The Mystic Humanism of Maria Maddalena de' Pazzi," in *Creative Women in Medieval and Early Modern Italy*, edited by E. Ann Matter and John Coakley (Philadelphia: University of Pennsylvania Press, 1994), 212–36; Karen-edis Barzman, "Cultural Production, Religious Devotion, and Subjectivity in Early Modern Italy: The Case Study of Maria Maddalena de' Pazzi," *Annali d'italianistica* 13 (1995): 283–305; Armando Maggi, "Blood as Language in the Visions of Saint Maria Maddalena de' Pazzi," *Rivista di letterature moderne e comparate* 3 (1995): 219–35. Compare my recent translation: *Maria Maddalena de' Pazzi: Selected Revelations* (New York: Paulist Press, 2000).

28. Claudio Catena, "Le malattie di S. Maria Maddalena de' Pazzi," *Carmelus* 16 (1969): 70–141.

29. Maggi, *Uttering the Word*, 8.

[T]he voice of the creatures is nothing but a little sound that one hears, and then it vanishes. But the voice of Jesus is eternal, so that Truth is God's being and His voice.

I will belch forth, I mean, I will pronounce the good word, the good Word, my Jesus, since I hold you in my heart.[30]

Although the human voice is only "a little sound that one hears, and then it vanishes," it has the power to embody God in its utterances. It is through the human voice that God may manifest himself. The Florentine mystic's daily monologues to the Word are rehearsals of a forthcoming visitation. The Word, Maria Maddalena is convinced, may and will invade her voice with his being. Given her obsessive focus on orality, Maria Maddalena de' Pazzi despises writing, including any recording of her words. Her sisters in the convent of Santa Maria degli Angeli developed a complex method of transcription to preserve her oral discourses, so that their confessor could evaluate their theological soundness. When the mystic entered a rapture and started to speak to the Word, a group of nuns gathered around her. The first sister would transcribe the first section of the mystic's discourse. As soon as she made a pause, the second nun would take over, and so on. At the end of the vision, the sisters would put together their notes, edit them according to their understanding, and finally rewrite the whole thing in a manuscript that would be submitted to the priest.

The manuscripts of Maria Maddalena's visions were published for the first time in 1960. The titles of the volumes are: *The Forty Days* (*I quaranta giorni*, the mystic's visions from May 27 to July 4, 1584); *The Dialogues* (*I colloqui*, in two volumes, containing her raptures from Christmas 1584 to June 4, 1585; altogether fifty visions); *Revelations and Knowledge* (*Rivelatione e intelligentie*, the visions Maria Maddalena had interruptedly during eight days beginning June 8, 1585); *Probation* (*Probatione*, two volumes); and *Renovation of the Church* (*Renovatione della Chiesa*, a miscellany, including letters and prayers).

These seven volumes do not offer a unified style and structure. If in *The Forty Days* we still find a rather traditional hagiographic narration in the third person, in the second part of *The Dialogues* the transcribers report the mystic's words as direct speech. The nuns even try to reproduce the orality of the mystic's discourses. For instance, they decide to report her si-

---

30. My translation is based on the only edition of the mystic's visions: *Tutte le opere di Santa Maria Maddalena de' Pazzi dai manoscritti originali* (Florence: Nardini, 1960–66). *The Dialogues* is divided into two books. The three quotations given here come from the first volume: 1:345; 1:172–73; 1:152.

lences, repetitions, and exclamations. One of the most powerful and moving sections of *The Dialogues* is vision 44, in which the mystic learns that the Word is about to withdraw from their daily conversations: Maria Maddalena's utterances are about to lose their addressee. If up to that moment her mysticism had been the attempt to turn a human "language of words" into a divine "language of things"—that is, if she had believed in the possibility of embodying the Word in the physicality of verbal expression— in vision 44 Maria Maddalena understands that from now on her daily monologues will be directed to no one. Speaking to no one, her verbal expressions will be nothing but solipsistic manifestations of sorrow.

The abandonment of the Word is the theme of vision 48, one of the last visions of *The Dialogues*. In this rapture, which lasted for more than forty hours (from Friday, May 17, to Sunday, May 19, 1585) and takes up more than eighty pages of the edited manuscript, Maria Maddalena experiences the moments following the death of the Word on the cross. As soon as she enters this rapture, the mystic walks to the choir of the chapel, which she sees as the place where the Word has been buried. She kneels down, indicating that now she finds herself in His sepulcher. She lies next to His corpse. Overwhelmed by sorrow, Maria Maddalena says:

> I won't be able to say anymore "Exultate filie Sion," but rather "plorate." One can now really say that the virgins have gone pale, and their faces have grown wan. And your ministers cry, because you, the highest minister, not only do you cry but you are dead and buried. And I, a virgin, have gone pale, since you don't gaze at my face any longer [*silence*] I was boastful and I believed that the virgins would follow me and could boast of having an immortal groom, but now I see you buried.

Mourning the loss of her Bridegroom the Word, Maria Maddalena is visited by a swarm of bad angels, like vultures flying around their prey. The mystic stands up and makes the gestures of grabbing these spirits and hurling them down to hell: "Go [*silence*] howl, scream as much as you want [*silence*] et sublimavit humanitatis nostre through their confusion[31] [*silence*] Non cognoscetur amplius."[32] When the subject loses her interlocutor, the "speakers of the mind" rush to articulate their idiom. How this linguistic substitution takes place is clearly explained in de' Pazzi's *Probation*. While the Word listened to the mystic even if He did not respond to her request for linguistic incarnation, the devils speak to and in the subject's mind without engaging in any interaction with their addressee, the

31. Read: "and elevated our humanity through their confusion."
32. "Nothing deeper will be known."

subject herself. We must remember that the speakers of the mind do speak, but do not have a language because, as Prierio has explained, they do not have memory. Since they say without actually saying anything, devils prevent the mind from reflecting on its own utterances—that is, they do not allow the mind to react to its own expressions. Like the *maleficiatus'* body of clay, the mind visited by its speakers is at the mercy of any possible (verbal) aggression. In vision 44 of *The Dialogues* the transcribers report the mystic's sudden realization of having been deprived of the Word:

> ["O]h holy archangel, please be close to me [*silence*] oh, the angelic spirit, when he became a devil, did he turn his purity into malice? [*silence*] magnificate Dominum mecum, et exaltamus nomen eius in idipsum."[33]
>
> And after these words, all of a sudden she became very upset, showing that she was seeing the devil. Thus, raising her voice she said: "Oh, oh, here he is [*silence*] et probavit me cum inimicum suum[34] [*silence*] fortitudo mea, and laus mea Dominus."[35]
>
> And stretching her hands on the altar, she said in a very anguished way: "Oh Word, oh Word! [*silence*] in te Domine speravi, non confundar in aeternum."[36] And giving a deep sigh, she turned to the devil and said:
>
> "And what do you want from me anyway? [*silence*] oh good Jesus!"[37]

"What do you want from me anyway?" is the question that synthesizes the mystic's experience of demonic possession. Like the Lacanian "Che vuoi?" that the subject directs to the Other, Maria Maddalena's inquiry has no answer.[38] Similar to the Lacanian Other, the speakers of the mind compel the mystic to focus on their demanding, though unuttered, discourse. It is indeed revealing that the mystic opens her question with a sigh ("And giving a deep sigh, she turned to the devil and said"). We have seen that, according to the *Thesaurus exorcismorum*, a sigh, a breath, emitted from one of the possessed person's orifices, reveals a demonic presence in the moment of its disappearance. Similarly, in this passage from *The Dialogues*, the mystic "sighs the Word away," so to speak, and "turns to the devil." A sigh tells of a sudden and melancholic isolation—the possessed bereft of his demons or the Florentine mystic abandoned by her Word.

33. Ps. 33:4: "Proclaim with me the greatness of God, and together let us extoll his name."

34. "And he tested me through his enemy."

35. Ps. 117:14: "My strength and my song, God."

36. Compare Ps. 30:2, 70:1: "In you, O Lord, I have taken refuge; let me never be put to shame."

37. *Maria Maddalena de' Pazzi: Selected Revelations* (trans. Maggi), 162.

38. Compare Jacques Lacan, *Écrits*, translated by Alan Sheridan (New York: W. W. Norton, 1977), 317.

Mentre ed ella è affinata nell'orazione da'Demoni vien dibattuta ed agitata con vrei e conpercosse con fierezza tale ede ne resta maleneia edenfiata notabilmte

Maria Maddalena de' Pazzi being attacked by devils; print by F. Curradi (1570–1661). (Courtesy of Istituto Germanico di Storia dell'Arte, Florence)

A sigh also marks the first page of *Probation*. Sister Maria Pacifica del Tovaglia, the nun elected to transcribe Maria Maddalena's words, reports that on June 16, 1585, the feast of the Holy Trinity, the "blessed soul" was rapt in spirit for many hours. When she came out of her ecstasy, she shook intensely and gave a very deep sigh (*Probation*, 1:31). As the transcriber explains, "she did so [sighed] because of the intense pain her soul felt when her Spouse the Word deprived her of the perception and the experience of His grace" (1:31–32). This sigh is also all we have of the first two years of the mystic's demonic melancholy, for she herself destroyed every record of her ordeal: "She happened to find those notebooks where we had written everything that had occurred during the first and most of the second year of her probation. When she realized that those notebooks concerned her, without even reading them through, she threw them into the fire and burned them." As the exorcist burns the name and the portrait of a possession (**N**) over the candle that **N**'s breath itself will eventually extinguish, so does Maria Maddalena's sigh signify the beginning of her melancholy (the withdrawal of the Word) and the silence ensuing from that melancholy (the act of throwing the transcriptions into the fire). Given this primary erasure, the scribe says, it is impossible to offer a faithful chronology of the mystic's probation. What she said and what she did during those first two years is lost. "Who reads the beginning of this book," the scribe writes, "should not be surprised if things are not narrated in a systematic manner." At the beginning of the book is the disorder of melancholy. What the transcriber does know is that from the outset "she [the blessed soul] heard with her ears the horrible screams, howls, and curses that the devils, and sometimes also the creatures, uttered to offend God. And sometimes these screams invaded her hearing to the point that she had difficulty in understanding us when we spoke to her" (1:33). As the body in pain passively registers the symptoms of a foreign presence within itself, the mystic's mind shuts off the external world and focuses on its own utterances, which exclusively express the mind's delirious resentment against itself. Sometimes, while she is in the chapel trying to praise the Lord along with her sisters, the devils start to recite blasphemous words in her ears, to the point that the mystic is unable to distinguish who is saying what (1:153). Her mind, Maria Maddalena herself says, is much louder than the chorus of her sisters praying with her.

It is essential to understand the exact meaning of the mind's sudden and deafening language. As I have pointed out in chapter 3, in the analysis of Visconti's exorcism, possession exposes existence as a paradox. The obsessed perceives his or her own presence as a symptom, as an opposing and dissenting "something" that prevents the subject from being him or herself.[39] It is, however, in that hostile "something" that the subject resides and exists. In a possession, identity reveals itself as the "place of negativity," as Giorgio Agamben defines Heidegger's concept of self.[40] This "place" is where the subject at once encounters itself and "falls out" of itself. According to the scribe of *Probation*, once her mind lost its bearings, the mystic literally stumbled and fell: "[T]hey [the devils] often pushed her down the stairs, made her fall down; and other times, like venomous vipers, they wrapped around her flesh biting her with a great cruelty. . . . Sometimes her sufferings kept her up until the 4th or the 5th hour in the morning" (1:33–34). Maria Maddalena's fall becomes the visible sign of her diabolical oppression: "[W]hen she was going to the choir for the mass, for Communion, or to similar places, almost always he [the devil] made her fall down the stairs" (1:115). In her repeated falls, the young mystic felt as if "she were falling apart inside, and outside as if her members were severed. And after these incidents she felt so drained and exhausted, that for quite a while she could neither move nor be fully alert." After one particularly severe attack at the beginning of her probation (July 12, 1585), Maria Maddalena turns to the sisters who have been taking care of her and says: "I tell you, I'm dying, I'm drowning. Help me! Don't you believe me?" (1:72).[41] The devils are "drowning" the young mystic in their vociferous images. Indeed, devils are enormous beasts rushing to devour her (1:73). Maria Maddalena yells back and tries to hide somewhere in her room. Her face is swollen. She feels as if she is about to suffocate. Trying to alleviate her despair, her sisters make the sign of the cross with relics. Another case of diabolical attack occurs a few months later in the chapel itself. While she is praying with her sisters, Maria Maddalena spots a horde of devils ready to invade that sacred place. In this case, instead of being overwhelmed by fear, the mystic grabs a crucifix and sways it like a big sword before the devils to discourage them from entering the chapel (1:179).

Asked to explain what she sees and feels during these ferocious attacks, the mystic states that "she does not [always see the devil with her corporeal eyes], although she always sees him with the sight of her mind with

39. Compare de Certeau, *The Possession at Loudun,* translated by Michael Smith (Chicago: University of Chicago Press, 2000), 46.

40. Giorgio Agamben, *Language and Death* (Minneapolis: University of minnesota Press, 1991), 1–5.

41. The mystic repeats a similar sentence two years later, on September 17, 1587: "I tell you that I am finishing and dying, but you don't believe me" (1:115).

DEVILS PUSH MARIA MADDALENA DOWN THE STAIRS AND TORMENT
HER BODY; PRINT BY F. CURRADI. (COURTESY OF ISTITUTO
GERMANICO DI STORIA DELL'ARTE, FLORENCE)

Crouandosi in loro à salmeggiare vede gran drappello di Demoni intorno all'vscio
di quelle, che stauan per entrar dentro, e già vno entrato tentaua le Suore. Ella
però tolta in mano vna Croce tutti li mette in fuga.

MARIA MADDALENA FIGHTS OFF THE DEVILS WHO ARE TRYING TO
INVADE THE CHAPEL; PRINT BY F. CURRADI. (COURTESY OF ISTITUTO
GERMANICO DI STORIA DELL'ARTE, FLORENCE)

no respite, as when (like a similitude) a creature sees something with her physical sight, and then that something stays in her mind so clearly that, even if she does not see it concretely, she has the impression that she always sees it. Her vision of the devil is so frequent, that he never departs from her eyes" (1:73–74). What "stays in the mind" and constantly shows itself to the intellect's internal sight is memory.[42] Memory rules over the melancholic's mind and blurs the distinction between external images and internal recollections of the primal trauma of possession. Memory, we may infer, is the sigh Maria Maddalena gave at the moment of the Word's departure from her. As the mystic explains to her sisters in a later passage, "when you direct your sight to a wall, what you actually see is not the wall itself, but rather the image of the wall that is already in your intellect" (1:210).

According to Maria Maddalena, the remembrances stored in our mind not only influence the way we perceive reality (the wall we remember versus the wall we see now), but are more present than reality itself.[43] Time past is paradoxically more present than time present. Time present is the actualization of the eternal presence of the past. Possession, and the subsequent split within the self, is indeed an act of memory. As Maria Maddalena emphasizes, in the case of a demonic melancholy the subject perceives the presence of memory even when memory does not visit the intellect ("even if she does not see it concretely, she has the impression that she always sees it"). Like the speakers of the mind, memory does not need to articulate any idiom (to summon images in the intellect) in order to make the melancholic sense its presence.

The unyielding persecution of memory, the transcriber writes, is a form of "exile": "No one could either describe this soul's exile and pains or communicate them, unless one sees her with his own eyes. I believe, though, that at least one can say—and I am totally sure about it—that her inner suffering and probation, similar to that which the Lord deigns to grant certain chosen creatures (like this blessed soul), can be only perceived by those who experience them" (1:156–57).[44] The only thing the

---

42. Compare de Certeau, *The Possession at Loudun*, 40–41.

43. In *Beiträge zu einer Kritik der Sprache* (Hildesheim, 1969), Fritz Mauthner holds that every linguistic sign is a "memory sign" *(Gedächtniszeichen)*, in that every sign necessarily embodies the speaker's remembrances connected with that specific word or expression (185–90).

44. As Czeslaw Milosz writes: "Despair [is] inseparable from the first stage of exile. . . . Exile is morally suspect because it breaks one's solidarity with a group, i.e., it sets apart an individual from the rest of his colleagues" ("Notes on Exile," in *Altogether Elsewhere: Writers on Exile*, edited by Marc Robinson [New York: Harcourt Brace, 1994], 37–38).

transcriber is able to say is that Maria Maddalena looks like someone "itinerant" in the two senses suggested by the Italian *in transito*, which refers both to a traveler and to someone who is about to pass away (1:154). She rolls her eyes, twists her mouth, shakes her arms, and all of a sudden lies completely still for a while. It looks as though her body is being undone from inside, as if it were devouring itself. Little worms *(vermini)* are eating her flesh (1:140).

Her being "itinerant" is also reflected in the way she envisions the path of her life. First of all, she feels "tempted by the devil with a great temptation of despair. He ma[kes] her believe that she [will] not be saved" (1:133). "She ha[s] the impression," the scribe continues, "that whatever she [does], both externally and internally, [will] deepen her damnation" (1:140). The mystic goes so far as to contemplate the idea of abandoning the convent and the religious life (1:124). Her daily practices and private challenges, such as walking barefoot and wearing only a gown throughout the year, have become senseless and even questionable.[45] In a vision that she immediately reports to her Mother Superior, Maria Maddalena sees two nuns, one dressed in white and the other in black, who "told her that God did not like her life style and was rather offended by her behavior, and that if she did not change it she would lose God's favor" (1:117). Satan goes so far as to appear to her as the Father, the Son, and the Holy Ghost, and as his blessed spirits (1:120).[46]

In a crucial passage of *Probation*, the young mystic asks first the Word and then herself why she can have no rest at all: "But, my dear Spouse, I'd like to know what prevents . . . this delicate bride of yours from finding any rest. I will say it to you, my soul, because I can't make anyone else understand it. . . . It is because of all the words which are pronounced neither to praise God nor to support one's neighbor" (1:98). What the mystic is undergoing is a linguistic exile. Her melancholy is linked to her realization that her voice fails to be what it was meant to be; that is, her words should

45. The scribe gives a short summary of Maria Maddalena's five-year melancholia, at the end of the second volume of *Probation* (2:229–31). The transcriber explains that on May 25, 1585, the mystic had started to feed only on bread and water and to walk barefoot.

46. Other women mystics experience a similar temptation. For instance, Caterina Viegri (1413–63) sees a crucified Jesus, who scolds her because she refuses to abide by her mother superior's orders. However, Caterina knows that she is right in defying her mother superior's decisions. In his reproach, the devil stresses humility and obedience, cardinal points of the religious life. Caterina understands that this Christ is an impostor by the way he expresses himself. This Jesus uses very violent and offensive language. Caterina replies as follows: "My Lord, what can I do? My heart is not free and I can't prevent thoughts from coming up in my mind" (Pozzi and Leonardi, *Scrittrici mistiche italiane*, 266–67).

be, but are not, a perpetual hymn to the Word, an incessant attempt to give birth to the "true word" in the physicality of her voice. I have already stressed the mystic's obsession with oral expression. Maria Maddalena's "exile," as the scribe defines her melancholy, is primarily a linguistic occurrence. We know that, according to Augustine and Thomas Aquinas, angelic beings do not have a language because they do not have memory. However, in Maria Maddalena's melancholy, memory itself paradoxically denies expression by invading the subject's mind. It is indeed a surplus of memory that makes the mystic into a speechless and deaf melancholic, similar to the young man possessed by a mute and deaf devil in Luke (9:37–43) and Mark (9).

The strict connection between remembrance and melancholy is a common trait of medieval and Renaissance theories on natural and artificial memory. As is well known, according to the humoral tradition that goes back to the fifth and fourth centuries B.C., melancholy was related to an excess of black bile, which was visualized as "viscous in nature and associated with the qualities of coldness and dryness." [47] Both the Aristotelian and Platonic schools thought that an excess of black bile also amplified the subject's poetic, rhetorical, and prophetic skills. [48] In particular, given its dry and cold nature, melancholy was supposed both to produce and to retain vivid memories. This aspect of melancholy became particularly relevant in medieval treatises that, stemming from the classical *Ad Herennium* and Cicero's *De oratore*, investigated the correlation between memory and speech. [49] According to classical rhetoric, in order to express himself fluently and accu-

---

47. Stanley W. Jackson, *Melancholia and Depression: From Hippocratic Times to Modern Times* (New Haven: Yale University Press, 1986), 31.

48. Compare Plato, *Phaedrus*, 244A–B, 245A, in *The Dialogues of Plato*, translated by B. Jowett, 2 vols. (New York: Random House, 1937), 1:248–50; Aristotle, *Problems*, 953a, 10, book 30, 1 ("Why is it that all those who have become eminent in philosophy or politics or poetry or the arts are clearly of an atrabilious temperament, and some of them to such an extent as to be affected by diseases caused by black bile . . . ?"), in *Complete Works* (ed. Barnes), 2:1498–99. Aristotle sees a fundamental connection between wine (especially red wine) and black bile, since both "are full of breath" (955a, 35, 1502). According to Aristotle, "sexual desire is due to the presence of breath, as is shown by the fact that the penis quickly increases from a small to a large size by inflation" (953b, 30, 1500). When black bile is overheated and reaches "the region of the intellect," it can bring about "frenzy and possession; and this is the origin of Sybils and soothsayers and all inspired persons" (954a, 30–35, 1501).

49. In *De memoria et reminiscentia*, a central text of this tradition, Thomas Aquinas himself upholds this theory. He believes that melancholics, given their "dry" nature, are more prone to retaining violent impressions. See Thomas Aquinas, *De memoria et reminiscentia*, in *Aristotelis libros de sensu et sensato, de memoria et reminiscentia commentarium*, edited by Raimondo Spiazzi (Turin: Marietti, 1949), lectio 8, chap. 403, 114.

rately, an orator was supposed to associate each section, each sentence, and even each word of his discourse to a specific area *(locus)* of a well-structured, albeit imaginary, place, such as a "house, an intercolumnar space, a recess, an arch."[50] The speaker would talk as if he were walking through a mental field. As we shall see later, in a critical stage of her melancholy Maria Maddalena de' Pazzi decides to walk around the kitchen garden of her convent, which in her mind has turned into purgatory, in order to retrieve and to speak (to) the memory of her deceased brother.

Melancholy's uncanny power of remembrance is discussed in Albertus Magnus' commentary on Aristotle's *De memoria and reminiscentia*.[51] In his attempt to distinguish between passive memory *(memoria)* and the active process of reminiscence *(reminiscentia)*, Albertus discusses two different forms of melancholy. While traditional melancholy is based on a dry and cold humor, a second form of melancholy *(melancholia fumosa)* may result from a dry and hot bile.[52] As Frances Yates explains in *The Art of Memory*, Albertus believes that this second kind of humor is responsible for "the intellectual, inspired melancholy."[53] Inspired melancholics can actively embark on a journey through memory. According to Albertus, it is undeniable that this form of melancholy also triggers a dramatic outpouring of verbal expression, which abounds with detailed memories.[54]

As I have noted, an excess of memory has made Maria Maddalena into a deaf and mute melancholic. The mystic becomes mute when she realizes that she repeatedly fails "to embody" the Word in her spoken language. As the transcriber emphasizes, the mystic is also deaf, in that she is often unable to hear what her sisters say because of the devils screaming in her ears. Devils, Maria Maddalena sees in a subsequent vision, "have certain notebooks" *(scartafacci)* in which they mark down what they have uttered in the mind; that is, they want to remember what they "have gained" (1:236).[55]

---

50. *Ad C. Herennium*, translated by Harry Caplan (Cambridge, Mass.: Harvard University Press, 1989), xvi, 29–30, 209. Compare Frances Yates, *The Art of Memory* (Chicago: University of Chicago Press, 1966), 1–26.

51. Compare Luciana de Bernart, *Immaginazione e scienza in Giordano Bruno* (Pisa: ETS Editrice, 1986), 16–17.

52. Albertus Magnus, *De memoria et reminiscentia*, in *Opera omnia*, edited by Auguste Borgnet, vol. 9 (Paris: Ludovicus Vives, 1890), part 2, chap. 7, 117.

53. Yates, *Art of Memory*, 69.

54. Albertus Magnus, *De memoria et reminiscentia*, 118.

55. In vision 39 of *The Dialogues*, the mystic sees an angel writing down the novice's words while she is taking the veil. The angel's notes will be used in favor of or against the novice at the moment of her death (*Selected Revelations* [trans. Maggi], 124–25).

The howls and screams in the mind are perverted signs. Although their phonemes mean nothing, they trigger fear and remorse in the subject's mind. The devils' screams are in fact the most eloquent signs of memory, for they summon the presence of memory without phrasing any particular remembrance. The mind affected by the devil of melancholy cannot help but perceive memory as a deafening scream.

We have said that the sudden invasion of memory makes the melancholic realize that time present is nothing but the unremitting persecution of time past. Obviously, suicide visits the mind as the most reassuring solution. But suicide itself is a form of active presence, for the melancholic must actively seek her end. More frequently, the melancholic commits a kind of mental self-murder. Still alive, the melancholic withdraws from her mind as the place infected by the plague of memory. The melancholic exists outside of her mind, since "mind" is where time present unleashes the persecution of remembrance.

In this form of mental suicide, the melancholic does not inhabit her mind any longer. The subject is "somewhere else." Facing no opposition, memory can finally conquer the mind and speak its being. In Maria Maddalena de' Pazzi's demonic melancholy, memory speaks the language of purgatory. The whole *Probation* is a meditation on the status and meaning of purgation and purgatory, as the place where the devils' screams finally acquire a syntactical meaning and convey a message.

Maria Maddalena's first encounter with purgatory occurs on June 14, 1585. Still suffering from the devils' physical and linguistic persecution, the mystic goes to the chapel to pray for the soul of her brother, who had passed away that very morning (1:41–42). She realizes that the pain she is still feeling reflects her brother's sufferings in purgatory, where he finds himself since the moment of his death. Brother and sister share the same agony. Thanks to her brother, Maria Maddalena is able to locate her distress, to see and narrate her anguish. His death and purgation are in fact hers. If an excess of memory had silenced her mind—that is, had deprived her suffering of any meaning—the young visionary now gives her distress a new name and a new, though "familiar," past. Maria Maddalena's is unlike most other religious and hagiographic narratives of journeys to purgatory. She is neither led to a particular place connecting this world to the nether regions of purgatory (as in the seminal *Saint Patrick's Purgatory*), nor visited by a soul in a series of haunting dreams (as in the fifteenth-century English prose *Revelation of Purgatory*), nor approached by an invisible but moaning ghost (as in the case of a French nun at the end of the nineteenth century).[56] We must bear in mind that, according to Peter Dinzelbacher's topological analysis of medieval mystical literature, Maria Maddalena's visions are exclusively "word revelations" *(Wortoffenbarungen)*—that is, her raptures are linguistic communications taking place in the visionary's mind.[57] As will become apparent, the mystic's healing coincides with the acquisition of a renewed, purified voice, a linguistic expression cleansed of the plague of memory. Maria Maddalena replies to her deceased brother as follows: "Oh, they're [the pains are] great, but not unbearable [*silence*] and I thought you didn't have them anymore [*silence*] oh, who has ever fathomed them! [*silence*] please, don't come too close to me [*silence*] when you were down here, you didn't want to listen to me and now you'd like me to listen to you? [*silence*] you, poor thing, what can I do for you?" (1:42). The mystic's brother asks her to respond to his pain. It is through his pain that Maria Maddalena's melancholy retrieves the faculty of language. The dialogue between the brother in purgatory and the sister afflicted by melancholy focuses on the theme of penance and the intrinsic empathy between the living and the dead, between suffering and enlightenment, between suffering and (linguistic) expression, according to the dogma of purgatory established by the Council of Trent only a few years before.[58]

56. According to the monk "H" who lived in the Cistercian monastery of Saltrey in the twelfth century, Patrick was shown a hole, which was a gate to purgatory itself. The monk also recounts the pilgrimage of the knight Owein, who literally walked down through purgatory (Jacques Le Goff, *The Birth of Purgatory*, translated by Arthur Goldhammer [Chicago: University of Chicago Press, 1984], 193–98). In *A Revelation of Purgatory by an Unknown, Fifteenth-Century Woman Visionary: Introduction, Critical Text, and Translation*, edited by Marta Powell Harley (Lewiston, Me.: Edwin Mellen Press, 1985), a nun describes to her father superior the dreams she had on the night of St. Lawrence's Day in 1422: "I went to bed at eight o'clock and fell asleep. And father, between nine and ten it seemed I was seized and carried into purgatory" (112). More similar to Maria Maddalena's experience is the experience of the French nun, Sister M., who in November 1873 perceived suddenly, very close to her, sounds of prolonged groaning. The text is constructed as a dialogue between the nun and the spirit who has been allowed to leave purgatory and follow the nun everywhere (*The Purgatory Manuscript: Le manuscrit du purgatoire*, translated by Alun Idris Jones [Lewiston, Me.: Edwin Mellen Press, 1990], 11).
57. Peter Dinzelbacher, *Vision und Visionsliteratur im Mittelalter* (Stuttgart: Anton Hiersemann, 1981), 163–64.
58. Compare Le Goff, *Birth of Purgatory*, 357–58; Michel Vovelle, *Les âmes du purgatoire* (Paris: Gallimard, 1996), 112–13; Caroline Walker Bynum, *The Resurrection of the Body* (New York: Columbia University Press, 1995), 280–83. As Le Goff notes, Innocent IV gave the first pontifical definition of purgatory in 1254 in a letter to his delegate in Cyprus (*Birth of Purgatory*, 283). Innocent IV states that "in th[e] temporary fire [of purgatory], sins, not of course crimes and capital errors, which could not previously have been forgiven through penance, but

The language of the melancholic Florentine mystic at once springs from a request ("now you'd like me to listen to you?") and results in one ("what can I do for you?"). Similarly, we know that for Maria Maddalena the speakers of the mind as well express a demand ("What do you want from me anyway?" [vision 44 in *The Dialogues*]). It is the Other that either subtracts (speakers of the mind) or grants (the mystic's brother) a language. The territory of these antithetical exchanges is purgatory. Purgatory is where silence and speech, physical presence and mental representation, oblivion and memory, temporality and eternity at once exclude each other and merge with each other. In Jacques Le Goff's words, purgatory is "an annex of the earth and extend[s] the time of life and memory." [59] However, as Richard K. Fenn stresses in his brilliant work, *The Persistence of Purgatory*, "the boundary between this world and the next, between the living and the dead, is as vague in purgatory as is the boundary between dream-states and waking consciousness . . . [I]t is not unusual for 'normal' individuals to be caught up in the same dream-states as Dante's figures in purgatory: caught between despair that they will never see again those from whom they have parted and dread of a final departure filled with the pains of death." [60]

Purgatory plays out the vague and torturous essence of memory. For the Florentine mystic, to be visited by a memory (the beloved brother) means to *be reminded* that being (the Word) has not been uttered yet, that life is the "persistence" of a longing. Indeed, we help a soul in purgatory through his or her journey toward the oblivion of heaven by assuming the burden of remembrance. Our responding to the other's request for memory (memorials, masses, prayers) means that his or her sudden visitation from purgatory has shown us our own "persistent" oblivion. A suffrage to a soul in purgatory is a tribute to our own absence, which has been re-

slightly minor sins, are purged" (*Birth of Purgatory*, 284). Obviously, in this analysis of de' Pazzi's visions, we exclusively refer to the concept of purgatory of the Counter-Reformation.

59. Le Goff, *Birth of Purgatory*, 233. In *Église, culture et société. Essai sur Réforme et Contre-réforme* (Paris: Société d'Édition d'Enseignement Supérieur, 1981), Pierre Chaunu examines how the Council of Trent theorizes the connection between the cult of purgatory and the Eucharist, which is of fundamental importance for Maria Maddalena de' Pazzi. Let us remember that she had chosen the convent of Santa Maria degli Angeli because there she could have daily access to this sacrament. As Chaunu explains, "if eternity is not perceived as . . . the negation and the transcendence of time any longer . . . , it is necessary to constantly reenact Christ's unique and perfect sacrifice. A strict link thus exists between Mass and the conception of transcendence invaded by duration" (378).

60. Richard K. Fenn, *The Persistence of Purgatory* (Cambridge: Cambridge University Press, 1995), 55.

vealed to us by the soul's visitation from purgatory.[61] Paradoxically, in some regions of southern Italy still today there are people who go to the souls in purgatory for assistance and guidance. In Naples, for instance, crypts, cemeteries, and catacombs underneath or connected to some churches are dedicated to this cult. People even know the names and biographies of the souls inhabiting each given space.[62]

The nuns witnessing the "dialogue" between the two siblings notice that Maria Maddalena is now counting with her fingers. Her brother has just asked her to have communion 107 times in his name: "I can do it every morning [*silence*] oh, dear, it'll take so long to erase it! But I would be blessed if I came there where you are. Oh, if all the creatures could avoid going down there! They would be blessed! [*silence*] I was right when I hoped you would get out of your miseries" (1:43). A repeated and ritualized act of remembrance (to take communion 107 times) aims to hasten the erasure of memory. Maria Maddalena expressly states that it will take a long time "to erase it." Both siblings are in fact persecuted by the devil of memory. If the mystic's mind has been "numbed," "dried up" by the devil through an excess of memory (1:121), her brother is tormented by a memory that is an incessant looking back on an unalterable past.[63] As Catherine of Genoa (1447–1510) writes in *Purgation and Purgatory*, a fundamental collection of teachings on the theme of spiritual purgation, the "only suffering [of a soul in purgatory] lies in what holds [her] back."[64]

61. Compare Fenn, *Persistence of Purgatory*, 22.

62. I refer to the fascinating study conducted by Patrizia Ciambelli in *Quelle figlie quelle spose. Il culto delle Anime Purganti a Napoli* (Rome: De Luca, 1980). In the introduction to *Antropologia delle anime in pena* (Lecce: Argo, 1997), Stefano de Matteis and Marino Niola explain that the Neapolitan cult of the souls in purgatory is based on a central complementarity: "The souls in purgatory and their devoted visitors share a common liminality. . . . Like the beggars in the seventeenth century, indigent people establish a contact with the purgatorial souls, whom they identify with the anonymous skulls scattered and exposed in several sacred places of the old city" (15). On the bonds between the living and the dead, see Le Goff, *Birth of Purgatory*, 293–94.

63. Teresa of Avila recounts a similar experience: "I forgot all the favours that the Lord had bestowed on me; all that was left was a memory, as of something in a dream, and this greatly distressed me" (*Life of Saint Teresa of Avila by Herself* [trans. Cohen], 215).

64. Catherine of Genoa, *Purgation and Purgatory: The Spiritual Dialogue*, translated by Serge Hughes (New York: Paulist Press, 1979), 74. We do not know whether or not Maria Maddalena de' Pazzi was familiar with this text. The only authors directly quoted in the biographies of the Florentine mystic are Catherine of Siena, Augustine, and Gaspar Loarte, a Spanish Jesuit who wrote several meditation manuals in Italian. Loarte's *Instrutione et avertimenti per meditare la passione di Cristo nostro Redentore, con alcune meditationi intorno ad esse* (Rome, 1571) was Maria Maddalena's very first reading.

We may infer that both siblings suffer from a vehement form of melancholy, to which they respond through an act of exchange, or better yet, of displacement. Maria Maddalena's brother needs her to activate his remembrance—that is, to reinsert his memory in the flow of time. In other words, the mystic's brother needs to be forgotten once and for all. For this to happen, he needs for his sister to visit the place of his melancholy and "to live it through." Conversely, given that the speakers of the mind have numbed the mystic with an excessive memory, the brother lends his sister the language of his own melancholy. To save herself and her brother, Maria Maddalena becomes the enactment of his memory.[65]

To clarify the intricate act of substitution between the young mystic and her brother, let us read a short passage from Catherine of Siena's *Dialogue*. Writing as if God had dictated these words to her, Catherine states: "And if you turn to purgatory, there you will find my gentle immeasurable providence toward those poor souls who foolishly wasted their time. Now, because they are separated from their bodies, they no longer have time in which to merit. Therefore I have provided that you who are still in mortal life should have time for them."[66] As Catherine explains, time is strictly connected with human physicality. The souls in purgatory have no time to modify their past because they "are separated from their bodies." Salvation lies in our flesh. Maria Maddalena knows that devils have a notebook in which they transcribe what they have gained (1:236); only the body is able to correct or even cancel the devils' written statements. This is why, in order to regain her own memory, which for the mystic is identified with an unyielding longing for the Word, Maria Maddalena must visit purgatory. Like the pilgrim Dante, Maria Maddalena de' Pazzi enters the realm of purgatory to interpret her (brother's) past.[67]

65. Following Maria Maddalena de' Pazzi, other Italian mystics experience a similar "purgatorial" substitution. The most eloquent case is St. Veronica Giuliani (1660–1727), who visited purgatory repeatedly in response to the souls' request for help. Veronica detailed her purgatorial journeys in her diary. I study Veronica Giuliani's view of de' Pazzi's "exchange" in "When the O. Moves in the Heart: The Annunciation of the End in the *Journal* of Saint Veronica Giuliani," *Annali d'italianistica* (forthcoming).

66. Catherine of Siena, *The Dialogue*, translated by Suzanne Noffke, O.P. (New York: Paulist Press, 1980), 313.

67. In his fascinating study of time in the *Purgatorio* ("Dall'antipurgatorio al paradiso terrestre: Il tempo ritrovato di Dante," *Letture classensi* 18 [1989]: 64–78), Franco Fido writes that "every friend, every colleague poet he [Dante] meets in purgatory . . . is a sort of 'double'" in that he offers the pilgrim Dante a chance to reflect (on) his own past (72). Compare Carlo Ossola, "'Coi piè ristretti e con gli occhi passai'. Sospensione e compimento del tempo nel *Purgatorio*," in *L'arte dell'interpretare* (Cuneo: L'Arciere, 1984), 45–66; Rudolf Palgen, *L'origine del "Purgatorio"* (Graz: Verlag Styria, 1967), 6–8.

The day following her first encounter with her brother (June 15), Maria Maddalena is granted a full perception of the "atrocious suffering" of purgatory (1:46). Indeed, purgatory is first and foremost its unfathomable and unique despair, at once a frantic longing for the past and a burning desire for annihilation.[68] Overwhelmed by the sudden perception of purgatory, Maria Maddalena bursts into scalding tears while she is in the workroom with her sisters. Rapt in spirit again in the middle of the night, the mystic sees that, thanks to her insight, her brother feels somehow alleviated, as if "she saw him in a fire and she pulled him up without being able to take him out of it" (1:47). The mystic understands that, to help her brother, she must visit purgatory without further delay: "I don't care, but since you want to, I'll go around the whole place. But who will come with me? [*silence*] my guardian angel, right?" (1:48).

After leaving her cell, Maria Maddalena rushes down the stairs to the kitchen garden. It is one o'clock in the morning. According to the transcriber of *Probation*, for more than two hours she walks around the garden, which for her has turned into the space of purgatory, stopping from time to time to observe the single souls who inhabit it. At the beginning of her journey, the mystic shivers and claps her hands. Looking very pale and troubled, she walks bent over, "as when one feels an immense fear." Like Dante, in visiting the circles of purgatory Maria Maddalena de' Pazzi pauses and then moves on, showing both terror and pity. Indeed, as she herself clarifies to her sisters after this rapture, the mystic's suffering results from her compassion for the souls.

It is not my intention to assess whether the Florentine visionary had any direct knowledge of Dante's *Purgatorio*. It is difficult to imagine that, as a member of the noble Florentine family de' Pazzi, Maria Maddalena was ignorant of the *Divine Comedy*. Still, according to her numerous biographies she had no familiarity with any lay book. What is absolutely relevant to my analysis is to see how the unquestionable analogies between de' Pazzi's *Probation* and Dante's *Purgatory* help us clarify the mystic's journey through the "circles" of memory.

To fully understand de' Pazzi's vision of purgatory, it is essential to remember that, for her, purgatory "takes place" in the kitchen garden of her convent. I have explained that the visions of this Florentine mystic are "word revelations"—linguistic visitations, we may say—which blur the boundaries between memory, imagination, and reality ("as when . . . a

---

68. Jacqueline Risset alludes to this aspect of Dante's purgatory in *Dante écrivain, ou "l'intelletto d'amore"* (Paris: Seuil, 1982), 147–48.

Camminando ella per l'orto del Monistero le mostra il Signore la diuersità delle gene del Purgatorio, nelle quali vede l'anima del suo fratello, eb in tal vista apparendole Sant'Agostino, Sant'Angelo Martire e Santa Caterina da Siena con cui fà diuoti e pietosi parlamenti.

MARIA MADDALENA SEES THE SOULS IN PURGATORY;
PRINT BY F. CURRADI. (COURTESY OF ISTITUTO
GERMANICO DI STORIA DELL'ARTE, FLORENCE)

creature sees something with her physical sight, and then that something stays in her mind so clearly that, even if she does not see it concretely, she has the impression that she always sees it" [1:73–74]). The kitchen garden is the space where the mystic performs her visit to purgatory. In the kitchen garden Maria Maddalena goes through and around the circles of her "exile," as the transcriber has defined her demonic melancholy. The kitchen garden, however, is not merely a stage on which the mystic performs her rapture; it *reminds* the mystic, and the nuns witnessing her performance, of a purgatorial garden. It is at once an actual area of her Florentine convent and the mental space that the mystic—similar to the classical orator theorized in *Ad Herennium* and *De oratore*—walks through during her linguistic performance. As Yates stresses, late medieval "memory treatises in the scholastic tradition usually include remembering Paradise and Hell, frequently with diagrams of those places."[69] As we shall see, Maria Maddalena at once enacts and retrieves her memory of purgatory, whose single areas are inhabited by different kinds of sinners.

In *Liber gratiae spiritualis* the German mystic Mechthild of Hackeborn (1241–99) had already visualized purgatory as a lovely garden, visited by a flock of cheerful souls. Through a divine insight, Mechtild had realized that each of these souls carried inside a worm chewing on its heart.[70] A year after the end of her probation (1591), Maria Maddalena has a very similar vision. The Word leads her to "the garden of our religion," which has wonderful bushes and trees (2:33). However, the mystic senses that the branches bend too low and risk being attacked by innumerable worms (2:34). We have seen that during her five-year demonic melancholy, Maria Maddalena de' Pazzi herself felt that little worms were eating her flesh (1:140). At the end of her probation, five years after her night journey to purgatory, the mystic will go back to the kitchen garden. There she will give voice to her resumed desire for the Word, whom she calls Love: "[S]he ran all around the kitchen garden several times. . . . She said that she was looking for some soul who knew and loved love. And she always either called love or spoke with love. Sometimes, when she met a nun, she grabbed her and holding her tight said to her: 'Soul, do you love love? How

69. Yates, *Art of Memory*, 94.
70. Mechtildis, *Liber specialis gratiae* (Paris: H. Oudin Fratres, 1877), chap. 17 ("De animis liberatis per eius orationes"), 345–47. For Mechtild, these worms represent the soul's conscience (346). Compare Erich Fleischhack, *Fegfeur. Die Christlichen Vorstellungen vom Geschick der Verstorbenen* (Tübingen: Katzmann Verlag, 1969), 83. For an analysis of Mechthild's spirituality, see Bernard McGinn, *The Flowering of Mysticism* (New York: Crossroad, 1998), 267–82.

can you live? Don't you feel as if you were consuming and dying for love?'" (2:189). The garden of purgatory is the space where the soul runs around begging for love. The mystic's quest for Love/Word is disturbed by the constant presence of devils, which inhabit her vision of purgatory and never recede from her sight (1:49). The garden of purgatory in the convent of Santa Maria degli Angeli is in fact a purgatorial inferno.

To gather a better understanding of de' Pazzi's conception of purgatory, we may turn our attention briefly to Dante's depiction of a purgatorial garden. My reference to the second part of the *Comedy*, however, does not mean that I believe in a direct, almost topographic, identification between de' Pazzi's vision of purgatory and the Dantean construction. Once again, I focus only on those analogies between the two narrations that can enhance our understanding of the Florentine mystic's process of verbal purification. We recall that for Maria Maddalena to exist primarily means to give a (linguistic) body to the Word. The persistent demonic eloquence in the mystic's mind results in a flood of memory, which paradoxically obfuscates her linguistic faculty. Maria Maddalena walks around the kitchen garden at once to assume the memories of her deceased brother, and thus to help him discard the remembrance of his own past, and to silence her own excess of memory generated by the speakers of the mind. Both in *Purgatory* and in *Probation*, the image of a garden coincides with a transitional, albeit essential, moment in the subject's journey toward God, who for Maria Maddalena is primarily the Word. Both in *Purgatory* and in *Probation*, the liminal character of purgatory is embodied in the image of a garden. I refer to the so-called "valley of the princes" of canto 8 and to the garden of Eden described in canto 28 of Dante's *Purgatory*.[71]

In canto 8 Dante and Virgil are still in what Dante calls "pre-purgatory," the area preceding the actual purgatory, which the pilgrim will enter after having walked through the valley of the princes. If transition characterizes the nature of purgatory, pre-purgatory speaks of time suspended in the expectation of a forthcoming process of passage and transformation. In

71. My reading of these two cantos is indebted to the following studies: Gabriele Rossetti, *Comento analitico al "Purgatorio"* (Florence: Olschki, 1967), 36–58; Fiorenzo Forti, "Il canto VIII del *Purgatorio*," *Letture classensi* 3 (1970): 297–322; Giovanni Fallani, "Il canto VIII del *Purgatorio*," in *Nuove letture dantesche*, vol. 4 (Florence: Le Monnier, 1970), 19–30; Marcello Aurigemma, "Il canto VIII del *Purgatorio*," in *Casa di Dante in Roma. Purgatorio. Letture degli anni 1976–79* (Rome: Bonacci, 1981), 155–74; Peter Armour, "*Purgatorio* XXVIII," in *Dante Commentaries: Eight Studies of the "Divine Comedy,"* edited by David Nolan (Dublin: Irish Academic Press, 1977), 115–41; Fidel Fajardo-Acosta, "*Purgatorio* XXVIII: Catharsis and Paradisal Visions as States of Dynamic Equilibrium," *Neophilologus* 75 (1991): 222–31; Victoria Kirkham, "*Purgatorio* XXVIII," *Lectura Dantis* 12 (1993): 411–32.

canto 7, since the sun was going down and it would be too strenuous to proceed in the dark, the pilgrim and his guide Virgil, accompanied by Dante's friend Sordello, walked down the valley to rest during the night. They would resume their journey in the morning.[72] The visitors were struck by the intense beauty and fragrance of the flowers and plants that adorned the valley.[73] After meeting with several monarchs whose lives had been ruled more by the senses than by reason, Dante, Virgil, and Sordello continued their walk along the slope of the valley.[74]

It is now dusk. In the opening of canto 8, the pilgrim is suddenly confounded by the melancholic perception of his being an outcast, an expatriate traveling through a land marked by passage and instability. Like Maria Maddalena de' Pazzi and her deceased brother, the nomad Dante is troubled by the burden of memory ("Era già l'ora che volge al disio / ai naviganti e 'ntenerisce il core / lo dì c'han detto ai dolci amici addio" [8:1–3]) and by the harrowing menace of the Enemy. Indeed, one of the souls who had welcomed the visitors raises her hand and starts to sing *Te lucis ante terminum*, the hymn performed at *compieta* to ask God for protection against the devils of the night (8:13).[75] The souls' chant is first and foremost an act of remembrance, for their very presence in purgatory testifies to their victory over the Foe. Devils linger in memory itself, as a following passage from the same canto confirms. While he is contemplating three bright stars shining in the night sky (8:89–90), Dante is suddenly confronted with the vision of a snake sliding down the slope of the valley. "Perhaps" *(forse)*, Dante writes, it was the same snake that gave the "sour food" to Eve (8:99). *Perhaps* speaks of the viewer's recognition of a primal memory "residing" in the mind. Before the Augustinian memory of an original happiness, in the garden of purgatory the mind reenacts the remembrance of its fall.

In the garden Dante sees the soul of his beloved friend Nino Visconte,

---

72. In his insightful "Gervase of Tilbury and the Birth of Purgatory" (*Medioevo Romanzo* 14, no. 1 [1989]: 97–110), Paolo Cherchi connects Dante's decision to place purgatory in the open air to the third section of Gervase of Tilbury's *Otia imperialia*, which were probably published in 1212–14. A "novelty in Gervase's Purgatory, also to appear in Dante's, is that in the third realm [Purgatory] day and night alternate. This feature . . . is very important because it brings with it the notion of time" (Cherchi, "Gervase of Tilbury," 108).

73. Dante Alighieri, *Purgatorio*, edited by Natalino Sapegno (Florence: La Nuova Italia, 1970), canto 7, vv. 76–81, 76.

74. On this subject see Edward M. Peters, "I Principi negligenti di Dante e le concezioni medioevali del 'rex inutilis,'" *Rivista storica italiana* 80 (1968): 741–58.

75. Compare Rossetti, *Comento analitico*, 38; Fallani, "Il canto VIII del *Purgatorio*," 20–21; Forti, "Il canto VIII del *Purgatorio*," 300.

who, like Maria Maddalena's brother, asks the living to take up the weight of his memory.[76] Indeed, as Maria Maddalena meets her brother the very night of his passage to purgatory, so does Dante encounter his friend at the end of his first day in the valley of the princes. Nino would like Dante to remind his only daughter Giovanna to mention him in her prayers (8:71– 73). The Florentine outcast and the mystic suffering from melancholy *arrive* in the garden of remembrance to listen and to be listened to, to save and to be saved, to welcome memory in order to bring about an everlasting oblivion. Writing on the "uncanniness" of the French term *arrivant,* Derrida states: "The new *arrivant,* this word can, indeed, . . . mean . . . the singularity of *who* arrives, he or she who comes, coming to be where s/he was not expected, where one was awaiting him or her without waiting for him or her, without expecting it. . . . One does not expect the event of whatever, of whoever comes, arrives, and crosses the threshold—the immigrant, the emigrant, the guest, or the stranger."[77] The absolute *arrivant,* Derrida continues, "surprises the host . . . enough to call into question, to the point of annihilating or rendering indeterminate, all the distinctive signs of a prior identity."[78] The space itself where the encounter occurs becomes "de-identified," a sort of nonplace, a transitional region where the host's historical identity is questioned and effaced. What Nino Visconte and Maria Maddalena's brother ask of their *arrivants* is their ultimate deletion from the garden of memory.

Oblivion is what "the emigrant, the guest, . . . the stranger" Dante finally encounters in the second garden of purgatory, the earthly paradise of canto 28, which had been foreshadowed by the valley of the princes.[79] In Jeffrey Burton Russell's words, "the garden is the most common metaphor [for heaven]. Its origin is in the Hebrew Bible: the garden of the earthly paradise at the beginning of the world. It was linked through the 'garden enclosed' of the Hebrew Bible to the Greco-Roman images of the *locus*

76. On Dante's conception of the purgatorial soul as an "aerial body," see Marianne Shapiro, "Dante's Twofold Representation of the Soul," *Lectura Dantis* 18–19 (1996): 49–90. Compare the entry "Anima" in *Enciclopedia dantesca* (Rome: Istituto della Enciclopedia Italiana, 1970), 1:278–85.

77. Jacques Derrida, *Aporias,* translated by Thomas Dutoit (Stanford: Stanford University Press, 1993), 33.

78. Derrida, *Aporias,* 34. On the fundamental concept of self as a "process of negotiation," see Steve Pile and Nigel Thrift, "Mapping the Subject," in *Mapping the Subject: Geographies of Cultural Transformation,* edited by Pile and Thrift (New York: Routledge, 1995), 13–51.

79. Jeffrey Burton Russell, *A History of Heaven* (Princeton: Princeton University Press, 1997), 161.

amoenus, the 'lovely place.'"[80] For Dante, to enter the "ancient forest" of Eden (28:23) equals going back to the primal oxymoron, as Victoria Kirkham says, where existence unfolds its perennial oblivion.[81] In canto 28, the marvelous garden of Eden does not expose the Florentine outcast to any encounter with his past. Initially, no familiar soul rushes to him begging him for remembrance. However, like the garden of canto 8, "Eden is itself an ambivalent terrain, a sort of split land . . . a field of tension."[82] Although Eden is a pretemporal land, what the pilgrim encounters is a place affected by a "persistent" memory, which is Adam and Eve's original banishment (28:91–96).[83] In Eden the exiled Dante visits the scene of an archetypal exile. The earthly paradise is indeed an "impossible" place, at once the land before and after the "invasion" of memory.

To be cleansed of the memory of exile, the pilgrim Dante is led by the mysterious and joyful Matelda to the banks of Lethe, the infernal river that the poet has transferred to the border of purgatory, and whose water erases the remembrance of one's sinful past. But before tasting the water of amnesia, Dante has the most humiliating and significant revelation of his entire purgatorial journey. In canto 30, his beloved Beatrice reveals herself to him and, addressing him by his first name, sternly reminds Dante how, right after her death, he had embarked on an "untrue" path and had followed "false images" (30:130–31). Afflicted by Beatrice's harsh accusations, Dante becomes unable to speak (31:7–9) and feels overwhelmed by "confusion and fear" (31:13).

It is only after this shattering confrontation with his past that Dante is taken to the river of forgetfulness. When he is already immersed in the water up to his throat, Dante hears the verse *Asperges me* (Ps. 50:9) coming from above (31:98). These words, recited during the consecration of a church, are meant to expel devils from the sacred place. In the garden of Eden, to forget means to undergo a second baptism, whose core is the exorcism of the devils of remembrance. Dante's baptismal cleansing in the river of oblivion is first and foremost an act of grace, which transcends the

80. Russell, *History of Heaven,* 13. Compare Colleen McDannell and Bernhard Lang, *Heaven: A History* (New Haven: Yale University Press, 1988), 70–71.

81. Kirkham, "*Purgatorio* XXVIII," 415.

82. Kirkham, "*Purgatorio* XXVIII," 415–16.

83. Armour, "*Purgatorio* XXVIII," 116. On Dante's interpretation of Adam's language both in *De vulgari eloquentia* and in *Paradiso* 26, see Umberto Eco, *Serendipities: Language and Lunacy,* translated by William Weaver (New York: Harcourt Brace, 1998), 23–51. Particularly interesting for our study of de' Pazzi's vision of linguistic expression is Eco's analysis of Dante's concept of *forma locutionis* in *De vulgari eloquentia.*

realm of human intervention. Matelda pushes Dante's head down into the river so that the pilgrim is forced to swallow its water (31:102). Dante understands that forgetfulness is in fact an unnatural occurrence. As in a demonic possession, oblivion overruns the mind's defenses, since the human mind cannot help but remember. This is what makes it so vulnerable to the speakers of the mind. In Dante's fictional rendition of the earthly garden, the banishment of memory takes the form of a ritual *reminiscent* of the sacrament of baptism, which is itself a form of exorcism. Before entering the river of oblivion, Dante has undergone a process of initiation, whose steps were embodied by the single souls the pilgrim encountered during his purgatorial journey.

In a similar manner, to be cured of the devil of melancholy, Maria Maddalena de' Pazzi goes around the "circles" of the kitchen garden trying to find the soul of her deceased brother:

> [T]hat place, as she has explained to us, is gloomy and extremely dark, although it is somehow illuminated by the brightness and splendor of the angels, which is a great consolation for the souls. That night she was looking for her brother's soul. We understood that because, when she stopped, she said: "Oh, where is my little soul? Isn't he here among these ones?" And, when she found him, she was very happy and, showing a great joy, she spoke to him in a compassionate way: "Poor one, you suffer so much and are still very happy? You burn and are so cheerful?" (1:51)

Maria Maddalena is unable to comprehend the nature of her brother's punishment. She only senses and participates in his suffering. The transcriber has indeed the impression that the mystic walks around and around having a hard time finding what she is looking for (1:53). Maria Maddalena walks and pauses, looks around and scrutinizes the ground. The purgatory of the Florentine visionary is thus articulated through the language of her gestures, movements, and pauses. Purgatory is indeed the dance of purgatory. As Maria Maddalena herself will explain at the end of the rapture, "she [is] not aware of her own walking, because her body simply follow[s] her soul's drive. Sometimes she [sees] the souls' torment from afar (that is, it is too distant from her), and she cannot perceive the nature and intensity of their pain. However, she raise[s] and elevate[s] her intellect in order to understand and feel it. Her gestures result from that understanding." In other words, if purgatory is the gesture of purgatory, the mystic's body enacts what the intellect has seen or has failed to see. Maria Maddalena literally moves toward the images her mind has perceived in an indistinct manner, as if she could walk closer to the object of her intellectual sight.

But devils endeavor to keep her sight out of focus: "Oh, this is indeed a horrible place, full of hideous and ugly demons" (1:52). Invoking the name of Catherine of Siena, a fundamental presence in all her visions, Maria Maddalena cries out: "Oh Catherine, where are you taking me to in this gloomy night? What is this dark place? Its inhabitants are surrounded by demons, served by demons, honored by demons, for they aspired to the glory and the honors of the world" (1:54–55).

The mystic is dismayed by what she sees. Devils pierce the souls with long shafts and then chop them up into small pieces with sharp knives (1:52). However, as Maria Maddalena herself explains to her sisters, these images are nothing but "similitudes" *(similitudini)* through which the souls convey their suffering to the mystic. Analogy allows a communication between the deceased and the melancholic mystic. The souls suffer *as if* they still had a body, *as if* their hypothetical bodies were subjected to the cruelest practices, according to what the mystic is able to imagine or to remember. The memory of these similitudes, Maria Maddalena says, never fails to speak to her. Let us keep in mind that similitudes are also a central tenet of the classical art of memory. To bring back to memory the images and the words of his discourse, the author of *Ad Herennium* suggests that an orator "establish likenesses as striking as possible. . . . The things we easily remember when they are real we likewise remember without difficulty when they are figment."[84] We may thus say that both the images summoned in the mystic's mind and her gestures and her walking in circles in the kitchen garden in the middle of the night are similitudes, whose goal is the communication of the purgatorial condition.

Maria Maddalena's purgatory is a rather systematic area of punishment and repentance. At the beginning of her journey through the kitchen garden, the mystic locates a sort of Dantean pre-purgatory, which is "very close" to hell and is thus filled with "its screams and noises, its grinding of teeth and its confusion." This is where hypocrites are tormented. After this introductory "similitude," the visionary faces a wide array of regions, in which the souls are tortured and dismembered according to their sins. Indeed, the common denominator of all these different "circles" (the mystic's actual walking around the perimeter of the garden) is the dissection of the "similitudes" of the souls. The impatient ones, for instance, are "consumed by an internal consumption" (1:53). The mystic sees them die and come back to life with no respite. Devils grab and squeeze their bodies "as

---

84. *Ad C. Herennium* (trans. Caplan), xxii, 37, 221.

when one wants to take the juice out of something." Snakes devour those who sinned because of their inner frailty (1:54). Some of these souls, Maria Maddalena says, are first melted like hot lead and then, when they solidify, are given to the serpents to be dismembered and eaten up again. Other souls, whose lives were "impure," roll in mud and filth. Devils poke their eyeballs and torture their eye sockets incessantly. Finally, those souls who had been ungrateful are merged and drowned in an immense and deep "chaos of lead" (*caos di piombo* [1:55]).

In de' Pazzi's purgatory, the soul identifies with the process through which his or her "similitude"—that is, the remembrance of his or her body—is dissected and reconstituted indefinitely.[85] We must bear in mind that the purgatory Maria Maddalena enacts through her walking around the kitchen garden is itself a "similitude," in that it is based on an act of memory. The kitchen garden reminds the mystic of the purgatorial garden, *as* the souls convey their affliction by summoning remembrances of physical suffering. In chapter 3 I stressed the fundamental role played by memory and metaphor in the healing process of exorcism. *Like* and *as* are the words connecting reality and memory, time present and time past, verbal language and things, melancholy and purgatorial purification. Indeed, after having walked around for more than two hours, at three o'clock in the morning Maria Maddalena stops at the border of the garden next to the back door of the convent, where the Word lets her know that her visit to the garden has certainly improved the condition of her brother (1:56). The Word even shows her his forthcoming glory. As a response, Maria Maddalena asks him for the salvation of every soul: "And what good does it make to see the glory of one soul only? If you want to free them all, please let me see it" (1:56).

A few days later (June 30) the Word visits the young mystic again to grant her a vision of her entire existence (1:59). The following day (July 1), He lets her know that her brother is about to ascend to heaven (1:64). Her passage through purgatory has hastened both her brother's and her own

---

85. The seminal studies of Caroline Walker Bynum have shown that the relationship between fragmentation and reconstitution is a central aspect of medieval and Renaissance spirituality. This is the topic of chap. 6 of her *Fragmentation and Redemption* (New York: Zone Books, 1991). Bynum recounts the story of the Franciscan reformer Colette of Corbie who, in the early fifteenth century, receives a vision of Christ. He appears to her "as a dish completely filled with carved-up flesh like that of a child" (181). Christ explains to the visionary that human depravity has brought about that image of his body. Bynum also offers a detailed analysis of the theological debate concerning the relationship between soul and body in Thomas Aquinas. Using "the Aristotelian form/matter dichotomy," Thomas believes that the soul is the *forma corporeitatis*, that is, "it is soul that accounts for the 'whatness' of the body" (228).

Vede in diuersi tempi molt'anime, e se libere dalle pene del Purgatorio son con=
dotte all'eterna felicità.

MARIA MADDALENA SEES SOULS ASCENDING FROM PURGATORY
TO HEAVEN; PRINT BY F. CURRADI. (COURTESY OF ISTITUTO
GERMANICO DI STORIA DELL'ARTE, FLORENCE)

healing. If the "similitude" of his physical self has almost suffered all the pains necessary to attain oblivion (the immersion in the Dantean Lethe), her existence has regained a sense of temporal perspective. The Word has let her see her own existence. In other words, unlike the melancholics mentioned in Weyer's *De praestigiis daemonum,* who perceive themselves as amorphous vessels of clay modified by any possible external intervention, the Florentine mystic is now able to move from the "chaos" of melancholy (the immense lake of lead where souls are melted and drowned) toward the physical consistency granted by remembrance.

The most striking aspect of de' Pazzi's healing process is its identification between memory and body, between spiritual purification and corporeal transformation. Indeed, the second and final section of *Probation* revolves around two major topics, which the transcriber considers as closely interrelated. First, thanks to the visit she has paid to her brother in purgatory, Maria Maddalena is now able to discern other human beings' nature and destiny. Second, according to the transcriber, after having been to the garden of purgation the mystic undergoes a process of spiritual and physical conversion, a sort of mystical rebirth. These two narrative threads are complementary, in that both show how the subject's ability to retrieve her voice—which for the mystic exclusively expresses a constant invocation to the Word—and thus to silence her speakers of the mind at once reflects and affects her relationship with others. We know that Maria Maddalena's probation is not a solipsistic occurrence. If the devils shouting in her ears prevented her from interacting with the other nuns, her brother has come to her both as a request and a gift. To recover her voice, the mystic has walked away from herself (the convent, the *locus* of the mind where the devils yell and swear) toward the garden where similitudes of violent acts of death have brought to the fore the memory of the violence she herself has been subject to.

Probation recounts a series of unexpected deaths, both inside and outside the convent. The duke of Florence passes away during the last weeks of 1587 (1:127). A sister of the convent dies on February 17, 1588, followed by another nun only a month later (1:218–19). In the spring of 1589 the convent experiences two more deaths. A nun dies in May, and another at the beginning of June (1:222–23). Maria Maddalena knows that all these souls have moved to purgatory, and she is able to predict the intensity of their pains and the length of their sojourn there. Moreover, during a conversation with St. Augustine, who in her visions is always associated with the act of recollection through writing, Maria Maddalena draws up a list of all the nuns in the convent. Reviewing her sisters' past with Augustine, the mystic sketches a brief outline of the character of each nun, including the youngest novices. For instance:

> Sister Mattea: Religious, under the shelter of Mary.
>
> Sister Piera: Very eager, even though she is unable to penetrate, because indeed she can't penetrate. But she will be rewarded for her effort. But what a bigger reward she would receive if she could penetrate! Simple, yes, but she wouldn't need to be it that much. Poor thing!
>
> Sister Giuliana: charitable toward her neighbor.
>
> Sister Raffaella: charitable, and very pious and patient.
>
> Sister Maria: humble, respectful of her Spouse's will, and grateful.
>
> (1:93)

In her journey through the garden of purgatory, Maria Maddalena has acquired the gift of listening. If during the most critical period of her probation she could hear neither what the other nuns told her nor what she herself uttered in her prayers, because devils yelled and cursed in her ears, now she is able to perceive the others' needs, weaknesses, and desires. She knows that the souls of the Florentine duke and of her sisters in purgatory need to be remembered in her prayer to the Word. She also knows that her sisters in the convent need her support and advice. Reporting what she has gleaned from her dialogue with Augustine, Maria Maddalena reassures her sisters, including the transcriber of *Probation*, and tells them that their efforts are appreciated and will be rewarded, even when, like Sister Piera, they are unable "to penetrate."

The essential theme of *Probation* is indeed transition and exile. The souls in purgatory, the mystic afflicted by melancholy, and the nuns of the convent of Santa Maria degli Angeli are what they are likely to become. A striking aspect of the book is that the mystic's body itself is not immune to a process of metamorphosis. According to the transcriber, after her visit to her deceased brother Maria Maddalena undergoes several partial or total transformations. Like her soul, her body needs to be cleansed of those demonic presences that have tormented her for five years, pushing her down the stairs, chewing on her entrails like worms, or biting her stomach and choking her like venomous snakes. In each case of "renewal" (*renovatione*), as the transcriber defines these occurrences of physical conversion, the mystic feels as if her old organs were being removed and new ones transplanted into her body. Maria Maddalena endures a first complete renovation on May 1, while she is meditating on the ascension of the Virgin

Mary (1:170). On this occasion, her body is given back its inner virginity, which is absolutely essential for her to be the Word's bride:

> She started to feel enormous pains inside. [We understood this] because she shook and trembled, and her gestures showed that she was suffering a great deal. Then, all her external organs were renewed, such as her head, her eyes, her ears, and others. And we understood this because, each time a member was renovated, she grasped it very tight, sighing and wriggling. And because of her great suffering she cried scalding tears, even though her face was still very beautiful and elevated toward the Virgin. She also said to this Virgin: "Oh Mary, I fear that my soul is going to be detached from my body, as it happened to you." (1:171)

A few months later (October 13), the mystic asks the Word to renew her heart, so that she can defend herself more effectively against the devils' attacks (1:196). As had happened in August, Maria Maddalena makes the gesture of grasping her heart with both hands and sighs deeply, as if the Word were taking it out of her breast.

The final, and most complete, "renovation" of the mystic's flesh and soul takes place at the very end of her five-year probation. On Monday, April 23, 1590, the day after Easter, the Word enters the mystic's mind to inform her that He is about to restore their past dialogue, which had come to a provisional end five years before (1:232). Maria Maddalena's utterances are about to regain their primary and sole interlocutor. However, Maria Maddalena has first to sustain a thorough process of mental and physical cleansing. The first organs to be purified are her eyes (1:232–33). The nuns have the impression that some sort of invisible balm is being poured into her pupils, because she opens and closes her eyelids slowly and carefully. Then, it is the turn of her ears, mouth, hands, and feet.

When "her external purification was over, [He] moved to purify her soul." The Word first takes care of her will (*volontà*). From that moment on, her will and the Word's are going to merge with each other. Then, the Word renews her memory, her heart, her desire, and her intention (*memoria, cuore, concupiscibile, intentione*, 1:233–35). The transcriber pays special attention to the mystic's transformed memory. As Matelda purifies Dante by plunging him into the river of oblivion, so does the Word cleanse the Florentine mystic of her sinful past by erasing her previous memory and by writing seven new remembrances (*ricordi*) in her mind:

> 1. Pacem relinquo vobis, pacem meam do vobis. ("Peace I bequeath to you, my own peace I give you" [John 14:17])

2. Regnum meum non est de hoc mundo. ("Mine is not a kingdom of this world" [John 18:36])

3. Meus cibus est ut faciam voluntatem eius qui misit me, ut perficiam opus eius. ("My food is to do the will of the one who sent me, and to complete his work" [John 4:34])

4. Quicunque enim fecerit voluntatem Patris mei qui in celis est, ipse meus frater et soror et mater est. ("Anyone who does the will of my Father in heaven, he is my brother and sister and mother" [Matt. 12:50])

5. Qui scandalizaverit unum de pusillis istis, qui in me credunt, expedit ei ut suspendatur mola asinaria in collo eius, et demergatur in profundum maris. ("Anyone who is an obstacle to bring down one of these little ones who have faith in me would be better drowned in the depths of the sea with a great millstone round his neck" [Matt. 18:6])

6. Pater, si possibile est. ("Father, if it is possible" [compare Matt. 26:42])

7. Pater, ignosce illis. ("Father, forgive them" [compare Luke 23:34])

The seven remembrances engraved in the mystic's mind mean more than a retrieved adherence to the Catholic creed. The Word has marked Maria Maddalena with the memory of his peace, the Augustinian recollection of an immemorial happiness, which cannot be separated from a vigilant listening to the other's needs. It is at this point that Maria Maddalena de' Pazzi recovers her voice, her deepest (in)vocation, her obsession with the articulation of the Word. Does not the pilgrim Dante as well receive the gift of a new or renewed idiom? After his immersion in amnesia, does not the sudden and blinding "splendor" of Beatrice manifest the (re)acquisition of a lost *vita nuova*, of a pristine language of poetry (31:139)?[86] Does not his beloved order Dante to communicate through writing the paradoxical event of a "new" memory, at once oblivion and regained remembrance (32:103–5)?

VERY SIMILAR TO MANY hagiographical accounts, the second and final section of *Probation* focuses on the miraculous effects of Maria Maddalena's "new" memory. Like a "living saint," both her body and her belongings have been soaked, so to speak, in the Word's divine memory.[87] For

---

86. Compare Salvatore Battaglia, *Esemplarità e antagonismo nel pensiero di Dante* (Naples: Liguori, 1967), 145–54.

87. With the expression "living saint" I refer to Gabriella Zarri's well-known analysis of holy women in Italy before the Counter-Reformation. These "living saints" played a significant role in the political life of their time, often becoming influential counselors and guides of monarchs. These women not only tried to emulate St. Catherine of Siena, they also possessed the

instance, in 1592 sister Cherubina falls extremely ill with a high fever and two bleeding wounds in her sides (2:253).[88] While she is confessing, this nun hears a voice suggesting that she sleep in Maria Maddalena's bed. As soon as her sisters carry the infirm Cherubina to the mystic's bed, she is cured of her disease. A year before, another nun contracted what the doctors believed was a serious case of leprosy, which spread from her ears to the rest of her body (2:256). Maria Maddalena cured her by licking her ears and the other spots of her head infected with the disease. Maria Maddalena also takes care of a twelve-year girl whose nickname is "Wild" (selvaggia), whom evil spirits have made at once restless and totally mute (2:254). After being exorcised by the mystic, the "Wild" girl confesses that being close to Maria Maddalena gives her an immense peace and protects her from the most insidious devils.

Before closing this chapter, let us go back for a moment to Monday, April 23, 1590, when the Word wrote seven memories in the mystic's mind. That day signifies Maria Maddalena's liberation from the speakers of the mind. To celebrate her recovered freedom, the mystic goes back to each place where her devils had "attempted to confound [her]" and starts to sing and dance around, expressing a complete and defiant joy: "[S]he danced and sang in such a beautiful, solemn, and powerful way that is truly impossible to describe it to those who have not seen her. She derided and sneered at the devils, singing the following and many other words: 'Despite your attempts, I will rejoice, and the day of the Lord I will laugh at you and will kneel before Him'" (1:240–41). The seven "remembrances" that the Word writes in the mystic's memory are indeed joyful and harmonious gestures, a dance of deliverance and reconciliation. If the melancholic body is a lump of clay molded and disfigured at random by the hostile remembrances summoned by the devils, the flesh marked with the seven memories of the Word is a dance that moves toward a full realization of those divine memories. The act of remembering the Word, his still unspoken being, is indeed a future event. At the end of her five-year demonic probation, Maria Maddalena de' Pazzi understands that to give voice to the Word means to dance his forthcoming memory.

This is the final insight the Word grants the mystic only a few weeks after her dance through the rooms of the convent (June 11). After her daily Mass, Maria Maddalena acquires a sudden "insight on herself" (intelli-

---

alleged gift of prophecy, which enhanced their social and political status. See Gabriella Zarri, *Le sante vive. Cultura e religiosità femminile nella prima età moderna* (Turin: Einaudi, 1990).

88. Compare Maggi, *Uttering the Word*, 136–37.

gentia di se stessa [1:242]). Feeling that the devils have finally lost any power over her, the mystic repeats three times "Ecce me, ecce me, ecce me" ("Here I am, here I am, here I am").

"Here" is where "I am" is a synonym for the Word, where a human voice has become the splendor of a divine word.

FIVE

To Dream *Insomnia:*

Human Mind and Demonic Enlightenment

in Cardano's *Metoposcopia*

Whence does our mind originate?
What is it?

Girolamo Cardano, *De arcanis aeternitatis*

O**UR ANALYSIS** of Maria Maddalena de' Pazzi's *Probation* has investigated the consequences of demonic possession for the human mind. If the devil endeavors to turn the subject against herself by infecting her with a devastating melancholy that spurs her toward her final annihilation (the body as a lump of clay; voices shouting in her ears; the mind echoing the devil's instigation to suicide), it is thanks to melancholy that the possessed mystic acquires a different language, which enables her to perceive her brother's request for oblivion. The fundamental paradox of a diabolical possession is that, once the devil has entered the mind, the subject becomes speechless and articulate, deafened and gifted with an exceptional hearing, oblivious of herself and fully aware of others' passions and remembrances.

Probation is unquestionably a cornerstone of sixteenth-century demonology. No other text of the European Renaissance offers a more detailed description of the distressing effects of a demonic invasion. However, it does not offer a theoretical or "scientific" analysis of this disturbing occurrence. Moreover, *Probation* posits the relationship between human mind and demonic presence as an "either-or" event in that, according to the transcribers of the mystic's visions, the devil is either in or out of the mind. In other words, in *Probation* the Enemy either takes over the self or is confronted by it from the outside. Does Renaissance demonology hypothesize other forms of diabolical influence over the mind? Does a demonic intervention necessarily mean possession and self-annihilation?

As I noted in my introduction, students of Renaissance culture usually apply the term *demonology* both to Christian, Catholic theology and to Florentine Neoplatonism. However, scholars tend to believe that a Ficinian "demon" has little or nothing to do with the biblical "devil" or "demon." We have seen that demonologists such as Prierio and de Moura are familiar with Marsilio Ficino's interpretation of a Platonic "daimon." Both Prierio and de Moura mention and discuss some of Ficino's major works (such as *Theologia platonica* or *Pimander*), to highlight his alleged "errors" and also to stress their points of agreement. Let us bear in mind that Christianity itself is built on Platonism. Furthermore, in their view of a demonic being, Italian Neoplatonic philosophers were inevitably affected by the dominant Catholic theology. As we shall see, a Neoplatonic "demon" may be at once similar to and different from the Socratic "daimon." The Neoplatonic "demon" is the result of a cultural contamination. In the Renaissance, what a Platonic "demon" does and knows is both "daimonic" and "diabolical."

To clarify this crucial point, we now turn to the Italian philosopher, physician, and astrologer Girolamo Cardano who, in Henry Lea's words, "may be regarded as exemplifying the highest intellect and culture of his age."[1] However, as Anthony Grafton stresses in his recent work on Cardano's astrology, "[his] vast intellectual territory . . . has remained largely unexplored."[2] This is due, Grafton is convinced, to the "technical density" of Cardano's books. In this chapter we will broach Cardano's "dense" philosophical system. After analyzing his psychology and demonology through several of his treatises, I will concentrate on *Metoposcopia libris tredecim, et octingentis faciei humanae eiconibus complexa*, Cardano's work on physiognomy published posthumously in Paris in 1658. In his vast and diverse production, which exceeds the ten-volume *Opera omnia* printed in Lyons in 1663, Cardano shows an unparalleled interest in defining and investigating how the mind's various areas and faculties relate both to each other and to the angelic beings. As we shall see, for Cardano the human intellect exists insofar as it detects, translates, and responds to the signs sent by what he calls the "superior minds." We could say that, according to the physician Cardano, human identity is a process of exegesis. We exist as an intellectual response.

BORN IN PAVIA IN 1501, Girolamo Cardano was the illegitimate son of Fazio Cardano, an elderly solicitor, and the young Chiara Micheri, who

1. Henry Charles Lea, *Materials toward a History of Witchcraft*, 3 vols. (Philadelphia: University of Pennsylvania Press, 1939), 2:435.

2. Anthony Grafton, *Cardano's Cosmos* (Cambridge, Mass.: Harvard University Press, 1999), 17.

attempted to terminate her pregnancy by taking "various abortive medicines," as Cardano himself writes in *The Book of My Life,* a masterpiece of Renaissance autobiography.[3] In being born, Cardano underscores, he was "taken by violent means from my mother; I was almost dead."[4] Indeed, although his mother had been in labor for three entire days, he had somehow managed to survive. Cardano always perceived the fact that his birth resulted from a failed abortion as a highly symbolic occurrence. As we shall see, Cardano's account of his troubled "nativity," as he defines it, is more than a personal interpretation of a trite topos of classical autobiography (the anomalous birth as a sign of exceptional or even divine qualities); it is a reflection of his philosophical view on the meaning and goal of human existence.

At the age of seventeen, Cardano attended the university of Pavia, specializing in medicine rathen than in law, as his father had hoped.[5] In 1531, after recovering from a sexual impotence that had afflicted him throughout the first part of his life, Cardano married Lucia Bandareni, who bore three children, Giovanni Battista (1534), Chiara (1537), and Aldo (1543). Cardano's wife died in 1546. Moving to Milan in 1532, Cardano unsuccessfully applied for membership in the College of Physicians. In 1536 he was finally offered a teaching position at the University of Pavia, but he could not accept it because it involved no financial remuneration. In 1543 Cardano accepted the chair of medicine at Pavia, where he discontinuously

---

3. I use Stoner's translation of Cardano's *De vita propria liber* (*The Book of My Life,* translated by Jean Stoner [New York: Dutton, 1930]), 4. I have also consulted these studies: Enrico Rivari, *La mente di Girolamo Cardano* (Bologna: Zanichelli, 1906); Antonio Corsano, "La 'dialectica' di Girolamo Cardano," *Giornale critico della filosofia italiana* 40 (1961): 175–80; Corsano, "Il Cardano e la storia," *Giornale critico della filosofia italiana* 40 (1961): 499–507; Corsano, "La psicologia del Cardano: 'De animi immortalitate,'" *Giornale critico della filosofia italiana* 41 (1962): 56–64; Oystein Ore, *Cardano: The Gambling Scholar* (Princeton: Princeton University Press, 1953); Eugenio Garin, *Storia della filosofia italiana,* 3 vols. (Bari: Laterza, 1966), 2:620–27; Alain Wykes, *Doctor Cardano: Physician Extraordinairy* (London: Muller, 1969); Alfonso Ingegno, *Saggio sulla filosofia di Cardano* (Florence: Nuova Italia, 1980); Markus Fierz, *Girolamo Cardano (1501–1576)* (Boston: Birkhäuser, 1983); Germana Ernst, *Religione, ragione e natura* (Milan, 1991); Eckhard Kessler, ed., *Girolamo Cardano. Philosoph, Naturforscher, Arzt* (Wiesbaden: Harrassowitz Verlag, 1994); Nancy G. Siraisi, *Girolamo Cardano and Renaissance Medicine* (Princeton: Princeton University Press, 1997); Siraisi, "Anatomizing the Past: Physicians and History in Renaissance Culture," *Renaissance Quarterly* 53, no. 1 (2000): 1–30.

4. *Book of My Life,* 5. On the role of astrology in Cardano's autobiography, see Grafton, *Cardano's Cosmos,* 178–98.

5. For this brief summary of Cardano's life, I quote from G. Gliozzi, "Gerolamo Cardano," in *Dizionario biografico degli italiani* (Rome: Istituto dell'Enciclopedia italiana, 1976), 19: 758–63.

taught until 1562. In 1560 he had the most devastating and significant experience of his life. At the age of twenty-six, his beloved son Giovanni Battista was arrested, tried, and beheaded for having poisoned his wife, whom he had married in 1557 against his parents' will. Giovanni Battista had discovered that he was not the father of their three children. As I will explain later, his first son's death plays an essential role in Cardano's philosophical system, and it is a recurrent theme in his texts. Cardano was convinced that the harshness of the sentence against his son was due in part to his colleagues' resentment of his own scientific successes and his attacks against the academic establishment in Pavia. He decided to move to Bologna, for this reason and also because of the insistent allusions to his sexual relationships with his students. In 1570 Cardano was temporarily arrested by the Inquisition for unknown reasons. He later settled down in Rome, where he was accepted in the Roman College of Physicians, but more than practicing his profession he dedicated himself to his philosophical investigations. He died in 1576. His collected works, apart from a few manuscripts still unpublished and his book on metoposcopy, were published posthumously in the seventeenth century.

IN RECENT YEARS, classical and Renaissance physiognomy has been the object of intense analysis.[6] More than one scholar, for instance, has highlighted the connection between the numerous arts of divination developed in the Renaissance and the new interest in human physical expression, which finds a superb synthesis in Leonardo's *Trattato della pittura*. Cardano's book on metoposcopy, the analysis of the signs marked on the human face, certainly follows the well-known Renaissance tradition of divinatory methods of *signaturae*, according to which every created thing exhibits the marks or "signature" of its internal qualities and potentials.[7] For Cardano, however, metoposcopy is not merely a procedure to foretell the future and destiny of a given individual. It is first and foremost one of the most fascinating manifestations of the dialogue between mind and memory, rationality and what we now would call "subconscious," and

---

6. For an introduction to Renaissance physiognomy, see the following: Flavio Caroli, *Storia della fisiognomica* (Milan: Leonardo, 1995), 9–79; Lucia Rodler, *I silenzi mimici del volto* (Pisa: Pacini, 1991), 19–55; Jean-Jacques Courtine and Claudine Haroche, *Histoire du visage* (Paris: Rivages, 1988), 41–85. For a history of physiognomy, I have consulted these studies: Claudia Schmölders, *Das Vorurteil im Leibe* (Berlin: Akademie Verlag, 1995); Rüdiger Campe and Manfred Schneider eds., *Geschichte der Physiognomik* (Freiburg: Rombach, 1996).

7. Courtine and Haroche, *Histoire du visage*, 57. Compare Michel Foucault, *The Order of Things* (New York: Pantheon Books, 1970), 34–42.

human self and angelic beings.[8] The art of metoposcopy became quite successful in the second half of the sixteenth century and throughout the seventeenth century, even though Pope Sixtus V forbade it in 1586 and Jean Bodin criticized the practice in his infamous *De la démonomanie des sorciers*.[9]

In the preface to *Metoposcopia*, Cardano points out that "every discipline and art that contemplates what is perishable principally insists on those things that occur more often."[10] For Cardano, to read any kind of mark as the signifier of a hidden discourse means to register the most frequent variables within a given field of occurrences. Cardano mentions the arts of navigation and agriculture, but first of all, "medicine, which is, albeit very ingenious, unable to predict the future with exactitude." We may infer that modern physiognomy had originally a strong medical connotation.[11] If not even medicine can attain a perfect understanding of a person's physical condition, Cardano infers, "we should expect to receive a perfect indication on future events neither from the shape of the human head, nor from the marks on the forehead." In terms of probability, these facial signs are "very clear about the qualities of the soul, very obscure about the future, and intermediate about their possible effects." Furthermore, a correct use of metoposcopy must take into consideration many other variables manifested in the subject himself, such as age, education, and parents' social, physical, and psychological condition. In other words, facial marks are

8. Caroli, *Storia della fisiognomica*, 9–10.

9. Caroli, *Storia della fisiognomica*, 47; Jean Bodin, *De la démonomanie des sorciers* (Hildesheim: Olms Verlag, 1988), 40v. Compare Pierre Nodé, *Déclamation contre l'erreur exécrable des maleficiers, sorciers, enchanteurs et semblables observateurs des superstitions* (Paris, 1578). Compare also Pierre de Lancre, *L'incrédulité et miscreance du sortilege plainement convaincue* (Paris: Nicolas Buon, 1622), 270: "Metoscopy or Metoposcopy or metopomanty is a form of physiognomic divination, because the physiognomist primarily considers the forehead and the face, since this part seems to reflect the subject's intellectual qualities." Among the most famous treatises on this subject are the following: Thaddaeus Hagecius, *Aphorismorum metoposcopicorum libellus unus* (Frankfurt, 1560); Rodolphus Glocenius the Young, *Uranoscopia, chiroscopia, et metoposcopia* (Frankfurt, 1603); Samuel Fuchs, *Metoposcopia et Ophtalmoscopia* (Strasbourg, 1615); Ludovico Settala, *De naevis* (Milan, 1626); Ciro Spontone, *La metoposcopia, overo Commensurazione delle linee della fronte* (Venice, 1626).

10. Girolamo Cardano, *Metoposcopia libris tredecim, et octingentis faciei humanae eiconibus complexa* (Paris: Thomas Iolly, 1658), iii. For a brief introduction to Cardano's book, see J.-P. Migne, *Encyclopédie théologique*, vol. 49, part 2 (Paris: Ateliers Catholiques du Petit-Montrouge, 1848), 125–28.

11. Medieval physiognomy starts at the beginning of the thirteenth century with the works of Peter of Abano and Michael Scotus. Both authors were published in the fifteenth century: Peter of Abano, *Liber compilationis physionomiae* (Padua, 1474); Michael Scotus, *Liber physionomiae* (Besançon, 1477). Compare Schmölders, *Das Vorurteil im Leibe*, 59.

"intermediate" signs in that their effects are contingent upon other external signs, primarily the subject's own relationship with his parents. We shall see later how Cardano grants an extraordinary importance to the connection between father and son.

Given metoposcopy's innumerable variables, Cardano states, "it seems that this art, unlike other divinatory disciplines, does not concede a great deal of reasoning *(rationem)*, since many of the things that happen in one's life escape human adroitness." In Cardano's view, metoposcopy lacks strong interpretative guidelines because it tries to determine and foresee even the most unexpected and unusual events. Although many condemn this practice because of its vague structure, Cardano continues, classical culture believed that metoposcopy was infallible in determining one's death within a year. For instance, in his biography of Titus, Suetonius reports that a practitioner of this art had predicted that Britannicus, son of Claudius, would never become emperor.[12] If metoposcopy becomes particularly accurate when the surface on which the marks are inscribed is about to be erased (the subject's death), we can infer that for Cardano metoposcopy posits the human face not as an oracle whose message is given once and for all, but rather as a text that writes itself out, as if a face progressively registers the signs of its own memory, including the awareness of its forthcoming death. The act of gathering any form of reasoning *(ratio)* from a human forehead thus translates a set of past phonemes (signs resulting from the subject's past, such as his upbringing, his parents, his traumas) into a future discourse inevitably narrating the subject's end.

Let us clarify at this point what Cardano means by "reasoning" *(ratio)*. In *Liber de animi immortalitate* Cardano defines this concept: "What is reasoning [*ratio*] but a certain capacity of leaping from one imagination [*imaginatione*] to another, from one thought to another, multiplied in no other way than as a net made of a series of knots?"[13] This subtle principle *(tenuis principium)* weaves *(nectet)* images together with great swiftness *(magna velocitate)*. Even when we are about to fall asleep and we discard every thought, Cardano stresses, even in this moment so similar to death, this subtle principle persists. Indeed, it is at the frontier between sleep and wakefulness that this faculty most clearly imposes itself on the mind.[14] In

---

12. Compare C. Suetonius Tranquillus, *The Lives of the Twelve Caesars*, translated by Alexander Thomson (New York: Worthington, 1883), 487.

13. Cardano, *Liber de animi immortalitate*, in *Opera omnia*, edited by Charles Spon, 10 vols. (Lyons, 1663), 2:459. Compare Cardano, *Mnemosynon*, in *Opera omnia*, ed. Spon, 1:231.

14. Ficino tackles the connection between divination, melancholy, and the state of "almost-

this passage Cardano identifies "reasoning" with the soul itself. For Cardano, the soul is its state of alertness and self-perception, which corresponds to its unremitting activity of "weaving" the images stored in its memory *(memoria)*. Memory, Cardano writes in the thirteenth book of *Paralipomenon,* is not only the "repository of all things, both eternal and ephemeral," it is first and foremost "the principal part and faculty of the soul."[15]

It is crucial to note that in Cardano's philosophical system key terms, such as *soul, memory, reasoning, intellect, mind, demons,* acquire specific, and sometimes contradictory, connotations.[16] Thus for Cardano *memory* and *reasoning* do not coincide with what we would understand as their ordinary definitions. Cardano paradoxically holds that reasoning *(ratio)* summons phantasmatic textures made of débris of different remembrances not through reason but rather through the seeming absence of it—that is, in a mental state that is almost *(quasi)* sleep. It is when thoughts are dispelled from the mind that the soul perceives its alertness. Only "wise men" *(sapientes),* Cardano states, are totally wakeful *(vigilant).*[17] Indeed, "those who are wakeful," Cardano explains in *Dialogus de morte,* are like those who suddenly "remember the things they saw when they were dreaming," and not like those "who dream about the things they saw when they were awake."[18] In other words, dreams themselves grant the soul its alertness, in that the soul is awake insofar as its *ratio* is able to recollect past dreams in a mental state that is similar to that preceding sleep.[19]

We have said that for Cardano memory is the central part and faculty of the soul. However, to fully understand what *memoria* is, we must first clarify how Cardano defines the soul. Cardano divides the soul into "soul" *(anima)* and "mind" *(mens).* The "soul" is simply "that substance that is the act of the body, which has only a potential life."[20] To see how the soul

---

sleep" in a crucial chapter of his *Platonic Theology (Theologia platonica,* in *Opera omnia,* 2 vols. [Turin: Bottega d'Erasmo, 1959], vol. 1, part 1, book 13, chap. 2 ("On Philosophers"), 293–95.

15. Cardano, *Paralipomenon,* in *Opera omnia,* ed. Spon, 10:541.

16. On the concept of *ratio* in Pomponazzi's *Tractatus de immortalitate animae,* see Ingegno, *Saggio sulla filosofia di Cardano,* 6.

17. *Paralipomenon,* in *Opera omnia,* ed. Spon, 10:468. Compare Alfonso Ingegno, "Cardano e Bruno. Altri spunti per una storia dell'uomo perfetto," in Kessler, ed., *Girolamo Cardano. Philosoph. Naturforscher. Arzt,* 77–90; Ingegno, "The New Philosophy of Nature," in *The Cambridge History of Renaissance Philosophy,* edited by Quentin Skinner and Eckhard Kessler (New York: Cambridge University Press, 1996), 236–63, in particular pages 247–50.

18. Cardano, *Dialogus de morte,* in *Opera omnia,* ed. Spon, 1:688.

19. As far as the classical interpretations of dreams, I am indebted to Patricia Cox Miller, *Dreams in Late Antiquity: Studies in the Imagination of a Culture* (Princeton: Princeton University Press, 1994).

20. *Liber de animi immortalitate,* in *Opera omnia,* ed. Spon, 2:469.

influences the body, says Cardano, we can look at demoniac people, who show a swollen neck, a reddish face, and tormented eyes.[21] If *anima* is what gives life and form to the body, in the fourth book of *Theonoston* Cardano states that "mind" *(mens)* is similar to the sun's rays, which enlighten us only when they succeed in breaking through the clouds.[22] Indeed, Cardano continues, what is absolutely surprising about mind is that it "learns *[cognosc(i)t]* even though we do not perceive that we are learning."[23]

Could not we say that mind visits us as the sudden memory of a past dream comes to us when we are almost asleep? Mind is certainly one of the most intricate elements of Cardano's philosophy. I will limit myself to highlighting only those aspects of this concept that are essential to Cardano's theory of demonology. We find a detailed analysis of mind in the fourteenth chapter of *De subtilitate,* Cardano's most famous and controversial work. According to Cardano, mind can be divided into four major parts: *iunctio, iudicium, intellectus,* and *voluntas.*[24] These four sections should be seen as two mental activities, each split into two different temporal segments. *Iunctio* (juncture) and *iudicium* (judgment) precede *intellectus* (intellect) and *voluntas* (will). *Iunctio,* Cardano writes, is one of the four essential components of human cognition *(cognitio),* which can be "external" *(exterior),* can tend to repeat itself in a passive manner *(conservatrix),* but can also produce a series of mental connections *(iunctio)* that formulate a conclusive deduction *(iudicium).*[25] The first pair *(exterior-conservatrix)* describes a form of memory that does not depend on a rational process, as when we play an instrument. We know how to reproduce a given melody without thinking about it. Yet *iunctio* is a sort of knowledge stemming from a "multiple memory," that is, from a blending of innumerable memorial units. *Iunctio* is the memory that makes an entire discourse into one intellectual perception, as when we look at a wall painted completely white. What strikes our attention, Cardano explains, is not a specific area of the wall but rather its uniform whiteness. From this unified apprehension we arrive at an intellectual reduction *(iudicium).*

21. *Dialogus de morte,* in *Opera omnia,* ed. Spon, 1:688.
22. Cardano, *Theonoston,* in *Opera omnia,* ed. Spon, 2:438. Cardano clearly borrows the concept of *mens* as the divine core of human identity from Neoplatonism. First of all, see Plotinus, *Enneads,* 5.5.4. The same idea is present in *Pimander* 10 (*Hermetica,* edited by Brian P. Copenhaver [New York: Cambridge University Press, 1998], 2). As far as Ficino is concerned, see his *Commentary on Plato's Symposium,* edited by Sears Jayne (Woodstock, Conn.: Spring Publications, 1985), chaps. 2.3 and 7.13, 47–49 and 169.
23. *Theonoston,* in *Opera omnia,* ed. Spon, 2:439.
24. Cardano, *De subtilitate,* in *Opera omnia,* ed. Spon, 3:583.
25. *De subtilitate,* in *Opera omnia,* ed. Spon, 3:582.

If *iunctio* and *iudicium* coincide with a form of memory that absorbs disparate physical and intellectual experiences into one unifying perception, *intellectus* and *voluntas* correspond to the subsequent process of moving from a mental reduction of the world to an external interaction with the world itself. *Intellectus*, a fundamental term of Cardano's philosophy, "is the apprehended thing itself. If I look at a horse, my intellect [*intellectus*] is the form of the horse."[26] Cardano further explains, "Now, while I am writing this text, my intellect is the things that you will apprehend through my writing."[27] It is evident that Cardano's notion of intellect has an inherently self-reflexive potentiality in that, if it is what the mind reflects upon (the page on which the subject writes out the process of cognition), it is also the act through which the mind perceives its own perceptions. Indeed, in a crucial passage from *Theonoston*, Cardano emphasizes that "to perceive how one's own intellect perceives itself is very different from perceiving how someone perceives his intellect."[28]

Cardano's notion of intellect is similar to contemplation. In the same chapter of *Theonoston*, he clarifies that there are three levels of intellect, according to three different objects of mental perception. The first form of intellect/contemplation is based upon imagination. Our mind sees/imagines what another mind is seeing/imagining. We shall see how this first stage applies to Cardano's intense relationship with his son executed in prison. Indeed, for Cardano the subject who reflects upon himself through someone else corresponds to the fundamental relationship between father and first son.

To say that we imagine what an external subject sees does not mean necessarily that the result of our apprehension is wrong. Later in this chapter we shall examine how for Cardano demonic presences can enlighten each level of our contemplation/intellect. The second level is when an intellect meditates upon itself. At this point intellect is still a process in which the subject perceives his own mind as an object of understanding distinct from himself. In other words, in this second form of contemplation I see myself perceiving my own mind. This differentiation disappears at the third and final stage, in which the subject and his mind become one and only one entity, "with no before and no after." The subject and his mind mirror each other in the surface of *intellectus*.

Cardano emphasizes that his notion of intellect is not far from what we

26. *De subtilitate*, in *Opera omnia*, ed. Spon, 3:583.
27. *De subtilitate*, in *Opera omnia*, ed. Spon, 3:586.
28. *Theonoston*, in *Opera omnia*, ed. Spon, 2:439.

call memory.[29] To see one's own mind in the mirror of intellect is an act of remembrance. The three degrees of contemplation sketched by Cardano are indeed similar to three forms of recollection. In particular, the first stage (to see someone else seeing his own mind) speaks of a conjectural form of remembrance. That someone else is both an external identity that the mind attempts to recall/understand and the subject's mind itself, still separate from its own memory. Thus, for Cardano to understand how another's (or one's own) mind perceives itself essentially means to recognize that my mind and the other's coincide.

For the physician Cardano, contemplation—which he defines as a form of "immortal life in a mortal body"—is not a solipsistic procedure, typical of Renaissance Neoplatonism.[30] Although Cardano does say that "we live as long as we contemplate," he sees contemplation as a form of remembrance arising from physical and mental reality.[31] Let us keep in mind that in Cardano's philosophical system, intellect is followed by *voluntas*, which projects the mind back to the reality of the world out there. To remember the world through meditation means to discern the signs of its perennial discourse.

Indeed, Cardano addresses what we could call the question of exegesis in several texts. In the third book of *Theonoston*, he states that there are eleven ways of learning *(modi cognoscendi)*. The first is a form of true knowledge and derives from the fact that the appearance of a given thing naturally imposes itself upon our senses.[32] The second and the third are erroneous forms of knowledge, either because of the presence of some kind of instrument that distorts our sight (for instance, a mirror) or because our sight itself is faulty.[33] The fourth kind of learning is when we imagine something that is not there. The fifth is when we at once imagine a thing and perceive its presence with our senses. This usually happens when we hypothesize something with our eyes closed. The sixth form of learning occurs if we picture something with our eyes open. According to Cardano, this is a perfect example of ecstasy. The seventh is when we are not sure that we are actually seeing what we are seeing. The eighth is when we

29. *De subtilitate,* in *Opera omnia,* ed. Spon, 3:586.

30. *Theonoston,* in *Opera omnia,* ed. Spon, 2:433.

31. *De subtilitate,* in *Opera omnia,* ed. Spon, 3:584. Compare Ingegno, *Saggio sulla filosofia di Cardano,* 256; Eugenio Garin, *Umanesimo italiano. Filosofia e vita civile nel Rinascimento* (Bari: Laterza, 1994), 214–16. For specific references to Plotinus' idea of contemplation, see the second part of this chapter.

32. *Theonoston,* in *Opera omnia,* ed. Spon, 2:417.

33. *Theonoston,* in *Opera omnia,* ed. Spon, 2:418.

think we see something, but we are not seeing what we think we are see-ing. The ninth form of learning is that of vain dreams, while the tenth con-cerns clear and truthful dreams. The eleventh and last one is a form of learning deriving from "natural causes," such as the voices of animals or the echoes produced in caves.

For Cardano, knowledge occurs when the image of the object analyzed mirrors the image perceived or "imagined" by the analyzer's mind. "True" interpretation is indeed a form of revelation or ecstasy, as Cardano says, in that in the act of contemplation the mind comes to see how the object sees itself. For Cardano this form of sight best takes place when the mind is about to fall asleep, but is not asleep yet.[34] However, in his taxonomy of possible forms of knowledge, dreams are listed after several different imaginary manifestations—as if dreams, fantasy, and true and false sight were expressions of a similar mental process.[35] In the first book of *Syne-siorum somniorum,* the most exhaustive treatise about dreams composed during the Renaissance, Cardano explains that there are three basic kinds of signs: *propria* (particular), *communia* (common), and *coniecturalia* (conjectural).[36] Cardano believes that the first category of signs can present itself both when we dream and when we are awake. When we have clear and distinct dreams, Cardano holds, signs are usually much better de-tectable than when we are awake. However, if we are not asleep, we can at-tain a similar level of clarity in those situations when our soul becomes "almost amazed" *(quasi admirata).*[37] The second group of signs depends

34. Compare *Hermetica,* ed. Copenhaver, treatise 9, 27–28.

35. For the relationship between dream theory and medicine in Cardano, see Nancy Siraisi, *The Clock and the Mirror: Girolamo Cardano and Renaissance Medicine* (Princeton: Princeton University Press, 1997), 174–91.

36. Cardano, *Synesiorum somniorum,* in *Opera omnia,* ed. Spon, 5:600. On this text see the following: Alice Brown, *Sixteenth Century Beliefs on Dreams, with Special Reference to Giro-lamo Cardano's "Somniorum libri IIII"* (London: Warburg Institute, 1971); Jacques Le Brun, "Jérôme Cardan et l'interprétation des songes," in Kessler, ed., *Girolamo Cardano. Philosoph. Naturforscher. Arzt,* 185–206. Nancy Siraisi relates Cardano's treatise to Auger Ferrier's *Liber de somnis* (Lyons, 1549), another fundamental Renaissance book on the meaning and interpre-tation of dreams (*Clock and the Mirror,* 180). The essential difference between Ferrier and Car-dano lies in their specific interpretation of demonic influence on vain or false visions. While for Ferrier "demons" simply coincide with devils and thus affect the mind only in a negative manner, for Cardano demons have a much more nuanced and even contradictory nature. Fer-rier is convinced that it is possible to detect demonic dreams by the images and feelings they stir in the mind. According to Ferrier, demonic dreams are marked with anguish and doubt. More-over, weird and mysterious figures are often characteristic of a dream sent by a demon. I refer to the following Latin/Spanish edition: Auger Ferrier, *Libro de los sueños (Liber de somnis),* edited by Francisco Calero (Madrid: Universidad Nacional de Educacion a Distancia, 1989), 13–14.

37. Let us read a passage from a letter Ficino sent to his friend Giovanni Cavalcanti (in *Meditations on the Soul: Selected Letters of Marsilio Ficino* [Rochester, Vt.: Inner Traditions

upon the subject's nature, age, deeds, customs, time, and ways of sleep.[38] For instance, young people usually have "unstable" dreams, whereas the dreams of pious and moral people are "true." Finally, the third kind of signs is the least clear and defined. One can gather some form of interpretation from the narrative structure of a given dream, such as its length (short dreams tend to be "truer" than long and convoluted ones), its frequency (recurrent dreams are certainly true), and its cohesiveness (sequences of dreams related to each other convey a truthful message). While the first kind refers both to dream-signs and to reality-signs, the second and third categories seem to be exclusively directed to the images seen in dreams.

But what does a "true" dream mean? A dream-image is true when and if the dreamer is capable of re-cognizing it as a recovered memory, as the sudden remembrance of a familiar face. An image or sign signifies its truth by revealing itself (its face) to the subject's intellect. Let us remember that for Cardano intellect is the surface through which the mind mirrors the object of its analysis (a dream, the lines of the forehead, the symptoms of an illness). This is why Cardano posits a fundamental connection between the act of dreaming and that of thinking.[39] Like a dream, Cardano explains, a thought is truthful if it is unquestionably "clear"—that is, if the mind receives it in an "ecstatic" manner.[40] In book 2, chapter 8 of *Synesiorum somniorum*, Cardano explains that "ecstasy is a state between sleep and wakefulness, as sleep is the state between death and wakefulness or life."[41] We recall that in the *Liber de animi immortalitate*, insight visits the mind when it is close to sleep. This stress on the mutual influence between sleep and alertness is a central element of Synesius' *De insomnis*, the text Cardano refers to in the title of his treatise. The fifth-century Neoplatonic thinker and Catholic bishop Synesius sees a fundamental connection between "the waking state of the dreamer [and] the sleeping state of the awakened, for both are concentrated upon the same underlying state"—

International, 1996], 45): "When in sleep the workings and movements of the external senses cease, then the imagination, which is fed by the rest of the senses, gathers so much strength that it paints pictures internally, which seem to represent what is real. What therefore will the intellect, which is so much more powerful than the imagination, do when it has escaped free from impediments to a far greater extent than the imagination of the dreaming man, and in pure truth and reason perceives the true principles of everything?"

38. In *Norma vitae consarcinata* Cardano states that, along with food and physical exercise, sleep is something we should consider with care (in *Opera omnia*, ed. Spon, 1:350).

39. *Synesiorum somniorum*, in *Opera omnia*, ed. Spon, 5:601.

40. Compare Rivari, *La mente di Girolamo Cardano*, 186–88.

41. *Synesiorum somniorum*, in *Opera omnia*, ed. Spon, 5:680.

the pursuit of knowledge through a semiotic reading of the creation.[42] As Patricia Cox Miller summarizes, "in Synesian theory, dreams can be a legitimization of experience insofar as they give self-awareness."[43] Indeed, for Synesius "all things are signs appearing through all things, inasmuch as they are brothers in a single living creature, the cosmos."[44] According to Synesius, in the "borderland between unreason and reason, between the bodiless and the body," the mind succeeds in gleaning some form of inner wisdom.[45] To interpret a dream is like learning a new language, says Synesius, "one reads [dreams] by syllables, another reads the complete phrase, another the whole story."[46]

The essential connection between Synesius' oneiric theory and Cardano's is now apparent. Cardano defines as "idols" *(idola)* those dreams that "simply show themselves" without requesting any further interpretation.[47] Dreams that trigger any form of exegesis or divination are *insomnia* or *visa* (appearances, visions).[48] *Insomnia* is the plural form of *insomnium*, a variation of *somnium* (dream), and is also a word meaning "sleeplessness." By this paradoxical word Cardano seems not only to refer to his primary source, Synesius' *De insomnis*, but also to hint at the state of alertness these images require.[49] In any case, unlike Synesius, in his treatise Cardano always uses *insomnia* as a technical term indicating visions *(visa)* that entail the dreamer's active presence, while *somnia* serves as the generic word referring to what the subject sees while asleep. Let us remember that for Cardano "ecstasy" best occurs when the mind is still awake but close to sleep. By *insomnia*, we could infer, Cardano means any

42. I quote from the Fitzgerald translation (*Concerning Dreams*, in *The Essays and Hymns of Synesius of Cyrene*, edited by Augustine Fitzgerald, vol. 2 [Oxford: Oxford University Press, 1930], 1305, 15–20, 346). Cardano knew Synesius through Ficino's translation (*Synesius de somnis translatus a Marsilii Ficini Florentino*, in *Opera omnia*, 2:1968–79).

43. Miller, *Dreams in Late Antiquity*, 70.

44. Synesius, *Concerning Dreams* (ed. Fitzgerald), 1284, 5–10, 328.

45. Synesius, *Concerning Dreams* (ed. Fitzgerald), 1289, 25, 334.

46. Synesius, *Concerning Dreams* (ed. Fitzgerald), 1284, 10–15, 328.

47. *Synesiorum somniorum*, in *Opera omnia*, ed. Spon, 5:604.

48. Compare Le Brun, "Jérôme Cardan et l'interprétation des songes," 190. In *On Divination in Sleep*, Aristotle is quite skeptical about the divinatory nature of dreams, even though he admits that "some of the images which come before the mind in sleep may even be causes of the actions cognate to each of them" (463a, 20, in *The Complete Works of Aristotle*, edited by Jonathan Barnes, 2 vols. [Princeton: Princeton University Press, 1985], 737). The reason is that, "when we are about to act, or are engaged in any course of action, or have already performed certain actions, we often find ourselves concerned with those actions, or performing them, in a vivid dream" (463a, 25). Thus, in some specific cases dreams are indeed "signs and causes" of forthcoming events (463a, 30). Compare Macrobius, *In somnium scipionis*, chap. 3.

49. *Synesiorum somniorum*, in *Opera omnia*, ed. Spon, 5:605.

phantasmatic manifestation that alludes to a possibly forthcoming revelation. Cardano is convinced that "idols" are in fact extremely rare, because there is almost always something "perverse" or "obscure" in dreams.[50] The inherent perversity of any dream, we shall see, in part results from the mind's constant dialogue with the "superior beings," angels and devils alike. On the other hand, Cardano holds that in some cases *insomnia* do convey a clear meaning, but only if the mind is "transparent like a mirror."[51] Indeed, Cardano is convinced that when we dream, we see things "as in a mirror, that is, what is on the right is in fact on the left and what is on the left is on the right . . . and if the mirror is not totally flat things look distorted."[52]

It should be evident by now that Cardano does not see any specific difference between dream-signs and reality-signs; that is, for Cardano in any act of exegesis or divination the human mind experiences only one form of alertness or ecstasy. Many scholars have pointed out how significant dreams were for Cardano, how influential they were in his interpretations of the most disparate events of his life.[53] However, we should understand that for Cardano reality and dreams speak the same idiom; they manipulate, hide, and reveal their signs in a very similar manner. We could say that, according to Cardano, both reality and dreams demand a state of "insomnia."[54]

To clarify this central point, let us mention one of the most uncanny events of Cardano's life, related in the third book of *Paralipomenon*. One

---

50. *Synesiorum somniorum*, in *Opera omnia*, ed. Spon, 5:689.

51. *Synesiorum somniorum*, in *Opera omnia*, ed. Spon, 5:675.

52. *Synesiorum somniorum*, in *Opera omnia*, ed. Spon, 5:688.

53. Ficino explores the connection between dreams, divination, and the soul's divine nature. See, for instance, the letter he wrote to the philosopher Matteo Corsini in which he justifies his belief in divination by recounting what had happened to his mother and his grandfather. One night, they both had the very same dream foretelling the death of Ficino's grandmother. For Ficino, "the souls of men . . . are almost separated from their bodies because of a temperate disposition and a pure life may in the abstraction of sleep divine many things" (*Meditations on the Soul*, 42–43).

54. My interpretation of Cardano's metoposcopy is clearly indebted to the philosophy of Emmanuel Levinas. I relate Cardano's concepts of "wakefulness" and "insomnia" to Levinas's fundamental "there is" (*il y a*), the state of insomnia in which the subject perceives the face of the other as an unremitting request. As an example, see Levinas's *Of God Who Comes to Mind*, translated by Bettina Bergo (Stanford: Stanford University Press, 1998), 58: "Far from being defined as a simple negation of the natural phenomenon of sleep, insomnia—as wakefulness or vigilance—comes out of the logic of the categories, prior to all anthropological attention and dullness. Always on the verge of awakening, sleep communicates with wakefulness; while attempting to escape from it, sleep remains attuned to it in *obedience to the wakefulness* that threatens and calls to it, the wakefulness that *demands*" (emphasis in original).

night in 1565 Cardano's bed suddenly and unexpectedly caught fire.[55] A boy who slept in a small bed next to Cardano's woke him up because the philosopher's bed was burning. As we might read in a Freudian story ("Father, don't you see I'm burning?"), Cardano goes back to sleep after extinguishing the mysterious fire.[56] Asleep, he has fearful dreams *(timorosa)* and sees himself running away from something. Because of the smoke and the flames, he wakes up again and realizes that an actual fire is again destroying his bed. However, the flames seem uninterested in burning his clothes.

What is absolutely remarkable in this story is that on this night in 1565 reality spoke to Cardano the language of dreams, while his dreams expressed only blurred and fearful sentences. "Smoke," Cardano analyzes, "means dishonor; fire [means] danger and fright." Moreover, "a fire can also refer to a magistrate." That his clothes were not burned meant that he would be able to escape the imminent danger related to some kind of conspiracy against him. Rather than examining reality only from a causal standpoint (how did the bed catch fire? why did the flames avoid his clothes?), Cardano believes in the possibility of reading existence also according to what it says.[57]

In the fourth book of *Synesiorum somniorum*, Cardano states that to understand a given event we can look at its "natural causes" or at its "signs, as in physiognomy or even more in metoposcopy."[58] The marks on a subject's forehead certainly say something, even if their listener/reader is unable to decode their message. In some cases, the meaning of a puzzling occurrence becomes intelligible thanks to some following events. Cardano makes it clear that reality's signs (a bed setting itself on fire, a set of obscure letters inscribed on the face) can be read as conveying a message concerning both/either the present and/or the past and/or the future. For in-

55. *Paralipomenon,* in *Opera omnia,* ed. Spon, 10:464.
56. Sigmund Freud, *The Interpretation of Dreams,* translated by James Stachey (New York: Basic Books, 1956), chap. 7 ("The Psychology of the Dream-Processes"), 509–11: "A father had been watching beside his child's sick-bed for days and nights on end. After the child had died, he went into the next room to lie down, but left the door open so that he could see from his bedroom into the room in which his child's body was laid out, with tall candles standing around it. An old man had been engaged to keep watch over it, and sat beside the body murmuring prayers. After a few hours' sleep, the father had a dream that *his child was standing beside his bed, caught him by the arm and whispered to him reproachfully: 'Father, don't you see I'm burning?'"* (509; emphasis in original).
57. Campanella attacks Cardano's interpretation of dreams in *Theologicorum liber XIV,* edited by Romano Amerio (Rome: Bocca, 1957), 80–83.
58. *Synesiorum somniorum,* in *Opera omnia,* ed. Spon, 5:705.

stance, says Cardano, let us imagine that we are visited by an acquaintance who wants to murder us. Now, the event of our death can be seen either in its causes, or in its present developments, or in its future consequences.[59] Reality may even send out a sign synthesizing all three temporal levels.

As a further example, consider an episode described in the chapter "Certain Natural Eccentricities" from *The Book of My Life.* Cardano writes: "A few weeks before my older son was arrested and then executed, one day looking at my hands, I observed on the ring finger on the right one, at the root, the image of a bloody sword. . . . That very evening a messenger appeared, afoot, bearing letters from my son-in-law, advising me that my son had been arrested." [60] From that moment on, that sign gradually ascended his finger up to the tip where "it blazed a blood-red flame." The mark disappeared after the execution of his son. What was the actual message of the blazing flame on the finger? As a warning, the blazing fire signified a state of sudden, "burning" crisis, in which a present event (his son under arrest), deriving from a violent past (his son's murder of his wife), portended an ominous conclusion (his son's death). Synthesizing all three occurrences, the blazing sword on the finger primarily meant its imminent extinction.

Rather than simply trying to understand how reality says what it says (how did his finger get that blazing mark? why did it move up to the tip of his finger?), Cardano investigates how human intellect may succeed in reflecting, echoing reality's discourse in order to respond to its warning signals.[61] Indeed, as I shall show, Cardano is convinced that every possible sign emitted by reality (through dreams, visions, metoposcopy, astrology) is first and foremost a gesture of admonition, an anticipation of adversity and chaos. Even when the intellect is an opaque surface, unable to mirror the text delivered by reality to the mind (an indistinct dream, a mole or an inscription on the forehead difficult to decipher), the subject still senses that reality is speaking to him with a solicitous and apprehensive voice.[62]

---

59. *Synesiorum somniorum,* in *Opera omnia,* ed. Spon, 5:603.

60. *Book of My Life,* 154.

61. Compare *Book of My Life,* 137.

62. Innumerable are the anthropological studies of how specific civilizations theorize the relationship between divination and time, physical signs and dreams. In her fascinating work *The Last Word: Women, Death, and Divination in Inner Mani* (Chicago: University of Chicago Press, 1989), Nadia Seremetakis examines the culture of Inner Mani, "the middle finger of the Morea, the trisected peninsula of the southern Peloponnese" (16). Analyzing how, in this rural region of Greece, women see the art of divination, dreams, and the care of the dead, Seremetakis writes: "In the Inner Maniat construction of self and body, the self, with the exception of the

Immediately after the story of the burning bed, in the third book of
Paralipomenon Cardano relates another unusual occurrence, one that is
very different from a semiotic point of view. In 1563, while he was in
Bologna, one evening Cardano saw the sky beautifully rippled with dense
white clouds, as if crafted with unique art.[63] It was an extremely rare event
that no one seemed to have remarked before. The sky, Cardano writes,
looked like a quiet ocean, curled with a variety of waves, some dark and
dense, others lighter and thinner. What was the purpose of such a mag-
nificent sky? What did the clouds/waves endeavor to communicate? The
viewer certainly perceived the materialization of an imposing message, but
his intellect was unable to translate its phonemes into an act of *voluntas*.
This kind of difficulty, Cardano explains in *Paralipomenon*, is typical of
dreams, when, for instance, we hear a voice but cannot understand what
it is saying.[64] However, he adds, when "the soul's senses are clear," in a
dream we manage to discern the words expressed by that imaginary voice.
Thus, Cardano asks himself, "what prevents [us] from having such experience also when we are awake?" It is true that when we are awake, our
senses can become distracted more easily.[65] However, if existence first
and foremost speaks the language of admonition, its different channels of
communication (reality, visions, dreams, thoughts) cannot represent essentially different alternatives of expression. What matters is that, in order "to see," or better yet to have visions *(visa* or *insomnia)*, the human
mind must have "clear senses"—that is, it must allow its vision *(visum)* to
speak itself.

Cardano believes that there are four basic forms of visions or "imaginations" (by this term he means not a fanciful and unreal mental product
but rather the act through which a phantasmatic message comes to the
mind). In the first kind of vision, we imagine something, but our eyes and
ears perceive something different.[66] In the second we imagine something
and actually see or hear the same thing. This form is superior to the first
and is called *spectrum* (appearance, specter). The third type of vision occurs if we neither imagine nor think about anything, but we see and hear

---

dream state, is tied to the present while the body and the flesh are tied to the invisible do-
mains of the past and the future—a dynamic that creates dissonance between the self and the
body" (64). Dreams, Seremetakis further explains, embody this blending of different time
levels (231–33).

63. *Paralipomenon,* in *Opera omnia,* ed. Spon, 10:464.
64. *Paralipomenon,* in *Opera omnia,* ed. Spon, 10:473.
65. *Paralipomenon,* in *Opera omnia,* ed. Spon, 10:472.
66. *Paralipomenon,* in *Opera omnia,* ed. Spon, 10:475.

something. Cardano defines this experience as *genius* (genius). The fourth and final vision is the highest and most powerful one and takes place while we are imagining nothing, although we are deeply immersed in thinking, reading, or reciting something. Suddenly we remember or sense a vision. This experience is called *daemonium* (demon) and is divided into two temporal sections, "invocation to demons" *(invocatio daemonum)* and "vision of a demon" *(visio daemonis).*

Before analyzing the four forms of "demonic" visitations, we should note that in *Paralipomenon* "specter," "genius," and "demon" are not the messengers of a given vision; rather, they coincide with a specific mode of sight. Further, only the last kind of vision involves the mind's active participation. Indeed, the "invocation to demons" (thinking, reading, or reciting something) is the part leading to the reception of the "demonic vision." In his definition of demonic manifestations Cardano refers to the complex and ambiguous notions of Platonic and Neoplatonic philosophy. In Renaissance culture the term *demon* covers a wide range of meanings, from the Socratic "daimon" to the Christian "devil." [67] It is thus impossible to reach a binding definition of Cardano's various "superior minds" (specter, genius, demon).[68] Clearly, however, Cardano did believe in the existence of

---

67. An interesting example of Renaissance syncretism can be found in the so-called *trattati d'amore* (treatises on love), the most popular philosophical genre of the Italian Renaissance. As is well known, given the enormous success of Ficino's commentary on Plato's *Symposium*, similar treatises were written in Italy until the end of the sixteenth century. These books discussed, according to a strictly Neoplatonic view, the nature and goal of love experience. However, a few texts merged Catholicism and Neoplatonism with very interesting results. For instance, Pompeo della Barba's *Spositione d'un sonetto platonico* (Florence, 1554) offers a fascinating interpretation of demonic beings. Expressing a sort of pre-Romantic sensibility, della Barba believes that the memory of an unrequited love stays in the soul even after its death. Tormented by this constant thought, this soul turns into a demon roaming around in search of the beloved. The demon goes back to the places where the beloved lives and even visits him in dreams. These demons often run into human beings who are deeply shocked and even die as a result of this demonic encounter (87). I study the connections between Ficino, Plotinus, and this treatise on love in "Demonologia e platonismo nel trattato d'amore *Spositione d'un sonetto platonico*," *Italianistica* 28, no. 1 (1999): 9–21. For an engaging analysis of Ficinian demonology, see Gary Tomlinson, *Music in Renaissance Magic* (Chicago: University of Chicago Press, 1993), 123–29.

68. In *Magiae omnifariae, vel potius, universae naturae theatrum* (Cologne: Conradus Butgenius, 1607), Strozzio Gigogna analyzes how "wise men" derive their knowledge from demonic beings (book 4, part 1, "On the demons' pact with magicians and wise men"). Gigogna stresses that demons often present themselves as "friends eager to help" (438). He applies the usual distinction between "explicit" and "implicit" pact not to the relationship between witches and demons, but rather to the deceptive enlightenment devils offer to "men of science." After describing the different forms of demonic beings, such as "genius" and "lemur" (book 3, chap. 8), Gigogna concludes by stressing that human knowledge is "inconstant" (560) and exclusively based on a rational interpretation of physical impressions (562).

"demons," whatever he thought they were.[69] In the famous nineteenth chapter of *De subtilitate* ("De daemonibus"), he notes that his father had a personal demon for more than thirty years; one day (August 20, 1491) seven demons in Greek costume visited Cardano's father to hold a scholastic debate on the eternity of the world.[70] When he asked them about their nature and age, the demons said that they were "almost ethereal men" *(homines . . . quasi aëreos),* and that their existence was not eternal but certainly much longer than a human being's (up to three hundred years).[71]

Cardano himself had a sort of private demon. In chapter 47 of his autobiography, he states that, like "Socrates, Plotinus, Synesius, Dio, Flavius Josephus," he had a "guardian spirit," who warned him about imminent dangers.[72] I have already stressed that for Cardano admonition is the ultimate topic of reality's speech. We have seen that for Cardano natural signs (metoposcopy, dreams, visions) primarily warn the viewer about some forthcoming disorder and ultimately about his own end. For instance, when his beloved son proposed to his future wife, Cardano's demon sent him palpitations of the heart.[73] In the same chapter, Cardano offers his synthesis of Renaissance syncretistic views on demonic beings:

> In general, the characters of these guardian spirits among the ancients have been manifold and diverse. There have been restraining spirits, as that of Socrates; admonishing as that of Cicero, which appeared to him in death; there have been spirits instructing mortals in what was yet to come, through dreams, through the actions of the lower creatures, through fateful events; influencing us as to where we should go; luring us on; now appealing to one sense, now to several at the same time. . . . Likewise there are good and evil spirits.[74]

69. Compare Stuart Clark, *Thinking with Demons: The Idea of Witchcraft in Early Modern Europe* (Oxford: Clarendon Press, 1997), 278.

70. *De subtilitate,* in *Opera omnia,* ed. Spon, 3:656.

71. Cardano mentions the same event in chap. 93 of book 15 of *De rerum varietate* (Avignon: Matthaeus Vincentius, 1558), 808–9. In *Tableau de l'inconstance des mauvais anges* (Paris: Nicolas Buon, 1613), Pierre de Lancre reports and attacks this episode. The alleged "profound mysteries" the demons revealed to Cardano's father were a "false doctrine" (422). De Lancre mentions Agrippa, Merlin, Nypho, and Cardano as examples of intellectuals who had some commerce with devils. Not only "ignorant women" *(femmelettes)* and "idiots," de Lancre says, but also well-read philosophers worship Satan (423). As far as the "almost ethereal" nature of demons, see Ficino's *In Plotinum,* in *Opera omnia,* vol. 2, part 2, chap. 10, 1553–54.

72. *Book of My Life,* 240. For an analysis of Socrates' demon, see Thomas C. Brickhouse and Nicholas D. Smith, *Plato's Socrates* (New York: Oxford University Press, 1994), 189–95. On the concept of "guardian spirit," see Plotinus, *Enneads* 3.4.

73. *Book of My Life,* 241. Compare Siraisi, *Clock and the Mirror,* 166–67.

74. *Book of My Life,* 242.

It is evident that for Cardano the superior minds (or "guardian spirits") exist insofar as they communicate to the human mind.[75] Adopting a Neoplatonic and thus heretical stance on the issue of angelic expression, in some passages Cardano maintains that demons are inferior to good angels, which he calls "celestial intellects."[76] In chapter 6 of *De arcanis aeternitatis*, he includes an illustration summarizing the relationship between angels, demons, humans, and the physical world.[77] Cardano posits the celestial intellects beyond the cir-

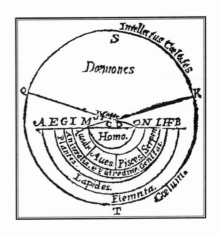

cumference of a sphere whose center is "mind." "Demons" take up the superior half of the sphere, while "man" shares the lower half with the rest of the created world, animals, plants, stones, and elements. However, Cardano makes it clear that "man," posited just beneath the center, is encompassed by "mind," as if "man" were an emanation of "mind." Therefore, according to this scheme, while the angelic intellects are completely inaccessible and out of reach, "mind" is the essential link between human beings and demons, the so-called "superior minds."[78]

For Cardano, to investigate the role and goal of demonic presences primarily entails an understanding of the concept of mind. "Whence does our mind originate?" Cardano asks himself in an earlier chapter of *De arcanis aeternitatis*. "What is it?" We have already analyzed how he interprets the relationship between soul and mind. If soul is the form of the body, mind is at once internal and external to the human mind in that, as Cardano writes in *Theonoston*, it visits the human mind as the sun's rays enlighten our sight. "I am aware," he says in *The Book of My Life*, "that I have received all things whatsoever I have known through the channels of the

75. In *Concerning Dreams*, Synesius states that an "oracle" is always with us and that "it is impossible to desert our oracle . . . even if we so desired. Nay, even if we remain at home, she dwells with us; if we go abroad she accompanies us; she is with us on the field of battle" ([ed. Fitzgerald], 1304, 5–10, 345).

76. Compare David Keck, *Angels and Angelology in the Middle Ages* (New York: Oxford University Press, 1998), 173–74.

77. *De arcanis aeternitatis*, in *Opera omnia*, ed. Spon, 10:7.

78. Compare Iamblichus, *De mysteriis*, 280–282.3.

spirits. To what end then are my senses? Do I know everything?"[79] Even the basest form of knowledge, that deriving from the senses, is processed through the mind.

In her seminal study of Cardano's medical treatises, Nancy Siraisi mentions a central passage from *Contradicentium medicorum*, which is of great use for our analysis.[80] At the end of chapter 6 ("Deus an singula quaque cognoscat"), in an attempt to reach a plausible definition of *genius*, Cardano states that a genius is either a "perpetual" being, or exists in man's mind as an "ethereal vehicle." In other words, a genius is either a constant state of mind or something that visits the mind from time to time. Cardano mentions a third, and much more significant, possibility. It could be that "two things know in us, the soul and the genius."[81] What the genius/soul "knows" is first of all the subject's past and destiny.[82] Indeed, although memory is at once a physical occurrence (marks on the face, scars, age signs) and an intellectual one, only the soul/genius "understands" memory, or more precisely, only that faculty of the mind called intellect with the aid of its genius can reflect the remembrances written both in the body and in the mind.

A fundamental question arises at this point. How does Cardano distinguish the different definitions of "superior minds," those "ethereal vehicles" that may exist within the human mind? What is the actual difference between specter, genius, demon, and guardian spirit? In the passage from *De arcanis aeternitatis* cited above, Cardano seems to subsume all these names under the term *daemones*.[83] We can find an insightful analysis of this linguistic problem in the chapter "On the Demons' Names" in *Paralipomenon*.[84] What does *daemon* mean? According to Cardano, it means "wise man" *(sapientem)*, which is similar to *cacodaemonem*, that is, "beautiful and auspicious wise man," and not *cachodaemonem*, which

79. *Book of My Life*, 245. Compare Plotinus, *Enneads* 3.3.4.

80. Siraisi, *Clock and the Mirror*, 168.

81. Cardano, *Contradicentium medicorum*, in *Opera omnia*, ed. Spon, 6:659.

82. Cardano's definition is very close to Apuleius' concept of "guardian daemons" in *On the God of Socrates*. Apuleius holds that guardian daemons are "lodged like an intimate guest deeply in the mind" (Apuleius, *De deo Socratis*, in *Apulée: Opuscules philosophiques et fragments*, edited by Jean Beaujeu (Paris: Les Belles Lettres, 1973), 16, 156, 36. I use Miller's translation (*Dreams in Late Antiquity*, 57). Compare Plotinus, *Enneads* 3.4.5. Plotinus states that the guardian spirit is at once ours and not ours.

83. For a brief discussion of Cardano's demonology, see Jean Céard, *La nature et les prodiges* (Geneva: Droz, 1977), 338–49; Terence Cave, *Pré-histoires. Texts troublés au seuil de la modernité* (Geneva: Droz, 1999), 65–68.

84. *Paralipomenon*, in *Opera omnia*, ed. Spon, 10:476.

means "bad and hostile genius." [85] In this passage, *daemon* acquires a fully human identity, while *genius* becomes the negative and ethereal alter ego of the positive and human "demon." Cardano also mentions the classical *lar*, the demon "of domestic help," and the *lemur*, which is strictly connected to us and whose original meaning is "shade or ghost of a departed." [86] In Cardano's interpretation, "[l]emur . . . is like our face reflected in a mirror" *(velut facies nostra in speculo visa).*

Cardano's detailed list of demonic beings (specter, genius, demon, lar, lemur), which seems reminiscent of Apuleius' classification, actually signifies different forms of vision, from the mere appearance of something (specter), to the imposition of a totally unexpected visual presence (demon), to the final unveiling of a phantasmatic coincidence between human and demonic identity (lemur as the representation of our own face).[87] As I have pointed out, for Cardano demons are less external entities than faculties (ethereal beings) residing in the subject's mind but independent

85. On *cacodaemones*, compare *Synesiorum somniorum,* in *Opera omnia,* ed. Spon, 5:615.

86. In the seventh book of *L'incredulité et miscreance du sortilege plainement convaincue,* De Lancre defines "lemures" as "the souls of evil and vile people, who had been banned from any hiererchy of good spirits." These "lemures" roam from place to place "to molest those who live badly" (364). De Lancre borrows what Augustine says about Platonic demonology in *The City of God,* book 9, chap. 11. Attacking Apuleius' *De deo Socratis,* Augustine states: "Apuleius indeed also says that the souls of men are demons and that, on ceasing to be men, they become *lares,* if they have deserved this reward for their good conduct, and *lemures* or *larvae* if they have been bad, while they are called *di manes* if it is uncertain whether they have behaved well or ill. What an abysmal pit of profligacy is opened up before men's feet by those who hold this belief" (Augustine, *The City of God,* book 9, chap. 11, translated by David Wiesen [Cambridge, Mass.: Harvard University Press, 1988], 189–91). Augustine continues his attack against Neoplatonism in chaps. 12 (On the three opposites by which the Platonists distinguish between the nature of demons and of men) and 13 (How the demons, if they share neither blessedness with the gods nor misery with men, can be midway between the two and have nothing in common with either).

87. Cardano speaks of *spectra* in chap. 86 of book 15 of *De rerum varietate.* Specters, he says, are illusions of the senses. This is why they usually "occur" at night, when the clarifying light of the sun is absent (760). In the same chapter he goes on to analyze the evocative procedures in cemeteries at night (761). In chap. 15 of *De deo Socratis,* Apuleius offers a detailed analysis of different forms of demonic beings. According to Apuleius, "Genius" or "Eudamion" may identify with the soul itself when it is still connected with the body. "Lemur" is the soul after leaving its body. "Lares" and "Larvae" are the demons who visit us with good (Lares) or noxious intentions (Larvae). In chap. 16 Apuleius also mentions the demons of love and sleep. See also his *Apology,* chap. 64 (*Apologia sive de magia liber,* edited by Giuseppe Augello [Turin: Utet, 1984], 262). On Apuleius' interpretation of dreams, see Miller, *Dreams in Late Antiquity,* 57–59; Frederick E. Brenk, "In the Light of the Moon: Demonology in the Early Imperial Period," in *Aufstieg und Niedergang der Römischen Welt, II, Principat,* edited by Wolfgang Haase (Berlin: De Gruyter, 1986), 16, 3, 2068–2145; Jacqueline Amat, *Songes et visions: L'Au-delà dans la littérature latine tardive* (Paris: Études Augustiniennes, 1985), 161–63.

from the mind itself. Demons are the "reflections" of our sight, in the sense that they are at once the manifestation and the exegesis of what we see. For Cardano, we may infer, demons ultimately participate in the human intellect.

The ethereal presences that inhabit our mind do not depend on our subjectivity. In the final sentence of his autobiography, Cardano explains that his "attendant spirit can neither be described nor alluded to and is not under my control."[88] According to Cardano, that demons linger in our mind without being part of it does not entail that our mind is always and inevitably foreign to itself, as in the case of a diabolical possession. Cardano responds to the Christian view of demonic presences in *De rerum varietate* (book 15, chap. 93).[89] He starts off by quoting Psellus' short treatise *De operatione daemonum*, one of the earliest Christian attacks on Neoplatonic demonology. In Cardano's description of this eleventh-century Byzantine text, all demons are said to be immortal and bad.[90] He notes that Psellus believes that once a demon has entered the mind, it corrupts its faculties and jeopardizes its deeds. As a consequence, the possessed person's body becomes the demon's passive instrument. The demoniac shakes, screams, and simply voices the demon's will.[91] Cardano is convinced that Christian theology has overlooked the infinite variety of demonic beings in that, like humans or animals, demons differ from each other according to their wisdom, qualities, and natural propensities.[92] Reconciling his Neoplatonic

88. *Book of My Life*, 292. Cardano repeats a similar concept in the opening pages of *De praeceptis ad filios* (in *Opera omnia*, ed. Spon, 1:475), when he warns his sons to be careful with demons and the spirits of the dead.

89. To find a clear and exhaustive discussion of the differences between the Aristotelian, Platonic, Neoplatonic, and Catholic concepts of "demon," we can refer to *Discorso dell'eccellentissimo filosofo Francesco de' Vieri intorno a' dimoni* (Florence: Sermantelli, 1576), a little known Italian text of the sixteenth century. To avoid any confusion, Vieri decides to use "spirit" (*spirito*) throughout his work (3). He notes that for Plato "demon" is "that power of our soul that governs us" (6). See also Francesco Cattani Diacceto, *De pulchro*, edited by Sylvain Matton (Pisa: Scuola Normale, 1986), 3.3, 179–89.

90. *De rerum varietate*, 805. I use an Italian edition of Psellus' *De operatione daemonum*: Psello, *Dell'attività dei demoni* (Genoa : Edizioni Culturali Internazionali Genova, 1985). This brief text opens with the casual encounter of two friends. The first section is dedicated not to the devils themselves, but rather to the heretics, who are Satan's servants. The actual discussion on the role and powers of demons takes up the second part of the book. Psellus gives a graphic description of the demons' horrible customs. In particular, he is convinced that demons do have a body (33). Like vampires, demons are drawn to the smell of blood (33–34).

91. *De rerum varietate*, 806.

92. *De rerum varietate*, 807. For a good summary of the classical view of demons' faculties, appearance, and functions, see Otto Böcher, *Dämonenfurcht und Dämonenabwehr* (Stuttgart: Kohlhammer, 1970), 40–79.

views with Catholic dogma, Cardano holds that bad demons succeed in invading our mind and our body only because of our sordid thoughts or negative actions.[93] In other words, bad angels come to us because we have called them.[94]

For Cardano, the essential distinction between good and bad demons lies in the visions they grant us.[95] I have already explained that for Cardano demons are less actual beings than forms of vision—that is, demons are what they make us see. Thus bad demons induce false and deceptive images, while good demons lead the mind toward ecstasy, which occurs when the mind succeeds in mirroring the received phantasmatic message—that is, when the subject re-cognizes, recalls the "truthfulness" of what he sees. I have also stressed that intellect—one of the four faculties of the mind according to Cardano (see above)—signifies this very act of mental reflection.[96] To Cardano, reflection is a human and a demonic activity alike. For a human being, to reflect (upon) a demonic visual communication is an act based on *spectra* (visual presences, appearances) and *ratio* (the faculty of weaving re-cognized images together).[97]

Demonic reflection is essentially different from ours. Indeed, Cardano emphasizes, demons do not understand in the way that human beings do.[98] We can find fascinating similarities between Prierio's position on demonic reasoning (the devil's perverted syllogism; see chapter 1) and Cardano's description of visual communication between demons and humans. While human beings reason through "discourse," Cardano explains, demons understand human beings by means of custom or predictability *(consuetudo)*. He means that demons do not need *ratio* as an instrument of comprehension. The truth of a given image offers itself to them at once and with no restriction. However, this immediate perception does not entail a comprehension of the rationale behind the image itself. This is why demons need to follow people's behaviors very closely. To clarify this point, in *De secretis* Cardano compares a demonic reasoning to our attempt to interpret what ants know of their huge subterranean constructions.[99] We are

93. *De rerum varietate*, 813.
94. Compare Plotinus, *Enneads* 1.8.4.
95. Compare Iamblichus, *De mysteriis*, 190.4–191.11.
96. Compare *De subtilitate*, in *Opera omnia*, ed. Spon, 3:583.
97. *De rerum varietate*, 815.
98. *De rerum varietate*, 835.
99. *De secretis*, in *Opera omnia*, ed. Spon, 2:548 (chap. 19). On this treatise, see William Eamon, *Science and the Secrets of Nature* (Princeton: Princeton University Press, 1994), 278–81.

certainly superior to ants, but we are still unable to understand them. In *De rerum varietate*, instead of ants Cardano mentions our relationship with dogs. Dogs sense things (through all the five senses) of which we are ignorant.[100] Similarly, demons are unable to decode our geometrical sketches or our mathematical schemes.

Cardano's interpretation of linguistic exchange between demons and humans does not contradict the traditional stance of Catholic theology on this matter. As we have seen in Prierio's work, Christian devils speak to us but do not share our language based on memory and desire. Likewise, Cardano is convinced that demons and human beings converse with each other without actually speaking to each other, if by speaking we mean the possession of a common linguistic field. More than understanding what each other says, demons and human beings gather some kind of "wisdom" by interpreting each other's linguistic gestures. Indeed, in the first book of *De sapientia*, Cardano states that human beings can attain four kinds of wisdom: divine, natural, human, and demonic.[101] In particular, we may apprehend demonic wisdom through dreams, ecstasies, visions of multiple forms, and arts of divination (metoposcopy, astrology), even though we always perceive the demons' signs as obscure "figures" and enigmas.[102]

But what kind of knowledge does demonic wisdom grant us? This is a particularly important point in Cardano's demonology. We have seen that for Cardano demons embody a variety of moral and intellectual positions. However, when he comes to describe the actual properties of demonic wisdom in chapter 4 of *De sapientia*, Cardano takes up the traditional Catholic view of demonic presences, interpreting *demon* as a synonym for *devil*. According to Cardano, demonic wisdom encompasses four major areas of activity, none of them positive or virtuous.[103] Demons may lead us to commit crimes, to pursue vain things, to attain something good but through bad means, and to deceive others. The first kind of wisdom involves incest, fire, and robbery. The second refers to various arts of divination. The third concerns incantations and sacrifices to idols. The fourth and final demonic wisdom corresponds to alchemy and forgery.

How can we possibly make sense of Cardano's contradictory statements on demonic influences? Even when demons coincide with guardian spirits,

---

100. *De rerum varietate*, book 16, chap. 93, 836 and 846. The same reference to dogs is found in *Hyperchen*, in *Opera omnia*, ed. Spon, 1:287.

101. *De sapientia*, in *Opera omnia*, ed. Spon, 1:496.

102. *Hyperchen*, in *Opera omnia*, ed. Spon, 1:287.

103. *De sapientia*, in *Opera omnia*, ed. Spon, 1:563.

they cannot be controlled, nor can their discourse (dreams, natural signs, visions, metoposcopy) be decoded in a clear and distinct manner. If ecstasy is for Cardano a truthful re-cognition, demonic wisdom is a possibly unstable reflection or mirroring. In other words, when we receive a demonic insight, we at once acknowledge and doubt its truth. Let us remember that Cardano, following Plotinus and Ficino, interprets demons as presences that inhabit the mind but are not the mind itself.[104] These mental visitors, Cardano states, speak to the mind through a language of figures and enigmas. Therefore, even a lemur, who is "like our face reflected in a mirror," carries a vision that requires an act of interpretation. Even the reflection of our own face must be read and reflected through the intellect.

Face is indeed a key term in Cardano's system of thought, since for him, to attain any form of knowledge means to reflect or "to face" a given visual message through an act of remembrance. The subject knows insofar as he recognizes the image facing his intellect, as if the wisdom gathered from an internal reflection were like a mirror placed in front of our internal sight. Indeed, the image of a human face best symbolizes the sudden recognition of a familiar but somehow forgotten vision.[105] In chapter 12 of *De subtilitate* ("On the Nature of Man"), Cardano states that a human face perfectly synthesizes his concept of "subtlety" *(subtilitas)* because it is impossible to find two identical faces.[106] Subtlety, let us remember, is for Cardano a certain *ratio*, which "is responsible for the difficulty the senses have to grasp the physical and the intellect has to comprehend the intelligibles." [107] The "subtle *ratio*" within a face is thus that something at once exposing the face and holding back its inner truth, that is, what that face can reveal to us. Moreover, Cardano says, a face is capable of infinite forms of expression, which multiply its possible messages. In a following chapter

---

104. Compare *De rerum varietate*, 813.

105. For an interesting analysis of the Latin *facies* in the Vulgata, see Jean Renson, *Les dénominations du visage en français et dans les autres langues romanes*, vol. 1 (Paris: Belles Lettres, 1962). In chap. 3 Renson shows how, unlike the classical writers, the Vulgate prefers *facies* over *os* or *vultus* (90–91). Quoting primarily from the Psalms, Renson explains that *facies* can mean both "face" (Gen. 32:30, "Vidi Deum *facie ad faciem*") and "presence" (Ps. 23:6, "Haec est generatio quarentium eum, / quaerentium *faciem* Dei Jacobi") (95).

106. *De subtilitate*, in *Opera omnia*, ed. Spon, 3:452. On Cardano's *subtilitas*, see Christoph Meinel, "Okkulte und exakte Wissenschaft," in *Die Okkulte Wissenschaft in der Renaissance*, edited by August Buck (Wiesbaden: Harrassowitz, 1992), 21–43.

107. I quote from Fierz, *Girolamo Cardano*, 91. I have modified Fierz's version in only two points. I translate *intellectu* as "intellect" and not as "mind," and *intelligibilia* as "intelligibles" and not as "spiritual things," given the philosophical relevance these two terms have in my study.

Cardano reiterates that it is extremely difficult to make a faithful portrait of a face and it is always better to work on a mental picture, that is, on how we remember a certain face.[108] Indeed, metoposcopy, the art of gathering the history and destiny of a face, is for Cardano an act of remembrance.[109] However, given that facial traits and marks (such as scars or wrinkles) are able to compose infinite messages, in his treatise on dreams Cardano holds that metoposcopy, along with other methods of divination, cannot reach "the ultimate things."[110] A human face, we may infer, is a cluster of infinite memories.

In several passages Cardano repeats that he is "inclined to be faulty of memory, though rather better in the matter of foreseeing events."[111] But, for Cardano, is not memory the central part of the mind? Is it not extremely similar to the intellect, the faculty of the mind that mirrors the truthfulness of any given vision? In fact, for Cardano, memory is of no use in itself. An act of remembrance "means"—that is, signifies—something only insofar as it reflects or hints at a future disclosure, at an "ecstatic" understanding. In *Synesiorum somniorum* (book 1, chap. 3), Cardano distinguishes between two forms of memory, the first springing from and residing in the body and the brain, what Cardano calls "first act" *(actus primus)*, the second being independent of the physicality of the mind. This second memory occurs as contemplation.[112] In this context, we may infer, contemplation corresponds to an act of abstraction from a physical, perishable image to an intellectual reflection.[113]

Cardano clarifies this process of "ecstatic mirroring" in two subsequent chapters of his treatise on dreams (book 2, chaps. 9 and 10). Here he analyzes the problem of duplication in dreams, both when the dreamer sees himself doubled (chap. 9) and when he sees his own face as if he were looking at himself in a mirror (chap. 10). Cardano calls this second vision a "specular dream."[114] To see oneself doubled is a warning about the dreamer's possibly imminent death. A human being becomes doubled, Cardano explains, when his body and his soul split. This admonition is vi-

108. *De subtilitate*, in *Opera omnia*, ed. Spon, 3: 601 and 603 (chap. 17).

109. *De sapientia*, in *Opera omnia*, ed. Spon, 1:526.

110. *Synesiorum somniorum*, in *Opera omnia*, ed. Spon, 5:671 (book 2, chap. 1).

111. *Book of My Life*, 6. Cardano also says that he did not dedicate himself to physiognomy because "it requires exceptional powers of memory" (168). Compare *De utilitate ex adversis capienda*, in *Opera omnia*, ed. Spon, 2:76 (book 2, chap. 9).

112. *Synesiorum somniorum*, in *Opera omnia*, ed. Spon, 5:598.

113. Compare Plotinus, *Enneads* 3.8.6, 3.8.7.

114. *Synesiorum somniorum*, in *Opera omnia*, ed. Spon, 5:681.

sualized through the images of people who are extremely close to us, such as a lover, a brother, a perfect friend, or in particular the son who resembles us the most. As we shall see in a moment, the face of one's son is of essential importance. As far as specular dreams are concerned, they present themselves when the dreamer looks at his face in a mirror and sees either himself or someone else's figure. In either case, the viewer knows that the reflected image is warning him about something that concerns him directly. The face we see in this kind of dream can be either an "idol"—that is, a self-explanatory picture—or an *insomnium*, if the viewer realizes that the dream has brought to the fore hidden connections between the traits of that face and his own. Let us remember that for Cardano *lemur* is the name of the demon that reflects our own face. This occurs both when we re-cognize ourselves in the reflection of our face and when we attempt to read in our face any warning about our future. Indeed, according to *Synesiorum somniorum* (book 1, chap. 50), in a dream metoposcopy means "servitude" and "to be submitted to a trial," in that servants usually try to interpret their master's wishes by looking at his forehead.[115]

In the fifth chapter of *The Book of My Life*, Cardano offers a fascinating description of his own face. First of all, he remarks that he has "a fixed gaze as in meditation."[116] However, if he looks at himself in a mirror, he realizes that he lacks any unique facial trait, to the point that "several painters who have come from afar to make my portrait have found no feature by which they could so characterize me, that I might be distinguished." In other words, Cardano's face is hard to remember and cannot easily be pictured in the mind. His face shows a subject constantly intent on the act of meditation, but which is "out of focus"—that is, it has difficulty in recalling and reflecting upon itself. If his face is a "blurred" picture, Cardano is convinced that his first and most beloved son had well-defined traits, "exactly resembling" Cardano's father.[117] His firstborn is the "specular" image of his grandfather, while Cardano himself is the medium, the surface in which his past (Cardano's father) and his future (Cardano's son) mirror each other.

The connection between father and son is certainly one of the most recurrent and influential themes of Cardano's writings. If we read the ten volumes of his *Opera omnia* carefully, we cannot help but notice Cardano's

115. *Synesiorum somniorum*, in *Opera omnia*, ed. Spon, 5:651.

116. *Book of My Life*, 20.

117. *Book of My Life*, 92. Compare *De utilitate ex adversis capienda*, in *Opera omnia*, ed. Spon, 2:267 (book 4, chap. 12).

obsession with his son and the young man's premature death. Indeed, most students of Cardano's thought consider his son's execution as the most traumatic experience of his life.[118] In *De utilitate ex adversis capienda*, the treatise in memory of his deceased son, Cardano writes that his anguish at his son's death "is incessant, and incessant are my tears."[119] But his first son is not only a central figure of Cardano's biography, he is also, and much more important, a fundamental reference in his philosophical system. The relationship between Girolamo Cardano and his firstborn Giovanni Battista at once summarizes and enacts Cardano's theories on the interaction between mind, soul, intellect, and demons, between reflection and "ecstatic" insight, between remembering, seeing, and foreseeing.

Throughout this chapter I have stressed that for Cardano, in an ecstasy the intellect becomes a surface mirroring the truthfulness of the other's visibility. The subject's face and the other's merge in the ecstatic event and manifest their essential affinity. I have also explained that the ecstatic event springs from the mind inhabited by demons but transcends the mind itself. Ecstasy is a synonym for a sight that has exceeded the dichotomy between seeing and being seen. Ecstasy is what sees its own truth.[120]

Cardano makes it clear that, in oneiric terms, "eyes" and "to see" mean "son." According to a process of "reciprocity" *(reciprocatio)*, "since an eye means a son, the loss of an eye means a son's death and a son's death means the loss of an eye."[121] If Cardano cannot see or remember his own face, his firstborn offers him a clear and distinct image of a face that looks familiar, similar to Cardano's. In other words, a father sees his face in the reflection of his son's image. According to Cardano, not only does a son inevitably resemble and somehow "clarify" his father's facial and physical traits, he is connected to his father at a mental and spiritual level. In *Paralipomenon* (book 13, chap. 3), focusing on the "activities of the mind and the soul," Cardano first restates the main differences between "soul" *(anima)* and "mind" *(mens)*. The soul, says Cardano, is neither "incorporeal," since it is "with the body," nor an accident of the body, because the soul is superior to any form of physicality.[122] The soul is "some form of corporeal substance." Concluding this analysis, Cardano writes that "a son is part of the

---

118. Cardano calls it "my supreme misfortune" in *Book of My Life* (93).

119. *De utilitate ex adversis capienda*, in *Opera omnia*, ed. Spon, 2:254 (book 4, chap. 7).

120. In *Enneads* 3.8.3 Plotinus writes that nature "possesses" contemplation, that is, nature "is" contemplation and is the object of contemplation.

121. *Synesiorum somniorum*, in *Opera omnia*, ed. Spon, 5:613 (book 1, chap. 15). Cardano repeats the same concept in chap. 42 (637).

122. *Paralipomenon*, in *Opera omnia*, ed. Spon, 10:540.

father in the soul." The same concept is present in a crucial passage of Cardano's *De sapientia*.[123] While the immaterial mind is where the subject and his demon(s) formulate their interpretation of any visible thing, soul is the presence of a bond demanding no explanation or exegesis. Although the father-son vinculum resides in the somehow material soul and exposes itself to visibility (the son's face is like his father's), its truth does not result from a mental process. The image of the son's face is within the father's soul, and a father's (blurred) image lives in his son. In a moving passage of *De utilitate*, Cardano writes that "this vinculum cannot be broken . . . we give birth to our sons, we extract them from our entrails . . . we educate them, we hold them as the visible image of our soul, mind, and will. We always have them before our eyes."[124]

According to Cardano, the essential "sympathy" *(sympathia)* between father and son becomes incontrovertible if one analyzes how divination originates and develops.[125] This is indeed a fundamental section of Cardano's thought. "Nothing," Cardano writes in *Paralipomenon*, "prevents us from assuming that the cause of divination is a humor." For Cardano, it is a fact that the perception of a forthcoming event manifests itself in a physical manner, even when it takes place solely in the mind. Not only the five senses (external or internal voices, smells, unusual tastes, visions), but also dreams and flashbacks can be vehicles of foresight. Cardano follows the traditional view on the connection between the humor of melancholy and any form of clairvoyance; although he believes that it is separate from blood *(alienus a sanguine)*, the melancholic humor shares blood's dry and cold nature.[126] This humor coalesces the images imprinted in the brain's spirits and turns them into something like a mirror *(in modum speculi)* revealing the sense of forthcoming or simply unknown occurrences. Clearly

123. Compare *De sapientia*, in *Opera omnia*, ed. Spon, 1: 509 (book 2).

124. *De utilitate ex adversis capienda*, in *Opera omnia*, ed. Spon, 2:202 (book 3, chap. 16).

125. *Paralipomenon*, in *Opera omnia*, ed. Spon, 10:469 (book 3, chap. 21).

126. In the popular *Commentarius de praecipuis generibus divinationum* (Wittenberg: Lufft, 1572), Caspar Peucer is also convinced that "cases of ecstasis without melancholy are rare" (127v). Peucer believes that devils can produce a "diabolical ecstasis" by affecting the melancholic humor in the brain (134r). If a divine ecstasis brings about inner enlightenment, a demonic ecstasis causes oblivion and alienation (129v). Jean Céard discusses Peucer's position on melancholy in "Folie et démonologie au XVIe siècle," in *Folie et déraison à la Renaissance*, 129–43. For a detailed discussion of the melancholic humor, see Tommaso Cornacchini, *Tabulae medicae* (Padua: Tozzi, 1605), 70–75. In sec. 26, Cornacchini offers an exhaustive summary of the medical theories of melancholy, which he defines as "delirium without fever" (70). For Cornacchini, the melancholic humor, which has "infinite species," is more dry than cold. It is dryness that affects the brain more seriously. Among the first symptoms of melancholy, Cornacchini mentions fear, sadness, "constant thinking," headache, and vertigo (72).

referring to Ficino's concept of melancholy, Cardano also emphasizes that divination as specular sight depends on the melancholic humor but is not necessarily a manifestation of melancholy.[127] In chapter 4, I quoted a passage from Weyer's *De praestigiis daemonum* in which possession is directly linked to this humor, which has the potential to invade the mind and turn the subject into "a lump of clay." In other words, melancholy, and thus demonic possession, is brought about by an excess of melancholic humor.[128]

But why and when does the humor of melancholy collect visual messages? Again, a specular seeing occurs only if seeing and being seen reflect each other through sympathy.[129] This is why divination is a "familiar" event, in that it primarily occurs between a father and his son. If a father is united to his son in the soul, both father and son will be able to perceive each other's traumas through the humor of melancholy. If a father (or his son) is killed, Cardano writes in the same chapter of *Paralipomenon*, the violence that has been inflicted upon the one will echo in the other's soul and will manifest itself through physical symptoms, given that the soul is "some sort of corporeal substance." More specifically, since our internal and external senses are always alert, if that violence takes place when the father (or his son) is asleep, he will see it in a dream.

127. Compare Ficino, *Theologia platonica*, in *Opera omnia*, book 13, chap. 2, 286–87. Among many other philosophers, Ficino mentions Plato and Plotinus who were often "abstracted" from their physical senses when they entered a deep state of meditation (286). The melancholic humor, Ficino stresses, enhances the soul's faculty of divination and contemplation (287). In his popular *De vita*, Ficino addresses such topics as "How Many Things Cause Learned People Either to Be Melancholy or to Eventually Become So" (book 1, chap. 4), "Why Melancolics Are Intelligent" (book 1, chap. 5), and "How Black Bile Makes People Intelligent" (book 1, chap. 6). From a suitable mixture of bile, blood, and black bile, Ficino holds, "come original philosophers, especially when their soul, hereby called away from external movements and from its own body, is made in the highest degree both a neighbor to the divine and an instrument of the divine. As a result, it is filled from above with divine influences and oracles." I quote from the following translation: Marsilio Ficino, *Three Books on Life*, edited by Carol V. Kaske and John R. Clark (Binghamton, N.Y.: Medieval and Renaissance Texts and Studies, 1989), 121–23. Still essential is the analysis of Ficino's "melancholic" ecstasy by Raymond Klibansky, Erwin Panofsky, and Fritz Saxl, in *Saturn and Melancholia: Studies in the History of Natural Philosophy, Religion, and Art* (New York: Basic Books, 1964), 254–74. Compare Winfried Schleiner, *Melancholy, Genius, and Utopia in the Renaissance* (Wolfenbüttel: Herzog August Bibliothek, 1991), 25. Porphyry describes Plotinus' contemplation in *The Life of Plotinus* (chap. 8).

128. On the dialogue between demonology and medicine in the Renaissance, see Jean Céard, "The Devil and Lovesickness: Views of Sixteenth-Century Physicians and Demonologists," in *Eros and Anteros: The Medical Traditions of Love in the Renaissance*, edited by Donald A. Beecher and Massimo Ciavolella (Toronto: Dovehouse Editions, 1992), 33–47.

129. On *sympathia* and *antipathia*, compare *Theonoston*, in *Opera omnia*, ed. Spon, 2:436.

Cardano reiterates that revelations best occur in the twilight zone between sleep and wakefulness *(inter somnium et vigiliam)*. In this in-between state the mind taps into what Cardano calls "fate" *(fatum)*. Echoing a distinctly Stoic vision that he could have found in Cicero's *On Divination (De divinatione)*, Cardano's concept of "fate" does not necessarily entail a negative, fatalistic view of human destiny. Although I have pointed out that for Cardano *sign* tends to mean "warning," in *Paralipomenon* the concept of "fate" is close to the Stoic "order and series of causes . . . the sempiternal truth flowing from eternity."[130] In other words, the seer perceives the fate of a given face when and if he comprehends its truthfulness. As a consequence, given their connection through the soul, for a father to see the truth of his son's fate means to gather a warning or insight into his own existence.[131] Indeed, Cardano continues, since a father and a son converse through the language of their souls, they also share similar "nature and thought."[132] This is even more evident if, as in Cardano's case, "father and son feel an intense love for each other."[133] For Cardano, a son is at once the subject's radical other and alter ego, that visible presence (a face) that brings the subject's fate to the surface of a language of obscure "figures and enigmas," as Cardano defines demonic idiom.

In the short treatise *De uno*, Cardano underscores that a wise man needs only one son to mirror the truth of his fate.[134] But what kind of lesson can a subject deduce from the reflection of his son's face? What does Cardano see in the remembrance of his son's image? We have seen that Cardano believes in the identification between knowledge or understanding and ecstatic contemplation, which occurs as an act of mirroring between the subject and his other. This ecstatic fusion between two gazes is symbolized by the relationship between father and son, since they are connected in the soul, the least spiritual and most physical part of a human being. A son is the materialization of his father's face and thus also of his fate.

---

130. Cicero, *M. Tulli Ciceronis De divinatione*, edited by A. S. Pease (New York: Arno Press, 1979), book 1, 125, 320–21. Compare Miller, *Dreams in Late Antiquity*, 52–53.

131. In *Commentarii in Ptolemaeum, De astrorum judiciis* (in *Opera omnia*, ed. Spon, 5:253–54), Cardano holds that, astrologically speaking, parents exert two different forms of influence on their children. While a mother has more power over a son's childhood and body, a father has a much deeper impact on a son. The father's horoscope affects his son's adult life, the qualities of his soul, and his destiny.

132. *Paralipomenon*, in *Opera omnia*, ed. Spon, 10:470.

133. Compare *De utilitate ex adversis capienda:* "I loved him [my son] . . . and he loved me" (in *Opera omnia*, ed. Spon, 2:270).

134. *De uno*, in *Opera omnia*, ed. Spon, 1:281.

loxically, it is in his son's image that a father reads the signs of his des-
ınd end. Let us remember that for Cardano a father has his son always
e his eyes.

e premature death of Giovanni Battista neither erases nor contradicts
no's faculty of contemplating his own fate in the recollection of
ı's face. In *De utilitate,* Cardano makes it clear that for him the act
ditation would be incomplete without the persistent memory of
ı's death.¹³⁵ The end or fate of a son is itself an ecstatic reflection
ɔeaks to us through obscure "figures and enigmas," as Cardano
fined demonic language. A dream in which we "know" a demon,
ıo writes in *Synesiorum somniorum,* is an unequivocal omen of our
:ath.¹³⁶ We could rephrase this point by saying that thanks to the
; inhabiting our mind, we are able to contemplate our own fate by
g the (internal) image of our son's face, fate, and end.

[etoposcopia,* we find an eloquent depiction of a father's contempla-
:. In the second section of this treatise, Cardano offers the picture
lderly man whose eyebrows are marked by two straight lines
crowned with two aureolas, similar to two rising suns [A]. The

[A]

author comments on this face as follows:
"These lines describe great tribulation and
pain because of his sons. For this reason, he
will undergo great hazards." ¹³⁷ Scholars of
physiognomy usually compare Cardano's abstract and even mechanical portraits with
della Porta's much more realistic and visu-
ally compelling studies of human and animal
physical expression. Although it is indisputable that modern physiognomy finds its
origin in della Porta's work and not in Cardano's, it is incorrect to assume that physiognomy or metoposcopy means the same thing
for the two Italian philosophers. Cardano's
sketches are not intended to define a gram-

al facial expressions, something that one could come across in
ıer, they are visual connectors between the viewer's memory

litate ex adversis capienda,* in *Opera omnia,* ed. Spon, 2:17.
iorum somniorum,* in *Opera omnia,* ed. Spon, 5:641.
ɔscopia,* book 2, fig. 123, 33.

and possible biographies or fates. Cardano's innumerable pictures are in fact based on one androgynous prototype, which he varies by adding or removing mustaches, beard, hair. Betraying no emotion whatsoever, this rudimentary face looks at the viewer with a blank and direct gaze.

We may say that Cardano's faces are clean slates marked with the demonic "enigmas" of memory. Like any visible event, the signs marked on the forehead of this essential face need the viewer to mirror them in his mind by means of his intellect. In his so doing, these marks will be allowed to speak their truthfulness—that is, they will be able to communicate their warning or fate. In *Metoposcopia*, each face, a variation of one essential face, is a different act of contemplation. Cardano's faces do not mean or express anything, in the sense that their meaning, their biography, is something that comes from the viewer and not from the faces themselves. As the mind is the place where the subject confronts his negation (demons as resident aliens), the face shows its meaning as an external, independent occurrence. The forehead is at once what contains the mind and is outside the mind, what shows the mind's discourse and is unable to understand its warning signs. In this regard, the image of the elderly man is particularly revealing. In this picture Cardano shows the face of a wise man absorbed in the act of contemplation. In other words, this is the face of the ecstatic reader of faces, someone who has achieved a transparent reflection between the face on the page and his own mind. Rather than alluding to possible biographical events, the aureolas above the old man's eyes signify the act itself of meditating upon someone else's face.

If the father has a face that has transcended the enigmatic, demonic language of metoposcopy, the son shows a much more eloquent forehead. An unmistakable reference to Cardano's son occurs in figure 149 of book 10 of *Metoposcopia* [B].[138] Cardano's comment on this picture reads as follows: "The man marked with these lines will kill his wife and will have a bad death." If we look at the face that follows this one, we notice that it describes a similar kind of

[B]

138. *Metoposcopia*, book 10, fig. 149, 131.

individual [C].[139] In this case, "the lines crossing the man's eyebrows indicate a murderer." We may say that the marks on the young man's face (Cardano's fig. 149) are able to recount a slightly more detailed biography, while the next face (Cardano's fig. 150) simply narrates that some individual may commit some kind of a homicide. A more specific description is given in another face [D], still from the same chapter of Cardano's work. Here we find a person who "will kill his parents and will die of a plague."[140] This face not only reveals a particular crime, it also details a kind of death. Only a few pictures later, we encounter the face of another future murderer [E], who "will die by a sword."[141] In the whole *Metoposcopia*, Cardano uses only one allegedly "real" face, again concerning a "famous thief" and murderer "who killed thirty men and then was flayed publicly" [F].[142] In fact, the intricacy of this forehead makes the whole picture much less realistic than the depictions of murderers' faces. As Cardano explains in his analysis of the next image ([G], Cardano's fig. 34), "vertical lines indicate murder."[143] The actual number of murders, says Cardano, can be inferred by the number of vertical lines on the forehead.

Just by looking at these few images, we can draw some fundamental conclusions about Cardano's metoposcopy. The inscriptions on a forehead are symbols whose code is both determined and interpreted by the interaction between intellect, its demons, and natural language. By "natural language" I mean any possible signifier produced by and in the created world. Let us remember that passage from *Paralipomenon* in which Cardano stares at a marvelous evening sky crossed by resplendent clouds and wonders what that vision in movement is trying to tell him. The act of reading the symbols on a forehead is certainly a form of remembrance, but a remembrance that comes to the viewer's mind from the face itself. The face remembers itself through an act of intellectual reflection. The ecstatic mind allows the "enigma," the riddle of obscure marks, to speak its language and manifest itself as the narration of a possible (past, present, or future) trauma. In this regard, the seer's mind is similar to the devil's in that, as Prierio explains in *De strigimagis*, devils do not have a memory and thus do not have an idiom of their own. We recall that, like the devils, the prophet Cardano suffers from a lack of memory. What he "knows" is what nature (dreams, visions, faces) tells him in its own language. Like the devils, the Italian

139. *Metoposcopia*, book 10, fig. 150, 131.
140. *Metoposcopia*, book 10, fig. 168, 135.
141. *Metoposcopia*, book 10, fig. 173, 137.
142. *Metoposcopia*, book 10, fig. 33, 102.
143. *Metoposcopia*, book 10, fig. 34, 102.

[C]

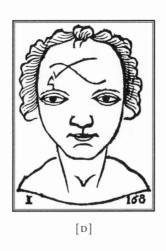

[D]

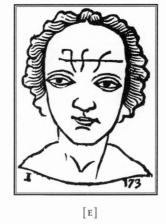

[E]

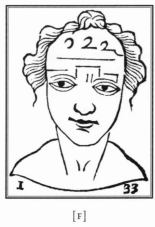

[F]

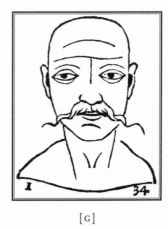

[G]

physician is essentially a semiotician. In *The Book of My Life*, Cardano remarks that his body has always exuded a rather peculiar smell, very similar to sulfur, the unquestionable trace of a demonic presence.[144]

The seemingly illegible lines on a forehead encapsulate an entire existence. As symbols, they first and foremost signify the presence of a hypothetical meaning, which cannot be inferred through the symbol itself.[145] In his introductory "Observations," Cardano does lay out a minimal grammar of linear expression, but in most cases these preliminary notes are very predictable and self-explanatory: "Bad [signs] always announce bad things, such as the characters of Saturn, the letter X, gridirons, irregular or badly shaped or confused signs. For instance, a divided circle, a broken or interrupted sign. . . . Good characters are those that have a certain quality, such as circles, stars, crosses, lines, parallels, triangles, quadrangles, cubes, and similar others."[146]

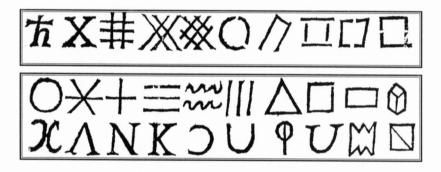

Cardano is also convinced that it is necessary to observe the "length, breadth, depth" of each line.[147] The length of a mark speaks of the duration of its meaning, its width reveals its intensity, and its depth corresponds to its stability.

---

144. *Book of My Life*, 155. Compare *De rerum varietate*, 847. On the figure of the magician / physician in the Renaissance, see Wolf-Dieter Müller-Jahncke, *Astrologisch-magische Theorie und Praxis in der Heilkunde der frühen Neuzeit* (Stuttgart: Steiner Verlag, 1985), 97–98.

145. Renaissance theory on emblematic expression strongly recommended that an emblem contain more than one figure, because meaning derives from the interaction between two or three visual elements. A picture reproducing only one figure was considered a "symbol" and not an emblem. While an emblem has a definite meaning, a symbolic image can mean anything. The Renaissance "summa" on this subject is certainly Ercole Tasso's *Della realtà e perfetione delle imprese* (Bergamo, 1612), 138–39. Compare my *Identità e impresa rinascimentale* (Ravenna: Longo, 1998), 42.

146. *Metoposcopia*, vii.

147. *Metoposcopia*, vi.

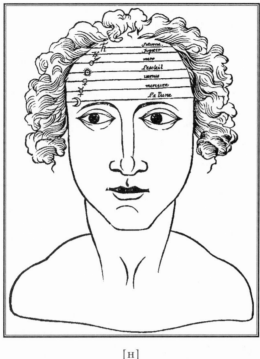

[H]

Another way to cast some light on the meaning of a sign is through astrology. The most famous picture from *Metoposcopia* is the opening illustration of a young-looking face on which Cardano has sketched seven lines, each affected by a different planet [H]. This clear-cut distinction between the particular influences exerted by Moon, Mercury, Venus, Sun, Mars, Jupiter, and Saturn, each analyzed in a separate chapter (chaps. 2–9), is indirectly questioned in the last four chapters, which altogether occupy more than half of the whole treatise. In particular, chapters 10 and 11 deal with "the lines on the forehead that have various positions" and with "the mixture of the lines on the forehead." [148] Cardano understands that a rational, astrological exegesis of a face inevitably clashes with the unpredictable formation of real foreheads. [149] While on the first face pictured Cardano marks the seven levels of the astral powers, toward the end of the same opening chapter he shows a similar forehead marked by a series

148. *Metoposcopia*, 93 and 143.
149. Compare Eugenio Garin, *Astrology in the Renaissance*, translated by Carolyn Jackson and June Allen (London: Routledge, 1983), 83–112.

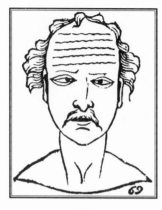

[I]

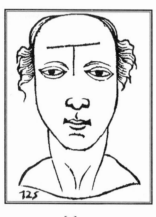

[J]

of undulating parallel lines [I]. For Cardano, this is the face of a "demented man" who will have a very short life, as if in this face the seven astrological influences had collided and thus failed to mold a plausible, readable fate.[150] Moreover, unlike any other picture in *Metoposcopia*, the man's inner condition is also expressed by his crossed eyes.

Although an astrological study and a grammar of linear expression certainly help elucidate the message conveyed through any facial mark, they are only secondary exegetical tools. More than reading a forehead, the ecstatic mind recognizes it through an intellectual reflection.[151] Otherwise, how could we possibly distinguish between the lines marked on the face of Cardano's figure 34 of chapter 10 (above, [G]) and the almost analogous ones inscribed on the face in figure 125 of book 2 [J]?[152] If in book 10 the T symbol is about a murderer, in book 2 it indicates a "strong and vigorous man, who will succeed in all his actions and over his enemies." Could we hypothesize that these quite different readings of the same symbol recount not two distinct identities but just two moments or aspects of a possibly similar or even identical biography? Or could it simply be that in metoposcopy the same character may signify two dissimilar occurrences? What is the actual influence exerted by the arched line in the face of Cardano's figure 34 of book 10? In book 2 (Cardano's fig. 107) the same arch describes not a murderer but a "very

150. *Metoposcopia*, book 2, fig. 69, 19.

151. Compare Emmanuel Levinas, *Totality and Infinity*, translated by Alphonso Lingis (Pittsburgh: Duquesne University Press, 1969), 202: "Language . . . presupposes the originality of the face without which, reduced to an action among actions whose meaning would require an infinite psychoanalysis or sociology, it could not commence" (202). For Levinas, "meaning is the face of the Other, and all recourses to words takes place already within the primordial face to face of language" (206).

152. *Metoposcopia*, book 2, fig. 125, 33.

lustful man" [K].[153] And what if these characters function like the names written on
tombstones, serving as indelible reminders
of erased existences? Two identical names can
indeed speak of two lives totally unrelated
to each other. We could thus see *Metoposcopia* as the map of a hypothetical cemetery,
where myriad unknown faces greet the seer
Cardano by pronouncing the name marked
on their foreheads. In the first book of *Synesiorum somniorum*, Cardano explains that
in a dream a first name means the subject
himself and "all his things," primarily his
sons and his homeland.[154]

[K]

The innumerable faces from *Metoposcopia* indeed establish a "filial"
relationship with the "prophet" Cardano in that, as the seer cannot help
but contemplate his son's existence, which is part of his own "name," so do
the faces ask Cardano that they be re-cognized and remembered.[155] Like
the soul of Maria Maddalena de' Pazzi's brother, infinite faces urge the
viewer to pronounce the name of their memory. And like the mystic's
brother and the seer's son, these faces' biographies are summarized in one
trauma, in a sin, in a premature death.

We must bear in mind that both Maria Maddalena de' Pazzi and Girolamo Cardano are capable of welcoming the face of the other because of the
demons inhabiting their minds. In *Probation*, the Florentine mystic sees
her brother when her demonic melancholy is most virulent and menacing.
Maria Maddalena feels as if she were thinking someone else's thoughts.
Similarly, Cardano is convinced that demons are integral parts of his mind.
These demonic presences are indeed the mark of his enlightenment. In the
moment when the mind faces its own alterity, when the I realizes that it is

153. *Metoposcopia*, book 2, fig. 107, 29.

154. *Synesiorum somniorum*, in *Opera omnia*, ed. Spon, 5:609 (book 1, chap. 14).

155. In *Totality and Infinity*, Levinas sees the mutual reflection between the subject and the
face as both a "fraternal" and a "paternal" encounter: "It is my responsibility before a face looking at me as absolutely foreign (and the epiphany of the face coincides with these two moments)
that constitutes the original fact of fraternity. Paternity is not a causality, but the establishment
of a unicity with which the unicity of the father does and does not coincide" (214). In other
words, Levinas believes that the "filial" connotation of the encounter with the other's face lies
in the fact that, although the other is always my brother, our relationship is absolutely unique:
"The I owes its unicity as an I to the paternal *Eros*. The father does not simply cause the son. *To
be* one's son means to be I in one's son. . . . The son resumes the unicity of the father and yet remains exterior to the father: the son is a unique son" (278–79, emphasis in original).

someone else's dwelling (as we have read in *Thesaurus exorcismorum*), then the mind is ready to discern the traumas that have marked the face of the other. This is, as I have noted repeatedly, the melancholic condition. "Is not melancholy a malady?" Cardano writes. "But has not it affected many wise and superior men, including Aristotle himself and a number of poets, prophets, and sibyls?"[156] The melancholic's ability to foresee the future,

[L]

[M]

Cardano writes in chapter 9 of *Paralipomenon*, "is confirmed by innumerable examples" and frequently occurs to those who are about to die.[157] As we find summarized in *De rerum varietate*, an overwhelming oneiric production, demonic presences, longing for death, solitude, divination, and sleeplessness are the main constituents of the melancholic condition.[158] The melancholic subject dreams too much but sleeps too little, cherishes isolation and his mental demons but senses the traumas and end of his neighbor. In *Metoposcopia* (book 11), Cardano offers two opposite portraits of the melancholic mind. Like any "demonic wisdom," melancholy can signify a wicked and criminal mind or a wise and clairvoyant one. If Cardano's figure 2 shows a "melancholic and contemplative man, prone to crime" and a disreputable life [L], the face in his figure 13 "indicates an ingenious man, with a great memory, interested in science, but melancholic, contemplative, and veracious" [M].[159] This second rendition of a melancholic man could be interpreted as a variation of the seer's face from book 2 (Cardano's

156. *Encomium podagrae*, in *Opera omnia*, ed. Spon, 1:224. On the connection between melancholy and art in the Renaissance, see Rudolf Wittkower and Margot Wittkower, *Born under Saturn: The Character and Conduct of Artists* (New York: W. W. Norton, 1963), 102–7.

157. *Paralipomenon*, in *Opera omnia*, ed. Spon, 10:462.

158. *De rerum varietate*, book 8, chap. 40 ("On Man"), 385.

159. *Metoposcopia*, 144 and 147. The two extremely similar faces also expose two different astrological influences. The first face is dominated by the "negative and oblique connection" between Saturn and Moon, while in the second one "the line of Saturn is united with that of Mercury."

fig. 123). If in book 2 Cardano had sketched the image of the (melancholic) seer in the act of mourning the loss of his son, in book 11 he gives a more general and descriptive version of the same melancholic and meditative face. I have already mentioned that for Cardano the melancholic subject is persecuted by the fear of death and foresees the death of the other.

[N]

The meeting between the seer and the face of the other is indeed a melancholic encounter. To welcome the other's name approaches an act of mourning, like the obsessive remembrance of a lost son. In *Metoposcopia*, the faces looking back at the reader almost exclusively speak of a protracted or sudden negativity, which is all the viewer is asked to remember.[160] In the chapter "On Mourning" ("De luctu") in *De utilitate ex adversis capienda*, Cardano writes that his persistent thoughts about his dead son are "like a lightning" invading his mind.[161] The memory of the other's trauma is an abrupt and harrowing disclosure. We could indeed say that *Metoposcopia* is a "book of revelations" revolving around a cluster of recurrent sufferings.

What makes a face an object of remembrance is indeed its "failure," that is, a visible mark of negativity. In book 12 of *Metoposcopia*, entirely dedicated to female faces, we come across women who will have children outside marriage (Cardano's figs. 1, 60, 61, 62, 63, 64, 67, 68, among many others), prostitutes (for instance, figs. 12, 14, 17, 19, 20, 21, 22, 30, 43, 80, 95), lascivious and "corrupt" women (see, for example, figs. 15, 16, 18, 23, 25, 27, 28, 33, 38), women involved in incestuous relationships (figs. 49, 51), women who will die in giving birth (fig. 100), women who will murder their own child (fig. 39), victims of sexual abuse (fig. 55), women who will cause the death of their husbands (fig. 76) or will be killed by them (figs. 78, 83), and women who will have an unspecified

160. Alphonso Lingis, the great interpreter and translator of Levinas's philosophy, synthesizes this point as follows: "The face of the other is a surface upon which the axes and directions of his posture and the intentions of his movements are exposed to me. . . . The face of the other is a surface of suffering, upon which . . . her vulnerability and mortality are exposed to me" (*The Community of Those Who Have Nothing in Common* [Bloomington: Indiana University Press, 1994], 131).

161. *De utilitate ex adversis capienda*, in *Opera omnia*, ed. Spon, 2: 271 (book 4, chap. 12).

violent death (fig. 102) or will be executed in a public space (fig. 90). Some female faces explicitly point to a brief life (Cardano's figs. 2, 5, 6, 57, 93) or to an ignominious death (fig. 91). Some others indicate women who will "be suffocated in water," as in the case of the only face depicting a witch ([N], Cardano's fig. 87).[162]

In most cases the event epitomizing the face's destiny is its death, as if for Cardano death coincided with the moment of a face's revelation.[163] We may say that Cardano's metoposcopy is a divinatory art unveiling the remembrance of a forthcoming annihilation. What the demons reveal to the seer's mind is the memory of the other's removal from the scene of visibility. In this regard, Cardano's philosophy does not contradict one of the fundamental tenets of Catholic demonology, that concerning the devils' ignorance about future events. Although they are not prophets, devils are certainly "perceptive" beings, for they fathom all the possible statements silently pronounced by the created world. "Demonic wisdom" takes place

162. *Metoposcopia*, 175. Cardano dedicates an entire chapter of *De rerum varietate* to witchcraft (book 15, chap. 80, 728–41). On Cardano's view of witches, see Lea, *Materials toward a History of Witchcraft*, 2:444–48. Lea rightly defines Cardano's ideas as "inconsistent" (448) in that, on the one hand, he claims to believe in the actual existence of demonic pacts between demons and human beings, while, on the other, he suggests that witches are simply unstable or even insane individuals. Cardano's position on witchcraft makes more sense if we look at it in the context of his ambiguous interpretation of demonology. Cardano posits two forms of "demonic wisdom," the first being the pernicious powers devils bestow upon their followers (witches), the second coinciding with inner enlightenment and divination. Cardano quotes two "absurd" stories from the famous dialogue *Strix sive de ludificatione daemonum* (1523) by Giovan Francesco Pico della Mirandola. Both stories are about priests who have some sexual contact with devils. The first tale concerns Benedetto Berna who, according to Pico, at the age of seventy-five confessed to having slept with a succubus called Hermelina for more than forty years. Pico writes that Berna's attachment to this devil was so intense that he even talked to her when he walked down the street. Not being able to see the devil, people thought the priest was crazy. The second case is about one Father Pinneto, who had an alleged relationship with a succubus for several decades as well. Cardano questions the theological soundness of these narrations. Devils do not have bodies, yet these stories are based on the carnal connection between a succubus and a human being (*De rerum varietate*, 733). Pico recounts these tales in the second dialogue of *Strix*. I refer to a nineteenth-century Italian edition: *La strega, ovvero degli inganni de' demoni*, translated by Turino Turini (Milan: Daelli, 1864), 79–80. In the same chapter of *De rerum varietate* Cardano is also adamant about the treatment witches deserve: "No one thinks that these blasphemous and heretical women, disciples of demons, murderers, do not deserve to die" (738). However, Cardano also stresses that superstition has created a lot of incredible and unreal stories. Witches, Cardano says, do not have the power to foretell the future. These women are "mad, foolish, wretched, impudent, inconsistent" (739).

163. Compare Alphonso Lingis, *Foreign Bodies* (New York: Routledge, 1994), 167: "To look upon faces is always to sense th[e] death that is latent, visible in the frail freshness of youth, the wrinkles of age. . . . A face turned to us is an appeal made to us, a demand put on us. . . . [On a face] lies the force of an imperative that touches us, caught sight of wherever we see a face turned to us."

in the perennial present of an act of "intellectual" listening, in that it is the subject's intellect that brings about the reflection (or echo) between past, present, or future reality and the seer's mind. What is about to happen does not intrinsically differ from what happened, because both time past and time future can only express themselves in the present of an ecstatic understanding. In a central passage from *Paralipomenon*, Cardano writes that memory is "something between a feeling and an act of imagination. . . . What results from memory and imagination is what we call 'reminiscence.'" [164]

"Reminiscence," we could say, is an "imagined memory" or a "recalled imagination." This is what metoposcopy is all about. To read on a witch's face her imminent execution undoubtedly involves imagination. But reminiscence is also a feeling, an inner recognition, what the intellect mirrors to the mind inhabited by demons. Reminiscence thus means identification or, better yet, self-revelation. In reminiscence the subject (the father) acknowledges that he cares for the other's (his son's) future or past erasure. In this sense, reminiscence is indeed a "familiar" language because it utters the mind's concern for the face of the other. Reminiscence is a lament.

Let us go back for a moment to the opening chapter of this book. Studying Prierio's *De strigimagis*, I said that for the Italian demonologist devils pronounce a language that devours both its speaker and its utterances. The language of the devils is like a fire burning its syllables. Devils indeed speak the language of death. Their insights, their ecstasies reveal how visible reality (the face of the other, of my beloved son) either burned, is burning, or is about to burn. But, we said, the devils' language erases both its words and the mouth uttering them. The devils of the mind first and foremost tell the seer that those innumerable faces bringing forth "reminiscence" are not different from the seer's, that by reading those faces the seer's mind is asking its demons for "reminiscence."

---

164. *Paralipomenon*, in *Opera omnia*, ed. Spon, 10:542 (book 13, chap. 5).

The Epic Triumph of the Church, Its Melancholy, and the Persistence of Sodom: A Conclusion

Now that you have finished the book, I need to take you back to the introduction. As you will remember, after a rather long quotation from a French treatise on the essential similarities between humans and devils (our common status as pariahs, our existence as perennial exiles), I stated that my work would probably incur the wrath or derision of more than one scholar. As you now realize, this study is neither strictly historical, nor psychoanalytical, nor anthropological. However, one could also argue that my introductory statement amounts to setting up a sort of straw man, since in recent years some scholars have shifted their attention from the *hows* to the *whys* of the persecution of Jews, witches, and sodomites. No one now can possibly deny the importance of studying the texts in which Catholicism—soon followed by Protestantism—laid out its murderous rationale. I must say, though, that the problem centers not on what books we read and discuss, but rather on how we read and discuss them. Again, the basic distinction is first and foremost a rhetorical one. It is one thing to believe that what we are studying belongs to the past—that is, it expresses itself in a language that is not *ours* any longer—and another thing to hold that *our* language and *theirs* is not intrinsically different. This is why I said that this book of mine is a translation, not an archeological investigation. In other words, I believe that the melancholy plaguing Renaissance Europe is *our* melancholy, that the souls of purgatory (whatever or whoever you think they are) are still calling us, that Satan (whatever or whoever you believe he is) is still watching and addressing us.

What I am trying to say is that the spiritual and philosophical issues examined in this book concern us, are relevant to us. We are still surrounded by demons and souls in pain. We are still visited and invaded by the "speakers of the mind," as the exorcist Visconti says in the *Thesaurus exorcismorum*. As in Cardano's *Metoposcopia*, faces still come up to us to be read and welcomed, to be saved and remembered.

A matter of rhetoric, I said. I would like to spend a moment clarifying where this book comes from—that is, which books and authors have molded my language and approach. In Michel de Certeau's *Mystic Fable* and *The Possession at Loudun* I found a first, essential teaching, primarily from a rhetorical point of view. De Certeau's dense and evocative work has always been of great importance to me. Louis Marin's *La critique du discours. Sur la "Logique de Port-Royal" et les "Pensées" de Pascal* has been my second point of reference. In particular, Marin was in the back of my mind throughout my writing on Menghi and Polidori's *Thesaurus exorcismorum*. Marin's often difficult text made me think about the connection between rhetoric and reality, between the "language of things," as Visconti writes in the *Thesaurus*, and the "language of words." Marin's book should be required reading for every student of rhetoric. I must also mention the work of Alphonso Lingis, whose texts I greatly admire. Lingis's interpretation of Levinas's philosophy is particularly present in the second half of this book, in my reading of Maria Maddalena de' Pazzi's mysticism and in Girolamo Cardano's *Metoposcopia*. The "face" of the other is a recurrent themes in Lingis's work. How we respond to the request spoken by the other's face is indeed, as Lingis teaches us, a matter of rhetoric. Finally, the Italian philosophical movement called Weak Thought (Pensiero debole) echoes throughout my book. Gianni Vattimo and Pier Aldo Rovatti are certainly two of its major and most vocal representatives.[1] In the introduction I quote a brief passage from a recent book of Vattimo's, in which he emphasizes that in our times "there are no facts, only interpretations." But interpretations, as Vattimo stresses repeatedly in his work, are the language they are expressed in—that is, history itself is a matter of rhetoric, as if the unfolding of history could be read as a sermon or discourse that delivers itself through our rhetorical translations.

WHILE I AM FINISHING THIS BOOK, the Catholic Church is celebrating its Jubilee, the two-thousandth anniversary of Christ's birth. It is no

---

1. Compare Gianni Vattimo and Pier Aldo Rovatti, eds., *Il pensiero debole* (Milan: Feltrinelli, 1983).

exaggeration to state that this "Holy Year" is a landmark in the history of Catholicism, and it is certainly an essential moment in the papacy of John Paul II. The term *celebration* does not fully convey the importance of the Catholic Jubilee. We usually associate this term with an act of remembrance, a festive memorial of a past event. But a celebration is also an event marking a new beginning (a wedding, a baptism, a homecoming). The Catholic Jubilee is at once the celebration of Christ's past victory over death and the original sin, and the celebration of a renewed mystical wedding between Christ and his bride, the Catholic Church. Let us remember that, following Catherine of Siena, women visionaries experience their mystical marriage to the Word as a repeated, constantly renewed celebration. Maria Maddalena de' Pazzi celebrates her marriage to the Word several times.

The Jubilee both recalls and shows the glory of the Catholic Church, as the embodiment of Christ's victory over Satan and his followers. To think of the Jubilee only as the memorial of Christ's incarnation would overshadow how Christ's glory *lives* in the Catholic Church here and now. The Catholic Church *is* Christ's glory. In studying de Moura's *De ensalmis* we have seen that, in its fight against the Protestant movement, the Catholic Church read relics, miracles, and angelic visitations as evidence for its mystical supremacy. Through relics and miracles, Christ spoke to his bride, confirmed his matrimonial pact, and thus supported the war of the Catholic Church against its traitors and the infidels.

Relics, miracles, and divine messages are not absent from this historic Jubilee. Consider, for instance, the role played by the Shroud of Turin. Although the Vatican has never officially recognized it as the actual cloth in which Christ's corpse was wrapped in the sepulcher, the shroud is treated as such both by the Catholic authorities and by the Catholic believers. The exposition of the "Holy Shroud," as it is normally called, is an essential part of this Catholic celebration (August 12–October 22, 2000). Catholics have been flocking to Turin to have a glimpse of this divine relic, and innumerable books are published to support the shroud's holiness against all scientific evidence.

But another, more powerful and more significant event has recently marked the celebration of this "Holy Year." On June 26 the Vatican revealed the content of the so-called Third Secret of Fátima during a news conference.[2] However, on May 13, the pope had already indicated the content of this mystery before an audience exceeding six hundred thousand

---

2. http://www.vatican.va/roman_curia/congregations/cfaith/documents/rc_con_cfaith_doc_20000626_mes-fatima_en.html

people in Fátima. The Vatican's interpretation of this third mystery is indeed of crucial importance. As is well known, in 1917 the Virgin Mary appeared to three young Portuguese shepherds in the poor village of Fátima.[3] The Virgin granted these children three mystical insights. If the first "secret" focused on World War I and the second spoke of the dangers of Soviet communism, the third message was kept hidden throughout the century. In the square of Fátima itself where the three children had allegedly seen the Virgin, on May 14 John Paul II announced the nature of this final mystery, whose core concerns the pope himself. Addressing the multitude gathered at the square of the Portuguese village, Cardinal Sodano stated that the third secret of Fátima was "a prophetic vision comparable to those present in the Holy Scriptures."[4] The third secret of Fátima, Cardinal Sodano is convinced, is a prophecy of such relevance and consequence that it can be likened to the Bible itself. Although the children received this fundamental insight in 1917, Sister Lucia, the only surviving member of the trio and now a Carmelite nun, wrote it down only in 1944. In the text of this revelation, we read that

> at the left of Our Lady and a little above, we saw an angel with a flaming sword in his left hand; flashing, it gave out flames that looked as though they would set the world on fire; but they died out in contact with the splendor that Our Lady radiated towards him from her right hand. Pointing to the earth with his right hand, the angel cried out in a loud voice: PENANCE PENANCE PENANCE. And we saw in an immense light, that is God, something similar to how people appear in a mirror when they pass in front of it a bishop dressed in white. We had the impression that it was the Holy Father. Other bishops, priests, men and women religious going up a steep mountain, at the top of which there was a big cross of rough-hewn trunks as of a cork-tree with the bark; before reaching there the Holy Father passed through a big city half in ruins and half trembling with halting step, afflicted with pain and sorrow, he prayed for the souls of the corpses he met on this way. Having reached the top of the mountain, on his knees at the foot of the big cross he was killed by a group of soldiers who fired bullets and arrows at him, and in the same way there died one after another the other bishops, priests, men and women religious and various lay people of different ranks and positions. Beneath the two arms of the cross there were two angels each with a crystal asperso-

---

3. Compare Ann E. Matter, "Apparitions of the Virgin Mary in the Late Twentieth Century: Apocalyptic, Representation, Politics," *Religion* (forthcoming).

4. I quote and translate from Marco Politi, "L'attentato del Papa nel segreto di Fátima," *La Repubblica*, May 14, 2000, 3.

rium in his hand, in which they gathered up the blood of the martyrs and with it sprinkled the souls that were making their way to God.[5]

According to the philosopher Gianni Vattimo, "the text is of a depressing banality. It is even hard to understand if it actually refers to the twentieth century."[6] If this clearly apocalyptic vision (the angel with a flaming sword, the two angels gathering the martyrs' blood) has the status of a biblical revelation, as Cardinal Sodano holds, its message should then be understood as a warning or omen. However, John Paul II is convinced that he is the "Holy Father" mentioned in the prophecy, and that the "group of soldiers" who kill "the Holy Father" is none other than Mehmet Ali Agca, the Turkish terrorist who shot John Paul II in Rome in 1981. But what about the other "bishops and priests, men and women religious and various lay people" who also die in the prophecy? To see John Paul II as the dead "Holy Father," two corrections must be made to the text of the revelation. First, the "Holy Father" does not really die, he looks *as if* he were dead. Second, the death of other religious and lay people in the prophecy is either irrelevant or a reference to a different temporal moment. According to the Vatican, the "other people" simply symbolize the present and future martyrdom of the Church, while the "Holy Father" is certainly John Paul II, who according to the third mystery would have died under Satan's attack, had the Virgin Mary not altered the very ending of the prophetic vision that she herself had granted to the three children. In other words, the Virgin Mary herself protected John Paul II from his assassin. The bullet from the Turkish terrorist's gun now lies in the crown of the Virgin's statue in the Fátima shrine.[7] The terrorist himself confessed that, when he made his attempt on the life of the pope, he felt that a diabolical force had taken hold of his mind.

It is essential to understand that the function of the third secret of Fátima is to exalt the person of John Paul II now in the year 2000. Although he had read this text in 1981 right after the attempted assassination, John Paul II made the third revelation of Fátima a fundamental moment of the Jubilee. Moreover, to stress its crucial relevance for the entire Church, in Fátima John Paul II at once disclosed the prophecy and beatified two of the three little shepherds, the third being still alive in Portugal. Thus, if the Jubilee celebrates the renewed alliance between Christ and the Catholic Church, the third mystery of Fátima celebrates John Paul II as the

5. CNN, June 26, 2000.
6. Gianni Vattimo, "Un grande flop," *La stampa*, June 27, 2000, 2.
7. Garry Wills, *Papal Sin* (New York: Doubleday, 2000), 205.

personification of the Church's triumph over evil. This apocalyptic prophecy indeed works as a form of exorcism. In my discussion of the *Thesaurus exorcismorum*, I pointed out that the exorcist expels a devil tormenting a body in pain by reminding him that his defeat has already taken place. The devil's expulsion has already been foreseen in the Scriptures. Similarly, the apocalypse described in the prophecy of Fátima shows that the Church *will be glorified* (the martyrs "making their way to God") because the Church (John Paul II) *was glorified* when the Virgin Mary changed the outcome of her own prophecy. If the "other people" ("bishops, priests, men and women religious") may die in the name of God, the Church as personified by John Paul II is a living glory.

It is thus undeniable that the Catholic Jubilee exalts the pope and his mystical and royal power. As the historian Garry Wills reminds us, to understand the role of the pope in contemporary Catholicism we must refer back to Pius IX's decree on papal infallibility. In the late nineteenth century Pope Pius IX declared himself infallible, to compensate for the loss of temporal power by the Catholic Church.[8] After Pius IX, Wills explains, "the Holy Spirit . . . speaks to only one person on earth, the omnicompetent head of the Church, a church that is all head and no limbs." The Church is the pope and the pope is the Church.[9] This is why, in the Fátima vision, the "others" (bishops, religious, and lay people) can die, but the Church/John Paul II survives in eternity. Since Pius IX's decree on papal infallibility, Wills writes, the pope has become an "oracle, replacing scripture and the Spirit."[10] More than a simple oracle, the pope is both a human and an angelic being, a semi-god. As we saw in chapter 1, in theory angels can err, since they are created beings, but God does not let them misinterpret his silent statements. With the decree of Pius IX, the pope has acquired a similar privilege.

It is thus understandable why the Jubilee of the Catholic Church is in reality the jubilee of John Paul II. Like the hero of an epic poem, John Paul II has been repeatedly described as an irresistible force of Truth. An indefatigable paladin of the Catholic faith, John Paul II defeated the beast of communism, spread the true faith throughout the world, overcame the power of evil (the Arab terrorist, the infidel), and victoriously returned to Jerusalem in the year of his jubilee. As in every epic poem, superior, more-than-human forces fight over the destiny of the epic hero (Satan through the Turkish infidel, against the Virgin Mary). It is impossible not

8. Compare Wills, *Papal Sin*, 246–59.
9. Wills, *Papal Sin*, 163.
10. Wills, *Papal Sin*, 174.

to think of Torquato Tasso's *Jerusalem Delivered,* the superb Italian epic "celebrat[ing] the triumph of the imperial, Counter-Reformation papacy."[11] As David Quint summarizes, "Tasso's epic portrays the taking of Jerusalem by the knights of the First Crusade under the leadership of Godefroi of Bouillon."[12]

Quint explains that in Tasso's epic, the pious Godefroi of Bouillon has to subjugate both internal and external enemies. The path of the hero toward assured triumph is questioned both by the resistance of the Enemy (Satan's direct intervention in favor of the Muslims holding Jerusalem) and by the presence of rebellious paladins (primarily symbolized by the character Rinaldo). Similarly, in his march toward its final glorification the Church/John Paul II cannot help but deal with those "brothers and sisters" who, in the history of the Catholic Church, meant well but unfortunately committed crimes against humanity. The pope has made it clear that the Church (the *Magisterium* that now corresponds to the person of the pope) is a holy entity, a Platonic idea whose sanctity cannot be questioned. The "others" (those who are and are not part of the Church—"bishops, men and women religious," as the Fátima prophecy says) may have failed in following the Church's (the pope's, the epic hero's) infallible instructions.

A fundamental obstacle in the march of the Church/pope toward epic triumph is thus the annoying presence of memory. For the "internal" enemies of the Church/pope are in fact its victims, all those who, throughout the centuries and in different ways, were persecuted and murdered by the "brothers and sisters" of the Church. The Church's "inner" enemy is a persistent melancholy. As we have seen in chapters 4 and 5, suffering souls come up to us, haunt us with a request for remembrance. The "souls in purgatory" and the faces looking back at us from the pages of Cardano's *Metaposcopia* ask us to take up and assume the weight of their tormenting memories. They want us to face them, to remember them, to become responsible for their suffering. I am of course alluding here to *Memory and Reconciliation,* the document formulating the alleged "apologies" of the Catholic Church for its crimes against humanity.[13] As the mystic Maria Maddalena de' Pazzi and the Neoplatonic philosopher Girolamo Cardano have shown, in order to welcome and to take up the pain of the other, to

11. David Quint, *Epic and Empire* (Princeton: Princeton University Press, 1993), 230.
12. Quint, *Epic and Empire,* 215.
13. *Memory and Reconciliation: The Church and the Faults of the Past,* issued by Cardinal Ratzinger, December 1999. I read this text at www.vatican.va/roman_curia/congregations/cfaith/documents/rc_con_cfaith_doc_20000307_memory-reconc-itc_en.html

perceive his request for remembrance, I must confront his "face," I must see that his face is a reflection of mine. But the Church/John Paul II has nothing to apologize for, since the Church's magisterial charisma (its angelic being) "is assured by the Lord to the Church's bishops, and consequently does not require any magisterial act of reparation." Thus, the "others" (the "brothers and sisters" who happen to be *in* the Church but are not the Church) may have momentarily misinterpreted and tainted the Church's mystical body. Recall again the few paladins who, in Tasso's epic poem, temporarily hold back Godefroi of Bouillon from his victorious conquest of the Holy City during the First Crusade.

Apologizing for the crimes committed by "others," John Paul II fights and defeats one more insidious enemy. With *Memory and Reconciliation*, the Church/pope buries the demons of melancholy. The victims of Catholicism are not the victims of the Catholic Church, and thus no melancholy should infest and mar the Church/pope's path of glory. The victims of Catholicism do not deserve to be remembered because the Catholic Church has no victims. *Memory and Reconciliation* works as the final prayer read at a funeral, or better yet, as the exorcism of the melancholy demons plaguing the Church's mind. In the words of Wills, "this is apology as propaganda."[14] But we all know that an epic narration is always a form of propaganda, for an epic saga always narrates the irresistible "propagation" of Truth.

Having expelled its last demons, having slain its inner and outer enemies, the Church/pope in the last chapter of this epic approaches its ultimate exaltation. Typical of an epic text, the Jubilee of the year 2000 then proclaims both the end of the Church's troubled past (its inner and outer demons and enemies) and the beginning of a new golden age in which the Catholic creed will impose its evident truthfulness. This final "celebration" of the Church's glory can only take place in the Holy City of Rome. During the Jubilee, the city of Rome thus reacquires its original status of New Jerusalem (capital of the state of the Church), welcoming its hero from his victorious conquests and suspending the city's lay nature.

But it is in the New Jerusalem that the Enemy unleashes his final, unexpected attack. It is in the "Holy City of Rome," as Cardinal Sodano stated on June 3, that the sodomites have decided to hold their Gay Pride 2000 event.[15] Clearly formulating a counter, demonic Jubilee, the sodom-

14. Garry Wills, "The Vatican Regrets," *New York Review of Books*, May 25, 2000, 20.
15. Alessandra Stanley, "Dueling Festivals: Gay Pride and Vatican Collide," *New York Times*, June 3, 2000, A4.

ites aim to infect the capital of the Catholic creed with their virus. Being unable to resort to the Church's more congenial means of repression and persecution, the highest ranks of the Catholic Church publicly and vigorously complained to the civil authorities, trying to convince them of the sinfulness of the planned sodomitical gathering. Cardinal Ruini, president of the Italian Conference of Bishops, communicated the pope's sadness and dismay, and warned that during Gay Pride 2000 "crimes would be committed." The essential "crime" would be certainly the identification between the Holy City of God and the city of Sodom. By allowing the sodomites and their supporters to march through the streets of Rome during the second week of July, the Italian authorities would turn Rome into a new or renewed Sodom.

In the words of Stanislaw Heymo, a Dominican priest who was in charge of the Polish pilgrimage to Rome, "[Gay Pride 2000] is a very bad thing. . . . It would be better to spend money on the poor and immigrants, because homosexuals are rich, from rich families. They do nothing other than travel throughout the world, flaunting their sickness."[16] It is impossible to avoid noticing the parallel between this description of the homosexuals and the traditional portrayal of the Jews, seen as sick, corrupt, and wealthy people. In our study of de Moura's *De ensalmis*, we saw that, for the Portuguese inquisitor, worldly wealth is the Jews' sole religion. But Heymo also points out that homosexuals "travel"—that is, they spread their sickness. A sickness that is, moreover, contagious. We recall what Prierio says in *De strigimagis* about the demonic local motion, the rhetorical connection (the movement from the two clauses to their possible conclusion) that enables the devil to fulfill his devastating syllogism. To complete his syllogism, the devil may need the support of his disciples, witches, magicians, sodomites, heretics, and Jews.

As we have also seen, according to de Moura, we should not distinguish between sodomites and Jews, since both sodomites and Jews act "against nature." However, after the Holocaust, it has become impossible to sustain the equation of sodomy and Judaism. After the Nazi persecution, the concept of sodomy has been purified, so to speak. The Foe now speaks exclusively through the sodomites. We recall that the language of Satan, as Prierio describes it, is a fire that devours both its listeners and its speakers. The Jewish community in Rome reminded the Vatican that the sodomites were also deported and executed in the concentration camps. But the Church/pope knows that no dialogue is possible with the Enemy. John

16. Quoted in Stanley, "Dueling Festivals."

Paul II officially forbade a French bishop to participate in a roundtable organized by sodomites during Gay Pride 2000.[17]

If the pope embodies the glory of the Church, the sodomites *embody* the errors of modernity. Indeed, "sodomy" is a concept that goes far beyond its strictly sexual content. Like "Church," "sodomy" is a Platonic idea. What is "against nature" and is incarnated in the sodomites are our modern times *tout court*. Again, we must go back to Pius IX and to his infamous *Syllabus of Errors* (1864) in which, as Wills summarizes, the pope "took on science, secularism, materialism, relativism, democracy, freedom of speech, and the competency of all modern governments."[18] Thus, the sodomites are the expression of modernity, and by attacking the sodomites the Church attacks the Idea of our "sodomitical" times. The sodomites are the visibility of "sodomy."

The Catholic view of sodomy is shared by other Christian denominations.[19] Pat Robertson, the leader of the Christian Coalition, has repeatedly stressed this essential point. Robertson senses the existence of a "Big Brother"—that is, of a conspiracy (liberalism, leftist universities, intellectuals, unidentified political forces)—against the values of Christianity. In *The Secret Kingdom*, speaking of this international machination against Truth, Robertson writes: "When homosexuals invade churches and cathedrals, as they have done in this country, screaming blasphemies at priests, pastors, and worshipers, defiling the very house of God, they have reached the depths of depravity."[20] A nation that "moves into blatant sexuality, especially homosexuality . . . ," Robertson writes in *The New Millennium*, "can expect the judgment of God and the full weight of God's wrath against them."[21] In June 1998 Robertson warned that the city of Orlando, Florida, might suffer from a number of possible divine punishments (terrorist bombs, earthquakes) if it allowed gay pride flags to be shown along the city

---

17. Marco Tosatti, "Gay Pride, stop del Papa a un vescovo," *La stampa*, July 3, 2000, 6.

18. Wills, *Papal Sin*, 74.

19. See Mark Jordan's analysis of the *Letter to All Catholic Bishops on the Pastoral Care of Homosexual Persons*, released by Cardinal Ratzinger in 1986 (in Mark D. Jordan, *The Silence of Sodom* [Chicago: University of Chicago Press, 2000]): "[In the *Letter*] an American reader will recognize . . . the allegation of a widely shared and covert 'gay agenda.' In fact the political analysis of the 1986 *Letter* much resembles the paranoid political phantasies of the American 'Christian Right'" (36). "If the sodomites are not stopped," Jordan continues in his description of the Catholic document, "they will bring on the destruction of any society that tolerates them. Sodomy will produce famines and plagues, floods and earthquakes, until God's own wrath is moved against it in final conflagration" (38).

20. Pat Robertson, *The Secret Kingdom*, in *The Collected Works* (New York: Inspirational Press, 1994), 560–61.

21. Pat Robertson, *The New Millennium*, in *The Collected Works*, 161–62.

streets. Again, the exposition of sodomy entails an infection, a mental and physical corruption. In this context, we may note that the current Catholic archbishop of New York, Edward Michael Egan, endorsed "a group affiliated with the Christian Coalition, the conservative political lobby founded by Pat Robertson and Ralph Reed."[22] Catholicism and the Christian Coalition indeed share the same enemy, the virus of sodomy, which is the virus of modernity.

If the created world has been tainted by the "speakers of the mind," if the created world has entered a "sodomitical" era of decadence, the Church and its epic narration is under the aegis of the luminous presence of Providence. The sodomites invading the Holy City of Rome will eventually be annihilated by their own virus. The purity of the New Jerusalem will be finally restored. Satan and his rhetoric will be silenced forever, along with all the souls in pain.

22. Laurie Goodstein, "Secure at the Helm: Bishop Edward Michael Egan," *New York Times*, May 12, 2000, C28

Agamben, Giorgio. *Language and Death: The Place of Negativity.* Translated by
    Karen E. Pinkus and Michael Hardt. Minneapolis: University of Minnesota
    Press, 1991.
————. *Stanzas: Word and Phantasm in Western Culture.* Translated by Ronald L.
    Martinez. Minneapolis: University of Minnesota Press, 1993.
Agnoletto, Attilio, Sergio Abbiate, and Maria Rosario Lazzati, eds. *La stregoneria.*
    Diavoli, streghe, inquisitori dal Trecento al Settecento. Milan: Mondadori,
    1991.
Albertus Magnus. *De memoria et reminiscentia.* In *Opera omnia,* edited by
    Auguste Borgnet, vol. 9. Paris: Ludovicus Vives, 1890.
Amat, Jacqueline. *Songes et visions: L'Au-delà dans la littérature latine tardive.*
    Paris: Études Augustiniennes, 1985.
Anglo, Sydney. "Melancholia and Witchcraft: The Debate between Wier, Bodin,
    and Scott." In *Folie et déraison à la Renaissance,* pp. 209–22. Brussels: Éditions
    de l'Université de Bruxelles, 1976.
Anon. *Ad C. Herennium.* Translated by Harry Caplan. Cambridge, Mass.: Harvard
    University Press, 1989.
Apuleius. *Apologia sive de magia liber.* Edited by Giuseppe Augello. Turin: Utet,
    1984.
————. *De deo Socratis.* In *Apulée: Opuscules philosophiques et fragments,* edited
    by Jean Beaujeu. Paris: Les Belles Lettres, 1973.
Aristotle. *The Complete Works of Aristotle.* Edited by Jonathan Barnes. 2 vols.
    Princeton: Princeton University Press, 1985.
————. *On the Soul.* In *Introduction to Aristotle,* edited by Richard McKeon.
    Chicago: University of Chicago Press, 1973.
————. *Politics.* Translated by Ernest Barker. Oxford: Clarendon Press, 1961.
Armour, Peter. "*Purgatorio* XXVIII." In *Dante Commentaries: Eight Studies of the*

Divine Comedy, edited by David Nolan, pp. 115–41. Dublin: Irish Academic Press, 1977.

Athanasius. *The Life of Saint Anthony*. Translated by Robert T. Meyer. Westminister, Md.: Newman Press, 1950.

Augustine. *The City of God*. Various translators. 7 vols. Cambridge, Mass.: Harvard University Press, 1957–72.

———. *De cura pro mortuis gerenda*. Vol. 40 of *Patrologia latina*, edited by J.-P. Migne. Paris: Garnier, 1887.

———. *De divinatione daemonum*. Vol. 40 of *Patrologia latina*, edited by J.-P. Migne. Paris: Garnier, 1887.

———. *De Genesi ad litteram*. Vol. 34 of *Patrologia latina*, edited by J.-P. Migne. Paris: D'Amboise, 1864.

———. *De spiritu et littera*. Vol. 44 of *Patrologia latina*, edited by J.-P. Migne. Paris: Thibaud, 1865.

———. *De trinitate*. Vol. 42 of *Patrologia latina*, edited by J.-P. Migne. Paris: Garnier, 1886.

———. *Enarratio in Psalmum CIII*. Vol. 37 of *Patrologia latina*, edited by J.-P. Migne. Paris: Garnier, 1900.

———. *Soliloquiorum libri duo*. Vol. 32 of *Patrologia latina*, edited by J.-P. Migne. Paris: Garnier, 1877.

Aurigemma, Marcello. "Il canto VIII del *Purgatorio*." In *Casa di Dante in Roma. Purgatorio. Letture degli anni 1976–79*. Rome: Bonacci, 1981.

Barzman, Karen-edis. "Cultural Production, Religious Devotion, and Subjectivity in Early Modern Italy: The Case Study of Maria Maddalena de' Pazzi." *Annali d'italianistica* 13 (1995): 283–305.

Battaglia, Salvatore. *Esemplarità e antagonismo nel pensiero di Dante*. Naples: Liguori, 1967.

Bernard of Clairvaux. *On the Song of Songs*. Kalamazoo, Mich.: Cistercian Publications, 1981.

Besnier, Liko. "Heteroglossic Discourses on Nukulaelae Spirits." In *Spirits in Culture, History, and Mind*, edited by Jeanette Marie Mageo and Alan Howard, pp. 75–97. New York: Routledge, 1996.

Bethencourt, Francisco. *L'inquisition à l'époque moderne*. Paris: Editions Fayard, 1995.

Binsfeldius, Petrus. *Tractatus de confessionibus maleficorum et sagarum*. Trier: Henricus Bock, 1605.

Böcher, Otto. *Dämonenfurcht und Dämonenabwehr*. Stuttgart: Kohlhammer, 1970.

Bodin, Jean. *De la démonomanie des sorciers*. Hildesheim: Olms Verlag, 1988.

Boguet, Henry. *Discours des sorciers*. 3rd ed. Lyons: Rigaud, 1610.

Boiron, Stéphane. *La controverse née de la querelle des reliques à l'époque du concile de Trent*. Paris: Presses Universitaires de France, 1989.

Borges Coelho, António. *Inquisição de Evora*. 2 vols. Lisbon: Caminho, 1987.

Borgna, Eugenio. *Malinconia*. Milan: Feltrinelli, 1992.

Bozio, Tommaso. *De signis ecclesiae Dei*. Cologne: Ioannes Gymnicus, 1593.

Brann, Noël. "Alchemy and Melancholy in Medieval and Renaissance Thought: A

Query into the Mystical Basis of Their Relationship." *Ambix* 32, no. 2 (1985): 127–48.

Brenk, Frederick E. "In the Light of the Moon: Demonology in the Early Imperial Period." In *Aufstieg und Niedergang der Römischen Welt, II, Principat.* Edited by Hildegard Temporini and Wolfgang Haase. Berlin: De Gruyter, 1986. Vol. 2, part 16, sec. 3, pp. 2068–2145.

Brickhouse, Thomas C., and Nicholas D. Smith. *Plato's Socrates.* New York: Oxford University Press, 1994.

Brown, Alice. *Sixteenth-Century Beliefs on Dreams, with Special Reference to Girolamo Cardano's "Somniorum libri IIII."* London: Warburg Institute, 1971.

Bruni de Sanseverino, Franciscus. *Tractatus de indiciis et tortura.* Venice, 1549.

Burton, Robert. *The Anatomy of Melancholy.* Edited by Floyd Dell and Paul Jordan-Smith. New York: Tudor Publishing House, 1938.

Bynum, Caroline Walker. *Fragmentation and Redemption.* New York: Zone Books, 1991.

———. *The Resurrection of The Body.* New York: Columbia University Press, 1995.

Cacciari, Massimo. *L'angelo necessario.* Milan: Adelphi, 1994.

Caciola, Nancy. "Wraiths, Revenants and Ritual in Medieval Culture." *Past and Present* 152 (August 1996): 3–45.

Caietanus. *In Scriptura commentarii.* In *Opera Omnia.* Lyons, 1639.

Campanella, Tommaso. *Theologicorum liber XIV.* Edited by Romano Amerio. Rome: Bocca, 1957.

———. *Theologicorum liber XXV.* Edited by Romano Amerio. Rome: Bocca, 1973.

Campe, Rüdiger, and Manfred Schneider, eds. *Geschichte der Physiognomik.* Freiburg: Rombach, 1996.

Cardano, Girolamo. *The Book of My Life.* Translated by Jean Stoner. New York: Dutton, 1930.

———. *De rerum varietate.* Avignon: Matthaeus Vincentius, 1558.

———. *Metoposcopia libris tredecim, et octingentis faciei humanae eiconibus complexa.* Paris: Thomas Iolly, 1658.

———. *Opera Omnia.* Edited by Charles Spon. 10 vols. Lyons, 1663.

Caroli, Flavio. *Storia della fisiognomica.* Milan: Leonardo, 1995.

Cassian. *De principatibus seu potestatibus.* In *Opera omnia.* Vol. 49 of *Patrologia latina,* edited by J.-P. Migne. Paris: Thibaud, 1874.

Catena, Claudio. "Ambiente del monastero di S. Maria degli Angeli ai tempi di S. Maria Maddalena de' Pazzi." *Carmelus* 13 (1966): 21–96.

———. "Le malattie di S. Maria Maddalena de' Pazzi." *Carmelus* 16 (1969): 70–141.

———. *Santa Maria Maddalena de' Pazzi carmelitana: Orientamenti spirituali e ambiente in cui visse.* Rome: Institutum carmelitanum, 1966.

Catherine of Genoa. *Purgation and Purgatory. The Spiritual Dialogue.* Translated by Serge Hughes. New York: Paulist Press, 1979.

Cave, Terence. *Pré-histoires. Texts troublés au seuil de la modernité.* Geneva: Droz, 1999.

Céard, Jean. "The Devil and Lovesickness: Views of Sixteenth-Century Physicians and Demonologists." In *Eros and Anteros: The Medical Traditions of Love in the Renaissance*. Edited by Donald A. Beecher and Massimo Ciavolella. Toronto: Dovehouse Editions, 1992.

―――. "Folie et démonologie au XVIe siècle." In *Folie et déraison à la Renaissance*, pp. 129–43. Brussels: Éditions de l'Université de Bruxelles, 1976.

―――. *La nature et les prodiges*. Geneva: Droz, 1977.

Cherchi, Paolo. "Gervase of Tilbury and the Birth of Purgatory." *Medioevo romanzo* 14, no. 1 (1989): 97–110.

Ciambelli, Patrizia. *Quelle figlie quelle spose. Il culto delle Anime Purganti a Napoli*. Rome: De Luca, 1980.

Cicero. *De divinatione*. Edited by A. S. Pease. New York: Arno Press, 1979.

Clark, Stuart. *Thinking with Demons: The Idea of Witchcraft in Early Modern Europe*. Oxford: Clarendon Press, 1997.

Col, Andrea del, and Marisa Milani. "'Senza effusione di sangue e senza pericolo di morte'. Intorno ad alcune condanne capitali delle inquisizioni di Venezia e di Verona nel Settecento e a quella veneziana del Cinquecento." In *Eretici, esuli e indemoniati nell'età moderna*, edited by Mario Rosa. Florence: Olschki, 1998.

Comensius, Bernardus. *Lucerna inquisitorum haereticae pravitatis*. Milan: Valerius et Hieronius fratres, 1566.

Copenhaver, Brian P., ed. *Hermetica*. New York: Cambridge University Press, 1998.

Corbin, Henry. *Avicenna and the Visionary Recital*. Translated by Willard R. Trask. Princeton: Princeton University Press, 1988.

Cornacchini, Tommaso. *Tabulae medicae*. Padua: Tozzi, 1605.

Corsano, Antonio. "Il Cardano e la storia." *Giornale critico della filosofia italiana* 40 (1961): 499–507.

―――. "La 'dialectica' di Girolamo Cardano." *Giornale critico della filosofia italiana* 40 (1961): 175–80.

―――. "La psicologia del Cardano: 'De animi immortalitate.'" *Giornale critico della filosofia italiana* 41 (1962): 56–64.

Courtine, Jean-Jacques, and Claudine Haroche. *Histoire du visage*. Paris: Rivages, 1988.

Csordas, Thomas J. "Imaginal Performance and Memory in Ritual Healing." In *The Performance of Healing*, edited by Carol Laderman and Marina Roseman, pp. 91–114. New York: Routledge, 1996.

―――. *Language, Charisma, and Creativity*. Berkeley: University of California Press, 1997.

D'Alexis, Leon. *Traicté des energumènes, suivi d'un discours sur la possession de Marthe Brossier: Contre les calomnies d'un medecin de Paris*. Troyes, 1599.

Dante Alighieri. *Purgatorio*. Edited by Natalino Sapegno. Florence: La Nuova Italia, 1970.

Davis, Eli. "The Psalms in Hebrew Medical Amulets." *Vetus Testamentum* 42 (1992): 173–78.

De Arles, Martin. *Tractatus de superstitionibus*. Frankfurt, 1581.

De Baucio, Carolus. *Modus interrogandi daemonem ab exorcista*. Venice: Turrinus, 1643.

De Bernart, Luciana. *Immaginazione e scienza in Giordano Bruno*. Pisa: ETS Editrice, 1986.

De Certeau, Michel. *Il parlare angelico*. Translated by Daniela de Agostini. Florence: Olschki, 1989.

———. *La possession de Loudun*. Paris: Julliard, 1970. English translation: *The Possession at Loudun*, translated by Michael B. Smith. Chicago: University of Chicago Press, 2000.

———. *The Writing of History*. Translated by Tom Conley. New York: Columbia University Press, 1988.

De Lancre, Pierre. *L'incredulité et miscreance du sortilege plainement convaincue*. Paris: Nicolas Buon, 1622.

———. *Tableau de l'inconstance des mauvais anges et demons*. Paris: Nicolas Buon, 1613.

De la Torre, Raphael. *De potestate Ecclesiae coercendi daemones circa obsessos*. In *Diversi Tractatus*. Cologne, 1629.

Della Barba, Pompeo. *Spositione d'un sonetto platonico*. Florence, 1554.

Della Mirandola, Giovan Francesco Pico. *La strega, ovvero degli inganni de' demoni*. 1st ed., 1523. Translated by Turino Turini. Milan: Daelli, 1864.

Del Rio, Martin. *Disquisitionum magicarum*. Mainz: Petrus Henningius, 1617.

De Matteis, Stefano, and Marino Niola. *Antropologia delle anime in pena*. Lecce: Argo, 1997.

De Mello e Souza, Laura. *Inferno atlântico. Demonologia e colonização. Séculos XVI–XVIII*. São Paulo: Companhia das Letras, 1993.

De Moura, Manuel do Valle. *De incantantionibus seu ensalmis*. Lisbon, 1620.

———. *Parodia ao primeiro canto dos Lusiadas de Camães por quatro esudantes de Evora*. Lisbon: Martins, 1589.

De' Pazzi, Maria Maddalena. *Maria Maddalena de' Pazzi: Selected Revelations*. Translated by Armando Maggi. New York: Paulist Press, 2000.

———. *Tutte le opere di Santa Maria Maddalena de' Pazzi dai manoscritti originali*. Florence: Nardini, 1960–66.

Derrida, Jacques. *Aporias*. Translated by Thomas Dutoit. Stanford: Stanford University Press, 1993.

Desjarlais, Robert R. "Presence." In *The Performance of Healing*, edited by Carol Laderman and Marina Roseman, pp. 143–64. New York: Routledge, 1996.

De' Vieri, Francesco. *Discorso dell'eccellentissimo filosofo Francesco de' Vieri intorno a' dimoni*. Florence: Sermantelli, 1576.

De Vio, Tommaso. *Summula caietani, S. Xisti Cardinalis Illustriss. Ord. Praedicat*. Venice: Nicolinus, 1584.

Diacceto, Francesco Cattani. *De pulchro*. Edited by Sylvain Matton. Pisa: Scuola Normale, 1986.

Dictionnaire de spiritualité. Paris: Beauchesne, 1932.

Dictionnaire de théologie catholique. Paris: Letouzey et Ané, 1928.

Di Nola, Alfonso. *Il Diavolo*. Rome: Newton and Compton, 1999.

Dinzelbacher, Peter. *Vision und Visionsliteratur im Mittelalter*. Stuttgart: Anton Hiersemann, 1981.

Dizionario biografico degli italiani. Rome: Istituto dell'Enciclopedia Italiana, 1976.

Eamon, William. *Science and the Secrets of Nature*. Princeton: Princeton University Press, 1994.

Eckhart, Johannes (Meister Eckhart). *Teacher and Preacher.* Edited by Bernard McGinn. New York: Paulist Press, 1986.

Eco, Umberto. *The Search for the Perfect Language.* Translated by James Fentress. Cambridge: Blackwell, 1997.

———. *Serendipities: Language and Lunacy.* Translated by William Weaver. New York: Harcourt Brace, 1998.

Edelman, Lee. *Homographesis.* New York: Routledge, 1994.

Elliott, Dyan. *Fallen Bodies: Pollution, Sexuality, and Demonology in the Middle Ages.* Philadelphia: University of Pennsylvania Press, 1999.

Enciclopedia dantesca. Rome: Istituto della Enciclopedia Italiana, 1970.

Ermanno del S. S. Sacramento. "I manoscritti originali di Santa Maria Maddalena de' Pazzi." *Ephemerides carmeliticae* 7 (1956): 323–400.

Ernst, Cécile. *Teufelaustreibungen. Die Praxis der katolischen Kirche im 16. und 17. Jahrhundert.* Bern: Huber, 1972.

Ernst, Germana. *Religione, ragione e natura.* Milan, 1991.

ps.-Eucherius. *Commentii in Genesim in tres libros distributi.* Vol. 50 of *Patrologia latina,* edited by J.-P. Migne. Paris: Thibaud, 1865.

Exorcismo mirabile da disfare ogni sorte de maleficii: et da caciare li demonii. Venice: Bernardinus Vercellensis de Lexona, 1532.

Eynatten, Maximilianus ab. *Manuale exorcismorum.* Antwerp: Balthasarius Moreti, 1648.

Fajardo-Acosta, Fidel. "*Purgatorio* XXVIII: Catharsis and Paradisal Visions as States of Dynamic Equilibrium." *Neophilologus* 75 (1991): 222–31.

Fallani, Giovanni. "Il canto VIII del *Purgatorio.*" In *Nuove letture dantesche,* vol. 4. Florence: Le Monnier, 1970.

Fenn, Richard K. *The Persistence of Purgatory.* Cambridge: Cambridge University Press, 1995.

Ferrier, Auger. *Libro de los sueños (Liber de somnis).* Edited by Francisco Calero. Madrid: Universidad Nacional de Educacion a Distancia, 1989.

Ficino, Marsilio. *Commentary on Plato's Symposium.* Edited by Sears Jayne. Woodstock, Conn.: Spring Publications, 1985.

———. *Meditations on the Soul: Selected Letters of Marsilio Ficino.* Rochester, Vt.: Inner Traditions International, 1996.

———. *Opera omnia.* 2 vols. Turin: Bottega d'Erasmo, 1959.

———. *Three Books on Life.* Edited by Carol V. Kaske and John R. Clark. Binghamton, N.Y.: Medieval and Renaissance Texts and Studies, 1989.

Fido, Franco. "Dall'antipurgatorio al paradiso terrestre: Il tempo ritrovato di Dante." *Letture classensi* 18 (1989): 64–78.

Fierz, Markus. *Girolamo Cardano (1501–1576).* Boston: Birkhäuser, 1983.

Fleischhack, Erich. *Fegfeur. Die Christlichen Vorstellungen vom Geschick der Verstorbenen.* Tübingen: Katzmann Verlag, 1969.

Flint, Valerie I. J. *The Rise of Magic in Early Medieval Europe.* Princeton: Princeton University Press, 1991.

Fodor, Alexander. "The Use of Psalms in Jewish and Christian Arabic Magic." In *Jubilee Volume of the Oriental Collection, 1951–1976,* pp. 67–71. Budapest: Library of the Hungarian Academy of Sciences, 1978.

Forti, Fiorenzo. "Il canto VIII del *Purgatorio.*" *Letture classensi* 3 (1970): 297–322.

Foucault, Michel. *The Order of Things*. New York: Pantheon Books, 1970.

Frank, Manfred. "Die Dichtung als 'Neue Mythologie'." In *Mythos und Moderne*. Frankfurt am Main, 1983.

———. *What Is Neo-structuralism?* Minneapolis: University of Minnesota Press, 1989.

Frede, Dorothea. "The Cognitive Role of *Phantasia* in Aristotle." In *Essays on Aristotle's "De Anima,"* edited by Martha C. Nussbaum and Amélie Oksenberg Rorty. Oxford: Clarendon Press, 1995.

Freud, Sigmund. *The Interpretation of Dreams*. Translated by James Stachey. New York: Basic Books, 1956.

Frick, Karl R. H. *Das Reich Satans*. Graz: Akademische Druck-u. Verlangsanstalt, 1982.

Friedrich, Paul. *The Language Parallax: Linguistic Relativism and Poetic Indeterminacy*. Austin: University of Texas Press, 1986.

Fuchs, Samuel. *Metoposcopia et Ophtalmoscopia*. Strasbourg, 1615.

Garin, Eugenio. *Astrology in the Renaissance*. Translated by Carolyn Jackson and June Allen. London: Routledge, 1983.

———. "*Phantasia* e *Imaginatio* fra Marsilio Ficino e Pietro Pomponazzi." In *Phantasia-Imagination*, edited by Eugenio Garin. Rome: Ateneo, 1988.

———. *Storia della filosofia italiana*. 3 vols. Bari: Laterza, 1966.

———. *Umanesimo italiano. Filosofia e vita civile nel Rinascimento*. Bari: Laterza, 1994.

Gigogna, Strozzio. *Magiae omnifariae, vel potius, universae naturae theatrum*. Cologne: Conradus Butgenius, 1607.

Glaser, Edward. "Portuguese Sermons at Autos-da-fé." *Studies in Bibliography and Booklore* 2 (1955–56).

Glocenius the Younger, Rodulphus. *Uranoscopia, chiroscopia, et metoposcopia*. Frankfurt, 1603.

Goddu, André. "The Failure of Exorcism in the Middle Ages." In *Possession and Exorcism*, edited by Brian P. Levack. New York: Garland, 1992.

Gonçalves Pires, Maria Lucília. *Xadrez de palavras. Estudos de literatura barroca*. Lisbon: Cosmos, 1996.

Goodstein, Laurie. "Secure at the Helm: Bishop Edward Michael Egan." *New York Times*, 12 May 2000, C28.

Goropius, Ioannes. *Hieroglyphica*. In *Opera omnia*. Brussels, 1574.

Grafton, Anthony. *Cardano's Cosmos*. Cambridge, Mass.: Harvard University Press, 1999.

Gregory the Great. *Homiliarum in Ezechielem*. In *Opera Omnia*. Vol. 76 of *Patrologia latina*, edited by J.-P. Migne. Paris: Garnier, 1878.

———. *Moralia*. In *Opera omnia*. Vol. 75 of *Patrologia latina*, edited by J.-P. Migne. Paris: D'Amboise, 1862.

Grillandus, Paulus. *Tractatus de sortilegiis*. 1st ed., 1536. Frankfurt, 1592.

Guazzo, Francesco. *Compendium maleficarum*. 1st ed., 1608. Translated by E. A. Ashwin. London: John Rodker, 1929.

Hagecius, Thaddaeus. *Metoposcopicorum libellus unus*. Frankfurt, 1560.

Hansen, Joseph. *Quellen und Untersuchungen zur Geschichte des Hexenwahns und der Hexenverfolgung im Mittelalter*. Bonn: Carl Georgi, 1901.

243

Harley, Marta Powell, ed. *A Revelation of Purgatory by an Unknown, Fifteenth-Century Woman Visionary: Introduction, Critical Text, and Translation.* Lewiston, Me.: Edwin Mellen Press, 1985.

Harsnett, Samuel. *A Declaration of Egregious Popish Impostures.* London, 1603.

Hildegard of Bingen. *Les causes et les remèdes.* Translated by Pierre Monat. Grenoble: Millon, 1997.

———. *The Letters of Hildegard of Bingen.* Translated by Joseph L. Baird and Radd K. Ehrman. New York: Oxford University Press, 1994.

Howard, Alan. "Speak of the Devils: Discourse and Belief in Spirits on Rotuma." In *Spirits in Culture, History, and Mind,* edited by Jeanette Marie Mageo and Alan Howard, pp. 121–45. New York: Routledge, 1996.

Husserl, Edmund. *Cartesian Meditations.* Translated by Dorion Cairns. The Hague: Martinus Nijhoff, 1960.

Iaquerio, Nicolao. *Flagellum haereticorum.* 1st ed., 1458. Frankfurt am Main, 1581.

Ingegno, Alfonso. "Cardano e Bruno. Altri spunti per una storia dell'uomo perfetto." In *Girolamo Cardano. Philosoph. Naturforscher. Arzt,* ed. Eckhard Kessler, pp. 77–90. Wiesbaden: Harrassowitz Verlag, 1994.

———. "The New Philosophy of Nature." In *The Cambridge History of Renaissance Philosophy,* edited by Quentin Skinner and Eckhard Kessler, pp. 236–63. New York: Cambridge University Press, 1996.

———. *Saggio sulla filosofia di Cardano.* Florence: Nuova Italia, 1980.

Jackson, Stanley W. *Melancholia and Depression: From Hippocratic Times to Modern Times.* New Haven: Yale University Press, 1986.

Jordan, Mark D. *The Silence of Sodom.* Chicago: University of Chicago Press, 2000.

Kamen, Henry. *The Spanish Inquisition.* New Haven: Yale University Press, 1998.

Keck, David. *Angels and Angelology in the Middle Ages.* New York: Oxford University Press, 1998.

Kelly, Henry Ansgar. "The Devil in the Desert." *Catholic Biblical Quarterly* 26 (1964): 190–220.

Kessler, Eckhard, ed. *Girolamo Cardano. Philosoph, Naturforscher, Arzt.* Wiesbaden: Harrassowitz Verlag, 1994.

Kieckhefer, Richard. "The Devil's Contemplatives: The *Liber Iuratus,* the *Liber Visionum* and the Christian Appropriation of Jewish Occultism." In *Conjuring Spirits: Texts and Traditions of Medieval Ritual Magic,* edited by Claire Fanger, pp. 250–65. University Park: Pennsylvania State University Press, 1998.

———. *Forbidden Rites: A Necromancer's Manual of the Fifteenth Century.* University Park: Pennsylvania State University Press, 1998.

———. *Magic in the Middle Ages.* New York: Cambridge University Press, 1989.

Kirkham, Victoria. "*Purgatorio* XXVIII." *Lectura Dantis* 12 (1993), 411–32.

Klibansky, Raymond, Erwin Panofsky, and Fritz Saxl. *Saturn and Melancholia: Studies in the History of Natural Philosophy, Religion, and Art.* New York: Basic Books, 1964.

Kramer, Heinrich, and James Sprenger. *Malleus maleficarum.* 1st ed., 1486. Translated by Montague Summers. New York: Dover, 1971.

Kristeva, Julia. "En deuil d'une langue?" In *Deuils: Vivre, c'est perdre*, edited by Nicole Czechowski and Claude Danzinger. Paris: Éditions Autrement, 1992.

Kuipers, Joel C. *Power in Performance*. Philadelphia: University of Pennsylvania Press, 1990.

Lacan, Jacques. *Écrits*. Translated by Alan Sheridan. New York: W. W. Norton, 1977.

———. *The Psychosis 1955–1956: The Seminar of Jacques Lacan: Book III*. Edited by Jacques-Alain Miller. New York: W. W. Norton, 1993.

———. "Seminar on 'The Purloined Letter.'" In *"The Purloined Letter,"* edited by John P. Muller and William J. Richardson. Baltimore: Johns Hopkins University Press, 1988.

Lachmann, Renate. *Memory and Literature*. Minneapolis: University of Minnesota Press, 1997.

Lausberg, Heinrich. *Elementi di retorica*. Bologna: Il Mulino, 1969.

Lavater, Ludovicus. *De spectris*. Lyons: Henricus Verbiest, 1669.

Lea, Henry Charles. *Materials toward a History of Witchcraft*. 3 vols. Philadelphia: University of Pennsylvania Press, 1939.

Le Brun, Jacques. "Jérôme Cardan et l'interprétation des songes." In *Girolamo Cardano. Philosoph. Naturforscher. Arzt*, ed. Eckhard Kessler, pp. 185–206.

Le Goff, Jacques. *The Birth of Purgatory*. Translated by Arthur Goldhammer. Chicago: University of Chicago Press, 1984.

Lengeling, Emil J. "Der Exorcismus der Katholischen Kirche." *Liturgisches Jahrbuch* 32 (1982): 248–57.

Lessius, Leonardus. *A Consultation about Religion*. Translated by Edmund Lechmere. London, 1693.

Levi, Giovanni. *Inheriting Power: The Story of an Exorcist*. Translated by Lydia G. Cochrane. Chicago: University of Chicago Press, 1988.

Levinas, Emmanuel. *Of God Who Comes to Mind*. Translated by Bettina Bergo. Stanford: Stanford University Press, 1998.

———. *Totality and Infinity*. Translated by Alphonso Lingis. Pittsburgh: Duquesne University Press, 1969.

Leysern D., Polycarpus. *Vom exorcismo. Ein Christlicher nötiger und in Gottes Wort wolgegründter Bericht*. Jena: Thobias Steinman, 1592.

Lingis, Alphonso. *The Community of Those Who Have Nothing in Common*. Bloomington: Indiana University Press, 1994.

———. *Foreign Bodies*. New York: Routledge, 1994.

Loarte, Gaspar. *Instrutione et avertimenti per meditare la passione di Cristo nostro Redentore, con alcune meditationi intorno ad esse*. Rome, 1571.

Lourenço D. De Mendonça, José, and António Joaquim Moreira. *História does principais actos e procedimentos da Inquisição em Portugal*. Lisbon: Imprensa Nacional–Casa da Moeda, 1980.

Macalpine, Ida, and Richard A. Hunter. *Schizophrenia 1677: A Psychiatric Study of an Illustrated Autobiographical Record of Demoniacal Possession*. London: Dawson, 1956.

Maccagni, Carlo. "Le razionalità, la razionalità." In *La strega, il teologo, lo scienziato*, edited by Maurizio Cuccu and Paolo Aldo Rossi, pp. 329–38. Genoa: Ed. Culturali Int., 1986.

Machado, Diogo Barboso. *Biblioteca lusitana.* 3 vols. 2nd ed. Lisbon, 1933.

Maggi, Armando. "Blood as Language in the Visions of Maria Maddalena de' Pazzi." *Rivista di letterature moderne e comparate* 48 (1995): 219–35.

———. "Demonologia e platonismo nel trattato d'amore *Spositione d'un sonetto platonico.*" *Italianistica* 28, no. 1 (1999): 9–21.

———. *Identità e impresa rinascimentale.* Ravenna: Longo, 1998.

———. "Impresa e misticismo nel *Settenario* di Alessandro Farra (1571)." *Rivista di storia e letteratura religiosa* (1997): 3–28.

———. "Performing/Annihilating the Word: Body as Erasure in the Visions of a Florentine Mystic." *TDR: The Drama Review* 41, no. 4 (1997): 110–27.

———. *Uttering the Word: The Mystical Performances of Maria Maddalena de' Pazzi, a Renaissance Visionary.* Albany: State University of New York Press, 1998.

———. "When the O. Moves in the Heart: The Annunciation of the End in the *Journal* of Saint Veronica Giuliani." *Annali d'italianistica* (forthcoming).

Marin, Louis. *La critique du discours. Sur la "Logique de Port-Royal" et les "Pensées" de Pascal.* Paris: Minuit, 1975.

———. *Food for Thought.* Translated by Mette Hjort. Baltimore: Johns Hopkins University Press, 1989.

Mattos, Vicente da Costa. *Breve discurso contra a heretica perfidia do iudaismo.* Lisbon, 1623.

Mauthner, Fritz. *Beiträge zu einer Kritik der Sprache.* 3 vols. Hildesheim: Olms, 1969.

McDannell, Colleen, and Bernhard Lang. *Heaven: A History.* New Haven: Yale University Press, 1988.

McGinn, Bernard. *The Flowering of Mysticism.* New York: Crossroad, 1998.

Mechtildis. *Liber specialis gratiae.* Paris: H. Oudin Fratres, 1877.

Meinel, Christoph. "Okkulte und exakte Wissenschaft." In *Die Okkulte Wissenschaft in der Renaissance,* edited by August Buck, pp. 21–43. Wiesbaden: Harrassowitz, 1992.

Menghi, Girolamo. *Compendio dell'arte essorcistica.* Venice: Bertano, 1605.

———. *Flagellum daemonum.* 1578.

———. *Fustis daemonum.* 1584.

Menghi, Girolamo, and Valerio Polidori, eds. *Thesaurus exorcismorum.* Cologne: Lazarus Zemerus, 1608.

Migne, J.-P. *Encyclopédie théologique.* Paris: Ateliers Catholiques du Petit-Montrouge, 1848.

Miller, Patricia Cox. *Dreams in Late Antiquity: Studies in the Imagination of a Culture.* Princeton: Princeton University Press, 1994.

Milosz, Czeslaw. "Notes on Exile." In *Altogether Elsewhere: Writers on Exile,* edited by Marc Robinson. New York: Harcourt Brace, 1994.

Mott, Luiz. *O sexo proibido. Virgens, Gays e Escravos nas garras da Inquisição.* Campina, Brazil: Papirus, 1988.

Müller-Jahncke, Wolf-Dieter. *Astrologisch-magische Theorie und Praxis in der Heilkunde der frühen Neuzeit.* Stuttgart: Steiner Verlag, 1985.

Murphy, John L. *Darkness and Devils: Exorcism and King Lear.* Athens, Ohio: Ohio University Press, 1984.

Nancy, Jean-Luc. *The Sense of the World*. Translated by Jeffrey S. Librett. Minneapolis: University of Minnesota Press, 1997.

Nicolsky, Nicolaj. *Spuren Magischer Formeln in den Psalmen*. Giessen: Alfred Töppelmann, 1927.

Nicuesa, Hilarius. *Exorcismarium in duos libros dispositum: quorum annuale alterum, alterum sanctuarium dicimus coniurationum*. Venice: Iuntas, 1639.

Nider, Johannes. *Formicarius*. Strasbourg, 1517.

Nodé, Pierre. *Déclamation contre l'erreur exécrable des maleficiers, sorciers, enchanteurs et semblables observateurs des superstitions*. Paris, 1578.

O'Neil, Mary R. "*Sacerdote ovvero strione*: Ecclesiastical and Superstitious Remedies in Sixteenth-Century Italy." In *Understanding Popular Culture: Europe from the Middle Ages to the Nineteenth Century*, edited by Steven L. Kaplan. New York: Mouton Publishers, 1984.

Ore, Oystein. *Cardano: The Gambling Scholar*. Princeton: Princeton University Press, 1953.

Origen. *Commentaria in evangelium Ioannis*. Vol. 14 of *Patrologia graeca*, edited by J.-P. Migne. Paris: D'Amboise, 1857.

———. *Contra Celsum*. Vol. 11 of *Patrologia graeca*, edited by J.-P. Migne. Paris: D'Amboise, 1857.

———. *An Exhortation to Martyrdom*. Translated by Rowan A. Grean. New York: Paulist Press, 1979.

———. *Homiliae in librum Iesu Nave*. Vol. 12 of *Patrologia graeca*, edited by J.-P. Migne. Paris: D'Amboise, 1857.

———. *Selecta in Genesis*. Vol. 12 of *Patrologia graeca*, edited by J.-P. Migne. Paris: D'Amboise, 1857.

Ossola, Carlo. "'Coi piè ristretti e con gli occhi passai'. Sospensione e compimento del tempo nel *Purgatorio*." In *L'arte dell'interpretare*, pp. 45–66. Cuneo, Italy: L'Arciere, 1984.

Pagels, Elaine. *The Origin of Satan*. New York: Vintage, 1995.

Palgen, Rudolf. *L'origine del "Purgatorio."* Graz: Verlag Styria, 1967.

Passavanti, Jacopo. *Specchio della vera penitenzia*. 1st ed., 1495. Florence: Tartini and Franchi, 1725.

Pastore, Federico. *La fabbrica delle streghe*. Paisian di Prato, Italy: Campanotto Editore, 1997.

Peters, Edward. *The Magician, the Witch and the Law*. Philadelphia: University of Pennsylvania Press, 1975.

———. "I Principi negligenti di Dante e le concezioni medioevali del 'rex inutilis'." *Rivista storica italiana* 80 (1968): 741–58.

Petrus Chrysologus. *Sermo 52*. In *Opera omnia*. Vol. 52 of *Patrologia latina*, edited by J.-P. Migne. Paris: Garnier, 1894.

Peucer, Caspar. *Commentarius de praecipuis generibus divinationum*. Wittenberg: Lufft, 1572.

Pile, Steve, and Nigel Thrift. "Mapping the Subject." In *Mapping the Subject: Geographies of Cultural Transformation*, edited by Steve Pile and Nigel Thrift, pp. 13–51. New York: Routledge, 1995.

Plato. *Philebus*. In *The Collected Dialogues of Plato*, edited by Edith Hamilton and Huntington Cairns. Princeton: Princeton University Press, 1996.

Polidori, Valerio. *Dispersio daemonum*. 1587.

———. *Practica exorcistarum*. 1585.

Politi, Marco. "L'attentato del Papa nel segreto di Fátima." *La Repubblica*, 14 May 2000.

Pozzi, Giovanni. *Le parole dell'estasi*. Milan: Adelphi, 1988.

Pozzi, Giovanni, and Claudio Leonardi, eds. *Scrittrici mistiche italiane*. Genoa: Marietti, 1989.

Prierio, Sylvester. *De strigimagarum daemonumque mirandis*. 1st ed., 1521. Rome, 1575.

———. *Sylvestrina summa, quae Summa summarum merito nuncupatur*. 2 vols. Bologna, 1514.

Psellus. *De operatione daemonum: Dell'attività dei demoni*. Genoa: Edizioni Culturali Internazionali Genova, 1985.

Quint, David. *Epic and Empire*. Princeton: Princeton University Press, 1993.

Remy, Nicolas. *Demonolatriae libri tres*. Translated by E. A. Ashwin. London: John Rodker, 1930.

Renson, Jean. *Les dénominations du visage en français et dans les autres langues romanes*. 2 vols. Vol. 1. Paris: Belles Lettres, 1962.

Riccardi, Antonio. "The Mystic Humanism of Maria Maddalena de' Pazzi." In *Creative Women in Medieval and Early Modern Italy*, edited by E. Ann Matter and John Coakley, pp. 212–36. Philadelphia: University of Pennsylvania Press, 1994.

Risset, Jacqueline. *Dante écrivain, ou "l'intelletto d'amore."* Paris: Seuil, 1982.

Rituale romanum. 1614.

Rivari, Enrico. *La mente di Girolamo Cardano*. Bologna: Zanichelli, 1906.

Robertson, Pat. *The Collected Works*. New York: Inspirational Press, 1994.

Rocke, Michael. *Forbidden Friendships: Homosexuality and Male Culture in Renaissance Florence*. New York: Oxford University Press, 1996.

Rodler, Lucia. *I silenzi mimici del volto*. Pisa: Pacini, 1991.

Romeo, Giovanni. *Esorcisti, confessori e sessualità femminile nell'Italia della controriforma*. Florence: Le Lettere, 1998.

———. *Inquisitori, esorcisti e streghe nell'Italia della Controriforma*. Florence: Sansoni, 1990.

Roper, Lyndal. *Oedipus and the Devil*. New York: Routledge, 1994.

Rossetti, Gabriele. *Comento analitico al "Purgatorio."* Florence: Olschki, 1967.

Rossi, Paolo. *Clavis universalis. Arti mnemoniche e logica combinatoria da Lullo a Leibniz*. Milan: Ricciardi, 1960.

Rovatti, Pier Aldo. *Abitare la distanza. Per un'etica del linguaggio*. Milan: Feltrinelli, 1994.

Ruggiero, Guido. *Boundaries of Eros: Sex, Crime, and Sexuality in Renaissance Venice*. Oxford: Oxford University Press, 1985.

Russell, Jeffrey Burton. *The Devil*. Ithaca: Cornell University Press, 1977.

———. *A History of Heaven*. Princeton: Princeton University Press, 1997.

———. *A History of Witchcraft*. London: Thames and Hudson, 1980.

———. *Lucifer: The Devil in the Middle Ages*. Ithaca: Cornell University Press, 1984.

————. *Mephistopheles: The Devil in the Modern World*. Ithaca: Cornell Uiversity Press, 1986.

————. *The Prince of Darkness*. Ithaca: Cornell University Press, 1988.

————. *Satan: The Early Christian Tradition*. Ithaca: Cornell University Press, 1981.

Sanchez, Thomas. *In praecepta decalogi*. 1st ed., 1615–22. Lyons: Laurentius Anisson, 1661.

Santi, Giorgio. *Dio e l'uomo. Conoscenza, memoria, linguaggio, ermeneutica in Agostino*. Rome: Città Nuova, 1989.

Saraiva, António José. *Inquisição e cristãos-novos*. Porto: Editorial Inova, 1969.

————. *A inquisição portuguesa*. Lisbon: Publicações Europa-America, 1956.

Scarry, Elaine. *The Body in Pain*. New York: Oxford University Press, 1985.

Schleiner, Winfreid. *Melancholy, Genius, and Utopia in the Renaissance*. Wolfenbüttel: Herzog August Bibliothek, 1991.

Schmölders, Claudia. *Das Vorurteil im Leibe*. Berlin: Akademie Verlag, 1995.

Scholz-Dürr, Adelbert. "Der traditionelle kirchliche Exorcismus im Rituale Romanum- biblisch-systematisch betrachtet." *Evangelische Theologie* 52 (1992): 56–65.

Secondin, Bruno. *Santa Maria Maddalena de' Pazzi: Esperienza e dottrina*. Rome: Institutum carmelitanum, 1974.

Seremetakis, Nadia. *The Last Word: Women, Death, and Divination in Inner Mani*. Chicago: University of Chicago Press, 1989.

Settala, Ludovico. *De naevis*. Milan, 1626.

Shapiro, Marianne. "Dante's Twofold Representation of the Soul." *Lectura Dantis* 18–19 (1996): 49–90.

Showalter, Elaine. *Hystories*. New York: Columbia University Press, 1997.

Siraisi, Nancy G. "Anatomizing the Past: Physicians and History in Renaissance Culture." *Renaissance Quarterly* 53, no. 1 (2000): 1–30.

————. *The Clock and the Mirror: Girolamo Cardano and Renaissance Medicine*. Princeton: Princeton University Press, 1997.

————. *Medieval and Early Renaissance Medicine*. Chicago: University of Chicago Press, 1990.

Spina, Bartholomeo. *Quaestio de strigibus*. Venice, 1523.

Spontone, Ciro. *La metoposcopia, overo Commensurazione delle linee della fronte*. Venice, 1626.

Stampa, Antonio. *Fuga Satanae*. 1597.

Stanley, Alessandra. "Dueling Festivals: Gay Pride and Vatican Collide." *New York Times*, 3 June 2000, A4.

Stewart, Charles. *Demons and the Devil*. Princeton: Princeton University Press, 1991.

Suarez, Christóbal de Figueroa. *Plaza universal de todas ciencias y artes*. Perpignan: Luys Roure, 1630.

Suarez, Franciscus. *Metaphysicarum disputationum*. Paris: Somnium, 1605.

Suetonius Tranquillus. *The Lives of the Twelve Caesars*. Translated by Alexander Thomson. New York: Worthington, 1883.

Sybilla, Bartolomeo. *Speculum peregrinarum quaestionum*. 1499.

Synesius. *The Essays and Hymns of Synesius of Cyrene.* Edited by Augustine Fitzgerald. xx vols. Vol. 2. Oxford: Oxford University Press, 1930.

Tanfani, Gustavo. "Il concetto di melancholia nel cinquecento." *Rivista di storia delle scienze mediche e naturali* 39 (1948): 145–68.

Tasso, Ercole. *Della realtà e perfetione delle imprese.* Bergamo, 1612.

Tavuzzi, Michael. *Prierias.* Durham, N.C.: Duke University Press, 1997.

Tedeschi, John. *The Prosecution of Heresy: Collected Studies on the Inquisition in Early Modern Italy.* Binghamton, New York: Medieval and Renaissance Texts and Studies, 1991.

Temkin, Owsei. *Galenism: Rise and Decline of a Medical Philosophy.* Ithaca: Cornell University Press, 1973.

Teresa of Avila. *The Life of Saint Teresa of Avila by Herself.* Translated by J. M. Cohen. New York: Penguin Books, 1957.

Thomas Aquinas. *Basic Writings of Saint Thomas Aquinas.* 2 vols. Edited and annotated, with an introduction by Anton C. Pegis. New York: Random House, 1945.

———. *De memoria et reminiscentia.* In *Aristotelis libros de sensu et sensato, de memoria et reminiscentia commentarium.* Edited by Raimondo Spiazzi. Turin: Marietti, 1949.

Thomas of Cantimpré. *Bonum universale de proprietatibus apuum.* Cologne: Koelhoff, 1478–80.

Thyraeus, Petrus. *Daemoniaci cum locis infestis et terriculamentis nocturnis.* Cologne, 1627.

Tomlinson, Gary. *Music in Renaissance Magic.* Chicago: University of Chicago Press, 1993.

Toorn, Karel van der, Bob Becking, and Pieter W. van der Horst, eds. *Dictionary of Deities and Demons in the Bible.* Leiden: E. J. Brill, 1995.

Tosatti, Marco. "Gay Pride, stop del Papa a un vescovo." *La stampa.* 3 July 2000, 6.

Tracy, David. "Metaphor and Religion: The Test Case of Christian Texts." In *On Metaphor,* edited by Sheldon Sacks. Chicago: University of Chicago Press, 1979.

Tristani, Jean-Louis. *Le stade du respir.* Paris: Minuit, 1978.

Tropianus, Thomas. *Compendium coniurationis contra daemones vexantes humana corpora.* Palermo: Baptista Maringhinus, 1598.

Vattimo, Gianni. "Un grande flop." *La stampa.* 27 June 2000, 2.

———. "The Trace of the Trace." In *Religion,* edited by Jacques Derrida and Gianni Vattimo. Stanford: Stanford University Press, 1998.

Vickers, Brian. "On the Function of Analogy in the Occult." In *Hermeticism and the Renaissance,* edited by Ingrid Merkel and Allen G. Debus, pp. 265–92. Washington, D.C.: Folger Books, 1988.

Vovelle, Michel. *Les âmes du purgatoire.* Paris: Gallimard, 1996.

Wagner-Egelhaaf, Martina. *Die Melancholie der Literatur.* Stuttgart: Verlag J. B. Metzler, 1997.

Walker, D. P. *Unclean Spirits.* Philadelphia: University of Pennsylvania Press, 1981.

Wenzel, Siegfried. *The Sin of Sloth: Acedia.* Chapel Hill: University of North Carolina Press, 1967.

Weyer, Johann. *De praestigiis daemonum et incantationibus ac veneficiis.* 1st ed., 1583. Edited by George Mora. Binghamton: State University of New York Press, 1991.

Wills, Garry. *Papal Sin.* New York: Doubleday, 2000.

————. "The Vatican Regrets." *New York Review of Books,* 25 May 2000, 19–20.

Wittkower, Rudolf, and Margot Wittkower. *Born under Saturn: The Character and Conduct of Artists.* New York: W. W. Norton, 1963.

Wykes, Alain. *Doctor Cardano: Physician Extraordinairy.* London: Muller, 1969.

Yates, Frances. *The Art of Memory.* Chicago: University of Chicago Press, 1966.

Zarri, Gabriella. "Living Saints: A Typology of Female Sanctity in the Early Sixteen Century." In *Women and Religion in Medieval and Renaissance Italy,* edited by Daniel Bornstein and Roberto Rusconi. Chicago: University of Chicago Press, 1996.

————. *Le sante vive. Cultura e religiosità femminile nella prima età moderna.* Turin: Einaudi, 1990.

Index